The Elementary School Teacher

THE ELEMENTARY SCHOOL TEACHER

VOLUME XII

SEPTEMBER, 1911—JUNE, 1912

The University of Chicago Press
CHICAGO, ILLINOIS

Published
September, October, November, December, 1911
January, February, March, April, May, June, 1912

Composed and Printed By
The University of Chicago Press
Chicago, Illinois, U.S.A.

INDEX TO VOLUME XII

INDEX TO ARTICLES

[The asterisk indicates authors of books reviewed]

INDEX TO AUTHORS

[The asterisk indicates authors of books reviewed]

VOLUME XII NUMBER 1

THE ELEMENTARY SCHOOL TEACHER

SEPTEMBER, 1911

SOME ISSUES IN THE TEACHING OF HANDWRITING. I

FRANK N. FREEMAN
The University of Chicago

The purpose of this article is to present some of the most important issues of the pedagogy of handwriting, and to discuss the psychological processes which may be appealed to for their solution. Psychological analysis cannot finally determine practical questions of this sort. It can, however, define the issue and lead to conclusions which may then be tested by means of practical experiment in the schoolroom. The discussion, therefore, does not aim to give a final settlement of these questions, but rather to offer tentative solutions and to lead to practical school experiments.[1]

I

The question in the pedagogy of writing which has been most widely agitated is probably that in regard to the slant of writing. A brief history of this agitation may be given.

Previous to the agitation for vertical writing which took place in the last quarter of the nineteenth century, rapid writing slanted, as a rule, to the right. There had been, it is true, some suggestions looking toward the adoption of vertical writing, but they did not have general influence until about 1875. What divergence there was, was due to an opposition between the aim of speed, which led to a slant in writing, and the aim of legibility without regard to speed, which led to a more vertical style. At about the time

[1] A more detailed account of the methods by which such practical investigation of writing problems may be made in the school will be published in a forthcoming number of the *Journal of Educational Psychology*.

mentioned, however, a number of physicians of Germany and France criticized the writing in the schools from the point of view of hygiene. In order to understand the basis of their criticisms we must realize that the pupil commonly took a position with his side toward the desk. This was held to cause curvature of the spine and eye-strain. The curvature of the spine was due to the fact that only the right elbow rested upon the desk, with the consequence that the right shoulder was lifted higher than the left. The eye-strain was due to the fact that the eyes were not at an equal distance from the writing, and that the lenses of the eyes had to be focused unequally.

In order to remedy these evils it was seen to be necessary to modify the position of the pupil at the desk, and it was concluded that this would require also that the writing be vertical. The demands of these investigators are well represented by the resolutions adopted by the Society of Public Medicine of France in 1879. This society recommended, first, that the pupil sit squarely on the chair, with the weight equally distributed, the shoulders parallel to the edge of the desk, and the back erect; second, that he preferably do not rest his elbows on the desk, but that if he does they should rest equally on the desk; third, that he should hold the paper in place with his left hand; and fourth, that vertical writing be adopted, but if not that the paper be inclined to the left to the same degree by which the writing inclines from the vertical. We see clearly then that vertical writing was regarded as a necessary consequence of the reform of the evils above mentioned.

It should be added that vertical writing has also been regarded as more legible than writing which has a slant, and as therefore preferably both from the point of view of the writer and of the reader. This consideration may be taken up separately.

The main arguments for vertical writing have been met in common practice by a modification of the position of the pupil at the desk. The pupil may sit directly facing the desk and still write either vertically or with a slant. The question of slant is to be decided not primarily upon the score of hygiene, then, but upon the score of ease and rapidity of movement and of the legibility of the resulting writing. We may take up the question of ease and rapidity of movement first.

The hand writing movement is made up ordinarily of a combination of arm and finger movement. To what extent the arm movement should be used is open to discussion, but at any rate it should co-operate to the extent of carrying the hand freely along the line. This it cannot do with the paper in the position which is commonly used for vertical writing, that is, with the paper parallel to the edge of the desk. In this position it is necessary that the arm be continually drawn back in order to avoid running off the line. In order then to make use of this valuable element of the writing movement, it is necessary that the paper be tilted to the left so that the base line of writing is about perpendicular to the forearm.

We have next to inquire what this position implies as to the direction of the main downward strokes of the letters, or, in other words, the slant of the writing. The fourth recommendation of the French society offers the solution to this question. It is found by experiment that the most natural direction for a downward stroke is toward the body, that is, in a line perpendicular to the edge of the desk when the writer sits facing it. If now the paper is parallel to the edge of the desk the writing will be vertical, but if it is inclined to the left the writing will be inclined to the right to the same degree. We have then the slant of the writing determined by two factors, first, the direction of the easiest movement of the arm in carrying the hand along the line, which determines the position of the paper, and second, the most natural direction of the downward stroke, which determines the direction of the downward strokes with reference to the paper.

There is, however, another consideration which favors some slant in writing. It has been remarked that historically rapid writing always tended to have more or less slant. This is not due in the main to the relative position of the arm and the paper, as just described, since this in all probability was not uniform but to the fact that as writing becomes rapid the different strokes of the letters tend to assume the same or nearly the same direction. It may readily be seen that it requires a more radical adjustment in the movement to make a succession of strokes alternating between a vertical stroke and one having a considerable slant than it does to make a series in which the downward stroke has a slant which is more nearly like that of the upward stroke. That is, the more nearly the successive strokes resemble each other in direction, the more quickly they can be made. Since the connecting strokes between the letters have a slant, naturally the downward strokes tend to approximate this slant.

It is evident that the question of legibility is intimately connected with this question of the relative direction of the upward and downward strokes. If the downward strokes incline so far as to have nearly the same slant as the upward strokes the different strokes become less easily distinguishable and consequently the writing becomes less legible. The maximum of legibility in so far as the directions of the strokes is concerned is attained by having a maximum difference in direction between the successive downward and upward strokes. This is attained by vertical writing and hence vertical writing is theoretically the most legible.

The theoretical advantage of vertical writing in legibility is not necessarily maintained in practice. It is an acknowledged truth that actual writing does not conform to the copy-book model. The degree of deviation from the theoretical model will depend to a large extent upon whether or not the writing conforms to the requirements for ease and rapidity of movement. Since vertical writing does not so conform it tends, when there is pressure for rapid writing, to depart from the model and to become illegible. One common way in which this happens is for the upward strokes, as well as the downward strokes, to be vertical and to be connected with the previous and succeeding downward strokes by semicircular curves. Thus the upward and downward strokes may here, as in writing which has a slant, approximate one another in direction, and the result for legibility is as disastrous in the one case as in the other.

The difference in the legibility between the theoretical model for vertical writing and for writing which has a moderate slant is not great enough to be of any importance. Writing only suffers in legibility when the slant becomes extreme and this condition is not found in present-day writing.

The psychological analysis then justifies the practice, which has been adopted by the majority of schools, of teaching writing which has a moderate degree of slant. The change has taken place largely as a result of unsatisfactory experience with the vertical writing. Changes which are made in this way, however, have not the same guarantee of stability as changes which are made with the consciousness of the psychological basis which underlies them. It is therefore of importance to determine the reasons why vertical writing was unsatisfactory in practice, and why writing with a slant is satisfactory.

II

We have now to consider a group of questions in the teaching of writing which may be described in general as growing out of the issue between the analytic and the synthetic method. The analytic method consists in training different processes or capacities simultaneously, and the synthetic method refers to the procedure of training different capacities one at a time. An example of the difference between these two methods is found, for instance, in reading. The analytic method is the so-called word or sentence method, in which the child first learns the whole and then proceeds from the whole to the parts. The synthetic method starts with the individual letters or the phonetic elements, and from these builds up the words and sentences. This general distinction between analytical and synthetic methods appears also in the teaching of writing.

The first question in this connection is in regard to the relation between the training for habits of movement and training for the production of correct form. That is, should the teacher aim from the beginning to train the child in correct habits of movement, and at the same time to train him to produce letters which are legible and correctly formed? The alternative is to lay stress first upon one of these aims and then after the first has been attained to emphasize the second. The consideration in favor of maintaining both of these aims together is that thereby we avoid the waste which results from a repetition, and from the necessity of undoing bad habits. That is, so long as the child is practicing, it would seem to be economical to require him to learn to use the best form of movement and to produce correct form at the same time. Economy, then, is the advantage of this form of procedure. On the other hand, this argument neglects the psychological conditions of learning. The child is capable of paying attention to only so much at once, and if we require him to distribute his attention too widely the result will be that he will neglect both elements of the task which he is performing. Accordingly, instead of training both the form and the movement at the same time, the result is that neither is thoroughly developed.

The problem then is reduced to the question of which component should be developed first, correct movement or form. The contention in favor of the prior development of the habit of movement is that the foundation of the habit should be laid early. By this means bad habits and the necessity of breaking them up will be avoided. The attention can afterward be given mainly to the perfection of the form of the writing. This argument when carried to the extreme leads to the use of strenuous movement drills from the beginning of the first grade up, and to the use of exactly the same kind of movement and the same writing materials throughout. The assumption underlying this practice is, further, that the acquirement of correct habits of movement is the main condition for the acquirement of legible writing. In other words, it is often assumed that legible writing will result without much attention being paid to the form when proper habits are trained. This assumption may be questioned, but it is not the place here to discuss it in detail.

The opposite procedure of paying chief attention at the beginning to the development of the form of the letters rests upon the facts which are known concerning the development of motor skill in the child. The facts at our command indicate that the child when he first enters school is very deficient in this respect. After two or three years his capacity for the acquirement of activities which involve skill and dexterity develops to a marked degree. If this is true, a given amount of drill undergone at the age of eight or nine will have a very much greater effect than the same amount given at the age of six or seven. In other words, it would be a waste of time and energy to train the child in an activity for which he has not yet developed sufficient motor control.

Evidence in support of this position is found in an examination of the writing of children in the different grades, all of whom have had the same form of training. This training consists in a strenuous drill in arm movement. Such examination reveals the fact that the children of the first three or four grades have profited little by the drill which they have undergone, but between the fourth and the fifth or sixth grade there is a sudden transition. Movement drill here begins to have marked results in the child's writing. This is not due to the accumulation of the results of the past four or five years, since the children who are the subjects of this investigation had not had the movement drill more than one year.

It might be concluded from these considerations that writing should be deferred entirely until the child had acquired sufficient natural motor skill to make its learning economical, but this would entail too great a sacrifice in view of the importance of writing as a means of expression in connection with reading and the other school subjects. Furthermore, the child may during the early years develop the perception of the form of the letters so that he may later have a standard to which he can bring his writing when movement drill is introduced.

If movement drill is deferred until the child is in the third or fourth grade he will employ during the first years a relatively slow movement in which the finger movement is the chief component. This will necessitate a marked readjustment of the co-ordination when arm movement drill is introduced, and the form of the writing will temporarily suffer. The child's nervous system is still sufficiently plastic, however, to permit of readjustment of his motor habit, and the sacrifice of form is only temporary. The contrary procedure, in which movement drill is introduced in the first grade, involves a sacrifice of form for a much longer period. From the point of view of its effect upon form, therefore, as well as from the point of view of the development of the co-ordination, strenuous movement drill may well be deferred until the third or fourth grade.

[*To be concluded*]

PESTALOZZIAN INDUSTRIAL EDUCATION FOR JUVENILE REFORM[1]

S. CHESTER PARKER
The University of Chicago

Recent agitation and experiments in connection with industrial education in public schools have developed a general interest in all aspects of industrial training. The present tendency to reject formal manual training as inadequate, and to substitute direct training in industrial processes, involves a reversion to the type of industrial education which Pestalozzi advocated. This Pestalozzian scheme finds its best embodiment in some of our juvenile reform schools, and in this form can be traced directly to Pestalozzi in its origin. It is the purpose of this paper to describe its development.

General appreciation of necessity of industrial training for juvenile delinquents.—The necessity and the value of providing industrial occupation and training for orphans and for neglected and delinquent children have been generally recognized. The provisions made for such training have assumed different forms corresponding to variations in fundamental principles at different times. The Pestalozzian basis was prominent during the nineteenth century. To indicate the general character of the social problem, however, earlier provisions in England and the American Colonies will be cited before discussing the Pestalozzian development.

American colonial laws required training in industry.—The early American colonists appreciated the importance of industrial training for children and in some cases provided for it by law. The necessity for this requirement and its nature was expressed in the Massachusetts law of 1642 as follows:

[1] In the last two volumes of the *Elementary School Teacher,* a number of articles appeared which were intended to illustrate a method of teaching the history of education by emphasizing school practice in its relation to social condition. This is the sixth article in this series. A textbook entitled *A History of Modern Elementary Education*, constructed on these principles, by the same author will appear in the near future.

> [The General Court of Massachusetts] taking into consideration the great neglect in many parents and masters in training up their children in learning and labor and other employments which may be profitable to the Commonwealth, do hereupon order and decree that in every town the chosen men appointed for managing the prudential affairs of the same . . . . shall have power . . . . to put forth [as] apprentices the children of such as shall not be able and fit to employ and bring them up . . . . and they are to take care that such as are set to keep cattle be set to some other employment withal, as spinning up on the rock, knitting, weaving tape, etc. . . . . They are also to provide that a sufficient quantity of materials, as hemp, flax, etc., may be raised in their several towns, and tools and implements provided for working out the same.

In Virginia colony: "in 1646 an elaborate plan for industrial education was advanced by the Assembly . . . . [which] marks out the settled policy of the State in the matter of industrial training."[1] This law refers back to English precedents in these words:

> WHEREAS sundry laws and statutes by Act of Parliament established, have with great wisdom ordained, for the better education of youth in honest and profitable trades and manufactures . . . . that the justices of peace should, at their discretion, bind out children to tradesmen or husbandmen to be brought up in some good and lawful calling . . . . be it therefore enacted by the authority of this Grand Assembly, according to the aforesaid laudable custom in the Kingdom of England. . . . .

The act provided that the commissioners of the several counties were to send two poor children from each county to James City to be "employed in the public flax houses under such master and mistresses as shall there be appointed in carding, knitting and spinning." Special dormitories were to be built and each county was to send food and other provisions for the children. In 1668 and other years, acts were passed empowering county courts to make similar provisions for educating and employing poor children.

Antecedent provisions in English laws.—That the colonial laws requiring industrial training were reproductions of antecedent English laws of the same nature was definitely stated in the preamble of the Virginia law of 1646 which we quoted. It is maintained by some authorities that such legislation as this constituted the fundamental basis of all English legislation for elementary education down to the nineteenth century; in other words, that

[1] Clewes, *Educational Legislation of Colonial Governments*, p. 355.

there is a very definite connection between legislation for poor relief and apprenticeship and legislation relative to elementary education.

The English social situation of the sixteenth and seventeenth centuries which necessitated such legislation was similar in character to the Swiss situation which confronted Pestalozzi later; namely, a very large number of unemployed, vagrant, shiftless, untrained children and adults. Many factors combined to cause the English situation, among them being the suppression of the monasteries by Henry VIII which abolished some of the dominant institutions for poor relief; and second, the abolishing of guilds by the Chantry acts which destroyed another of the important forms of poor relief. Other economic factors were causes also, notably the consolidation of small farms for grazing purposes, and the consequent eviction of hundreds of small farmers who were thus deprived of their means of livelihood. As a consequence we find important legislation in the reign of Queen Elizabeth, which included the same elements to which we have called attention in the colonial laws.

Domestic industries the basis of Pestalozzian industrial education.—The Pestalozzian industrial education was originally planned to meet industrial conditions which existed in places where factory systems had not developed; in other words it was based on the conditions of domestic industries and handicrafts which prevailed generally down to the beginning of the nineteenth century. The factory system with the attendant industrial and social revolution, necessitated a change in the type of industrial work but not in the general scheme which Pestalozzi advocated.

Factories did not destroy possibilities of Pestalozzi's scheme.—Factories were early introduced into Switzerland in certain select districts, and Pestalozzi himself commented on the new and peculiar social problems which they created. But many parts of Switzerland continued in the stage of home or domestic industries and handicrafts, even as they do to the present day. The same was true of the United States during the early nineteenth century. The more primitive forms of industry continued to be practiced in some places at the same time that the factory development was dominant in others.

Included in the domestic industries and the handicrafts were farming, work with textiles, namely, spinning, weaving, and dyeing of cotton and wool, and work with wood, metal, and leather. Examples of leather work were the shoe-making and nail- and tack-making which many New England farmers engaged in at home during the winter months. The early Pestalozzian industrial education emphasized especially farming and work with textiles. In the later development, under Fellenberg, other trades were taught. The enormous development of textile factories soon eliminated this form of labor from such schemes of education, but there remain, even at the present day, many forms of manual labor which are suited to the general purposes of the Pestalozzian industrial education.

Moreover, many intellectual and social leaders who have been impressed with the social evils that have attended factory development have idealized the former conditions of industry and have endeavored to reproduce them on a limited scale. This endeavor is represented in the arts-and-crafts movement of the present day. Many who consider this reaction against the factory system to be utopian believe, however, in the educative value of industrial training along the lines of domestic activities, agriculture, and handicrafts.

Pestalozzi's writings described the degraded condition of Swiss peasantry.—Two phases of Pestalozzi's own work directly related to industrial education were the publication of *Leonard and Gertrude* (1781) and his experiments at Neuhof and Stanz. Every student should spend a few hours reading *Leonard and Gertrude* to get an appreciation of the low moral standards which prevailed in the Swiss villages.

The typical village which Pestalozzi described was governed by semi-feudal customs, being under the control of a nobleman who lived in a castle outside of the town. Owing to the dishonest administration and oppression by his subordinates, the most degraded conditions had developed. The elements of viciousness in this life, as described by Pestalozzi, included all forms of public and private dishonesty, graft and oppression, intrigue and perjury, cheating and lying, gambling, drunkenness, hypocrisy in religious matters, superstition—including belief in witchcraft and ghosts—domestic disorder, idleness, laziness, general shiftlessness, and filthiness.

In contrast with all these, Pestalozzi presented examples of possible social reforms which would result in a fair, honest, and efficient management of the public affairs, in real piety and charity, domestic peace, cleanliness and order, appreciation of responsibility, industry, economy and general thrift, and more intelligent methods of labor.

Condition of neglected and vagrant children.—Other striking examples of the prevailing social conditions are contained in Pestalozzi's descriptions of the individual children in this establishment at Neuhof and Stanz. These examples and others show that many of the children had not even profited by the meager instruction offered in the village schools. When we recall that this instruction consisted in a bare memorizing of the catechism, and the acquirement of a stumbling facility in reading, we see how hopelessly inadequate it was to cope with the social conditions that Pestalozzi described.

School to reproduce conditions of ideal home.—Pestalozzi's plan for social reform through training in domestic industries was described in *Leonard and Gertrude.* The central idea was that the school should reproduce the typical conditions of a well-ordered peasant's or artisan's home. This idea is expressed in the following quotations:

> The school ought really to stand in the closest connection with the life of the home, instead of, as now, in strong contradiction to it. . . . . The school ought to be brought into harmony with the developing influence of domestic life. . . . . All verbal instruction, in so far as it aims at true human wisdom and at the highest goal of this wisdom, true religion, ought to be subordinated to a constant training in practical domestic labor.

Domestic labor in Gertrude's home.—The home of Gertrude, which Pestalozzi described, was his ideal. In addition to receiving careful religious and moral training, the children spent a large part of the time spinning under the direction of their mother. The following quotation presents the picture seen when Gertrude, the mason's wife, brings home some children of an unfortunate neighbor, Rudy.

The mason's children were all at their spinning wheels and although they greeted their guests joyfully, they did not stop working for a moment. "Hurry and get through and then you can play with your little friends till six o'clock," said Gertrude. Rudy's children stood in open-mouthed wonder at the beautiful work and the cheerful aspect of the room. "Can you spin?" she asked. "No," they answered. "Then you must learn, my dears. My children wouldn't sell their knowledge of it at any price, and are happy enough on Saturday, when they get their few kreutzers. The year is long, my dears, and if we earn something every week, at the end of the year there is a lot of money, without our knowing how we came by it."

Supplemented by intellectual and religious instruction.—This domestic labor constituted the central activity of the home, but it was supplemented by intellectual training much of which was carried on while the children were doing the manual work. The following quotation describes how this was done:

The children all helped wash the dishes, and then seated themselves at their customary places before their work. . . . . First the children sang their morning hymns, and then Gertrude read a chapter of the Bible aloud, which they repeated after her, while they were spinning, rehearsing the most instructive passages until they knew them by heart.

The instruction she [Gertrude] gave them in the rudiments of arithmetic was intimately connected with the realities of life. . . . . She made them count their threads while spinning, and the number of turns on the reel when they wound the yarn into skeins.

Instruction in spinning in the ideal village school.—Pestalozzi believed it possible to organize the village school in imitation of Gertrude's home as indicated in the following quotation:

The lieutenant began his school, and Gertrude helped him in the arrangement of it. They examined the children with regard to their previous studies. . . . . Besides reading, all were to learn writing and arithmetic, which previously had only been taught to the more wealthy in private lessons. . . . . A good, capable woman who came to take charge of the sewing, spinning, etc., proved a most valuable and conscientious helper in the work. Whenever a child's hand or wheel stopped she would step up and restore things to their former condition. If the children's hair was in disorder she would braid it while they studied and worked . . . . and she showed them how to fasten their shoes and stockings properly, besides many other things they did not understand.

Educative labor to be taught in reformatories.—Finally, Pestalozzi indicated his belief that such training should be provided, not only in the ordinary schools, but also in orphan asylums and houses of correction where the inmates should be given definite education in manual trades.

Pestalozzi taught farming and textile work at Neuhof.—The plan which Pestalozzi described in *Leonard and Gertrude* (1781) he had tried to put into practice on his farm at Neuhof from 1774 to 1780. When he proposed this experiment, although he had just failed as a farmer, several philanthropists provided the necessary funds.

Most of the children that Pestalozzi took in were vagrants and beggars. Many of them were vicious and improved little in the short time spent under his care. Others, however, were honest and capable and needed only the opportunity which he offered to develop into efficient persons. At one time he had thirty-seven children, at another fifty, and later eighty. Describing the management of the institution he said:

> I get very valuable help from Miss M. of Strassberg, who is both highly gifted and of untiring activity. I have, besides, a master to teach weaving, and two skilled weavers; a mistress to teach spinning, and two good spinners; a man who winds for the weavers and teaches reading at the same time; and two men and two women who are almost always employed on the land.

Pestalozzi had no administrative ability and the management of such an enterprise, calling for unusual skill, was beyond his powers. Consequently the experiment was abandoned. In spite of its failure, it had served a valuable purpose in demonstrating the lines along which industrial education might develop. It remained for Emmanuel Fellenberg to organize a successful institution on these same lines.

Emmanuel Fellenberg's Pestalozzian Institutions. Early acquaintance with Pestalozzi.—Pestalozzi carried on an intimate correspondence with Emmanuel Fellenberg in 1792 concerning the French Revolution; and in 1804, for a few months, Pestalozzi tried to conduct his school under the business management of Fellenberg at Münchenbuchsee.

Fellenberg active in Swiss social reform.—Fellenberg's father, a high governmental official in Switzerland, was interested in Pestalozzi's experiments, and thus Emmanuel, while quite young, became acquainted with the latter. His mother early directed his attention to the care of the poor and unfortunate. He pursued political and social studies in German universities; visited Paris in 1795 to ascertain the French intentions with regard to Switzerland; tried in vain to arouse his country to appreciate its danger; led Swiss troops against the French when they invaded Switzerland in 1798, but was defeated and had to flee the country. Later he was permitted to return. He occupied important administrative offices for a while, but he soon became disgusted with the general dishonesty and lack of interest in public affairs, and turned his attention to education. He became convinced that legislation in favor of improvements in education was too slow a process and decided to use his ample fortune in establishing "a model institution in which it should be proved what education could accomplish for humanity." For this purpose he purchased a large country estate at Hofwyl, near Berne. Here he conducted, from 1806 to 1844, educational experiments along Pestalozzian lines which were as successful from an administrative and economic standpoint as Pestalozzi's were unsuccessful.[1]

Included industrial training of rich as well as poor.—Fellenberg's aim was to establish an institution in which the poor would be trained to work, and the rich trained to appreciate the work of the poor and to be efficient in directing it for the public good. He believed that agriculture, as the principal occupation of the people, was best adapted to produce the harmonious physical and intellectual development at which he aimed. His aim was broader than Pestalozzi's had been at Neuhof, inasmuch as it included not only the industrial education of the poor, but also the training of teachers for rural schools and the training of the rich.

Many successful phases of the Hofwyl institution.—The Hofwyl institution was organized gradually, each element in the organization being well established before another was added. By 1829, according to William Woodbridge's contemporary description, the institution included the following elements: (1) a farm of about 600 acres; (2) workshops for manufacturing agricultural implements and clothing for the inhabitants; (3) a lithographing

[1] *Am. Annals of Education*, Vol. I (1830), based on a letter from Fellenberg to Woodbridge, August 24, 1829.

establishment where music and other things were printed; (4) a literary institution for the education of the wealthy and higher classes; (5) an intermediate or practical institution training for handicrafts and middle-class occupations; (6) an agricultural institution for the education of the poor to be farm laborers and for the training of rural school teachers.

The agricultural institution most significant for elementary education.—It was this sixth phase of the work that was generally copied in Switzerland and other European countries. Just as Pestalozzi had intended, agriculture was to be used as a means of moral and practical education for the poor. It also made their labors defray the expense of their education. In addition to training in agriculture, the institution provided training for cart-makers, carpenters, joiners, blacksmiths, locksmiths, shoemakers, tailors, etc. Fellenberg's practice of giving intending rural school teachers a thorough training in scientific agriculture was copied in many of the normal schools of Switzerland. The practice of training poor children in agriculture and other occupations under the conditions of family life was soon copied in most countries except the United States.

General adoption of Fellenberg's plan. Farm schools established in all cantons of Switzerland.—Henry Barnard wrote in his *National Education in Europe* (1854, p. 488):

> In each of the cantons of Switzerland, in 1852, there was at least one rural or farm school conducted on the basis of a well regulated family. The school is open both to girls and boys. . . . . The number of inmates averages from twenty to forty, and when the entire family exceed twenty, it is subdivided into lesser ones of twelve or more, who are placed under an assistant "father." The school instruction occupies three hours in summer and four in winter; the remainder of the day being devoted to work in the field or garden, or at certain seasons of the year and for a class of pupils, in some indoor trade or craft.

Redemption industrial plan imitated in other European countries.—The above-described scheme was imitated in many parts of Europe. In Germany, one of the most interesting examples was Redemption Institute or "Rauhe Haus," established in 1833, near Hamburg. This was a private charity admitting boys and girls of the worst type. Ordinarily such children would have been identified with the criminal class and would have developed as criminals.

At the beginning of 1844, of 81 children who had left the establishment, 33 were apprenticed to artisans or mechanics, 7 entered at service as farm-laborers or domestics, 7 had become day laborers, 11 (girls) had become servants, 9 had become sailors, 3 entered the army, 1 prepared himself for the university, 5 continued at school; the occupation of 3 is unknown, and 2 children belonging to a family of vagrants could not be kept at any regular occupation.

Only 6 or 7 of these had misbehaved after leaving the school.

In England the famous Battersea Training Establishment for teachers was founded in 1839 in definite imitation of the Swiss normal schools. A noted reform school and farm for juvenile criminals was established at Red Hill in 1849 by the Philanthropic Society. On a farm of 140 acres, without bars or walls or gates, criminal children, including some of the most vicious, were trained and reformed according to the Pestalozzian-Fellenberg plan.

Fellenberg manual-labor scheme popularized in the United States by Woodbridge (1830).—One of the chief factors in popularizing the Fellenberg idea in the United States were the letters of William C. Woodbridge describing the Hofwyl institution, which started in the *American Journal of Education*, and ran for almost two years (1831–32) in the early volumes of its successor, the *American Annals of Education.* Henry Barnard said that of more than one hundred reports concerning Fellenberg's establishment "the most particular account and that in which the spirit of the institutions was considered by their founder to be best exhibited" was the one by Mr. Woodbridge.

American manual-labor schools mostly for higher education.—In the United States, the original Pestalozzian element (moral redemption through manual labor) in the Fellenberg scheme was not copied until much later than in most European countries. On the other hand, Fellenberg's idea was carried out in manual-labor institutions, organized to provide secondary or higher education along literary lines. These were very common during the second quarter of the nineteenth century. The two ideas most prominent in this development were: (1) the necessity of physical exercise;

and (2) the possibility of self-support for poor students. Theological seminaries, colleges, and many less important schools were established upon these principles from Maine to Tennessee. The movement began actively about 1825 and continued for about a quarter of a century. In general, it did not realize the hopes of its advocates, although some phases of it persist today in the farm work for self-support that students carry on in some of the agricultural colleges. Another phase of the development in the United States which is more directly related to elementary education remains to be discussed.

Industrial work in American reformatories. Early reformatories organized on prison principles.—We noted in an earlier paragraph that industrial training in reform schools on the family plan was copied from Switzerland in several European countries but was adopted very tardily in the United States.

In 1824 the House of Refuge for delinquent boys was established in New York City and similar institutions were organized in Philadelphia in 1826 and in Boston in 1827. Only a few others were established before 1850, but between 1850 and 1860 over a dozen were established. These institutions were the results of the movement which had started in England in the latter part of the eighteenth century, to provide separate institutions for juvenile delinquents instead of confining them with adult criminals, as was the general practice. These new institutions differed from those established on the Pestalozzian plan in two fundamental respects: (1) they were not homes, but were simply separate prisons for children; (2) although they provided industrial work it was not "educative labor," but prison-contract labor. The principal factor in this labor was the amount of money that the institution could make from it.

American reformatories little affected by Pestalozzian principles before 1873.—In 1873, Miss Mary Carpenter, one of the leaders in juvenile reform work in England, visited America and criticized the prison-like character of the reform schools. This criticism was one of the influences which was operative in stimulating the movement to reorganize these institutions on the Pestalozzian basis. I have found no general account of this development but the following items are fair examples of it. They are taken from the report of the United States Commissioner of Education for 1882–83:

Pestalozzian basis of organization common in the eighties. Cottage plan.

The reform school of the present is a decided improvement on those which were first established sixty years ago. The changes effected have been stated as follows in a pamphlet issued by the Colorado State Industrial School:

"In the earlier history of these schools, all inmates were classed together. For their safe-keeping it was thought necessary to fasten them in cells at night; strong iron bars guarded the windows, etc. . . . . In the modern reformatory neither high walls, cells, bolts or bars are found. Nothing in the surroundings distinguishes them from first-class public schools."

The Ohio Industrial School for Boys, opened at Lancaster, Ohio, in 1856, was the pioneer American institution on the cottage plan. These cottages were described in 1882 as follows:

The family buildings are arranged in a segment of a circle around the main building with the exception of a double building, called the Ohio, for the use of the very youngest boys, which is separated from the main and other buildings nearly half a mile, but is connected with the rest of the institution by a good board walk. These family buildings are named after the rivers in the state.

The building for the youngest children accommodated 100 boys, those for the older children accommodated 50. The large building for younger children contained schoolrooms for the "elder brother and his family," sitting-rooms for boys in the evening, sleeping-rooms for teachers and pupils, a playroom, workshop, etc. Here "home life more attractive than they had ever known awaited most of the inmates."

Pestalozzian educative labor replaces prison contract labor.—These quotations indicate the change from the spirit of prison life to the Pestalozzian spirit of home life. A similar change has taken place in the industrial work. On the old plan, this consisted of contract sewing and tailoring, cigar-making, brush-making, glove-making, knitting, shirt-making, the cane-seating of chairs, etc. These were factory industries of little educative or economic value for the individual child. For these have been substituted the domestic industries of the institutions, and other activities connected with the maintenance of the plant, such as farming, gardening, care of stock, carpentering, blacksmithing, plumbing, painting, brickmaking, furniture making, etc. In addition to these, other special trades, such as printing and telegraphy, have been added.

General educational significance of Pestalozzian industrial education.—The special significance of this movement has been sufficiently indicated in the previous discussion. Its general significance appears when it is compared with the "manual training" movement, and with the recent tendencies to introduce direct industrial training into the public schools. The Pestalozzian movement, as successfully organized in practice, antedated the manual training movement by over half a century. It differed from the latter in aiming, to a considerable degree, directly at special efficiency in some trade or occupation. The manual training movement emphasized, on the other hand, general or formal values as opposed to specialized efficiency, "making the hand the obedient servant of the brain, training the eye for good form and shape, and teaching neatness and correctness in the execution of their work." The Pestalozzian system has proven effective in special institutions, but has not had a chance in the American public schools. Manual training has had some opportunity to be tested out in the public schools, and many educators affirm that the results have not been satisfactory from the standpoint of industrial education. The recent movement for industrial education in the United States has tended to emphasize the necessity of training in specific industrial processes, which was the prominent element in the Pestalozzian system. The present tendency seems to be to experiment in the public schools with the modified Pestalozzian system as it is found in some juvenile reform schools.

LEARNING TO READ[1]

JOSEPHINE HORTON BOWDEN

The adult gives no more thought to his reading than he gives to his walking. The process has become automatic; when he sees the printed symbols he reads in spite of himself. He can no more tell how he reads than he can tell how he walks; he simply reads. He has so far forgotten the time and energy he spent mastering the process that he is not even aware of its complexity. Reading sometimes tires his brain and sometimes tires his eyes; further in the analysis he does not go. He may think that his eyes do not move across the page with each line but that he takes in two or more lines at once; he may believe that the movement is a continuous one and that he experiences no difficulty in gauging the length of the line or in fixating any given point in the line. When the psychologist tells him that he reads but a line at a time, that the movement across the page is a succession of short movements and brief pauses, and that even after the movements have become automatic, the eyes sometimes fail to fixate the correct point, he realizes that learning to read is a difficult task for the eyes, and he understands why the beginner's finger follows the line word by word as he reads. Tachistoscopic readings and photographic records of the movements of the eyes tell him that instead of reading whole sentences or even whole phrases at a glance, in those brief reading pauses he takes in, on the average, but a word or two regardless of sentence structure. He is not so much at a loss to understand why the child reads haltingly, a word at a time. He knows that there is a relation between reading and speech, though he may not realize how close it is. He may have observed lip-movement in others and have been unconscious of the inner speech that accompanies his own silent reading. He may even have believed himself to be a pure visual reader, though there is no proof that that type exists. When he has become conscious

[1] From the Laboratory of Experimental Education, The University of Chicago.

of that form of inner speech which is present in all his reading, he ceases to marvel that the beginner should, when he reads to himself, whisper the words or at least go through the motions of pronouncing them. Add to these processes that still more difficult one by which the printed words arouse thought in the mind of the reader and one realizes in a way the problem that confronts the child when he begins to read.

We have been learning to read for so many centuries that one might think that the technique had long since been perfected but primary reading still presents its problems and there are almost as many methods as there are teachers and almost as many theories as there are psychologists and educators interested in the matter.

There is still opportunity and need for careful observation and analysis of the way in which children learn to read under the various methods employed. We know surprisingly little about the methods that *children* use in contrast to the abundance of teacher's methods. Observant teachers of reading have doubtless accumulated in their own experience many pertinent facts, but they have not written them down or attempted to relate their observations, so that there are no accounts of the ways, to be specific, in which beginners learn to recognize words as wholes. When the children were taught their letters first, they supposedly learned words by recognizing some of the letters and letter combinations, building up the word concepts on the basis of their previous analysis. What happens now that they are supposed to recognize the words as wholes from the start, or with only such analysis as, for example, the drill in phonics necessarily supplies? It was with the hope of making some contribution to the study of such a question that these experiments were undertaken.

A number of experimental studies in recognition of words by adults has been made. The purpose of the following experiments is to determine how children recognize words. There are two experiments: first, an individual study; and second, a class study.

The child in the first study was a girl six years old, a normal child, who was interested in learning to read, but who had had almost no instruction in reading. She was not attending school and had never attended school; she was receiving no instruction during the period of the experiment save the instruction in reading. The problem was to determine how a child learns to read with only printed words in context and out of context, with no assistance save the direction of the work. There was no analysis, either letter or phonic, and no use of script. The time of the experiment was eight weeks, from February 7 to April 13, with a week's vacation; the study period was from 10:30 to 11, five days in the week. The material, which was home-made, i.e., made primarily by the child, had as its subject-matter incidents of home-life—dolls, etc. The story, made one day, was typewritten for the next day's lesson with each new word on a separate card. The story was first read by the child; the words she did not know were given her, then the words were read from the cards. This was repeated until the lesson was mastered or until the child asked for new material. A record of each day's work was kept in which were recorded the rate of learning, any interesting comments of the child, and the tests that were given. At the end of each week the child read the material of the week and a record of the words known and not known was kept. Then all of the words of the week on the separate cards were gone through and the words known and not known recorded. At the end of each month a similar test was given of the work of the month.

The rate of learning in words for each week was as follows: 11, 6, 12, 10, 17, 14, 12, 18. The first week's record was rather high because it included the words the child had already learned. During the first month 53 words were presented, of which the child knew in context 45, or 83 per cent, and out of context 28, or 52.8 per cent. The second month 96 words were presented, of which she knew in context 85, or 88.5 per cent, and out of context 60, or 62.5 per cent. These figures show the significance of context as a cue in the recognition of words. Even from the first, when she did not know the word on the card, she asked for the story, that she might find it in context. If this was not allowed, she sometimes said the sentence to herself until she came to the word.

As evidence of the methods employed by the child the following may be cited. First, incidents; for example, one day when the child was given the cards to read from, it was observed that she read with equal ease whether the card was right side up or upside down. This incident suggested a test which was later given. Second, comments of the child; for example, when she was asked to find in the context the word "shoes," she said that "dress" looked so much like "shoes" that she was afraid she would make a mistake. Third, questioning; for example, she had trouble to distinguish between "sing" and "song." When she had mastered the words she was asked how she knew which was which. Her reply was, "by the looks." When questioned further she put her finger on the "i" and the "o." These three types of evidence correspond to introspection with the adult. The fourth type of evidence is a comparison of the words learned with the words not learned as to the parts of speech, geometric form, internal form, and length. Fifth, misreadings; for example, "dogs" was read "twigs," and "feathers," "fur." Sixth, mutilations; for example, "dogs" was printed "digs," "lilac" was written "lalci."

The class consisted of five children, six years old, just from the kindergarten, who had had no experience in reading. The problem was the same as in the former study though the conditions were different. The words were presented in both script and print; there was no phonics, but the names of the letters were freely used, though without an effort to teach them. The time of the experiment was the same; but there were two study periods, one from 8:45 to 9:15, when the material was presented by the teacher in charge, and the other from 10:20 to 10:40, when the writing exercise took place and when word drill and testing were given by the experimenter. The method of teaching reading in this school is the imitation method, the basis of which is that reading should be learned as talking is learned. There is no reading period but words are presented in connection with all the work given, though particularly with nature-study and history. The teacher presented the material for the day, writing the words on the board as she used them. When the presentation was finished, the matter was put into sentences which were written on the board and then read by the children. Sometimes these groups of sentences were printed on charts and read a second or third time. The teacher also had the important words printed on cards which she showed the children as she presented the material. The testing and recording were similar in method to those in the former experiment except that not all the words presented in context were used as drill words.

This experiment gave opportunity for the study of the influence of writing upon the learning of words, however, since the writing lesson was not under the control of the experimenter and since oftentimes words that were already known were written, the results are not so reliable as they might be. It was the impression of the experimenter that the writing did not assist in the learning, probably because the child was concerned with the operation of writing so far that he did not think about what he was writing. The number of words written by the class during the period was 25. Of this number "C" learned 17, or 68 per cent; "S" learned 15, or 60 per cent; "D" learned 12, or 48 per cent, "P" learned 14, or 56 per cent; and "Sp" learned 15, or 60 per cent—an average of 58.4 per cent, a figure which does not tell anything in particular about the influence of writing. With the idea in mind that possibly a comparison of the whole number of words learned with those learned and written might show more definite results, the following percentages were worked out. "C" learned 41 words of which 17, or 41.4 per cent were written; "S" learned 30 words of which 15, or 50 per cent were written; "D" learned 21 words of which 12, or 57.1 per cent were written; "P" learned 25 words of which 14, or 52 per cent were written; and "Sp" learned 27 words of which 15, or 55.5 per cent were written. The average is 51.2 per cent, which gives even less influence to writing than the preceding percentages.

The results of the experiments are discussed in the following order: parts ot speech; word form, significance of misreadings, significance of mutilations, and methods of learning.

Table I gives results with regard to parts of speech and word form. Since the drill words of the class were selected, there is not enough variety in parts of speech to give definite results. In the case of "E," the child of the individual study, there is variety enough to show that nouns and adjectives are more easily learned than other parts of speech. This would seem to indicate that the content of the word and its use in the sentence are factors which influence the ease with which it is learned.

TABLE IA

COMPARISON OF WORDS LEARNED WITH WORDS NOT LEARNED

	E			C			S		
	Cases	Learned	Per-centage	Cases	Learned	Per-centage	Cases	Learned	Per-centage
Parts of Speech—									
Nouns	64	51	76.9	44	29	65.8	44	20	45.4
Verbs	33	11	33.3	10	6	66.6	10	4	40.
Adjectives	21	17	80.9	6	3	50.	6	3	50.
Pronouns	9	8	88.9	3	2	....	3	2	....
Adverbs	8	1	12.5	1	..	....	1	..	....
Prepositions	4	1	....	2	1	....	2	1	....
Conjunctions	2	1	....	..	..	....	..	..	....
Geometric Form—									
Linear	20	9	45	11	7	63.6	11	6	54.5
Superlinear	76	48	63.1	37	22	56.7	36	16	43.2
Sublinear	19	14	73.6	2	1	....	2	1	....
Super-and sub-linear	26	19	73.	16	11	62.5	16	71	45.
Internal Form—									
Straight	43	32	74.4	20	16	80.	20	13	65.
Curved	36	21	58.3	19	9	47.3	19	7	36.7
Neither	62	37	59.6	27	16	59.2	27	10	37.
Length—									
One	2	2	....	1	1	....	1	1	....
Two	7	6	85.7	4	2	....	4	2	....
Three	23	16	69.5	11	8	72.7	11	7	63.6
Four	39	22	56.4	20	10	50.	20	8	40.
Five	26	14	53.8	12	7	58.3	12	5	41.6
Six	17	10	58.8	7	4	57.1	7	2	25.9
Seven	13	9	62.2	3	3	....	3	2	....
Eight	1	1	....	4	3	....	4	..	....
Nine	8	5	62.5	4	3	....	4	3	....
Ten	3	3	....	..	..	....	..	..	....
Eleven	1	1	....	..	..	....	..	..	....
Twelve	1	1	....	..	..	....	..	..	....

Messmer[1] makes two classes of words, according to geometric form. The first class is linear words, like "acorns," "saw," and "were," words with no high letters. Into this group he also puts

[1] Oskar Messmer, "Zur Psychologie des Lesens bei Kindern und Erwachsenen," *Archiv für die gesamte Psychologie*, Bd. II, Hefte 2 u. 3; cf. Huey, *Psychology of Reading*, pp. 93 ff.

words with letters that extend below the line because, he says, the eye does not notice the projection and the effect is as though the letters were all letters of the line. The second class is superlinear,

TABLE I*B*

COMPARISON OF WORDS LEARNED WITH WORDS NOT LEARNED

	D			P			SP			
	Cases	Learned	Percentage	Cases	Learned	Percentage	Cases	Learned	Percentage	Average
Parts of Speech—										
Nouns	41	15	36.5	44	21	47.7	41	20	48.7	53.5
Verbs	5	1	....	8	..	....	3	1	....	34.9
Adjectives	6	3	....	6	1	16.6	6	4	66.6	52.8
Pronouns	2	2	....	3	2	....	2	1	....	....
Adverbs	..	..	....	1	..	....	..	..	....	....
Prepositions	1	..	....	2	1	....	1	1	....	....
Conjunctions										
Geometric Form—										
Linear	8	3	37.5	9	5	55.5	6	5	83.3	56.5
Superlinear	34	15	44.1	36	15	41.6	33	16	48.4	50.
Sublinear	..	..	....	2	..	....	1	1	....	....
Super- and sub-linear	13	3	23.	16	5	31.2	13	5	38.4	45.8
Internal Form—										
Straight	16	7	43.7	19	10	52.6	15	10	66.6	65.3
Curved	17	6	35.2	18	5	27.7	16	7	43.7	41.4
Neither	22	8	36.3	26	10	38.4	21	10	47.6	45.4
Length—										
One	1	1	....	1	1	....	1	..	....	....
Two	3	1	....	1	1	....	3	2	....	....
Three	9	4	44.4	9	3	33.3	9	5	55.5	56.5
Four	15	8	53.3	20	8	40.	15	8	53.3	48.8
Five	11	1	9.9	12	3	25.	11	3	27.2	35.9
Six	6	3	50.	7	3	42.8	6	3	50.	48.1
Seven	3	1	....	3	2	....	3	2	....	....
Eight	4	..	....	4	..	....	4	1	....	....
Nine	4	2	4	4	3	....	4	3	....	....
Ten	..	..	....	..	..	....	..	..	....	....
Eleven	..	..	....	..	..	....	..	..	....	....
Twelve	..	..	....	..	..	....	..	..	....	....

like "Eskimo" and "coat," words with high letters. Since the child's eye has not been trained to follow the line, two other classes not proposed by Messmer have been added: sublinear—like "primrose," "my," and "going," words containing letters that extend below the line; and super- and sublinear—like "dogs," "polar-bear," and "yesterday," words with letters that extend both above and below the line. Messmer says that the linear words are less easily recognized because the contour is unbroken. However, four of the six children learned more of the linear words than of the other groups. Except in the case of "E," the child of the individual study, there were not sublinear words enough to show any results; but in her case, these words were read somewhat more readily than those of any other group. In only one case were the superlinear words, which Messmer holds to be more easily recognized, learned more readily than those of any other group.

Messmer makes a second classification of words according to internal form based on the type of line of which the letters of the word are made. He speaks of letters of straight lines like "n" and "f," letters of curved lines like "o" and "s," letters of curved and straight lines, like "d" and "p," and letters of oblique lines, like "w" and "y." He holds that words in which straight lines predominate are least easily recognized because most of the letters belong to this class and the word has no distinctive character. He holds that words containing both letters of straight lines and letters of curved lines are most easily recognized. In the table given, by preponderance of straight lines is meant that more than one-half of the letters of the word are straight-line letters, like "ferns" which contains three straight-line letters and two curved-line letters. By preponderance of curved lines is meant that more than one-half of the letters of the word are curved-line letters, like "dogs" which contains no straight-line letters, three curved-line letters, and one straight- and curved-line letter. By preponderance of neither is meant that the letters of the word are distributed among the classes, no one of which contains more than one-half, like "worm," which has two straight-line letters, one curved-line letter, and one oblique letter. Without exception words of straight lines were most easily learned; words of curved lines less easily learned; and words of neither just a little more readily than those of curved lines.

The significance of the length of the word does not come out very plainly in this comparison, except in the case of the child in the individual study, probably because there was not variety enough in the length of the drill words. In the case of "E" the figures show that the short words and the long words were most readily learned and that the words of five letters gave most difficulty.

TABLE II

POINTS OF RESEMBLANCE BETWEEN THE WORD AND ITS MISREADING

PUPIL	MISREADINGS	LENGTH		COMMON LETTER		INITIAL LETTER		FINAL LETTER		CONTOUR		ASSOCIATION		TOTAL POINTS OF RESEMBLANCE
		Cases	Percentage	Cases	Percentage	Cases	Percentage	Cases	Percentage	Cases	Percentage	Cases	Percentage	
C..........	38	16	23.5	16	23.5	17	25.	9	13.2	5	7.4	5	7.4	68
S..........	37	26	41.9	17	27.4	2	3.2	7	11.2	6	9.6	4	6.7	62
D..........	30	17	36.1	13	27.6	13	27.6	1	2.1	3	6.4	..	...	47
P..........	27	13	35.2	7	19.4	8	22.2	4	11.1	2	5.5	2	5.5	36
Average..........			34.1	..	24.4	..	19.5	..	12.6	..	7.2	..	4.9	..
E..........	45	27	27.5	12	12.2	17	17.3	24	24.4	10	10.1	8	8.5	98

The significance of misreadings is brought out in Table II. The misreadings of each child were tabulated and points of resemblance between the word and its misreading were recorded. Of these points of resemblance, length is most common, with an average of 34.1 per cent for the class, and 27.5 per cent for "E." The common letter, for example, the "g" and "o" in "igloo," which was read "dogs," comes second for the class with an average of 24.4 per cent, though not for "E," probably because she knew the names of no letters. The initial letter is third; the final letter is fourth with the class and second with "E." The contour of the word and the association of one word with another, for example, "horse" and "wagon," are of little significance. The table brings out, however, that length, which Messmer says the child does not appreciate, is appreciated more than any other feature of the word.

The most significant table is that of mutilations (No. III). The classes of mutilations are arranged in order of least disturbance to the individual. In the first group, inversion, the words were shown to the children right side up, and after five or ten minutes they were shown again, upside down. This exercise took place in the sixth week. Only two of the five children noticed that the words were upside down; and the other three when questioned said the words looked just as they had before. This mutilation, though

TABLE III*A*

MUTILATIONS OF THE WORD AS A WHOLE

Pupil	Inversion			Transposition			Script			Substitution		
	Cases	Read as Word	Percentage	Cases	Read as Word	Percentage	Cases	Read as Word	Percentage	Cases	Read as Word	Percentage
C........	17	12	70.5	16	10	62.5	11	8	72.7	32	12	37.5
S........	16	14	87.5	16	11	68.7	14	10	71.4	29	17	58.6
D........	12	9	75.	6	4	66.6	11	9	81.8	24	7	29.1
P........	13	10	76.9	11	9	81.8	14	9	64.2	17	7	41.1
Sp.......	16	16	100.	11	11	100.	13	10	76.9	17	8	47.
Average .	14.2	12.5	81.5	12	9	75.9 *62.5	12.6	9.6	73.4	23.8	10.2	42.6
E........				8	3	37.5				21.	8.	38.4

* Average without "D."

TABLE III*B*

MUTILATIONS

Pupil	Of the Word as a Whole						Of a Part of the Word						Average
	Length and Addition, Omission or Substitution			*Contour* and Substitution or Transposition			*Final Letter* and Substitution or Transposition			*Initial Letter* and Substitution or Transposition			
	Cases	Read as Word	Percentage	Cases	Read as Word	Percentage	Cases	Read as Word	Percentage	Cases	Read as Word	Percentage	
C............	20	4	20.	19	5	26.3	22	11	50.	9	2	22.2	45.2
S............	16	6	37.5	19	9	47.3	22	12	54.5	21	14	66.6	61.5
D............	15	6	40.	16	7	43.7	13	7	53.8	18	6	33.3	53.2
P............	7	5	71.4	9	2	18.1	14	10	71.5	5	1	20.	55.6
Sp...........	7	2	28.5	9	2	18.1	14	8	57.1	5	1	20.	57.7
Average......	11.4	4.8	37.4 32.5*	14.4	.5	30.7	16.8	9.4	57.1	11.6	4.8	32.2 40.6*	
E............	14	3	21.5	9.	..	..	13	2	15.3	21.	4.	19.	20.2

* Without P and Sp.

it gave the least difficulty to the children, would probably be most difficult for the adult. It would seem that the child sees the word as a whole and recognizes it upside down, just as he would recognize a toy upside down. In the second group of mutilations, transposition, the letters of the word were shifted about, but the contour of the word was preserved; i.e., a letter of the line was put in place of a letter of the line and a high letter in place of a high letter, e.g., "nettims" for "mittens." This mutilation disturbed the children but little more than inversion. The reason may be that, up to this time at any rate, these children had made no connection between the letter and its sound and did not realize that by shifting the position of the letter a new word was made; they merely noticed that the whole word was there. From the first, script and print were used and no comment was made about the difference between the two. Almost from the first the pupils could match the word in script with the printed word and vice versa. The adult, without thinking about the matter, sees no particular resemblance between the word in script and the word in print but to the child evidently the script is merely another form of print. This may be the reason why children learn to read script and print with less effort when they are taught simultaneously than when one is taught after the other is learned and after children have come to examine word forms with some care. In the group of mutilations in which other letters were substituted for those of the word, the contour was preserved as it was in transposition, e.g., "lihac" for "lilac"; but the percentage of mutilations read as words falls from 75.9 per cent in transposition to 42.6 per cent in substitution. This would seem to show that while these children have some pretty definite conceptions of the appearance of the word as a whole, they are also conscious of the parts of the word and notice their presence or absence. In mutilations affecting the length and contour of the word more than one factor enters in, for one cannot change the length of the word without adding, omitting, or substituting a letter; e.g., "cat," "coast," and "coact" for "coat"; and he cannot change the contour of the word without transposing or substituting letters; e.g., "fed" and "der" for "red." It is to be expected that these mutilations would disturb the child more than the preceding ones and they do so—the percentages falling to 37.4 for length and 30.7 for contour. The last two groups of mutilations affected the part of the word only, though in each case there was either substitution or transposition. The figures show that for these pupils up to the time of the tests the final letter is a little more significant than the initial letter; the opposite is true with adults, probably because through training they have come to depend on the first part of the word for its recognition. It is unfortunate that no mutilations of the middle of the word were presented to determine its significance. The conclusion drawn from these mutilations is that the children saw the words as wholes and, while not conscious of the position of the parts, were conscious of their presence or absence.

The comments and the questions, as well as the misreadings, seem to show that children learn to read words by the trial and error method. It may be the length of the word, the initial letter, the final letter, a characteristic letter, the position of the word in the sentence, or even the blackness of the type that serves as the cue. There were surprisingly few instances of learning by imitation. The first occurred in the fifth week, when one child pointed out the word "the" and two other children pointed out other "the's," though similar opportunities had been presented before. Suggestion, which is a noticeable element in the reading of young children, also played a minor part. There is no evidence in any of the cases studied that the child works out a system by which he learns to recognize words. That he does not work out phonics for himself comes out quite clearly in the transposition test. Furthermore, only once did a child divide a word even into its syllables. There is some evidence that the child is conscious of the letter, though there is none that he analyzes the word letter by letter, except in the case of "E," who so analyzed the word "six." Sometimes, when the child seemed to have made a letter analysis, he failed to recognize the word a second time, and in some cases did not learn it at all.

The scope of this study does not warrant general conclusions. The purpose has been to present some concrete observations of what children do in learning to read, and to suggest some means by which such observations may be analyzed and interpreted. Some considerations which seem to the writer to be at least suggested by the results of this study may, however, be mentioned.

Under the methods of instruction employed with this class as outlined above, it appears that these beginners in reading have after two months or more of instruction secured a sufficient conception of the general appearance of a very limited number of words to recognize them as wholes, that in doing this they made use of only very general cues or points of differentiation between words and have not noticed the finer points of distinction between words and parts of words. It appeared very doubtful to the experimenter whether, under this method of teaching words as visual wholes, the pupils would, of themselves, have come to make this latter necessary analysis with much success. Without some foregoing analysis and subsequent synthesis, the differences between words are not great enough to be recognized merely from the total visual appearance. The early introduction of phonics may supply, in some measure, this analysis. There is an undoubted advantage in having words presented at the start as units and wholes, as contrasted with the discarded teaching by letters. But that a word method can be used very long without some detailed analysis of the structure and parts of the words is altogether too common a notion in the theory if not in the practice of teaching.

STUDIES OF EDUCATIONAL PRINCIPLES

CHARLES H. JUDD
The University of Chicago

I. TYPES OF CORRELATION

When the doctrine of correlation was first stated it carried with it a kind of immediate conviction. Everyone realizes that mental processes get their character from their associations. The same fact falls into two different minds. In one mind it branches out into a score of productive lines of thought; in the other it falls lifeless because there are no suggestive associations. By all means let us group around every item of experience productive associations.

The schools took up the suggestion with avidity. Teachers devoted themselves to the discovery of new and interesting associations. They even went farther. They began to invent associations. The writer has a clipping which sets forth the possibility of a novel nature-study lesson to be given on Lincoln's birthday. Because Lincoln freed the slaves, and because the slaves came from Africa, from whence the elephant also comes, the elephant is to be made a subject of special study on February 12. Of course this is not a typical example of that which the advocates of correlation would have us do in the schools, but it makes clear by its extreme character the necessity of defining what is the limit of productive correlation.

Our problem, accordingly, is not to find possible correlations, but to find productive correlations. To this end let us draw a distinction which will be helpful in marking off productive from unproductive associations.

All human experience has justified the bringing together of certain typical methods of thought without reference to the objects to which these methods of thought are applied. The most obvious case of this development of a method of thought is to be found in the science of geometry. All triangles have certain common characteristics, whether they are made of wood or stone or paper or air. We come therefore to think of triangles without reference to the material which fills them. We reason about triangles. We relate triangles to quadrilateral figures and to many-sided figures. The reason for thinking about all of these different figures together is that we thus cultivate a type of thought, a method of reasoning. In a very proper sense all triangles are correlated with each other and all triangles are correlated with all lines and all quadrilaterals.

In like manner all number relations are correlated with each other. As soon as one establishes a method of adding three and five, he has established a method of adding three and fifteen, three and twenty-five, and so on. The method of adding three is a uniform intellectual operation whether it occurs today or tomorrow, whether it is applied to apples or houses.

Differences in methods of thought explain many of our distinctions between the sciences. Thus if I think about the formation of land areas and their relations to bodies of water and other land areas I am in a geographical attitude of mind. My method of thinking is the same, whether I deal with Africa or Asia or America. I can lay down certain broad definitions which apply alike to all countries and all times. While I am interested in these geographical matters the correlations which are most obvious are all of the geographical type.

The interesting fact about many discussions of correlation is that the obvious lines of correlation just described are ignored. To many thinkers correlation of number facts means the taking of these facts out of their arithmetical connection and the placing of them in some other connection. Thus the fraction $\frac{1}{2}$ is part of a number scheme. It may be also a part of a cooking lesson, as when one wishes to divide a cupful or a quart into equal parts. Many thinkers would regard it as a true example of correlation to bring the fraction $\frac{1}{2}$ into the cooking lesson, but would fail to recognize that there is just as much correlation in relating $\frac{1}{2}$ to $\frac{1}{4}$ or to $\frac{1}{6}$.

Again the facts of history may be correlated in temporal order or they may be taken out of their temporal order to be coupled with facts of location. Many teachers would be conscious of an effort to correlate if they coupled a geographical fact with a historical fact, but would never think of using the term correlation if they proceeded from one point in history to the next.

For the purpose of defining the two types of connection which have been under discussion in the foregoing examples, let us speak of longitudinal correlations and transverse correlations. The following diagram will illustrate what is meant by the terms longitudinal and transverse.

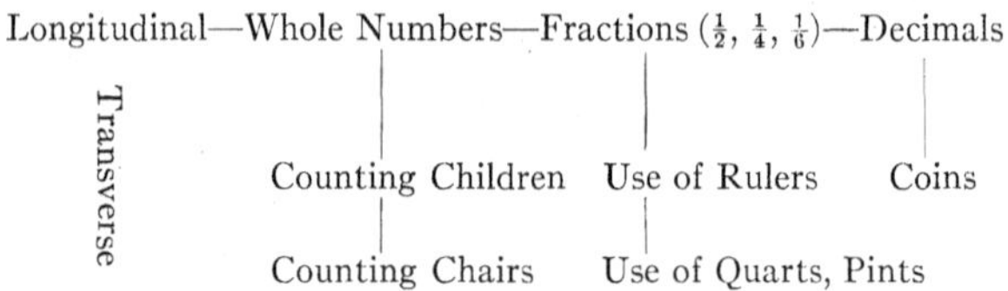

With the distinction between longitudinal correlations and transverse correlations clearly in mind, it will readily be seen that the longitudinal connections are much more systematic and orderly while the transverse connections are illustrative and concrete. The longitudinal connections depend, it will be remembered, on certain methods of thought.

Our problem in any particular case is: Which type of connection will contribute most to the training of the pupil? We need not stop to ask whether there is correlation or not, for there will always be some correlation, some connection in the mind between experiences. For no experience can ever stand alone. There will always be either forward movement in some system of well-organized knowledge or transverse movement crossing over from systematic knowledge to concrete application.

If the case is put in terms of our ordinary discussion of school problems we should say, arithmetic is a progressive system of knowledge about number facts. When the pupil learns a little about numbers he can go farther by following the same method of thinking and can thus master more and more fully the system of strictly arithmetical ideas. We stop, however, all along the line and let the child note not merely the arithmetical facts but their application also. Thus we teach the child to add, and then we teach him that adding will help him to count more rapidly all his possessions. Then we teach him that men add in stores and on the stock exchange. We relate his arithmetic to things which he knows and to many things which he does not know. In these applications we go outside of arithmetic and exemplify transverse correlation.

There are two reasons given for the emphasis of transverse correlations. First, the incidental concrete facts, such as use of rulers and quart measures, are supposed to furnish strong motives which impel the pupil to follow more willingly than he otherwise would the longitudinal series. The longitudinal series is supposed to be difficult and devoid of all natural interest.

Second, the transition from arithmetic to concrete facts is supposed to train in the applications of arithmetic. In later life, we are told, the facts will not present themselves in orderly arithmetical procession. They will come incidentally in the form of things to be measured and weighed. Children should therefore prepare to deal with the facts as they come.

These reasons for emphasizing transverse correlations can and should be met by cogent reasons for the emphasis of longitudinal systems of thought.

First, children have a great aptitude for what we call purely logical relations. Thus the child who was interested in discovering the last number was absorbed in a purely arithmetical problem. Again, the child is filled with interest when he first discovers that the order of the numerals is the same in the fifties and sixties as it is before he reaches ten. The properties of fractions are of absorbing concern to the child who grows up in a social environment which is at all commendatory of his efforts. It is a mistake to assume that children are not capable of longitudinal associations. The race has moved along these longitudinal lines in its intellectual evolution. In the schools of every generation it has been possible to train children in these longitudinal lines, as is evidenced by the criticism of the schools for cultivating exclusively these associations.

These facts may not justify us in repeating the mistake of the earlier school which trained exclusively in longitudinal correlations, but they certainly justify us in emphasizing the fact that longitudinal systems of thought are not wholly foreign to the pupil's nature.

With regard to the plea that children should apply the principles of arithmetic, there can hardly be any disagreement. Do applications interfere with the longitudinal correlation? Not at all. Indeed, it is not until the pupil has some command of the principles of arithmetic that he is in a position to apply these principles. Thus a child who has no real knowledge or appreciation of a fraction will be very much confused by the effort of the teacher to apply the fraction to a problem in cooking. The problem in cooking is so complicated in itself and it has so many natural associations with other problems in cooking that the mind does not travel readily from the kitchen to the abstract methods of reasoning suggested in number. The race to which the advocates of the mixture of cooking and number so often refer, did not mix the two issues. There was a time and place for cooking and a time and place for the cultivation of number. Indeed, in the experience of the race these two interests were usually taken care of by entirely separate people. Only in the latest stages of culture when arithmetic was a mature science and the practice of cooking was well established, did the race apply the methods of exact measurement to the practical problem. In other words, application of arithmetical science is a late stage of development. Put in terms of our earlier diagram, number was matured as a longitudinal system before transverse relations became possible.

This paper is a plea for the recognition of longitudinal systems of training. It should not be regarded as an attack upon all transverse correlations. Transverse correlations are legitimate when the mind is ready to carry over productively its matured systems of thought. The need of emphasis in educational thought of our day does not seem to lie in the direction of these transverse correlations. Our generation needs to consider the importance of certain fundamental longitudinal correlations. These are natural and legitimate. They have grown up as a result of racial experience. They are the traditional lines along which training in the schools has moved. We should not abandon them lightly.

In a subsequent paper the problem of applications will be

treated more fully. It is not assumed that the examples cited above have disposed of the matter. It is contended, however, that the possibility of a productive longitudinal association has been fully established, even when one is looking forward to practical applications. The conclusion to which we have arrived is that longitudinal correlations are at least as legitimate and productive as any other type.

[*To be continued*]

EDITORIAL NOTES

The New Commissioner of Education

When President Taft appointed Professor Claxton to the Commissionership of Education, his act was recognized on all sides not merely as a very fitting compliment to Mr. Claxton's personal qualifications for that important office, but also as a clear and timely recognition of national interest in southern education. The enthusiasm of the South for all that is new and vital in education is personified in the new Commissioner. The national office will profit by his wide acquaintance with schools and school men and women. The South will continue to benefit by his teachings and influence and the other sections of the country will gain in equal degree by his succession to the office which has up to this time been so ably filled.

The Educational System in Baltimore

The City of Baltimore has passed through a series of experiences during the last year which have been observed by educators in all parts of the country with more than ordinary interest. In 1898 a city charter was adopted which aimed to put the control of the schools out of politics. Mr. Van Sickle was appointed in 1900 to the superintendency of the newly organized school system and an era of educational progress opened. Since 1900 the course of study has been enlarged. Baltimore has become widely and favorably known for its special attention to children of unusually good ability. The supervision of schools has been extended. The teaching force has been steadily improved by judicious selection at the time of appointment and by a carefully planned system of promotional tests. All this has been done in the face of conservatism on the part of the community, inadequate financial support, and the opposition of a large number of the teachers. During the last year an acute political situation arose which resulted in the removal of Mr. Van Sickle to Springfield, Mass., where he will be less hampered by unfavorable conditions. Another result of the political crisis was the examination of the city system by a commission which rendered a full report on the educational operations of the system and set an example which is likely to be followed in many other systems. Other consequences will doubtless issue from the political activities of the past few months. It requires no prophet to foretell that Baltimore will suffer just in so far as politics continue to play a part in the school life of the city. It is equally evident that Baltimore may profit greatly by the recommendations of the commission.

Politics Have No Place in School Affairs

It is not the purpose of this editorial comment to deal further with the local issues referred to in the foregoing paragraph. All who are engaged in teaching are vitally concerned that politics shall be kept out of school affairs and are therefore distressed to see that happen which has happened in Baltimore. In the history of American education this controversy will probably come to be known more because it gave rise to a Commission of Examination than because of any of the unfortunate blunders which it made possible. Dr. Brown, commissioner of education of the United States, was invited to organize a group of educators who with himself should examine the situation in Baltimore and render a report on the efficiency of the school system.

Personnel of the Commission

Dr. Brown associated with himself Professor Cubberley of the Department of Education of Stanford University and Superintendent Kendall of Indianapolis. These gentlemen together with their assistants went to Baltimore, held hearings, visited the schools, inspected records, made comparisons of Baltimore with other cities, and rendered through the Bureau of Education a full report.

The Report

The report is evidently drafted with a view to the need of the citizen for broader information regarding school movements in all parts of the country. How money is spent, how supervision is worked out, how the course of study has grown, are all shown in clear form. This Bulletin No. 450 is a model on which Superintendents may very well pattern their reports. No community can appreciate either the virtues or defects of its school system until it has the comparative figures which show how the local system ranks with others of like size. In the second place the report is an example of scientific study of education. Facts are here presented which cannot be overthrown by mere prejudices. Baltimore must face squarely the inadequacy of her educational budget, the inadequacy of her sanitary arrangements, the absence of any progressive social movements for the larger use of her school plant, the inadequacy of her provision for supervision. It is great wisdom to face facts of this kind frankly and openly. When the value of such impartial examinations is fully realized we shall undoubtedly see many schools examining themselves in a similar manner.

The Example of New York

New York City is giving another example to the educational world of scientific study of school affairs. The financial authorities of New York have initiated an inquiry into the efficiency of the educational system of that city. Professor Hanus of the Department of Education of Harvard has taken a leave of absence for a year from the work of his department to carry on this investigation. As in Baltimore so also in New York practical interests of a complicated character are at stake. The educational world will note with profound interest the development of the New York investigation. The interest which will attach to this inquiry will not be limited, however, to the immediate issues which it raises or settles. The matter of largest importance to the history of education is the method of scientific investigation which is at once illustrated and cultivated by such an investigation. The student of the science of education notes these studies of school efficiency with satisfaction. They mark the opening of a new and productive attitude toward school problems.

BOOK REVIEWS

A Cyclopedia of Education. Edited by PAUL MONROE, with the assistance of Departmental Editors, etc. Vol. I. New York: Macmillan, 1911.

It would be difficult to overestimate the importance of this first *Cyclopedia of Education* in English. This is true either from a consideration of the need of such a work or of the manner in which it is being carried out. The editor, in the preface to the first volume, gives as evidence of the need the "vast and varied character of educational literature," "the growing importance of the school as a social factor," and "the great numerical strength of the teaching profession, and its rapidly changing personnel." The *Cyclopedia* will serve as a unifier of the varied literature, and as an introduction and guide to its further study; it will be a means of acquainting the general public with the school and its problems; and it will prove an indispensable instrument for the advancement of the teachers in their professional equipment.

That the work will be efficiently carried out is guaranteed by the character of its editors. The editor-in-chief, Professor Monroe, is well known as the chief authority in the history of education in America. Each of the departmental editors is well known in his field as may be seen from a glance at their names: Elmer E. Brown, Edward F. Buchner, William H. Burnham, Gabriel Compayré, Ellwood P. Cubberley, John Dewey, Charles H. Judd, Arthur F. Leach, Will S. Monroe, J. E. G. de Montmorency, Wilhelm Münch, David Snedden, Henry Suzzallo, and Foster Watson. These are asisted by over one thousand individual contributors, many of whom are themselves eminent. The general scholarly standing of the work leaves nothing to be desired.

The *Cyclopedia* aims to treat of all of the topics which are in any way connected with education in any of its branches. Topics of historical importance include a discussion of types of schools, such as the Abbey Schools, or individual schools, as Abbotsholme; an account of prominent educators, as Abelard; of educational devices or methods, as the Abacus or the A-B-C method. Besides this, many other topics are treated historically—such, for example, as arithmetic. Another type of topic treats of the philosophy of education, as Adaptation, or of educational psychology, as Attention or Adolescence. Administration is treated in Accredited Schools and similar topics. The use of the book not merely as a work of reference, but also as a collection of systematic treatises on such topics as these, is facilitated by a full system of cross references. This plan is still further carried out by listing the main subtopics under the general topic as a heading. Thus, by turning to the title Administration one is referred to a series of articles which together give a systematic treatment of this subject.

Another type of discussion which is of great value in bringing together a large mass of scattered information is the description of current educational systems and organizations. Thus the education in each country in the civilized world, each state and important city in the United States is presented. Also each prominent university in the world is described. One function of the *Cyclopedia* is to serve as a dictionary of educational terms, including foreign words. For example, in the first volume are defined Anschauung, Arbiturientenprüfung, and Aggregation. One article which should prove very convenient consists in a list of educational bibliographies under the title Bibliography.

The only criticisms to be offered of the work refer to details rather than to its general plan or character. The most obvious type of question in the mind of the reviewer of a cyclopedia is in regard to the proportion in the treatment of various topics. It is recognized also, of course, that this is one of the most difficult problems of the editors on account of the great number and variety of the contributors. A few examples may be given, however, which indicate rather glaring inequality of treatment. Arithmetic, for example, is given four pages, while Archaeology is given eleven pages, School Architecture (together with the allied subject of Blackboards), eighteen pages, and Architectural Education, six pages. Some other contrasts are Apprenticeship and Education, twelve pages, and Aptitude, less than one-half of a page; Athletics, eighteen pages; Backward Pupils, one-sixth of a page; Alcuin, less than one and one-half pages; Chesterfield, three pages. One and one-half pages are given to a historical curiosity, the Boy Bishop. Not only are some of the articles too detailed and technical for their purpose, but some of the bibliographies would be a better guide to the reader of such a work if they were shorter and more selective. For example, the article on Botanical Gardens gives thirty-seven titles in the bibliography and Archaeology sixty-one titles.

The reviewer noticed the omission of three names from the list of contributors: C. S. G., author of Botanical Gardens; S. M. L., author of Childhood; and A. F. C., author of Children, Criminality in. As these cases were discovered at random, there are doubtless others. Only two misprints were noticed. In general, the mechanical features of the book are excellent.

In conclusion, it may be said that no public or educational library can afford to be without this cyclopedia, and everybody in any way connected with education should have it at his disposal.

FRANK N. FREEMAN

THE UNIVERSITY OF CHICAGO

BOOKS RECEIVED

AMERICAN BOOK CO., NEW YORK

English Composition. Book I. By STRATTON D. BROOKS. Cloth. Pp. 294. $0.75.
Essentials of Biology. By GEORGE WILLIAM HUNTER. Cloth. Illustrated. Pp. 448. $1.25.
Elements of Geology. By ELIOT BLACKWELDER AND HARLAN H. BARROWS. Cloth. Illustrated. Pp. 475. $1.40.
Ekkehard—Audifax und Hadumoth. By JOSEPH VICTOR VON SCHEFFEL. Edited by CHARLES HART HANDSCHIN AND WILLIAM F. LUEBKE. Cloth. Pp. 251. $0.60.
How the World Is Housed. By FRANK GEORGE CARPENTER. Cloth. Illustrated. Pp. 352. $0.60.
Makers and Defenders of America. By ANNA ELIZABETH FOOTE. Cloth. Illustrated. Pp. 342. $0.60.
The Story of Modern France. By H. A. GUERBER. Cloth. Illustrated. Pp. 350. $0.65.
Laboratory Manual in Biology. By RICHARD W. SHARPE. Cloth. Illustrated. Pp. 353. $0.75.
School Hymnal. By HOLLIS DANN. Cloth. Pp. 191. $0.50.
A Language Series. Book II. By ROBERT C. METCALF AND AUGUSTINE L. RAFTER. Cloth. Illustrated. Pp. 365. $0.60.
Argumentation and Debate. By JOSEPH VILLIERS DENNEY. Cloth. Pp. 400. $1.25.
Old Testament Narratives. By EDWARD CHAUNCEY BALDWIN. Cloth. Maps. Pp. 192. $0.20.
Don Quixote for Young People. By JAMES BALDWIN. Cloth. Illustrated. Pp. 287. $0.50.
Les origines de la France contemporaine. By H. A. TAINE. Edited by J. F. L. RASCHEN. Cloth. Pp. 272. $0.60.
Historical Reader. By HORACE L. BRITTAIN AND JAMES G. HARRIS. Cloth. Pp. 266. $0.75.
Molière: Les femmes savantes. By CHARLES A. EGGERT. Cloth. Pp. 187. $0.40.
First Year Algebra. By WILLIAM J. MILNE. Cloth. Pp. 321. $0.85.
Inland Voyage and Travels with a Donkey. By GILBERT SYKES BLAKELY. Cloth. Pp. 303. $0.40.
History of American Literature. By REUBEN POST HALLECK. Illustrated. Cloth. Pp. 432. $1.25.
The Eleanor Smith Music Primer. By ELEANOR SMITH. Cloth. Pp. 128. $0.25.
Horace : Satires and Epistles. By EDWARD P. MORRIS. Cloth. Pp. 493. $1.25.

D. APPLETON & CO.

A History of the United States. By ANDREW C. McLAUGHLIN AND CLAUDE HALSTEAD VAN TYNE. Cloth. Pp. 430.

FORBES & CO., CHICAGO

Truths. Talks with a Boy concerning Himself. By E. B. LOWRY, M.D. Cloth. Pp. 95. $0.50.

GINN & CO., BOSTON

The Quest of the Four-Leaved Clover. Adapted from the French of Laboulaye's "Abdullah," by WALTER TAYLOR FIELD. Cloth. Illustrated. Pp. 209. $0.40.

Education as Growth; or the Culture of Character. By L. H. JONES. Cloth. Pp. 275.

Barbarian and Noble. By MARION FLORENCE LANSING. Cloth. Pp. 183. $0.35.

GOVERNMENT PRINTING OFFICE, WASHINGTON

Annual Report of the Board of Regents of the Smithsonian Institution. Cloth. Illustrated. Pp. 751.

GUNTHORP-WARREN CO., CHICAGO

The Social Evil in Chicago: A Study of Existing Conditions, with Recommendations by the Vice Commission of Chicago. Paper. Illustrated. Pp. 358.

HOUGHTON MIFFLIN CO., BOSTON

The Story of the Roman People. By EVA MARCH TAPPAN. Cloth. Illustrated. Pp. 251. $0.65.

The Night Before Thanksgiving, A White Heron, and Selected Stories. By SARAH ORNE JEWETT. Cloth. Pp. 119. $0.25.

Children's Classics in Dramatic Form. Book I. By AUGUSTA STEVENSON. Cloth. Illustrated by CLARA E. ATWOOD. Pp. 116. $0.30.

Teaching Poetry in the Grades. By MARGARET W. HALIBURTON AND AGNES G. SMITH. Cloth. Pp. 116. $0.60.

Primer. By JAMES H. VAN SICKLE AND WILHELMINA SEEGMILLER. Cloth. Pp. 128. $0.30.

First Reader. By JAMES H. VAN SICKLE AND WILHELMINA SEEGMILLER. Cloth. Pp. 128. $0.35.

B. F. JOHNSON PUBLISHING CO., RICHMOND

Elementary Algebra. By JOHN M. COLAW AND JAMES K. POWERS. Cloth. Pp. 344. $0.90

Fifty Famous Fables. By LIDA BROWN MCMURRY. Cloth. Illustrated. Pp. 126. $0.30.

LITTLE, BROWN & CO.

Fanciful Flower Tales. By MADGE A. BIGHAM. Cloth. Pp. 162. Illustrated. $0.50.

Smoky Days' Wigwam Evenings. By CHARLES A. EASTMAN AND ELAINE GOODALE EASTMAN. Illustrated. Cloth. Pp. 148. $0.60.

Children of History. By MARY S. HANCOCK. Cloth. Pp. 142. Illustrated. $0.50.

CURRENT EDUCATIONAL LITERATURE IN THE PERIODICALS[1]

IRENE WARREN
Librarian, School of Education, The University of Chicago

ABERDEEN, THE COUNTESS OF. The woman's national health association of Ireland and infant welfare. Child 1:759–72. (Je. '11.)

ANDREWS, BENJAMIN R. The girl of tomorrow: what the school will do for her. World's Work 22:14526–30. (Je. '11.)

ARNOLD, F. S. Thomas Arnold of Rugby. Child 1:711–14. (My. '11.)

BALDWIN, BIRD T. The psychology of mental deficiency. Pop. Sci. Mo. 79:82–93. (Jl. '11.)

BARKER, D. WILSON. The Thames nautical training college, H.M.S. "Worcester." Child 1:715–22. (My. '11.)

BERGENGREN, RALPH. Free dentistry for poor children. Tech. World M. 15:664–66. (Ag. '11.)

BETZ, W. College entrance requirements in modern languages. School R. 19:406–9. (Je. '11.)

BIGELOW, MARGUERITE OGDEN. The girl of tomorrow and her education. Craftsman 20:241–49. (Je. '11.)

BILLIARDE, F. J. Winnipeg and the child welfare exhibit. Child 1:845–58. (Jl. '11.)

BISHOP, J. REMSEN. The poor results in Latin teaching. Educa. R. 41:489–98. (My. '11.)

BLAYNEY, THOMAS LINDSEY. The modern languages as cultural college disciplines. Educa. R. 41:478–88. (My. '11.)

BRIDGE, JOHN C. The Dunfermline school clinic. Child 1:680–86. (My. '11.)

BROOME, EDWIN C. The attitude of the teacher towards his profession. Educa. 31:604–13. (My. '11.)

[1] *Abbreviations.*—Amer. Physical Educa. Rev., American Physical Education Review; Atlan., Atlantic; Cent., Century; Chaut., Chautauquan; Educa., Education; Educa. Bi-mo., Educational Bi-monthly; Educa. R., Educational Review; Educa. T., Educational Times; Journ. of Educa. (Bost.), Journal of Education (Boston); Journ. of Educa. Psychol., Journal of Educational Psychology; Kind. Mag., Kindergarten Magazine; Lit. D., Literary Digest; Liv. Age, Living Age; Nature Study Rev., Nature Study Review; Out., Outlook; Pedagog. Sem., Pedagogical Seminary; Pop. Sci. Mo., Popular Science Monthly; Psychol. Clinic, Psychological Clinic; Pub. Lib., Public Libraries; Relig. Educa., Religious Education; R. of Rs., Review of Reviews; School R., School Review; School W., School World; Tech. World M., Technical World Magazine.

BUTLER, NICHOLAS M. The Kahn foundation for the foreign travel of American teachers. R. of Rs., 44:47–48. (Jl. '11.)

BYERS, J. P. Needed legislation. Training School (N.J.) 8:33–37. (My. '11.)

CARRIGAN, THOMAS C. The law and the American child. Pedagog. Sem. 18:121–83. (Jl. '11.)

CASSIDY, M. A. The common schools. Educa. 31:646–51. (Je. '11.)

CLEGHORN, ISABEL. A system of national education. School W. 13:181–84. (My. '11.)

CLOUSTON, T. S. The mental effects of a child's environment (1, 2). Child 1:663–71, 779–86. (My., Je. '11.)

CURTIS, HENRY S. Playground training. Amer. Physical Educa. Rev. 16:302–8. (My. '11.)

DEAN OF NORWICH. On being more Froebelian than Froebel. Child Life 13:135–39. (Je. '11.)

EDER, M. D. Training colleges of the future. Child Life 13:105–8. (My. '11.)

ELIOT, CHARLES W. The differentiation of the high-school course in English. Educa. 31:639–45. (Je. '11.)

ELLIOTT, ORRIS LESLIE. University standards and student activities. Pop. Sci. Mo. 79:68–81. (Jl. '11.)

FARRINGTON, FREDERICK ERNEST. National union of teachers of England and Wales. Educa. R. 42:54–59. (Je. '11.)

FAUNCE, W. H. P. Choosing teaching as a profession. Educa. 31:599–603. (My. '11.)

FELMLEY, DAVID. What share shall the normal schools take in a general movement towards vocational training? Educa. Bi-mo. 5:395–401. (Je. '11.)

GIBSON, CHARLES R. The teaching of science for children. Child 1:693–95. (My. '11.)

GILES, FREDERIC M. Conversion and moral instruction. Relig. Educa. 6:268–76. (Ag. '11.)

GLYNN, FRANK L. The practical public school. World's Work 22:14721–25. (Ag. '11.)

GODDARD, HENRY H. Two thousand normal children measured by the Binet measuring scale of intelligence. Pedagog. Sem. 18:232–59. (Jl. '11.)

GRAY, HENRY DAVID. The poor professor. Educa. R. 42:29–47. (Je. '11.)

GROSSMAN, LOUIS. Jewish religious education. Relig. Educa. 6:276–81. (Ag. '11.)

GULICK, LUTHER H. Measurements as applied to school hygiene. Journ. of Educa. Psychol. 2:301–5. (Je. '11.)

HALE, WILLIAM GARDNER. The harmonizing of grammatical nomenclature in high-school study. School R. 19:361–82. (Je. '11.)

HANCOCK, JOHN A. The place of reasoning in teaching. Pedagog. Sem. 18:184–96. (Jl. '11.)

HARPER, CHARLES F. What constitutes preparation for college: the high-school view. Educa. 31:585–98. (My. '11.)

HEMENWAY, H. D. Gardens for children. Child 1:787–90. (Je. '11.)

HICKMAN, J. E. How to reach the individual student. Educa. 31:663–68. (Je. '11.)

HILL, DAVID S. Comparative study of children's ideals. Pedagog. Sem. 18:219–31. (Jl. '11.)

HILLIS, MRS. NEWELL D. The girl graduate. Out. 98:548–52. (8 Jl. '11.)

HOLMES, W. H. How the college entrance certificate board can help the high school. Educa. 31:567–77. (My. '11.)

HOPPER, FRANKLIN F. The basis of support for the public-library work. Pub. Lib. 16:238–44. (Je. '11).

How Chicago manages her art. Lit. D. 42:1199. (17 Je. '11.)

JESSE, RICHARD HENRY. Some helpful educators. Educa. R. 42:20–28. (Je. '11.)

JOHNSON, G. E. Play as a moral equivalent of war. Amer. Physical Educa. Rev. 16:291–301. (My. '11.)

JOHNSON, RALPH L. A score of difficult boys. Psychol. Clinic 5:121–27. (Jl. '11.)

JONAS, J. E. B. Intra-national exchange of teachers. Educa. R. 42:60–70. (Je. '11.)

JONES, W. FRANKLIN. An experimental-critical study of the problem of grading and promotion (1, 2). Psychol. Clinic 5:63–96, 99–120. (My., Je. '11.)

KING, CHARLES A. Vocational training in the public schools. Educa. 31:657–62. (Je. '11.)

KIRK, JOHN, AND OTHERS. Child problems: the national insurance bill and child welfare. Child 1:885–88. (Jl. '11.)

KOCH, MRS. C. VON. Chautauqua—a center of popular education. Chaut. 63:32–39. (Je. '11.)

LANKESTER, RAY. Compulsory science versus compulsory Greek. Liv. Age 51:606–18. (3 Je. '11.)

MCCURDY, J. H. Play and physical education for boys over ten. Amer. Physical Educa. Rev. 16:315–20. (My. '11.)

MACKENZIE, WM. D. Standardization of theological education. Relig. Educa. 6:253–61. (Ag. '11.)

MCMILLAN, MARGARET. The Deptford clinic, or health centre, for school children. Child 1:672–79. (My. '11.)

MANNY, FRANK A. The elementary school curriculum. Kind. Mag. 23:247–52. (My. '11.)

MATHENY, W. A. The common drinking cup. Pedagog. Sem. 18:205–13. (Jl. '11.)

MEIKLEJOHN, ALEXANDER. What constitutes preparation for college: the college view. Educa. 31:578–98. (My. '11.)

MEISSNER, AMELIA. Educational museum of St. Louis public schools. Nature Study Rev. 7:113–16. (My. '11.)

MILLER, WILLIAM T. What is wrong with our boys? Atlan. 107:789–93. (Je. '11.)

MILLNER, A. The problem of Jewish education. Pedagog. Sem. 18:214–18. (Jl. '11.)

MONTGOMERY, THOMAS H., JR. Expansion of the usefulness of natural history museums. Pop. Sci. Mo. 79:36–44. (Jl. '11.)

MOORE, CLIFFORD H. A new plan of admission to Harvard college. Educa. R. 42:71–78. (Je. '11.)

MOSES, MONTROSE J. The New York public library. R. of Rs. 43:701–8. (Je. '11.)

MOULTON, PRESTON S. Some uses of the classics to a modern student. Educa. 31:652–56. (Je. '11.)

MURRAY, E. R. A short history of infant schools and kindergartens in England. (4, 5.) Child Life 13:108–10, 141–45. (My., Je. '11.)

MUZZEY, DAVID SAVILLE. State, church, and school in France. IV. Moral education as an ideal of the French republic. School R. 19:383–97. (Je. '11.)

NICE, LEONARD B. The disinfection of books. Pedagog. Sem. 18:197–204. (Jl. '11.)

O'SHEA, M. V. Psychology in the normal school. Journ. of Educa. Psychol. 2:322–33. (Je. '11.)

PATTEN, SIMON N. An economic measure of school efficiency. Educa. R. 41:467–77. (My. '11.)

PHILLIPSON, J. T. The school-leaving age. School W. 13:169–72. (My. '11.)

PORRITT, ANNIE G. The feminization of our schools and its political consequences. Educa. R. 41:441–48. (My. '11.)

PORTER, MARY W. The boys' club in our town. Out. 98:591–93. (15 Jl. '11.)

PRENTICE, E. PARMALEE. The new opportunity of the small college. Harper 123:133–37. (Je. '11.)

PUTNAM, HELEN C. Education for parenthood. Relig. Educa. 6:159–66. (Je. '11.) Journ. of Educa. (Bost.) 74:33–35, 47–48. (Jl. '11.)

PYLE, WILLIAM H. Retention as related to repetition. Journ. of Educa. Psychol. 2:311–21. (Je. '11.)

(The) qualification of inspectors of schools. School W. 13:161–63. (My. '11.)

RANGER, WALTER E. Higher recognition for the teacher. Educa. 31:614–20. (My. '11.)

REAVIS, W. C. The importance of a study-program for high-school pupils. School R. 19:398–405. (Je. '11.)

RITSON, JOHN H. The Bible and the child. Child 1:773–78. (Je. '11.)

SACHS, JULIUS. The training of the teacher of the classics in Germany. Educa. R. 41:449–66. (My. '11.)

SADLER, MICHAEL E. Education according to Tolstoy. Educa. R. 41:433–40. (My. '11.)

ST. HELIER, LADY. The training of English children. Cent. 82:175–81. (Je. '11.)

SALISBURY, ROLLIN D. The Round Table conference of the Association of American Geographers on the teaching of geography. Educa. Bi-mo. 5:402–6. (Je. '11.)

SAVAGE, GEORGE H. Backward children. Child 1:859–64. (Jl. '11.)

Schools for cripples. Lit. D. 43:134. (22 Jl. '11.)

(The) secret of precocity. Lit. D. 43:100–101. (15 Jl. '11.)

SHERLOCK, ANNIE. Pioneers and benefactors: Dickens and the welfare of children. Child 1:889–92. (Jl. '11.)

SHERLOCK, E. B. Intelligence tests for the feeble-minded. Child 1:791–95. (Je. '11.)

SMITH, GRANT. The school museum. Nature Study Rev. 7:117–23. (My. '11.)

SPRANGER, EDUARD. The significance of the continuation school for the educational system and the educational ideal of Germany. Educa. R. 42:1–19. (Je. '11.)

STARCH, DANIEL. Transfer of training in arithmetical operations. Journ. of Educa. Psychol. 2:306–10. (Je. '11.)

STORY, A. J. The deaf child. Child 1:875–81. (Jl. '11.)

STRIBLING, E. H. The school museum. Child Life 13:114–17. (My. '11.)

TAYLOR, JAMES M. The problem of the larger college. Educa. R. 42:79–84. (Je. '11.)

TERMAN, LEWIS M. Medical inspection of schools in California. Psychol. Clinic 5:57–62. (My. '11.)

Tests of child-intelligence. Lit. D. 42:999–1000. (20 My. '11.)

THORNTON, J. S. The first people's high school in England. Educa. T. 64:194–95. (My. '11.)

TUCKER, WILLIAM JEWETT. Undergraduate scholarship. Atlan. 107:740–50. (Je. '11.)

TYLER, ALICE S. The effect of the commission plan of government on public libraries. Pub. Lib. 16:281–84. (Jl. '11.)

University aid for the drama. Lit. D. 43:141. (22 Jl. '11.)

VINCENT, RALPH. The infants' hospital and its work. Child 1:723–31. (My. '11.)

WARNER, ALLAN. The problem of the neglected child. Child 1:865–74. (Jl. '11.)

WEBB, WILDRED MARK. The Selborne society—what it does for children. Child 1:696–701. (My. '11.)

WELLMAN, H. C. The library as an investment. Pub. Lib. 16:277–280. (Jl. '11.)

WHITBECK, R. H. High-school geography: what of its future. Educa. Bi-mo. 5:407–12. (Je. '11)

WHITNEY, FRANK P. The "American idea" and the American high school. School R. 19:410–11. (Je. '11.)

WHITNEY, FRANK P. The teaching of natural science in our American high schools. Educa. 31:674–87. (Je. '11.)

WINCHESTER, BENJ. S. The religious element in public education. Relig. Educa. 6:261–67. (Ag. '11.)

WOOD, E. B. The constitution and work of industrial and reformatory schools. School W. 13:166–69. (My. '11.)

WOODWORTH, R. S. Psychology in the college course. Educa. R. 41:499–506. (My. '11.)

WYER, J. I., JR. What the community owes the library. Pub. Lib. 16:244–45. (Je. '11.)

YONGE, EUGENE S. Throat conditions in infancy and childhood. Child 1:882–84. (Jl. '11.)

VOLUME XII NUMBER 2

THE ELEMENTARY SCHOOL TEACHER

OCTOBER, 1911

SOME ISSUES IN THE TEACHING OF HANDWRITING. II

FRANK N. FREEMAN
The University of Chicago

III

The previous article closed with a discussion of the application of the general issue between the analytic and the synthetic methods to the relation of form and movement.

A question which is closely related to the one which has just been discussed concerns the advisability of training all of the elements of the writing movement simultaneously, or training first one and then the other. The same answer may probably be given here as in the question of the relation of form and movement. The writing movement is so complex that it is doubtless better (unless indeed we attempt to confine it to one component) to lay emphasis first upon one of the components and then upon the other. The question then remains whether it is better to train first the finger component or the arm component. This question has already been touched upon. It may be added to what has already been said that although the child may use the finger movements predominantly in his early writing at the desk, the arm movements may be advantageously employed in writing at the board or even in writing with wax crayon or pencil upon paper. That is, when the child is using materials which call for large rough movements he may readily employ the arm movements. But when he is attempting to write letters in smaller compass and to produce letters correct in form it is probably well to allow him at first to follow his natural inclination to use the finger movement.

The use of the arm component in conjunction with the finger movements may then be deferred until the child has developed greater motor skill and control.

IV

The third application of the alternative between the analytic and the synthetic methods is found in the development of the letter forms. That is, the procedure may be to begin with words or groups of letters and lead the child to perfect the individual details of form by a subsequent analysis. This procedure has the advantage of eliciting the interest of the child from the beginning, and of training not merely the separate letters, but also at the same time the connections between them. The advantages then of this method are based upon the considerations of interest and economy.

The synthetic method, on the other hand, begins with the individual letters or even the so-called "elements of the letters." The extreme form of this method is now very seldom used, but was quite common two or three decades ago, and we still find traces of it. The extreme synthetic method is fallacious in supposing that the elements into which the letters are analyzed are the psychological elements of the letters. It therefore puts an unnecessary burden upon the mind of the child by calling to his attention these artificial parts of the letters. The letter is a psychological unit and defects in its form may be remedied by calling attention to them without the burden of the procedure of developing a series of elements. The question, then, is concerned with the alternative between the use of letters or of words at the beginning of the writing drill. The use of the letters—that is, the synthetic method—has the advantage of thoroughness in the training of the perception of form. It is a question, however, whether it is necessary to use the one or the other of these two methods exclusively. If words are used as the main basis of writing, then this procedure may be supplemented by the introduction of drill upon the letters whenever this seems to be necessary to remedy defects which may be found, or systematic drill upon the letters may be used to supplement the writing of words.

V

The final question in the teaching of writing to be discussed concerns the best form of movement to be employed. Several different forms of movement are distinguished in ordinary practice. These may be designated as the free-arm movement, the arm movement with rest, the finger movement, and the combined movement. The free-arm movement is made by swinging the arm freely from the shoulder. The arm movement with rest is the same as the free arm movement, except that the forearm rests upon the desk. This is often called the muscular movement, because the arm moves upon the muscle pad in the forearm as a sort of pivot. This term, however, is clearly a misnomer, since all movements are muscular, and the term "arm movememt with rest" is a much better one.

The arm movement and the arm movement with rest are made without the co-operation of the fingers in the formation of the letters. In the finger movement, on the other hand, the fingers form the letters without the co-operation of the movement of the arm. The arm is only used so far as is necessary to carry the hand across the page. In the combined movement the arm carries the hand freely across the page, and co-operates to a certain extent in the individual strokes of the letters, but the fingers produce for the most part the details of the letters.

There is a third movement which is not included in the catalogue given above, but which may co-operate to a considerable extent in carrying the hand from one letter to another, and even in making the longer strokes of the letters. This movement is the rotation about the wrist joint.

The question now is, whether it is better to seek to develop one or the other of the extreme types of movement, or the combined movement. Extreme finger movement may be left out of account, since its disadvantages are manifest. The issue is between the exclusive use of the arm movement and a use of the combined arm, finger, and wrist movement.

The discovery of the advantages of the arm movement by teachers of commercial penmanship has led to its very general adoption. It is a question, however, whether there are not disadvantages in this type of movement which minimize its advantages when it is used to the exclusion of the finger movement. The extreme emphasis on arm movement may be natural as a reaction against exclusive finger movement, but the whole question may now be thrown open for psychological analysis and for impartial investigation.

The arguments for the arm movement may be reviewed briefly. In the first place, arm movement is held to be superior because it involves so-called fundamental movements in distinction to the finger movements which are described as accessory. The meaning of fundamental and accessory movements in current use is not always clear. Several different meanings may, however, be distinguished. A fundamental movement is sometimes described as one which involves the larger muscles. If this is the basis of the distinction, it is clear that fundamental movements are by no means exclusively characteristic of the earlier period of the child's development, and cannot therefore be held to be more natural because of priority. The infant possesses very early many movements which involve small muscles. Among these are, for example, movements of the eyes, movements used in facial expression, the movements of the lips, tongue, and throat in sucking and swallowing, and the movements of the hand in grasping. These all develop before there is control over the large muscles of the trunk and legs in sitting, standing, or walking.

The second distinction which is sometimes made is that between central and peripheral movements. Central movements are those of the trunk or near the trunk, and peripheral movements those toward the extremity of the limbs. Thus finger movements would be peripheral. It is by no means certain, however, that the child shows a decided preference for central as distinguished from peripheral movements. The grasping reflex often appears during the first few days of life. Movements of the toes and feet are also very common in early infancy, and the abundant movements of the face may be regarded as peripheral in comparison with body movements.

These are the more common interpretations of fundamental and accessory movement. A third distinction is more important. This distinction relates to the degree to which a movement is developed as an instinct early in the evolution of the race. Thus grasping is a fundamental movement, while writing is an accessory movement. As a consequence of this principle, the more a habit which is to be acquired has in common with instinctive movements, the more easily it may be learned. This distinction, however, does not affect the issue between finger and arm movements since writing by either form of movement is not instructive.

The ease or difficulty with which a new movement is learned, then, is not determined to a great extent by the degree to which it is fundamental or accessory in the above senses of the terms. The conditions which do render a new movement difficult are, in general, the degree of its complexity and the degree of delicacy of adjustment which it demands. A movement which involves the co-ordination of a large number of different elementary movements is very much more difficult to learn than one which involves fewer elementary movements. Again, the movement which must be made within very narrowly defined limits is more difficult than a large coarse movement. From this point of view the arm movement possesses both an advantage and a disadvantage, in comparison with the finger movement. The arm movement clearly is less complex than the combined arm and finger movement, and so far forth is easier. On the other hand, the fingers are capable of a more delicate adjustment than the arm, and in this respect they have the advantage. We must therefore appeal to other considerations in order to arrive at a solution of the question.

Another reason which is offered why the arm movement should be preferred to the finger movement is that it is less fatiguing. There are no tests by which this question has been investigated, but general experience would seem to bear out the contention. It is found, for example, that writer's cramp may be prevented or to a certain extent relieved by an emphasis on the freer arm movements. It should be pointed out, however, that this consideration is not entirely conclusive. The use of the arm movement may render the total movement less fatiguing partly because it renders the writing freer and more open, and partly because it distributes the work by dividing it between the fingers and the arm. Another reason that this procedure relieves cramping is that the larger muscles are not so easily set in motion by the nervous impulse as the smaller muscles. It is observed, for example, that in some forms of general nervous excitation it is the smaller muscles which are first affected. There seems then to be a tendency to overemphasize the use of the smaller muscles, and it is therefore worth while to counteract this tendency by consciously emphasizing the use of the larger muscles. The evidence then indicates that the arm movement should be employed, but not necessarily to the exclusion of the finger movements.

A further reason which is advanced for the use of the arm movements is that they are more rapid than the finger movements. The fact which is here appealed to is doubtful. Experiments which have been made to determine the relative speed of movement of different joints of the arm and hand have shown that one can tap with the finger the most rapidly, and with the wrist, elbow, and shoulder successively less rapidly in the order named. The comparison of a rapid succession of up and down strokes made with the finger movement and with the arm movement also shows that the finger movement is slightly more rapid than the arm movement.

The arguments which may be advanced then in favor of the exclusive use of arm movement are not conclusive. They do indicate that the arm movement is a necessary element in the best form of writing movement.

There are further some considerations against the exclusive use of the arm movement. It is a fact which may readily be confirmed by observation that even when the exclusive arm movement is taught in the school, the pupils revert to a combined movement. That is, the teaching is not successful in training the exclusive use of the arm movement. This would seem to indicate on the face of it that it is natural to use the fingers to perform part of the work of writing.

This inference from general practice is confirmed by experiments upon the relative accuracy or delicacy of control of the fingers and of the arm. It has been found that the fingers are capable of a much more exact and delicate adjustment than the arm. It has also been found that when it is necessary to make a delicate adjustment there is a tendency to emphasize the use of the fingers in contrast to the arm. This would indicate that the fingers are well adapted to perform the parts in the production of the letters which require the more delicate adjustment.

A further general consideration is that the movement of the arm requires the expenditure of much greater energy than the movement of the fingers, on account of the larger mass which must be set in motion. There is consequently more inertia to be overcome when the whole arm is used to make the details of the letters.

It would seem from a psychological analysis of the writing movement, then, that the most favorable type of movement is one which combines the use of the arm, of the wrist, and of the fingers, in such a way that each does the work for which it is best adapted. The arm is clearly adapted to carry the hand along the line. Rotation about the wrist may readily carry the fingers along during the course of the formation of a group of letters or of a word. The fingers may co-operate by producing the details of the letters. In general the best condition for an efficient movement is one in which the various joints are not held in a rigid position, but in which there is such flexibility that there may be smooth and harmonious co-operation between them. The suppression of one component movement on the part of the hand which is naturally flexible requires a condition of continual muscular tension and this interferes with ease and rapidity of the whole movement. The condition which is most favorable, then, to a rapid and easy movement is one of general flexibility and of harmonious co-operation of the different joints.

Such then are some of the issues which confront the teacher of writing, and such are at least some of the psychological principles which must be taken account of in their solution. Whether the solutions are correct or not may be decided by the trial of the alternative methods under standard conditions, and with a measurement of the results obtained by them. The writer would repeat, then, the suggestion made at the beginning of these articles, that these or other questions be submitted to practical tests and to a measurement of the results of these tests so that some definite check may be made upon the theoretical considerations.

REPORT ON THE STUDY OF RETARDATION IN THE SCHOOLS OF INDIANAPOLIS, 1908-1911

GEORGE A. MIRICK
Acting Superintendent of Schools, Indianapolis

In the spring of 1908, as a result of discussions in the meetings of the supervising principals, and of some informal investigations, the superintendent of schools, Dr. C. N. Kendall, arranged that a full report of retarded pupils be made at the time of the term promotions in June. (The school year is divided into two terms, one closing January 31, the other closing June 15.)

In carrying out this arrangement, the following blank was prepared:

INDIANAPOLIS PUBLIC SCHOOLS

REPORT ON PUPILS WHO HAVE BEEN RETARDED IN THEIR PROMOTION

This report is to be made out in duplicate at the close of each term. One copy is to be filed with the principal of the building, the other to be sent to the school office.

This report is for statistical purposes only. All pupils therefore should be included in the reckoning who have been registered during the term, provided they have not left school, moved from the city, or been transferred to another building.

C. N. KENDALL, Sup't of Schools.

Name	Age*	Grade	Years in Indianapolis Public Schools	Terms in Present Grade	Causes of Retardation†						Subjects Failed in†							Remarks
					Ill-health	Idleness	Slowness	Absence	New to City Schools	Mental Defect ‡	Math.	Geog.	History	Oral Reading	Silent Reading	Composition	Spelling	

* A pupil is five years old until he is six, etc.

† Indicate the causes which apply to each case and the subjects failed in with an X in the proper column.

‡ No child should be classed as mentally defective who has been able to reach the sixth grade. Below the sixth grade, class those as mentally defective only whom the Director of Physical Training or the Supervising Principal has so classed.

Number of Pupils belonging to Grade ....

School..

Date..

Teacher...

Reports on these blanks have been made by each teacher in the city each half-year since June, 1908.

Reduced to percentages, the retardations may be tabulated as follows: The 1B record is not here included, for reasons explained later. The June, 1909, record has been accidentally destroyed.

TABLE OF RETARDATIONS

FIGURES REPRESENT PERCENTAGES

WHITE SCHOOLS

Grades	June 1908	Jan. 1909	June 1909	Jan. 1910	June 1910	Jan. 1911	June 1911
1B......	....	...	....	...	...	...	...
1A......	8.0	5.8	....	5.9	7.0	6.3	4.7
2B......	9.6	5.1	....	8.3	5.2	6.6	2.8
2A......	12.0	7.1	....	7.2	6.2	4.9	2.8
3B......	13.8	8.2	....	9.7	6.8	6.1	4.5
3A......	14.0	8.3	....	8.3	8.9	7.8	4.7
4B......	16.7	8.3	....	9.2	8.5	8.0	5.6
4A......	14.0	8.1	....	7.8	8.8	6.3	4.5
5B......	14.0	8.6	....	8.1	7.5	5.0	3.8
5A......	14.5	6.5	....	6.8	6.0	4.8	3.7
6B......	13.0	6.0	....	7.8	6.2	4.6	3.7
6A......	13.0	6.2	....	4.9	4.7	5.6	3.1
7B......	15.0	7.0	....	4.1	3.3	4.0	4.3
7A......	13.1	5.0	....	4.3	4.1	2.6	4.1
8B......	10.8	4.6	....	3.0	2.3	1.8	4.7
8A......	3.0	1.0	....	0.7	0.1	0.4	0.6

COLORED SCHOOLS

Grades	June 1908	Jan. 1909	June 1909	Jan. 1910	June 1910	Jan. 1911	June 1911
1B......	....	....	....	...	...	....	....
1A......	4.6	11.4	....	6.5	6.1	6.5	7.8
2B......	6.9	7.2	....	7.1	6.1	10.2	10.5
2A......	8.0	9.0	....	7.9	7.9	4.7	7.6
3B......	8.7	7.2	....	6.2	3.7	8.4	18.5
3A......	11.0	9.6	....	6.8	4.2	4.4	9.6
4B......	9.0	9.6	....	9.9	10.6	6.5	5.6
4A......	6.9	8.4	....	5.1	0.5	6.3	5.8
5B......	6.7	7.5	....	8.8	8.7	4.4	10.3
5A......	7.0	4.8	....	5.6	6.3	3.4	11.1
6B......	5.4	3.6	....	7.6	4.2	4.4	9.3
6A......	5.4	2.7	....	4.8	4.2	5.8	9.6
7B......	4.8	5.1	....	0.8	4.2	5.2	18.0
7A......	2.0	3.9	....	3.6	4.2	1.5	27.5
8B......	1.8	3.0	....	2.8	2.1	4.7	27.0
8A......	0.7	0.0	....	3.4	0.7	2.8	14.7

As the table for white schools includes the records of approximately 24,000 children and that for the colored schools includes the records of only about 2,500 children, the table for the white schools has been taken for purposes of general study.

TABLE OF RETARDATIONS IN WHITE SCHOOLS GRAPHICALLY REPRESENTED

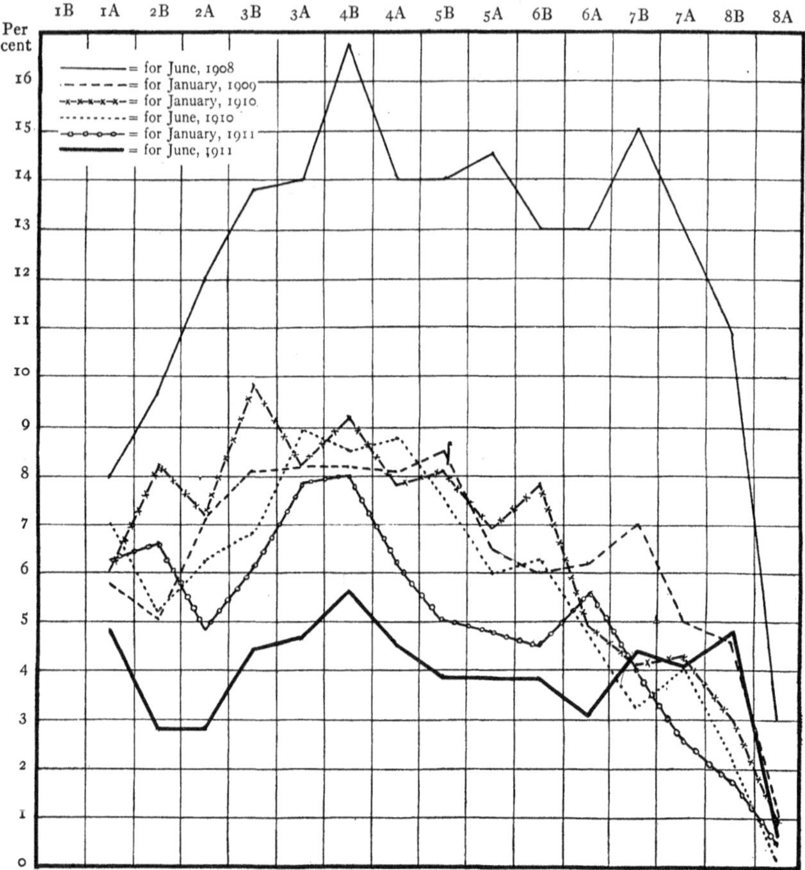

The reports of the "Retardation" of June, 1908, were tabulated and were studied in the meetings of the supervising principals during the fall term. Some of the facts brought to light were:

1. An excessive retardation was reported in a few schools.

2. The "crests" of retardation were in the 4B and 7B grades.

3. Among the causes of retardation "mental defect" was frequently given, even in the seventh and eighth grades. (The

first blank has no footnote limiting the use of the term "mental defect.")

4. Among the causes of retardation "mathematics" was very prominent, with attention called to "lack of reasoning power."

5. Another prominent cause of retardation was "oral reading."

6. Many cases of retardation were reported of pupils several years over age for their grades, although they were not reported as mentally defective.

The results of this study of the "Retardation Reports" were:

1. An investigation by the supervising principal of these facts and of their causes in each district. (In Indianapolis a supervising principal is assigned to a district varying in size from fifteen to fifty teachers. The supervising principal is responsible for efficiency of instruction and grading of pupils in the district.)

2. A recognition of the fact that supervising principals and teachers were not thinking alike on the matter of the promotion of doubtful children.

3. A confirmation of the suspicion that the real mentally defective child was a factor in general retardation.

4. The opening of two additional schools for mentally defective children and the fixing of a standard for judging of such children. One school for mentally defective pupils had been started before 1908. The next blank contained the footnote regarding this class of children.

5. The placing of "special teachers" in buildings where the need was greatest, to study and help retarded pupils. There are now eight such teachers in the city. A careful record is kept of the work of each teacher, and it appears from these records, made by the supervising principals, that each teacher helps from fifty to seventy-five children to make their promotion each term.

6. That two studies stood out prominently as stumbling blocks: mathematics and oral reading. In mathematics much of the "explanation" or "reasoning" work required proved to be poorly graded and too elaborate.

7. Evidence was seen that in determining promotions too much emphasis was placed on memory proficiency, especially in the upper grades, and too little credit was given to the child's

mental ability, general interests, bodily conditions, and possible improvement during vacation.

8. The discovery that a particularly high standard was held in mind at certain grades because of the assumed special difficulties or hazards to be met in the next grade. This was conspicuously true in grades 4B and 7B.

In general, there was evident on the part of all in charge of the children an attitude toward accepted standards of judgment and toward habitual practices by which they were restudied and the course of study was somewhat modified.

It became evident early in this investigation into retardation that the first grade was a problem by itself. In Indianapolis the first-grade pupils enter in largest numbers in September and April. If they are six years of age they may enter at other times, and somewhat large additions are registered at the beginning of the winter term, February 1. The first-grade pupils go to school one session only—one group of forty-five in the morning and another group of thirty in the afternoon. The first-grade teacher therefore has under her instruction about seventy-five pupils. Many of these pupils are so irregular in attendance that this first term is of little tangible value. The first-grade teachers have found it difficult to classify these pupils for statistical purposes. The reports were so various that they gave little reliable information. In June a report was made on the following blank:

Indianapolis Public Schools

REPORT ON PROMOTIONS AND RETARDATIONS

Grades 1B and 1A

Note.—Teachers are asked to report all 1B and 1A pupils on this blank. The individual report of retarded pupils need not be made out for these grades.

Note.—Please make these reports in duplicate—one copy to be given to supervising principal and one to be sent to school office with blank entitled Report of Retarded Pupils.

1B Grade

	Less than 2 Mo.	2–3 Mo.	3–4 Mo.	4–5 Mo.	5–6 Mo.	6–7 Mo.	7–8 Mo.	8–9 Mo.	More than 9 Mo.
Total number present*......									
Number not advanced to 1A grade..................									

1A Grade

Total number present......									
Number not advanced to 2B grade..................									

* Children are here scheduled by their *attendance*, not by their membership. A full and accurate account of all first-grade pupils is desired. This report should therefore include all the *different* 1B and 1A pupils who have been enrolled during the current term, except those transferred to other schools. Those who are not members when this report is made out, but who will return, should be included.

Date............................... School No...............

Supervising Principal......................... Teacher..........................

The increased interest in the retarded child resulted in some very interesting experiments and related investigations by several supervising principals and teachers. There was a clear and uniform suggestion lurking in all these experiments and inquiries—namely, that our promotions were based too largely on a small number of the factors involved in the problem of the child's fitness to go on; too exclusive attention seemed to have been given to the factors enumerated below in column "A," while the factors enumerated in column "B" had not been given due consideration.

A

1. In how many of the required subjects of study has the pupil *failed?* Daily marks. Tests.
2. How much has been the absence?
3. What have been the delinquencies of conduct?

B

1. In which of the required subjects of study has the pupil *succeeded?*
2. In those subjects in which a pupil failed, was the failure total or partial?
3. If the failure was either total or partial could it be made good in next grade provided pupil worked?
4. Provided the failure was complete in one subject, as in mathematics, does the failure appear to be due to inability to comprehend or to slow maturing? If the latter, may this failure be made good at time of review in later grades?
5. If failure is due to omission of some parts of curriculum, as in geography, may omissions be made good in later grades?
6. Has the pupil "gotten on" with the present teacher? How much of the failure is due to unadaptability to teachers

or to accidental environment in the school-room?

7. What is the general intelligence of the child?

8. Is the child a "static" or a "developing" individual? May the possibilities of change of environment and teachers, a summer's vacation, or the stimulus of "trial" be legitimately given large consideration in determining promotion?

The first column contains the tangible, measurable, markable factors in the problem. They are also largely negative in character—an inventory of failures rather than of successes.

The second column contains the factors which are more vital, but less visible. It seemed to be true that we were judging that a child could not succeed in the grade beyond, provided he had failed in two or more of the fundamental studies of the school curriculum—this failure established in case of doubt by written or oral tests. The question persistently formulated itself, "Are we judging right?"

Light had been thrown on this question by a rough study which was made by one of the supervising principals. He wished to find out the effect of retardation on pupils of fourteen years of age and over. He found that in a relatively large number of instances these children had not returned to school. Those who had returned seemed indifferent. After a private talk with groups of those who were yet in school he advanced them arbitrari y on trial. The teachers understood and were sympathetic. The largest part of those then advanced did as well as they had previously done. A few took a higher standing in school than they had before taken. Some failed.

Thus it appeared to be true that where it was judged the child could not succeed by promotion and on trial he *did* succeed, in every such case, we had judged wrong. To bring this phase of the retardation problem strikingly to the attention of all and to enlarge the study of it the following blank was sent to each teacher:

INDIANAPOLIS PUBLIC SCHOOLS

REPORT ON PUPILS PROMOTED OUT OF THE REGULAR ORDER AND ON TRIAL

DURING TERM FEBRUARY 1 TO JUNE 16, 1911

IRREGULAR PROMOTIONS

NOTE.—By Irregular Promotions is meant promotions made after the term has opened. These may have been on trial, but if made after the term has opened, they should be recorded in this schedule.

NOTE.—Please make out in duplicate—one copy to be given to supervising principal, the other copy to be sent to the school office with the blank on Report of Retarded Pupils.

Grades	1B	1A	2B	2A	3B	3A	4B	4A	5B	5A	6B	6A	7B	7A	8B	8A
Total...............																
Failures																

PROMOTIONS ON TRIAL

NOTE.—By Promotions on Trial is meant promotions made with trial conditions in January at time regular promotions were made.

Grades	1B	1A	2B	2A	3B	3A	4B	4A	5B	5A	6B	6A	7B	7A	8B	8A
Total...............																
Failures																

DATE................................ SCHOOL NO.............

SUPERVISING PRINCIPAL............................ TEACHER.........................

It was inevitable that the entire problem of grading should be drawn into discussion as a result of this study of retardation. Supervising principals and teachers began to compare the relative ability of the pupils and to test whether or not each was working at his educative best.

Several deductions of importance were drawn from this discussion:

1. The course of study should be thought of as a means by which the development of a growing child may be helped, not as an end at which the child stops or a standard by which this development is to be exclusively measured. It is not a ladder by which a human mind is to climb, but a dietary by which it is to be nourished. Inasmuch as the course of study is in process of constant change it should not be taken too seriously.

2. The teacher who has had the child for an entire term is not the best final judge of the question of the promotion of a "doubtful" pupil. The "personal equation," the fear of the criticism of the next teacher, the schoolroom standards, influence too often when the matter is left entirely to the teacher.

There seemed to be only one way of determining with certainty whether or not a pupil should be promoted. That way was to "put it up to him," to let him try.

Seven schools were chosen in different parts of the city in which, in June of this year, every child was promoted. Those who would not have been promoted or who would have been promoted on trial if the customary plan had been followed were tabulated, so that they could be identified the following term.

The plan involves a six weeks' period of trial. The teachers are asked not to force these children to unusual efforts during the trial period. At the end of six weeks those whom the teachers feel would be benefited by repeating the previous grade work will be put back.

The results of this experiment will not be known until about November 1.

An analysis was made of the reports on retardation for the term closing January, 1911, to find out what effect large numbers in a room had on retardation.

A single table is given in full showing the facts for 42 fourth grades throughout the city. This detailed table is followed by a general table summarizing the results for all other grades. The letters A and B designate respectively schools made up of 35 to 40 pupils (A) and schools made up of from 44 to 51 pupils (B).

GRADE IV

School Membership		Total Retarded		School Membership		Total Retarded	
A	*B*	*A*	*B*	*A*	*B*	*A*	*B*
..	46	..	8	37	..	7	..
..	45	..	3	37	..	3	..
39	..	3	..	38	..	8	..
..	45	..	12	38	..	3	..
..	46	..	13	35	..	2	..
..	44	..	5	37	..	1	..
35	..	2	..	39	..	6	..
..	46	..	8	39	..	2	..
36	..	1	7	40	..	4	..
..	45	..	..	..	46	..	8
38	..	8	..	40	..	6	..
..	45	..	7	36	..	3	..
..	51	..	9	..	47	..	6
..	46	..	6	..	46	..	4
..	47	..	7	37	..	2	..
..	45	..	6	36	..	2	..
38	..	5	..	..	46	..	5
..	45	..	3	..	45	..	1
40	..	5	..	..	47	..	2
38	..	4	..				
40	..	2	..	Pupils...868	873	86	120
40	..	3	..	Schools.. 23	19	..	...
39	..	4	..				

Average retardation in 23 schools, 35–40 pupils.....................3.8 pupils
Average retardation in 19 schools, 44–51 pupils.....................6.3 pupils
Per cent of retardation in 23 schools, 35–40 pupils.................. .09$\frac{8}{10}$ pupil
Per cent of retardation in 19 schools, 44–51 pupils.................. .13$\frac{7}{10}$ pupil

Grade	Total Number of Schools Considered	A	B	Total Pupils in A	Total Pupils in B	Retarded in A	Retarded in B	Percentage in A	Percentage in B	Average in A	Average in B
II..........	34	16	18	615	836	56	119	9.1	14.2	3.5	6.6
III.........	56	26	30	996	1397	73	133	7.3	9.5	2.8	4.4
IV..........	42	23	19	868	873	86	120	9.8	13.7	3.8	6.3
V...........	38	25	13	955	608	72	56	7.6	9.2	2.9	4.3
VI..........	31	20	11	765	509	75	40	9.8	8.0	3.7	3.6
VII.........	28	18	10	682	470	60	47	8.8	10.0	3.3	4.7
VIII........	23	15	8	557	383	32	20	5.7	5.2	2.1	2.5

SUMMARY

Schools, Grades II–VI

110 schools with membership 35–40
91 schools with membership 44–51

Number of schools in which not more than 3 pupils were retarded	
Membership 35–40	74
Membership 44–51	35
Number of schools retarding 4, 5, or 6 pupils	
Membership 35–40	25
Membership 44–51	30
Number of schools retarding 7 or 8 pupils	
Membership 35–40	8
Membership 44–51	15
Number of schools retarding more than 8 pupils	
Membership 35–40	3
Membership 44–51	11

Note.—Attention is called to the fact that the June retardation line on the graphic representation is possibly affected by the experiment referred to in the report—of promoting all the children "on trial" in eight buildings. The retardation of this term may be increased by later demotions due to the failure of some of these children to keep their places.

It should be understood that this article is of the nature of a report simply; that the statistics are considered as suggestive only; that in no sense are conclusions final; that these figures are not the statistics of the most important factors, but only of partial results, which we consider valuable merely as a basis for further discussion and investigation.

SOME FACTORS THAT DETERMINE THE HABITS OF STUDY OF GRADE PUPILS

WILLIAM CLAUDE REAVIS
Oakland City, Indiana

Investigations by Dr. Earhart[1] of Columbia University have shown that a very large per cent of the pupils of our public schools do not study properly or profitably, and that as a result much energy is dissipated and a great deal of waste in time and effort is incurred. The cause is not to be found in the motives and purposes of the pupils, but in their ignorance of correct habits and methods of study. The term study is an enigma to many children, and when told to study a lesson they generally do everything but the right thing. I have frequently heard pupils respond, when asked if they had studied their lesson, that they had read it over a certain number of times. The recitation showed distinctly that their preparation had been entirely wanting in the zeal, thoroughness, and definite motivation essential to the mastery of an assignment. They had no doubt wasted more energy in aimless efforts than would have been required to master two or three similar lessons, if judicious habits of study had been made use of.

Of course, this will mean new and increased responsibilities for the teachers. It will require on their part a more accurate knowledge of home environments, a greater familiarity with schoolroom hygiene, and a more intimate knowledge of the mental traits and characteristics of the pupils as individuals. "However, if as the result of this endeavor we teach the child how to study effectively, we do the most useful thing that could be done to help him to adjust himself to any environment of modern civilized life into which he may be thrown."

[1] *Teaching Children to Study.*

The following study is an attempt to find out some of the factors both in and out of school that may influence and perhaps determine the habits of study of grade pupils, and to suggest ways by which these influences may be modified and even controlled by the class teacher. The material upon which the discussions are based is the result of a year's observations and carefully kept records in a typical town school system of five hundred pupils. The teachers who took the records were well qualified on the grounds of scholarship, successful experience in the school system, knowledge of the individuality of the pupils, and familiarity with home conditions. Furthermore, the opinion of the individual teacher is corroborated in almost every case by the opinion of at least one other teacher.

In the first place, each teacher was asked to make a very careful study of the methods and habits of study of the pupils in her grade, taking into consideration their habits of application, perseverance, and thoroughness in mastering assignments and their ability to select, organize, and retain. Considerable time was given to the grading of the pupils according to the above points, and in cases in which there was some doubt, judgment was not passed without consultation with other teachers who knew the individuality of the particular pupil under consideration, equally well. When the grading was completed, each grade was divided into three equal tertiles, designated as Class I, Class II, and Class III. By this method of classification, the variation of standards of judgment among the different teachers was reduced to a minimum, so far as the results as a whole were concerned, because each teacher's Class I was grouped with the same class of the other teacher's, and similarly, all pupils of Class II were grouped together, and likewise Class III.

HOME ENVIRONMENT

In the next place, an effort was made to get the exact status of the home environment of each pupil, in order to ascertain, if possible, what relations obtained between the habits of study of the pupil and the rank of his home surroundings. Data concerning the homes of 393 children were gathered and graded according to the following points: educational interest on the part of parents, means to provide adequate food, clothing, medical attention, books, papers, magazines, and entertainment, and moral atmosphere that would encourage honesty, earnest effort, regard for the rights of others, and a due measure of self-respect. The homes were then divided into three equal tertiles and designated as Rank I, Rank II, Rank III.

TABLE I

Habits of Study	Class I	Class II	Class III
	Per cent	Per cent	Per cent
Environment Rank I	75	19.7	5.3
Environment Rank II	32.4	48.2	19.4
Environment Rank III	15.3	40.7	44

In the above table, it is observed that 75 per cent of the pupils of environments of the first rank, 32.4 per cent of the second rank, and 15.3 per cent of the third rank have habits of study of the first class. The large percentage of first-class students in the environments of the second and third rank is due to two things: first, the home conditions of the town are extraordinarily good, and secondly, by grouping in tertiles the character of the homes of the third rank are much better than if grouped according to some fixed standard of grading, because the number of poor homes being relatively few, the third rank includes many homes that would be ranked higher under the other system of classification. In this particular school the pupils coming from an environment of the first rank have two and three tenths the chances of having first-class habits of study that a pupil has coming from an environment of the second rank. A further examination of the percentages shows that there is a marked correlation between the rank of the home environment and the habits of study of the pupil.

If these results stand for anything, they indicate that home environment is a potent factor in fastening upon the child habits of behavior that are utilized in other kinds of activity. Certain parents said to the teachers when spoken to concerning the habits of work of their children, "That is just the way they do everything at home." One good mother in conversation with the teacher of her son remarked, when told that her son was very careless about his habits of study, "That is a family failing, he takes it after his father."

It may be true that an element of heredity enters into the problem, but for the purposes of this study, it will be passed by with the explanation that the pupil may adopt many of his habits of behavior through imitating activities seen in the home, or that he unconsciously takes up bad habits and the home unwittingly permits them to become established in his conduct. At least, the study points out the fact that the possible origin of many of the habits and attitudes of school children is in the home.

TABLE II

HOME STUDY

Environment	Rank I	Rank II	Rank III
	Per cent	Per cent	Per cent
Home study	35.5	54.2	7.3
No home study	4.1	43.8	42.1

In Table II, we see 179 pupils who did home study and 207 who did no home study, distributed according to their home environment. It is interesting to see that the large percentage of pupils doing home study come from environments of the first and second rank, and that the large percentage doing no home study come from environments of the second and third rank. The percentages indicate that the large number of pupils coming from homes of the first rank do home study, while the large majority of those coming from homes of the third rank do no home study. The pupils who come from homes of the second class are very evenly divided. From an analysis of the above table, it is easy to see what class of pupils is kept under parental discipline, and what class is permitted to loaf on the streets during their out-of-school hours. For some time I have recorded my observations of the pupils who seem to spend the greater part of their time on the streets, when out of school, and I find that the great majority come from homes of the third rank. Is it any wonder, then, that more than 50 per cent of the pupils doing no home study belong to homes of the lowest rank?

In a previous study,[1] I have shown that high-school pupils who do regular home study take higher standing in school than those who do no home study. I take the same position with reference to grade pupils. While I know that there are conditions under which home study is not advisable, yet in the large majority of cases it is advisable, as is shown by Table III.

TABLE III

Habits of Study	Class I	Class II	Class III
	Per cent	Per cent	Per cent
Home study	57.7	36.5	6.5
No home study	17.3	45.5	37.2

Table III shows the pupils of Table II distributed according to their habits of study. The large percentage of pupils doing home study have habits of study of the first and second class, and the large percentage who do no home study have habits of the second and third class. The small percentage of home-study pupils having habits of study of the third class and the small number of pupils who do no home study, having habits of study of the first class, convinces me that so far as this particular school is concerned home study is of great value.

The objection is sometimes made that it is not within the power of the teacher to control the home study of the pupils, and therefore, it is better to have them do none. Under the old method of schoolroom procedure, there may have been some validity to this objection, but under the changing methods, I am led to believe that a great deal of home study can be very satisfactorily done. Formerly the chief work of the teacher was to test by means of recitations the character of the pupils' study, and little attention was given to the direction and supervision of study. Now, the work of the class hour is often given up to study recitations, and to teaching the pupils how to study particular lessons or, in a word, to teaching them how to think. Consequently, the pupil may now engage in home study with some degree of efficiency, and if par-

[1] *School Review*, XIX, 395.

ticipated in by the parent, the work may take the form of a recitation rather than teaching.

The problems of school and home study may be rendered more effective by finding out home conditions and securing the intelligent co-operation of the parents through home visitation by the teachers. It is one of the best means of gaining the confidence of parents, for, when they find that the teacher is more than a salaried official, as a rule the majority are both ready and anxious to co-operate in any way the teacher may suggest. Thus, through a mutual understanding between parents and teacher, the work of the pupil in school may be greatly improved.

TRAITS TO BE CULTIVATED

An analysis of the study process will reveal nine mental traits that should be thoroughly understood and made to function as habits in the mental work of a student. The interpretation of these traits are as follows:

1. Speed—the rate of accomplishment.
2. Neatness—orderly arrangement of all written material.
3. Accuracy—reliability of results.
4. Initiative—power to originate, opposite of imitative.
5. Self-reliance—self-confidence, as opposed to self-depreciation and subservience to teacher, books, and classmates.
6. Perseverance—continuity of attention and effort.
7. Ability to organize—power to arrange things according to some definite sequence or order.
8. Ability to select—i.e., to arrange or pick out facts according to their relative value, or with reference to some given theme.
9. Ability to retain—power of making associations.

In order that it might be ascertained whether or not there was a relation between these characteristics and the pupils' school work, the teachers above the fourth grade were asked to study each pupil carefully and grade him according to the nine traits, using the following scale:

I. When the trait was decidedly pronounced.

II. When the trait was noticeable, yet not distinctly marked.

III. When the trait was very weak.

This task was faithfully performed. Although it was done in a quantitative rather than a qualitative way, I attach much value to the judgments. As a matter of fact, the teacher's judgment of the intelligence of elementary-school children is more reliable than any qualitative standards yet devised have been able to give. This has been clearly demonstrated by David Heron of the Galton Laboratory of Eugenics. While the personal equation of the teacher enters into the judgments, still they probably furnish the most reliable data that could be obtained.

The tables and the discussions that follow will show the possibility of modifying or changing the habits of the pupils that are factors in the process of study, and will open up a field of new work for the teachers who have made no effort to direct and control the study of their pupils.

Table IV shows the correlation of the pupils' habits of speed, neatness, and accuracy, and the distribution of the grades in arithmetic according to the correlation involved. The habits were grouped in threes, because of the facility gained in tabulating the results, and because of the possibility of discovering the relative value of the various habits. Arithmetic was selected for the reason that there were more pupils ranking low and high in that subject than in any other, consequently, the correlation obtained between the marks in arithmetic and the habits of study would be more significant than if the pupils' grades had been relatively uniform in character.

In correlating the three habits, it was found that there were twenty-seven different combinations. Of these there were three perfect correlations in which each of the three habits had equal development, six in which the relation between neatness and accuracy was uniform with speed as a recessive character, six in which the relation between speed and accuracy harmonized and neatness was the varying factor, six in which the relation between speed and neatness obtained and accuracy passed into recession, and six in which each of the three habits were different in character of development.

From this grouping, I was able to find the combination of habits that gave the best results, and thus was able to study the pre-eminence or the recessive character of the different habits as they appeared in the results of the marks in arithmetic, which were obtained through the teacher's judgment of the pupil's worth in that subject, after a consideration of the daily class record and the written work. The results, therefore, ought to be reliable, and should throw some light on the question under discussion.

TABLE IV

Speed Neatness Accuracy	No. of Pupils in		
	Rank I	Rank II	Rank III
AAA	15	4	1
BBB	8	19	4
CCC	0	4	11
bAA	19	4	1
cAA	1	2	0
aBB	1	4	2
cBB	2	5	7
aCC	0	0	0
bCC	0	1	4
AAb	2	4	1
AAc	0	0	1
BBa	2	4	1
BBc	0	0	11
CCa	0	0	0
CCb	3	2	1
AbA	2	4	1
AcA	0	0	1
BaB	7	5	3
BcB	1	5	2
CaC	0	0	0
CbC	0	2	7
ABC	0	0	3
ACB	0	0	0
BAC	0	3	4
BCA	0	1	0
CAB	0	4	0
CBA	1	0	0

NOTE.—In the above table, the recessive trait is written in small letters, the correlating traits in capitals, and the combinations in which the correlation is perfect or in which the three traits differ i written in capitals.

By bringing certain habits to the foreground, either individually or in correlation with another, and by reducing, similarly, the other habit or habits to the background, we are able to see in

Table IV that the best combination of habits for arithmetic are first-class habits of accuracy, first-class habits of neatness, and second-class habits of speed. This conclusion may seem somewhat absurd, because the above combination is placed ahead of the group of three first-class habits between which the correlation is perfect; but after a careful consideration and an analysis of individual cases, it is easy to verify. When speed is too highly developed in elementary pupils, it often defeats its own end by interfering with the pupil's accuracy and neatness. Thus, by over-development, it becomes negative in character with reference to the other habits.

The table also shows that habits of neatness are a very close second in importance to the habits of accuracy. This is not at all strange, when we take into consideration that in doing work neatly, the pupil must necessarily be more attentive to processes and results. Hence, habits of neatness are very intimately associated with habits of accuracy in efficient work; and by cultivating the one, improvement is likely to be gained in the other.

By following Table IV through carefully, a teacher can easily locate a pupil with reference to his habits of study, and may be able to meet in an efficient way the individual need. To illustrate, a pupil may be exceedingly rapid in his habits of work and as a result fall low in his marks, because of inaccuracies and slovenly work. The teacher should hold the speed in check to a certain extent, and insist upon neat workmanship and reliable results, instead of indulging the habits of speed and permitting the pupil to pay the penalty in classmarks. Such a scheme, although possessing some limitations, is a step toward the control and direction of the pupils' methods and habits of study, and will no doubt bring beneficial results, if consistently followed by the class teacher.

Similar tables were prepared to show the significance of (*a*) initiative, self-reliance, and perseverance; and (*b*) of habits of organization, selection, and retention.

The results of the comparison (*a*) show that perseverance is slightly more important than self-reliance, and that self-reliance is a shade more important than initiative. However, the table shows that after the group containing the three first-class habits, the combination of first-class habits of initiative, second-class habits of self-reliance, and first-class habits of perseverance probably make the best group.

To anyone who has studied carefully the mental traits of children, it is evident that the above triad of habits is a character-making group. The pupil who possesses any one of them in a marked degree is fortunate, for with any one as a basis the other two may be developed. In school work, then, the three should receive practically equal attention from the teacher, for the pupil who fails to develop strength along some one of these lines, at least, loses a very valuable asset for later life.

The charge has often been made against much of our teaching —and with some justice—that in the school the pupils are entertained rather than exercised, that they are guests of the school rather than hosts, and that they are taught imitativeness and dependence rather than initiative, self-reliance, and perseverance. I have no doubt that these conditions, when they do exist, are due primarily to neglect on the part of the parents and teachers to cultivate and encourage self-activity in the pupils. Self-activity and a feeling of responsibility are the foundation of initiative, self-reliance, and perseverance, and unless these traits receive some direction and gratuitous exercise or, in a word, made to function as habits, they are likely to become dwarfed or abnormally developed.

The two groups of habits discussed in connection with Table IV and in the last few paragraphs are general in character, and although of great value in study, they are equally valuable in any field of human activity. But the habits considered in the final subdivision (*b*) are more specialized in character, and their chief value is to be found in mental activity. Measured according to the traditional purpose and aim of education, this group of habits is *THE* group that ought to be most thoroughly understood and most carefully directed by the teacher, for the success of the pupil in mastering book material will depend very largely upon his ability to select, organize, and retain.

The investigation showed that the factor of greatest importance is retentiveness. The other two are very similar in value, although the power to organize seems to be slightly more important than the ability to select. This should not appear strange, for the power of establishing and mastering associations carries with it more or less of the ability to organize, while selection is more of an analytical process. An extended discussion of these habits would involve a consideration of apperception, a topic with which every reader should be somewhat familiar. Suffice it to say that by directing and supervising the study of the pupils, as a part of school work, the teacher can give attention to the development of these special habits in special subjects, so that they may be carried over to a certain extent into any mental work that the pupil may have to do.

CONCLUSIONS

In concluding this study I am thoroughly conscious of the limited character of the investigations I have made. Some of the points I hope to work out more fully at some future time. However, I do think that the data warrant several conclusions that should enable the teacher to supervise more effectively the habits of study of the pupils, during a period nascent to habit formation.

1. Home environment is a factor in the formation of study habits. Its influence may be either for good or for bad. It is possible for the teacher to exert some modifying influence over environmental conditions.

2. Home study is desirable, because it acts as a check on the formation of habits out of school, that would be negative in their influence on habits in school. Furthermore, the pupils who do home study are as a rule stronger students than those who do none.

3. By analyzing the habits of study of a pupil, his weakness may be discovered and active and conscious steps may be taken to form, strengthen, or inhibit certain habits that may need attention. This work is entirely within the province of teaching and should receive as careful attention as the teaching of the formal subjects.

STUDIES OF EDUCATIONAL PRINCIPLES

CHARLES H. JUDD
The University of Chicago

II. THE CONCRETE IN EDUCATION

For something over a generation, there has been a very definite reaction in our educational system against the abstractions which had grown up during the earlier period when education was primarily literary in its character. The charge is often made today that the older school which dealt chiefly with writing and reading gave children no sensory experiences, and no concrete material which they could carry in mind while they were learning the words in books, and while they were learning the elaborate forms of expression which were sometimes demanded of them in their reading lessons. The reaction against literary education has, in some cases, been so extreme as to suggest that reading and writing can be very largely left to take care of themselves; that the main business of the school consists in giving children new ideas about the material and social worlds. It is asserted that this larger information will stimulate a sufficient desire for reading, and will, at the same time, give the material knowledge for the interpretation of everything that is found in the books.

Certain changes in the methods of teaching reading have tended to encourage this reaction toward concrete experiences. Thus, we no longer give instruction in the alphabet as the first step in teaching reading because the letters of the alphabet are in no wise connected with the children's experiences of things and with their experiences of spoken words. We begin rather by giving the word-wholes which are directly related to objects and to the spoken words which children know. The word-whole thus has a concrete meaning attached to it from the very first, and the process of analysis into the separate letters is allowed to come at a later stage. This method of teaching reading emphasizes the value of the concrete.

Various types of concrete material have been welcomed into the course of study. In the first place, nature material has been regarded as entirely suitable for even the earliest grades. Children should have their attention turned to plants and animals because these are the most useful and attractive objects in the world, and observation of them fills the mind with material for later intelligent interpretation of the world.

Concrete material of the social type has also been suggested, and children have been encouraged to note the details of the manufacturing processes in which the community is engaged. Pupils have been encouraged to go to the markets where they can see the different products of the factories, and can become acquainted with importations from other parts of the country.

Further than this, children have been encouraged to see the importance of all kinds of constructive work. Here they are in contact with reality in a very direct fashion. When they take materials into their hands, and mold these into useful articles, they get a type of experience which is often described as very much more important than that which can be derived from descriptive accounts given in books.

Even the more abstract subjects which it is regarded as necessary to take up in the school have been given as concrete a character as possible. Thus, we find the books on algebra, and especially the books on arithmetic, filled with all sorts of examples about objects which are thought to be present in the child's experience, and doubtless have appeared before his eyes or have come into his hands. These objects are to be thought of as adjusted and readjusted in greater or less quantities, and the abstractness of mathematics is supposed to be corrected and the difficulty reduced because the child's interest is retained by reference to his ordinary experience.

Devotion to concrete experience is so typical of the educational thought of our day that it may seem bold to suggest any criticism of the interpretation which has been put upon the term "concrete" in our ordinary educational thinking. Furthermore, when one begins to call the concrete in question, he runs some risk of being regarded as opposed to all use of the concrete. It may be well to state, therefore, at the very beginning of this paper, that the present writer wishes to be distinctly understood as advocating the proper use of all the concrete material that can be employed in the early and in the later stages of education. No return is advocated to the earlier type of formalism against which our present educational tendencies are a protest. This paper, however, aims to draw attention to the fact that the mere presentation of an object to the senses is in no wise a complete educational process; and the eliminating of language, or even its relegation to a place of secondary importance, is not justified by any careful analysis of the child's consciousness or by the demands for complete experience in any proper interpretation of that term.

Let us analyze a simple case which illustrates all of the advantages of concrete experience. The child is brought into contact with some external object, such, for example, as a piece of furniture. This piece of furniture may be forced upon his attentive recognition in a variety of ways. It will be very completely understood if he tries to go through the process of constructing the furniture. He will then become aware of the fact that the different parts of the chair are joined together, and that the joints each represent certain difficult problems in uniting the material which is employed in the construction of the chair. He will also realize that each line of the chair is the result of some careful constructive thought. He will see that the combination of materials is significant; that the different materials employed in different parts of the chair all have special justification. When the chair has been completed, he will have a large amount of direct personal experience which will attach itself to any image of a chair that now comes to his eyes. This fuller experience of chairs will be in part of the sensory type, but it will be in very large measure of the memory type; that is, all later chairs will be more fully recognized because of the one which he made. Furthermore, a very large part of this memory experience will be motor in its character; that is, it will consist of memories of certain types of behavior through which he has passed. The more completely these various types of personal behavior are aroused in his contact with things, the more completely will objects have concrete and vivid meaning to him.

This illustration makes it clear that the meaning of the term "concrete" is not confined at all to that which appears before the senses at any given moment, nor is it confined entirely to visual or tactual experience. The weaving together of a large number of sensory experiences in some definite relation to personal memories is what is meant by concrete in such a case as this.

Let us turn from this illustration to the wholly different experience which is presented when objects are discussed in arithmetic as a means of giving concrete character to number problems. The child is asked to represent to himself three men working on a certain piece of work which requires their combined effort for two days and a half; the problem being to discover how many men will be necessary to complete the work in half the time if all worked at the same rate as the three who were originally given in the problem. If the child is able to deal with such situations at all he will instantly turn each of these statements into symbols which convert the situation into an arithmetical situation rather than into a situation to be worked out in any concrete, personal way. Indeed, it is the intention of the arithmetic lesson to show him a method of treating this problem of work which is wholly at variance with the method that he would employ if he came into contact with it through his own personal efforts. It is not that he is to dig the ditch, nor to go and see men dig the ditch. He is not to sympathize with their efforts. He is shown through his study of arithmetic a short cut which has been devised at great intellectual expense by the race for the purpose of making it unnecessaay for him or any of his friends to go through the concrete experience of working out the ditch in the two ways contrasted in the problem. He can work out the readjustment of the men and work, as Professor Stout puts it "in his head." Arithmetic is a short abstract method of working out a problem which it would be quite impossible to work out with anything like the same rapidity "in the concrete."

One sees from such examples that just in so far as a child is trained in the methods of dealing with objects through arithmetical rules, he is taken away from the concrete manipulation of objects.

Another very good illustration of similar type is to be found in our ordinary experience with spatial dimensions. If one wishes to find out how much paper he needs to cover a certain wall, he does not take the rolls of paper in his hand, and by long and laborious experiments, find out how much of that paper will be needed to cover the wall. He would indeed derive many very concrete experiences in an effort to cover the wall with the paper. He would learn some of the difficulties of handling and manipulating the paper. He would become acquainted with the different devices for making the paper stick to the wall, and would see the difficulty of keeping it smooth, etc. He might have the concrete experience of the paper-hanger, but the ordinary individual needs such experience, if at all, only as an introduction to another and more abstract form of knowledge. He usually wishes to know how far he, as the purchaser of paper, must go in preparing for the fuller concrete experience of someone else who will do the hanging of the paper on the wall. Fortunately he finds himself supplied through racial experience with the very convenient device of measurement. He measures one roll of paper, he measures the wall, and he finds without any actual handling of the paper, or further consideration of it in detail, that he is able through arithmetical devices to work out the amount of paper that he must purchase.

Arithmetic is thus a substitute for concrete experience and a very convenient substitute. When we are trying to cultivate the methods of arithmetical reasoning, we find ourselves continually drifting away from the necessity of handling concrete objects with which we deal. Any observation of children in the schools will make it perfectly clear that where examples have been mastered, they are taken up, not in a concrete way but in an abstract arithmetical way, which is entirely legitimate, and highly economical of human energy.

What has been said with regard to arithmetic may be repeated in kind for our treatment of experiences through the use of words. If one owns a piece of farm-land he may go over the ground very carefully, and become acquainted with its character by actual contact with it. Its distances may be measured by actual movement across it. The thickness of the soil may be tested by actual labor. In these and other ways one may gain concrete knowledge of land. It does not follow, however, that one will have the highest and most complete knowledge of his farm through this direct contact with it. Indeed, all of our experience with scientific improvement of farming shows us that it is not the person who is most concretely acquainted with a piece of land who is usually in a position to make the most important suggestions about it. It is more important that one should be able to apply to the land a vast body of knowledge which has been written down in the books of science, in the form of words. These words are not actual pictures of the landscape, nor are they the concrete experience which would be derived by going over the land. The problems of farming have all been turned into certain verbal symbols which help us to concentrate many different kinds of experience first "in our heads." The land is rolling, for example, or it is very level; the land has a thick soil or a thin soil; the land has good drainage or poor drainage. As soon as these various words have been substituted for an actual muscular experience of contact with the land itself, we are in a position to bring to bear upon the problem of dealing with the land much descriptive material which has been carefully worked out and recorded in bulletins of the Agricultural Department or in books on agriculture. To be sure, these books on agriculture never can be complete substitutes for the kind of experience that one would get in actual contact with the soil, but the two types of experience are supplementary and not identical in character. They were never intended to be substitutes for each other, and he who would neglect the ability to turn experience into words and work them over "in the head," is forgetting an important fact of human nature just as much as he who would deal with words alone is neglecting an important fact of human nature.

The words are means and devices for a most significant mode of dealing with the world, and just in so far as this significant mode of dealing with problems is cultivated, and its methods are mastered, will the learner become superior to the person who merely comes into concrete contact with objects and does not think about them.

Putting the matter which has been discussed in the last paragraph in a more general form, we may say that science is superior to mere contact with objects just because science is more comprehensive and general than the concrete. The scientist who knows about birds and plants does not merely have more sensory experiences than the ordinary individual. Such a scientist is indeed likely to come into contact with more objects than the ordinary individual because he goes and seeks this kind of experience; but the essential fact in his scientific thinking is that he takes some common experience and relates it to the large body of knowledge which the ordinary individual never takes up. The methods by which this large body of additional knowledge is brought to bear upon present experience is not the method of mere sensory contact with the object, it is rather the method of reasoning. Such thoughtful reasoning involves the use of a highly developed scientific terminology and a body of reference material which would be utterly unmanageable without the aid of language.

It is time that someone suggested in regard to the nature-study movement, that it is not the bringing of objects into the schoolroom which will give the scientific attitude: it is rather thought about these objects, and careful inference based upon objects that will train children in scientific modes of thought. Careful inference can in no proper sense of the word be described under the term "concrete." No scientist is satisfied to look at the things about him. His largest generalizations always carry him away from these concrete facts, into the realms of thinking. It is into these realms of thinking that the child must be carried if he would see the large significance of the experiences that are presented to him. The turning of experiences into words is therefore to be recognized as an abstract method of dealing with the world supplementary to the concrete manipulation of objects. He who stops and thinks about the situation is not dealing with that situation primarily through his senses or with his hands.

Let us consider another type of illustration which is very common in our schools today. A great effort is being made in some of the schools to combine elementary science and cooking. Children are brought into contact with the operations of the kitchen on the assumption that as soon as these operations involve certain scientific principles the scientific principles should be worked out both as cooking and as science.

A brief review of the history of the race would seem to be enough to convince the enthusiast that cooking and science are not necessarily related. Practical operations in cooking were brought to a degree of perfection long before there was a chemistry of foods. On the other hand, the chemistry of foods has gradually arisen in remote laboratories which are very far from the kitchens where most of the actual food of the race has been prepared. The chemistry of organic substances is a highly developed form of science which involves some of the most elaborate technique that is at the command of trained scientists.

Any psychological analysis of the cooking activity and of the thought processes on the part of the organic chemist, ought to convince the student of domestic science that these two forms of experience are at least not identical. To boil common potatoes in water on the one hand and to recognize starch in unboiled potatoes by the iodine test on the other, are two totally different attitudes toward potatoes. It is very doubtful whether, in the earlier years of the child's life, there is any possibility of bringing together these two attitudes. They are likely to be disturbing to each other. They are undoubtedly capable of being related to each other at some stage of education, but they do not flow at once into each other.

The above examples have been chosen for the purpose of making it as clear as possible that in our school work we are constantly training a great variety of different attitudes towards things. In the use of tools and in the use of words we are training different modes of treatment of the world. One of these modes of treatment is the constructive mode, another mode is the arithmetical mode of treatment, a third is the verbal mode of treatment, and so on down the list. The reason why the school has to treat these different types of relation to the world separately is that each has its own independent justification, and its own definite character. We ought not to make the mistake of thinking that we can substitute the arithmetical attitude for the constructive attitude. On the other hand, it should be noted with perfect clearness that there is no remote possibility of substituting the constructive attitude for the arithmetical attitude. While the school of the last generation was in some danger of assuming that its work was done when it taught the arithmetical attitude, there are certain examples in our generation of a tendency to make the mistake of believing that the work of the school is done when the constructive attitude has been trained.

We must recognize that the term "concrete" has its place in our education just so far as we can show the legitimacy of concrete reactions upon the external world. Abstract training can be justified with equal emphasis and we are justified whenever we point out that abstract methods of treating the external world are of advantage to the individual. We should no more eliminate abstractions from our school work than we eliminate abstractions from our ordinary life. Indeed the abstract has superior virtues which have been touched upon in the foregoing illustrations. There is danger that these virtues will be overlooked in the enthusiasm for concrete experience which is characteristic of our present-day education.

[*To be continued*]

EDITORIAL NOTES

Mr. Mirick's article in the present number of the *Elementary School Teacher* raises in a very concrete way a number of questions regarding promotion which are of vital importance to every member of the school system. The interest of the superintendent and principal is so obvious that it calls for no comment. The individual teacher cannot do her work successfully if the children in the class are so different in maturity and previous equipment that they cannot work together. The backward child is discouraged; the forward child learns habits of neglect and forms a false estimate of the importance of all intellectual tasks. The parents are dissatisfied with the associations into which the child is brought, and are critical of a system which holds a child back for reasons which do not tally with the evident needs of the child.

Significance of the Problem of Promotion

The fundamental difficulty in this matter as in many of the other aspects of educational organization is the lack of any clear guiding principles underlying practice. The individual teacher sometimes recommends promotion not because of any clearly statable reasons; or, what is worse, the teacher recommends the holding back of a child on the weakest of pretexts. Thus, some teachers undoubtedly recommend that a given child go forward when their patience and resources are exhausted. They have perhaps done all that they can for the child in question and look upon promotion as a device for putting an end to what seems to be fruitless effort. On the other hand, some teachers hold children back unduly because they wish to avoid criticism from the teacher next above. They send forward only those children of whom they are perfectly sure, so that the next teacher may be impressed with the proficiency of the preparation given in the lower grade. Such reasons as these are seldom stated in these bald terms and they are certainly not generally acceptable when put in this form.

Vague Reasons for Promotion

Another serious defect in the promotion system is to be found

How Can Uniformity Be Gained?

in the fact that practice, even within the bounds of a single school building, is not uniform. The principal may intend to supervise the school in such a way as to make all promotions on the same basis, but he does not know the pupils intimately, and his information from the teachers differs in value and differs in the expectations which lie back of each teacher's personal judgments. If the principal cannot judge accurately, certainly the superintendent cannot. The only hope of securing uniformity is to begin a full study of the matter involving every school and every teacher.

Value of the Indianapolis Study

It requires some courage to face all these facts as is done in the Indianapolis system. Most school officers are timid about admitting that they have ever made mistakes. Of course, the Indianapolis schools have been no more guilty than other systems. So far, however, this system has been the first to take up for its own sake, and incidentally for the sake of other school systems, a systematic study of the whole problem. Furthermore, this system is in advance of others in opening up a rational and carefully organized experiment to correct the evils discovered, and to study the effects of newer, and what seem to be better, practices.

Scientific School Organization

Reform is significant wherever it is conscientiously made. The difficulty with most reforms, however, is that there is no adequate evidence on which to base a judgment either of the needs of reform or its effects. Here is a most significant change in practice backed up by a clear-headed statement of the reasons for the change and by a series of investigations that make it possible to evaluate with perfect precision the outcome. Such reform rises to the level of scientific organization. That a great system of schools, recognized as one of the most efficient in the country, should give an example of scientific organization such as we have here is a matter of congratulation. Others of less courage and initiative will undoubtedly be induced to follow this example. Mr. Mirick's report is a long step in advance in the administration of schools. He and his associates in that city, as well as their former leader, Mr. Kendall, have done a large public service in this study.

BOOK REVIEWS

Introduction to Psychology. By ROBERT M. YERKES, Assistant Professor of Comparative Psychology, Harvard University. New York: Henry Holt & Co., 1911.

The Essentials of Psychology. By W. B. PILLSBURY, Professor of Psychology, University of Michigan. New York: Macmillan, 1911.

The appearance of two new introductory texts in psychology will be of interest to educational readers. These books contain the new material which has been worked out in recent years and they give new emphasis to the scientific spirit which now characterizes psychology as an independent discipline.

Professor Yerkes has adopted a somewhat unique view regarding the function of a textbook which is to serve as an introduction. Most writers regard it as the function of such a book to furnish the reader with the fundamental results of the science. Professor Yerkes, on the other hand, has pushed the results of the science somewhat into the background and has devoted much attention to discussion of what the science is from a logical point of view. What are the methods of the science? What are the characteristics in which psychology resembles physics and chemistry? How far can psychology establish generalization? What is the nature of a psychological law? These and similar questions are the matters chiefly discussed.

One wonders whether the elementary student will be able to take this "outside" point of view toward a science which he approaches for the first time. One cannot but be skeptical about the ability of an elementary student to follow the elaborate discussions of physical and chemical analogies and contrasts. In short, it seems to the present reviewer that the book has little to recommend it as an elementary text. Students who wish to critically discuss the logic of the science may take the book in hand. The teacher who is looking for applications may find suggestions here and there, but in the main the book should not be used as a first text even by mature readers.

Professor Pillsbury's book is wholly different in type. The essential results of psychological investigation are here presented in a simple and very usable form. The book reminds one strongly of James's *Briefer Course* or Angell's *Psychology*. The general concepts of Attention and Association are taken up early in the text and the particular processes of perception and memory, etc., are taken up later. There is a very good introductory treatment of the nervous system. The structural aspects of consciousness are emphasized.

This book will undoubtedly be very useful as an introductory text. Teachers will find little or no effort to suggest applications but they will find a very satisfactory statement of the most recent results on which to base educational applications.

C. H. J.

BOOKS RECEIVED

THE MACMILLAN CO., NEW YORK

The English Language. Book I. By Sarah Withers and James P. Kinard. Cloth. Illustrated. Pp. 289. $0.40.

The English Language. Book II. By James P. Kinard and Sarah Withers. Cloth. Illustrated. Pp. 270. $0.55.

The Study of History in Secondary Schools. Report of the American History Association by a Committee of Five. Cloth. Pp. 72. $0.25.

Dictation Day by Day. By Kate Van Wagenen. Cloth. Pp. 127. Illustrated. $0.20.

Educational Values. By William Chandler Bagley. Cloth. Pp. 259. $1.10.

Select Orations. Edited with Introduction by Archibald McClelland Hall. Cloth. Pp. 207. $0.25.

A Short History of the American People. By Edna Henry Lee Turpin. Cloth. Illustrated. Pp. 478. $0.90.

The Pupil's Arithmetic. Book III. By James C. Byrnes; Julia Richman; John S. Roberts. Cloth. Pp. 256. $0.35.

The Pupil's Arithmetic. Book IV. By James C. Byrnes; Julia Richman; John S. Roberts. Cloth. Pp. 235. $0.35.

Proceedings of the Fourth Annual Meeting of the Association of Life Insurance Presidents, Held in the Hotel La Salle, Chicago, Ill., December 9 and 10, 1910. Paper. Pp. 215.

Principles of Education Applied to Practice. By W. Franklin Jones. Cloth. Pp. 293. $1.00.

American History for Grammar Schools. By Marguerite Stockman Dickson. Cloth. Pp. 531. $1.00.

The Continents and Their People: North America, A Supplementary Geography. By James Franklin Chamberlain and Arthur Henry Chamberlain. Cloth. Pp. 295. $0.55.

CHARLES E. MERRILL CO.

Culture Readers. Book I. By Ellen E. Kenyon-Warner. Cloth. Pp. 128. $0.30.

Alice's Adventures in Wonderland. By Lewis Carroll. Cloth. Pp. 187. $0.30.

RAND, McNALLY & CO., CHICAGO

A Dog of Flanders. By Louise de la Ramée (Ouida). Edited by Rose C. Swart. Cloth. Illustrated. Pp. 100. $0.25.

ROW, PETERSON & CO.

First Reader. By Harriette Taylor Treadwell and Margaret Free. Cloth. Pp. 134.

THE SALEM PRESS CO.

Vanished Arizona. By MARTHA SUMMERHAYS. Cloth. Pp. 319. $1.50.

CHARLES SCRIBNER'S SONS, NEW YORK

Indoors and Out. By SARAH M. MOTT AND PERCIVAL CHUBB. Illustrated. Cloth. Pp. 118.

THE UNIVERSITY OF CHICAGO PRESS, CHICAGO

The Unfolding of Personality as the Chief Aim in Education. By THISELTON MARK. Cloth. Pp. 224. $1.07 postpaid.

Alumni Directory, The University of Chicago. 1861–1910. Cloth. Pp. 297.

The Elementary Course in English. By JAMES FLEMING HOSIC. Cloth. Pp. 150. $0.82.

WARWICK & YORK

Educational Psychology Monographs. By J. E. WALLACE WALLIN. Cloth. Pp. 86.

Educational Psychology Monographs. By W. H. WINCH. Cloth. Pp. 98.

CURRENT EDUCATIONAL LITERATURE IN THE PERIODICALS[1]

IRENE WARREN
Librarian, School of Education, The University of Chicago

ANDREWS, FANNIE FERN. The American school peace league. Child 1:969–70. (Ag. '11.)

BADLEY, J. H. Handwork in education. Child 1:939–50. (Ag. '11.)

COCKERELL, T. D. A. The university in politics. Pop. Sci. Mo. 79:160–64. (Ag. '11.)

(A) fund for public school betterment in Pittsburgh. Science 34:47. (14 Jl. '11.)

Growth of our art institutions. Lit. D. 43:207–8. (5 Ag. '11.)

HARRIS, J. ARTHUR. Francis Galton. Pop. Sci. Mo. 79:171–90. (Ag. '11.)

HITCHING, WILENA. The teaching of home management in elementary schools. Child 1:951–55. (Ag. '11.)

HOWERTH, IRA W. The classification of the sciences. Pop. Sci. Mo. 79:165–70. (Ag. '11.)

HUTCHINSON, WOODS. Can the child survive civilization? Child 1:966–68. (Ag.'11.)

Insurgent educators. Lit. D. 43:175. (29 Jl. '11.)

JACOB, MARY S. The colour-sense of children. Child 1:962–65. (Ag.'11.)

LOEB, JACQUES. The significance of tropisms for psychology. Pop. Sci. Mo. 79:105–25. (Ag. '11.)

MACLAURIN, RICHARD C. Darwin at an American university. Atlan. 108:192–98. (Ag. '11.)

MANGOLD, GEORGE B. Child welfare and street trades in the United States of America. Child 1:956–61. (Ag. '11.)

MAYER, MARY JOSEPHINE. Our public schools as social centers. R. of Rs. 43:201–8. (Ag. '11.)

ROLKER, A. W. (The) college woman in business. Good Housekeeping 53:147–53. (Ag. '11.)

ROYCE, JOSIAH. James as a philosopher. Science 34:33–45. (14 Jl. '11.)

SWIFT, EDGAR J. The genesis of the attention in the educative process. Science 33:1–5. (7 Jl. '11.)

Technical libraries for employees. Print. Art 17:469–70. (Ag. '11.)

WOLFE, A. B. What makes a college? Pop. Sci. Mo. 79:151–59. (Ag. '11.)

[1] *Abbreviations.*—Atlan., Atlantic Monthly; Lit. D., Literary Digest; Pop. Sci. Mo., Popular Science Monthly; Print. Art, Printing Art; R. of Rs., Review of Reviews.

VOLUME XII NUMBER 3

THE ELEMENTARY SCHOOL TEACHER

NOVEMBER, 1911

PESTALOZZIAN FORMALISM

DEGENERATE OBJECT-TEACHING; SIMPLE TO COMPLEX

S. CHESTER PARKER
The University of Chicago

In the last two volumes of the *Elementary School Teacher*, a number of articles appeared which were intended to illustrate a method of teaching the history of education by emphasizing school practice in its relation to social conditions. This is the seventh article in this series. A textbook entitled *A History of Modern Elementary Education*, constructed on this principle, by the same author will appear in the near future.

In the history of educational changes, it is not uncommon to find that a reform which has been initiated as a protest against the formalism of words, of teaching devices, and of excessive routine, often degenerates very rapidly into the same kind of formalism that called forth the protest. This degeneration is well illustrated by the developments in Pestalozzian object-teaching, which became as pernicious in some of its aspects as it was beneficial in others. The tendency to formalism was also inherent in another phase of Pestalozzian reforms, namely in the application of the principle of proceeding from the simple to the complex in the teaching of all subjects. It is the purpose of this paper to discuss these two forms of Pestalozzian formalism. The discussion has a practical bearing on many present practices in elementary schools, practices which are essentially Pestalozzian in character and to a certain extent in origin.

Pestalozzi realized the danger of formalism.—Pestalozzi realized clearly the danger of degeneration into formalism and said:

I know too well how it will be; this poor husk, which is but the mere outward form of my method, will appear to be its real substance to a great number of men, who will endeavor to introduce this form into the narrow circle of their own ideas, and will judge of the value of the method according to the effects it produces in this strange association. I cannot prevent the forms of my method from having the same fate as all other forms, which inevitably perish in the hands of men who are neither desirous nor capable of grasping their spirit.

Herbert Spencer described Pestalozzian formalism in England.—One of the best accounts of Pestalozzian formalism versus the Pestalozzian spirit is found in the second chapter of the work by Herbert Spencer (1820–1903) on *Education*, published in 1861. Spencer's chapter contains an exposition of English Pestalozzianism which, as we noticed in an earlier article, tended toward this formal type. Spencer rejected the particular forms while approving strongly of the fundamental principles. He said:

While, therefore, we would defend in its entire extent the general doctrine which Pestalozzi inaugurated, we think great evil likely to result from an uncritical reception of his specific devices. That tendency which mankind constantly exhibit to canonize the forms and practices along with which any great truth has been bequeathed to them—their liability to prostrate their intellects before the prophet and swear by his every word—their proneness to mistake the clothing of the idea for the idea itself renders it needful to insist strongly upon the distinction between the fundamental principles of the Pestalozzian system, and the set of expedients derived for its practice.

This Pestalozzian formalism can be discussed to advantage under two main heads: (1) degenerate object-teaching, and (2) extreme and false applications of the theory of proceeding from the simple to the complex.

Degenerate object-teaching. Pestalozzi recommended memorizing words.—Strange as it may seem, Pestalozzi recommended and carried out in his school the practice of having children memorize lists of words. Herbart, von Raumer, and other visitors to Pestalozzi's schools commented on this anomaly. Lists of nouns and adjectives were made up from the dictionary by the teacher and memorized by the children. Pestalozzi said:

These lists of words are placed in the hands of the child, merely as exercises in learning to read, immediately after he has gone through his spelling-book; and experience has shown me that it is possible to make the children so thoroughly acquainted with these lists of words that they shall be able to repeat them from memory, merely in the time that is required to perfect them in reading; the gain of what at this age is so complete a knowledge of lists of names, so various and comprehensive, is immeasurable in facilitating the subsequent instruction of children.

This memorized material included such phrases as "slippery, wormshaped, thick-skinned eel," "crawling, amphibious animals," "long-tailed monkeys," etc. In geography the children memorized long alphabetical lists of the names of German towns before studying their locations on the map. Many other examples of such absurd practices could be cited which were utterly inconsistent with the theory of basing all instruction on sense perception which Pestalozzi emphasized as his most important principle.

English books of object-lessons became manuals for memorizing.— It was in England that Pestalozzian verbal formalism was most influential in actual practice, resulting in what Spencer called "the well-conceived but ill-conducted system of *object-lessons*." In an earlier article it was pointed out that one reason why Pestalozzian methods took such a strong hold on English schools was because of the early preparation of a textbook, *Lessons on Objects*, by Elizabeth Mayo (1793–1865) and her brother. This textbook was published in 1830 and was very successful. By 1855 it had reached the fourteenth edition, a copy of which I have examined. It was a veritable little encyclopedia of the arts and sciences. The lessons were arranged in five series. The first series contained simple lists of qualities, for example, in the case of leather, it was stated that it was flexible, odorous, waterproof, tough, smooth, durable, opaque. The second series gave parts of complicated objects as well as qualities; the third series included non-sensory qualities such as *valuable*, and such classifications as *artificial* and *natural;* the fourth series continued the classifications and proceeded to discover analogies between physical and moral or spiritual qualities; the fifth series provided exercises for composition, containing lessons on various chemical substances, on solubility, on the five senses, etc. Finally there was a vocabulary of words beginning with *aromatic*, *adhesive*, *affinity*, and ending with *vitrifiable*, *volatile*, *unctuous*. All of this, according to the title-page, was intended for children from six to eight years of age.

The motive of the Mayos in preparing this text was to provide a method of object-teaching that was not limited by the dearth of suitable objects in the schoolroom, or by the uncertainties of excursions. They realized clearly the danger of the books being used in unprofitable ways. Thus in the Preface it was stated that—

Those who fall into a mechanical way of giving such instruction, and do not perceive the principle involved, completely defeat its intention, and they had far better keep to old plans and old books.

Miss Mayo intended that the facts should be discovered by the children by an actual examination of the objects, the teacher giving new names where necessary. After advising against too much telling by the teacher she said:

The writer desires particularly to enforce this remark, having in one or two instances seen the lessons entirely misused. The qualities were told, and the explanation of the terms given, instead of the object being presented to the children that they might make their own observations upon it, and learn from the teacher how to express qualities clearly discovered by them, though unknown by name.

Dickens satirized formal memorizing of Mayo books.—The practice which Miss Mayo said she had seen "in one or two instances" was really very common and led to the following classic satire on these methods by Charles Dickens in his story entitled *Hard Times.*

Mr. Gradgrind, the town magnate and school patron, is present in the model school of his own creation, where Mr. McChoakumchild surcharges the youthful Coke-towners with grim facts. After a preliminary address to the teachers in this vein—

"Now what I want is facts. Teach these boys and girls nothing but facts. Facts alone are wanted in life. Plant nothing else, and root out everything else. You can only form the mind of reasoning animals upon facts; nothing else ever will be of any service to them. This is the principle upon which I bring up my own children, and this is the principle upon which I bring up these children. Stick to facts, Sir!"

Having thus relieved himself, that his self-love may be gratified by witnessing the triumphs of his own educational scheming, he calls out, by an appropriate management and catechizing, its distinctive features.

Sissy Jupe, Girl No. 20, the daughter of a strolling circus actor, whose life, no small share of it, has been passed under the canvas; whose knowledge of horse, generic and specific, extends back as far as memory reaches; familiar with the form and food, the powers and habits and everything relating to the horse; knowing it through several senses; Sissy Jupe has been asked to define horse. Astonished at hearing her father stigmatized as a veterinary surgeon, a farrier, and horse-breaker; bewildered by the striking want of resemblance between the horse of her own conceptions and the prescribed formula that represents the animal in the books of the Home and Colonial Society, she dares not trust herself with the confusing description, and shrinks from it in silence and alarm.

"Girl No. 20 unable to define a horse," said Mr. Gradgrind.

Girl No. 20 is declared possessed of no facts in reference to one of the commonest of animals, and appeal is made to one red-eyed Bitzer, who knows horse practically only as he has seen a picture of a horse or as he has, perhaps, sometimes safely weathered the perils of a crowded street-crossing.

"Bitzer," (said Thomas Gradgrind,) "your definition of a horse!" "Quadruped. Graminivorous. Forty teeth, namely: twenty-four grinders, four eye teeth, and twelve incisive. Sheds coat in the Spring; in marshy countries sheds hoofs too. Hoofs hard, but requiring to be shod with iron. Age known by marks in mouth." Thus (and much more) Bitzer.

"Now Girl No. 20," said Mr. Gradgrind, "you know what a horse is."

The methods of the Home and Colonial Infant School Society, mentioned by Dickens, were copied at Oswego, New York, and encountered considerable criticism of a similar sort. Many of the papers on object-teaching published during this period (1860), contain comments on the tendency of teachers to have children merely memorize facts about objects instead of providing real experiences with them.

Proceeding from simple to complex. Favored by Spencer.—The second large group of formalized Pestalozzian practices resulted from the extreme application of the principle that in the process of instruction the teacher should proceed from the simple to the complex. The validity of this principle will be discussed later in this section. It is open to a variety of interpretations. Thus Herbert Spencer states it as the first of the Pestalozzian principles which he would "defend in its entire extent" but rejects the practices which Pestalozzi described for its application. Spencer defended the principle in these words:

That in education we should proceed from the simple to the complex is a truth which has always been to some extent acted upon; not professedly, indeed, nor by any means consistently. The mind grows. Like all things that grow it progresses from the homogeneous to the heterogeneous; and a normal training system being an objective counterpart of this subjective process, must exhibit the like progression. Moreover, regarding it from this point of view we may see that this formula has much wider applications than at first appears. For its *rationale* involves not only that we should proceed from the simple to the combined in the teaching of each branch of knowledge, but that we should do the like with knowledge as a whole.

Pestalozzi desired to mechanize instruction.—With Pestalozzi this principle was bound up with his desire to mechanize instruction. Describing his work in the second school in which he taught at Burgdorf (1799), Pestalozzi said:

> I once more began crying my ABC from morning to night. . . . . I was indefatigable in putting syllables together and arranging them in a graduated series; I did the same for numbers; I filled whole notebooks with them; I sought by every means to simplify the elements of reading and arithmetic, and by grouping them psychologically, enable the child to pass easily and surely from the first step to the second, from the second to the third, and so on. The pupils no longer drew letters on their slates, but lines, curves, angles, and squares.

Shortly after this, when Pestalozzi was explaining his experiments to a visiting French-Swiss official, the latter said, "I see, you want to mechanize instruction." "He had hit the nail on the head," said Pestalozzi, "and supplied me with the very word I wanted to express my aim and the means I employed."

Later, Pestalozzi said that he meant that he desired to psychologize instruction; but the fact remains that what he really did was to reduce much of instruction to a mechanical routine by application of the principle of proceeding from the simple to the complex.

Would organize an alphabet of every subject.—In one of Pestalozzi's last publications, *The Song of the Swan*, he said:

> I now came to consider the idea of elementary education from the point of view of means of instruction. From its very nature, it demands the general simplification of its means, which simplification was the starting-point of all the educational labors of my life. At first I desired nothing else, but merely sought to render the ordinary means of instruction for the people as simple as to permit of their being employed in every family. And so in every branch of popular knowledge or talent, I set to work to organize a graduated series of exercises, the starting-point of which was within everybody's comprehension, and the unbroken action of which always exercising the child's powers without exhausting them, resulted in a continuous easy and attractive progress, in which knowledge and the application of knowledge were always intimately connected.

Pestalozzi said that these graduated series of exercises would make teaching so easy that "schools would gradually almost cease to be necessary, so far as the first elements are concerned."

Thorough mastery of each step required.—Closely connected with the practice of using a minutely graduated series in each subject was the emphasis on the mastery of each step or element before proceeding to the next. This notion of thoroughness was another factor in establishing mechanized routine among the Pestalozzians.

The influence of these principles in the teaching of special subjects in the elementary schools was very great, particularly in the case of reading, arithmetic, drawing, writing, and form study.

From simple to complex in teaching reading.—In the teaching of reading the influence of Pestalozzi was to fix and stereotype the synthetic method of beginning with long drills on the letters, then proceeding to syllables, to words, phrases, etc. The first steps in this alphabet-syllable-spelling method of teaching reading, Pestalozzi described in these words:

> The spelling-book must contain the entire range of sounds of which the language consists, and portions of it should be repeated daily in every family. . . . . No one imagines to what a degree the attention of infants is aroused by the repetition of such simple sounds as *ba*, *ba*, *ba*, *da*, *da*, *da*, *ma*, *ma*, *ma*, *la*, *la*, *la*, etc.

The spelling-book contained all the possible combinations of vowels and consonants for such drill. After these had been mastered, words were to be learned by spelling them. As was the case in Salzman's school, Pestalozzi provided large movable letters to be inserted in a frame by the teacher as a means of class instruction. These methods were copied in the Prussian schools which were described in Professor Stowe's report to the Ohio legislature in 1839. After telling how the children were drilled on the elementary sounds of letters and syllables till they were mastered, Stowe said:

> They were now prepared to commence reading. The letters are printed in large form on square cards; the class stands up before a sort of rack, the teacher places one upon the rack . . . . [and says], What letter is that? [Pupils answer] *H*. He places another. What letter is that? *A*. I now move these two letters together, thus: *HA*. What sound do these letters signify? *Ha*. [And so on adding a letter at a time, the teacher proceeded until he had formed *hard, hard fist, hard fisted, hardfistedness*.]

In the next higher grade the reading proceeded as follows according to Mr. Stowe:

> The sentence is first gone through with in the class, by distinctly spelling each word as it occurs; then by pronouncing each word distinctly without spelling it; a third time by pronouncing the words and mentioning the punctuation pöints as they occur [and so on until the sentence is finally read with expression]. Thus one thing is taken at a time, and pupils must become thorough in each as it occurs, before they proceed to the next.

In the Oswego schools, similar synthetic methods were used but with special emphasis on the phonic values instead of the names of the letters.

Study of form, drawing and writing.—Applying the general principle of reducing each subject to its elements, Pestalozzi maintained that the elements of drawing and writing are lines and geometrical figures of various sorts and that long drill in these elements as arranged in his "alphabet of form" should be the first step in instruction. These practices were copied in England and America.

The elements of form with which the children were to be made acquainted occupied sixty pages in N. A. Calkins' *Primary Object Lessons* (1861), one of the best of the numerous books on object-teaching published in America at about the time of the Oswego movement. This included instruction about corners, sides, straight and curved lines, plane and curved surfaces, right, acute and obtuse angles, equilateral and right-angled triangles, perpendicular, horizontal, and parallel lines, the square, rhomb, and parallelogram, pyramids, prisms, cubes, circles, semicircles, circumferences, arcs, center, radius, diameter, cylinders, cones, spheres, hemispheres, and ovals. Calkins' book was largely an imitation of Miss Mayo's which included in addition to the above the tetrahedron, octahedron, pentagonal dodecahedron, icosahedron, rhombic dodecahedron. All of this was to be taught in infant or primary schools and was partly correlated with the teaching of drawing.

The teaching of drawing was to begin with the making of these geometrical figures, starting with various kinds of lines, etc. Spencer, while defending the principle of proceeding from the simple to the complex, said that he wholly disapproved of this "formal discipline in making straight lines and compound lines." A drawing-book constructed on these principles he denounced as "the most vicious in principle" which he had seen.

Writing was taught in connection with drawing in the Pestalozzian methods. The letters were analyzed into straight, curved, and slanting lines, into acute and obtuse angles, etc., and drill given on these before proceeding to write letters, words, and phrases.

Thorough mastery of elements in arithmetic. Grube method.—In an earlier article improvements in the teaching of arithmetic by applying the Pestalozzian principle of sense perception were discussed in connection with Warren Colburn's *Arithmetic*, published in Boston, in 1821. The Pestalozzian principle of reducing each subject to its elements and requiring thorough mastery of each element before taking up the next was also very influential as applied to the teaching of arithmetic This application was emphasized by a German, Grube (1816–84), in a work published in 1842. Grube was not original in his system of teaching arithmetic. He copied a number of Pestalozzi's characteristics, notably the sense-perception basis, as well as ideas from other sources. The essential characteristic for our present purposes and the one by which the system is most commonly known is the practice of considering each number as an individual, and mastering all the possible operations with it, namely, addition, subtraction, multiplication, and division before taking up the next number. This differs radically from the common practice of first teaching counting, sometimes clear up into the millions, then addition of all numbers, then subtraction of all numbers, then multiplication and division. In as much as Grube began with the number one, which was mastered, before proceeding to number two, and so on up to ten, counting was definitely eliminated. The first year was to be spent on the numbers from one to ten in order, and the first three years on the numbers up to one hundred.

Grube method popularized in America, 1870.—One of the chief influences in popularizing the Grube method in the United States was an essay describing it, read by Mr. L. Soldan before the St. Louis Teacher's Association in 1870. According to its author this essay was "republished extensively in state and city school reports and educational magazines . . . . from California (see San Francisco Report of 1872) to New Hampshire (see State Report of 1876)." A larger treatment of the subject was contained in *Grube's Method of Teaching Arithmetic*, by Levy Seeley, published in New York, in 1888. According to Professor Smith,

it thus became . . . . almost the only German "method" known in America. Thus it has come about that Grube has been looked upon as a name to conjure by, and neither the faults nor the virtues (much less the originality) of the system seem to have been well considered.

Grube method unnecessarily thorough.—The Grube method has been severely criticized by the two leading American writers on the theory of teaching arithmetic. Professor D. E. Smith says:

> To know all there is about a number before advancing to the next one is as unnecessary as it is illogical, as impossible as it is uninteresting. . . . . [Two of] the chief defects of the system are these: 1. It carries objective illustration to an extreme, studying numbers by the aid of objects for three years, until 100 is reached. 2. It attempts to master each number before taking up the next, as if it were a matter of importance to know the factors of 51 before the child knows anything of 75, or as if it were possible to keep children studying 4 when the majority know something of 8 before they enter school.

Professor John Dewey, the other prominent critic of the Grube method, says:

> It seems absurd, or even worse than absurd, to insist on thoroughness, on perfect number concepts, at a time when perfection is impossible. . . . . If the child knows 3, if he has an intelligent working conception of 3, he can proceed in a few lessons to the number 10, and will have all higher numbers within comparatively easy reach.

Criticism of proceeding from simple to complex.—Pestalozzi thought he was psychologizing instruction by having the teacher analyze each subject into a graduated series of elements which were to be learned by the pupil in order. He thought that the work of the educator should be analytic and that of the learner synthetic. This implied that the natural process of learning which he was trying to discover, consisted in building up complex wholes from elements which could not be further analyzed.

Pestalozzian theory held by English associationists.—This theory of the way in which we learn was not unique with Pestalozzi.

Many psychologists have believed it. Prominent among these were the whole English school of "associationists" and Herbart, the German follower of Pestalozzi. The subject is too involved to be discussed here in a clear and satisfactory manner, but a little must be said to suggest the recent criticisms of Pestalozzi's fundamental principle. Reference has been made several times to Spencer's discussion of this theory. What he believed is not perfectly clear, but certainly, one of his most important contentions would be rejected by many modern psychologists as being just the opposite of the truth. I refer to his statement that—

> Manifestly decomposable states of consciousness cannot exist before the states of consciousness out of which they are composed . . . . [thus] no articulate sound is cognizable until the inarticulate sounds which go to make it up have been learned.

It was on this theory that Pestalozzi said that the mother should address the infant with *ba*, *ba*, *ba*, *da*, *da*, *da*, etc., before she tried to teach him to recognize whole words like "bottle," "mother," etc.

William James rejected associationist theory of learning.—The best criticism of this theory occurs in William James's chapter on "Discrimination and Comparison" in his *Principles of Psychology*. In direct opposition to Spencer's point he says that the child's experience instead of beginning with nicely separated elements is

> one big, blooming, buzzing confusion. That confusion is the baby's universe; and the universe of all of us is still to a great extent such a confusion, potentially resolvable, and demanding to be resolved, but not yet actually resolved into parts. . . . .
>
> Experience from the very first presents us with concreted objects vaguely continuous with the rest of the world which envelops them in space and time, and potentially divisible into inward elements and parts. These objects we break asunder and reunite.

Analysis by the learner prominent in ordinary learning.—As a rule in the ordinary process of learning, the individual things with which we become acquainted are complex wholes; we recognize, identify, and remember them without completely analyzing them, and may never analyze them unless some practical necessity requires it. Thus in the case of the so-called taste of coffee or onions, this necessity usually does not arise, and as a consequence we do not ordinarily know how much of the so-called "taste" is really taste and how much is odor. Or to take the example that Spencer suggests, as a matter of fact, the child recognizes spoken words as wholes long before he has gotten separately acquainted with the articulate elements which compose these words. In the same way the child recognizes visual wholes (doors, windows, etc.), long before he has gotten acquainted with the various kinds of lines, angles, and shades of color which are fused in the total experience.

In mastering any new situation or material, for example, in becoming familiar with a strange city, or in solving a geometry exercise, or in studying pictures to determine their artistic qualities, the following process takes place. The mind begins by apprehending the situation as a vague, unanalyzed whole; proceeds by comparison or selective attention to break this whole up into its parts (as far as necessary for the practical purpose of the moment); and then reconstructs (synthetizes) these parts into an organized whole in which the relation of the parts is more or less clearly perceived.

Partly as a consequence of this change in psychological theory, the Pestalozzian methods of teaching reading and drawing by proceeding from simplified elements to complex wholes have been rejected in many places, and methods substituted which are more in harmony with the theory of the psychology of learning maintained by James and his followers.

CORRELATION OF ELEMENTARY SCHOOLS AND HIGH SCHOOLS

RALPH E. CARTER
The University of Chicago

Many superintendents of city schools would be glad to make a close study of the correlation of their elementary and secondary schools if they knew some simple, economic way of recording and tabulating results. Without any recognized method of procedure it seems like a hopeless task to most of them to undertake to evaluate the educational product of each of their various elementary schools through the high school.

The method to be outlined in this article is the outgrowth of a study of the correlation of the Milwaukee public schools. The study was rendered possible by the co-operation of Superintendent Pearse who made the wealth of well-preserved records in that city accessible to the investigator. There were naturally difficulties in organizing the material of such a scope into a simple, compact form. Undoubtedly the plans of tabulation and method of procedure which proved, after more or less experimentation, to be the best suited to such a problem may constitute a suggestive working basis for similar studies in other systems.

The study in question proposed to judge the preparation of pupils from each elementary school upon the basis of the ability exhibited by its pupils to retain their rank or relative position in the high school. That is, if a pupil has taken high rank in the elementary school, does he continue in the highest rank in the high-school class to which he is promoted?

The use of rank instead of absolute marks as the basis of all comparisons is very important for two reasons. In the first place, the group of pupils who never enter high school ought to be considered. If the pupils who go to high school from any given elementary school are not truly representative—that is, about equally divided between poor, average, and superior pupils—this fact will be taken into consideration in the investigation by using the marks of all the original eighth grade to determine rank in that school. What is the wisdom in comparing two schools on the basis of the future marks of their pupils in high school if one-half of the pupils from one school were originally in the lowest division of the class and only one-tenth of the pupils from the other school came from the lowest division of the class? This difference in representation existed in two schools in Milwaukee and the difference in many cases was quite marked. Some schools did not have any of their poorest pupils going on to high school and, on the other hand, several schools had as many go from the low as from the high third of their classes.

The second important reason for the use of rank is found in the lack of uniformity of marking. The teacher whose pupils received the lowest marks in arithmetic (only one-third of the class got a mark above 78 per cent) must have marked very low, for the ability of her pupils was shown by an excellent record in mathematics in high school. More detailed illustrations of the lack of uniformity of standard will be given later. There is sufficient evidence to convince one that absolute marks may easily be misinterpreted by the high-school teacher if he attempts to gain any idea of the ability of pupils from different schools by the absolute marks used by different teachers.

ELEMENTARY-SCHOOL GRADES AND RANK

Elementary-school marks were taken from thirty-nine schools. In order to make this a comparative study, the entire outgoing class of a given year was taken as the basis for the study. There can be no doubt but that all of these pupils had pursued the same course of study in the elementary school and would have the same texts and subject-matter in high school. A class that graduated from the eighth grade in June, 1907, was selected, so that the progress of those entering high school could be followed for a considerable time. There were report sheets showing the marks, in a numerical percentage system of each pupil in all of his subjects.

(The scope of this article precludes a detailed description of the system of records as kept in Milwaukee and the minor details of technique in arranging this material.)

The marks in reading, arithmetic, language, and German were selected as typical. In each of the subjects the pupils were arranged in the order of superiority as indicated by the teacher's marks. Lines were then drawn marking off the third of the class having the highest marks, the third having medium marks, and the third having the lowest.

The special method used in tabulating these data is illustrated by the distributions of arithmetic marks for three schools in Table I.

TABLE I

					70	71	72	73	74	75	76	77	78	79	80	81	82
School 16	//		//	/	/						//	//	//		// ////		/
			/		///			//	/			//	//		/////	///	///
School 14		///	/	/		/	///	//	/	/	/	/			/		
	/		//	/	/////	/	/			/			//	/	/		
School 7		/	/		/						/						/
			/	//				/	/	/						/	//

TABLE I.—*Continued*

	83	84	85	86	87	88	89	90	91	92	93	94	95	96	97	98	Totals
School 16	/	/		//	/	/		/	/		/						=24
	///	//	//	//	//	//	//	/	/	//	///		/				=49
																	73
School 14			/		/	//								/			=21
		/	/	/	//		/										=22
																	43
School 7	/	/	/			/		/					/		/		=13
	/			/		///	//	///		/		/					=20
																	33

Every numerical percentage from 70 to 100 has a separate vertical column. There are also four groupings for lower marks. The record for each school is placed on a double horizontal column. The lists had been previously checked to show which pupils entered high school in the following autumn. These pupils were differentiated from the others by placing their record on the lower half of the column. It is a simple matter to take a list of final marks for a class in a given subject and represent the mark of each pupil by a tally in the column designated by that per cent and, at the same time, keep the records of the high school and non-high school separate.

This form of tabulation serves several purposes: (1) With all the data on one sheet, totals can easily be obtained showing the distribution of marks for the entire city. And the total can be obtained either for those who went to high schools or for those who did not, as well as for the entire class. (2) It affords an excellent opportunity to compare in a graphic way characteristic features such as (*a*) a preponderance of marks in the upper or lower range of the scale; (*b*) a wide or narrow range of marks given; (*c*) an unusual use of certain marks, and (*d*) the difference between the marks of those entering high school and those who did not. (3) An intensive study can be made of each school. The plan facilitates the work of determining the rank of each pupil.

The entire class of each school is divided into three groups or tertiles, as nearly equal as possible on the basis of position in the scale of marks. For instance, if we establish three divisions or tertiles to determine high, middle, and low rank in arithmetic in School 14 (see Table I) there will be fourteen pupils in each tertile, with an extra one in the middle group. Heavy vertical lines are used to designate the limits of the tertiles. After the middle range—the inclusive percentages of the middle tertile—is known, the rank of each pupil may be set down opposite his name.

The example given in Table I also shows the impossibility of dependence on absolute marks. Pupils receiving a mark of 80 to 81 per cent in School 14[1] would be in the highest tertile (first mark); the pupils getting these marks in School 16 would be in the middle tertile, and the same marks would place pupils of School 7 in the lowest tertile. "Yes," someone may say, "That may not show that standards of marking were different but that there was actually a corresponding difference in the ability of the pupils in the different schools." The latter part of the study shows conclusively that

[1] The numeral used here to designate a school does not correspond with the numeral employed in the Milwaukee system but is part of a simplified system used throughout the study.

such was not the case. When the rank of the pupils in arithmetic was compared with their rank in algebra it was found that a greater percentage of School 14 (the school which gave the lowest marks) excelled in maintaining their original rank or increasing it. In fact there was a complete reversal of things from what the absolute marks alone might indicate. School 14 with a middle range 71–78 had 61 per cent of the pupils in algebra remaining in the relative position they had in the elementary school, while School 16 with a middle range 79–84 had 56 per cent remaining in their original rank, and School 7 with the highest middle range had the lowest retention—only 44 per cent.

HIGH-SCHOOL GRADES AND RANKS

The high-school rank which was used in these comparisons was determined in the following way. The distribution of marks for the whole class in the high school and divisions into tertiles was made just as with the elementary data. A pupil's rank in this case is his relative position among all of the Freshmen in his high school.

It is a good plan to transfer the high-school records of all pupils considered to individual cards which have spaces also for elementary marks and rank. And it is well for comparative purposes to have the data from one school placed on the right side of the card and that of the other school on the left. In this way subjects of natural sequence or close relationship can be placed in close juxtaposition. Thus arithmetic and algebra can be compared. Then the cards can be shuffled to arrange the material with reference to any problem that may come up. Most of the time the cards of pupils from each elementary school will be kept together in one group; sometimes the point of interest may require a grouping by high schools; or a separation of those failing may be needed in order to make a special study of them; or again, those irregular in other ways may be selected for special study.

The material in some form like this may soon be the starting-point of studies in correlation. The work involved in the preliminary steps of a study using existing material is necessitated by our failure in the past to recognize the value of continuous records.

One could take the cards from any school, if made according to the suggestion above, and by a careful examination get a good general impression of its correlation with the higher institution, or of any marked peculiarities of its pupils as a group. But there is need for a more concise definite and graphic tabulation of results, especially if a superintendent is to make close comparisons of schools.

All of the material for any correlation can easily and simply be represented "on the square," as shown in Tables II, III, and IV.

TABLE II

School 18—Algebra

	1st	2d	3d	Total
Arithmetic— 1st	/////	/	/	(7)
2d	//	//		(4)
3d		/////	//	(7)
Total	(7)	(8)	(3)	

TABLE III

School 17—Algebra

	1st	2d	3d	Total
Arithmetic— 1st	///// /////	////	//	(16)
2d	//	///	// /////	(12)
3d	/	///	/ /////	(10)
Total	(13)	(10)	(15)	

These show retention and fluctuations of rank in mathematics for pupils of three different schools of Milwaukee. Each individual is again, as in Table I, represented by a tally. The small square in which this tally is placed depends upon the pupil's rank in arithmetic and in algebra. His rank in the elementary subject will determine in which horizontal column the tally will be placed, but at the same time the tally must have position in a vertical column. The vertical column shows the pupil's rank in the subsequent high-school subject. To illustrate, a rank of first in both is represented in the upper horizontal and first vertical column; a rank of second in the elementary and third in the high-school subject is denoted by a tally in the second horizontal and third vertical column.

With just a little practice one can see all of the significant features at a glance. It is evident that a diagonal line from the upper left to the lower right corner would pass through the three spaces which indicate that students hold in the high school the same

TABLE IV

School 4—Algebra

	1st	2d	3d	Total
Arithmetic— 1st	//// /////	/		(10)
2d		/////	//	(7)
3d		/	//	(3)
Total	(9)	(7)	(4)	

rank that they had in the elementary school. The three small squares below the imaginary diagonal show the gains in rank—from second to first; third to second; and from third to first. The corresponding squares above show losses in the reverse order.

School 4 is an example of a school that has good retention—only four have shifted from the rank obtained in the elementary school and no one has fluctuated more than one point. School 18, on the other hand, shows many gains in rank; while School 17 has a preponderance of losses.

The question of the kind of representation from each school is clearly set forth on this diagram. The group from School 18 is very representative of the original class. On the basis of their early work we could expect about seven pupils in the lowest tertile in high school. School 4 has more pupils in this low tertile and yet had comparatively very few of their poor pupils enter high school (three out of forty-two). The people who are satisfied with knowing only what kind of marks each delegation made in high school can see at a glance whether the right or the left side of the square has the most tallies.

The foregoing correlations in single subjects may be compiled into a composite card upon which all the correlations in all subjects are recorded for a given school. The same card may be used to record the withdrawals from the school. The general plan devised for this larger "school card" is shown in Table V. It shows the correlation in the sequences, reading and English; language and English, arithmetic and algebra, reading and Latin, language and Latin, and in elementary arithmetic and commercial arithmetic. The first three are the more important in considering

SUMMARY SHOWING RETENTION AND GAINS AND LOSSES IN RANK

Subject	Same	G. 1.	L. 1.	G. 2	L. 2
Reading and English	11	5	8	0	0
Language and English	12	4	7	1	0
Mathematics	18	3	3	0	0
Language and Latin	5	0	3	0	1

only a single class because the number of individuals taking the electives such as Latin and commercial arithmetic is often small. (The last correlation mentioned above is omitted in the accompanying summary.)

Such a card in addition to accumulating all the data for a given school offers an excellent opportunity to compare retention in different subjects.

There are several well-marked cases of the same group of pupils showing better preparation in one study than in another although they have been taught by the same teacher. The reason for such a condition may be perfectly obvious in any given case. For instance, a school in a foreign section of the city would often have difficulty with English. But there are in any system teachers who slight some subject that they do not like or in which their preparation is weak. When it is shown definitely that her pupils

TABLE V

SCHOOL 20

	English			Algebra			Latin			Failures	
	1	2	3	1	2	3	1	2	3	1" Sem.	2" Sem.
Reading— 1	//////	///////					//	/	///	L.	
2	//	//	/				/		/		E.
3		///	///						/	L.E.	E.
Arithmetic— 1				///////	///						A.
2				/	//////						
3					//	/////				A.A.	A.A.
Language— 1	//////	/////					///	/	/	L.	
2	/	////	//						//		E.
3	/	///	//						//	L.E.	E.E.

differ materially in preparation in different subjects it will be much easier to remedy the situation.

The double column at the extreme right of Table V needs some explanation and deserves some comment. Initial letters are used to show each failure in a given subject. Their position indicates in which semester the failure was made and the original rank of the pupil making the failure. This last point is usually overlooked but is vitally important in a comparative study of the efficiency of schools. Let us take an illustration which shows the bearing of this information on the question of failures—or rather "judgment by failures." One school in this study had six pupils fail in high-school mathematics. There is nothing alarming about that, some other schools had as many. But the tabulation shows that three of the pupils who failed came to high school with marks which indicated that they were the best of their elementary class; the other three came from the second or middle tertile. There were no failures from the lowest tertile because none of their poorest pupils had elected to go to high school. It is more to the discredit of a school to have six failures under those conditions than it would be to have six of its poorest pupils fail—pupils recognized as poor and labeled that way before they entered the higher institution. The illustration given is an extreme case, but there was an unwarranted number of failures from the higher tertiles of some schools. Such failures were rare in schools that were shown to be better in the point of retention.

The results found in any system by such a method of correlation as the one here outlined will show that there are differences between the different elementary schools. Whether the particular condition in any school is due to some cause inherent in the constituency of that school or to the plan of organization of the school and the quality of instruction given is a matter for further investigation. But as long as a deficiency in any respect is unknown or merely a matter of conjecture and not an established fact there is little hope for the betterment of that condition. Facts of the type above reported certainly have this importance, that they make clear to any principal in a wholly impersonal way the problems which he ought to face as a member of a school system.

A CITY SCHOOL AS A COMMUNITY ART AND MUSICAL CENTER

JOHN FRANKLIN BOBBITT
The University of Chicago

It appears that a considerable amount of leisure is normal for the human race, whether savage or civilized. Under the primitive conditions in which man's nature was originally shaped, his struggle for existence was by no means continuous, especially in easy climates. Yet the struggle made it necessary that he possess a supply of energy sufficient to overcome all hostile forces during the period of greatest stress. The result was that during the periods of relaxed struggle, he possessed a very considerable surplus of energy that had to be expended in leisure occupations. In our recently developed civilization the struggle has been still more relaxed and regulated, with the result that most social classes have acquired a relatively large amount of leisure. This is especially the case during the last few decades, when the burden of heavy labor has been transferred from human shoulders and placed upon labor-saving machines. The great mass of the people are emancipated from heavy labor for a considerable portion of the day. Where workmen are engaged eight hours a day or forty-eight hours per week, after allowing twelve hours a day for sleep and meals, there yet remains a surplus of thirty-six hours a week to be devoted to leisure occupations. This is three-quarters of the time given to regular economic industry. It is the portion of the man's time that is most subject to his own disposition, and it is also probably the portion of his time for which he needs the greatest amount of education unless he happens to be of the managerial class. As a workman, he has directors, foremen, superintendents. As a citizen he has political leaders to direct him, and teach him what is to be done, as he goes along. As a parent he has the school to advise him as to the training of his children and the physician to advise him as to the health of the family. But in the matter of recreation he is free to do as he will, and this is therefore the region in which men most easily go wrong. Moral education probably consists for the most part in education for the right use of leisure.

Recognition of these matters is responsible for the extremely rapid development of civic, social, and recreative centers in our larger cities and for the wider use of the school plant by the community. The activity of these centers consists for the most part of healthy, leisure occupations—quiet games, athletic games, the gymnasium, the swimming-pool, the library and reading-room, public lectures and entertainments, and the like.

Among leisure occupations of a healthy sort there is certainly none of a wider appeal than music. Its power is recognized by both the forces of good and the forces of evil. It is one of the chief attractions both of the church and of the saloon. In fact, wherever men are gathered together, the pleasures of social intercourse are greatly heightened by the influence of stimulating and appropriate music.

Notwithstanding this almost universal appeal of music, it has been given relatively little attention in the development of our social centers. In Perry's book on *The Wider Use of the School Plant*, for example, in a very complete index of twenty-seven pages, "music" is not to be found. It is employed certainly in the social centers since chorus classes are not infrequent, pianos are common, and occasionally the center has an amateur orchestra that furnishes the music for dancing, for theatricals, and for other special occasions. But the music in these cases is subsidiary and is used not for its own sake or for the development of the musical appreciation of the community, but rather as an aid to other activities.

It is probable that the reason for this neglect in large measure lies in the presence of a number of obstacles of a serious sort. Professional music is expensive as compared with other forms of healthy activity that can be introduced; and the musical traditions of the community are usually so little developed that a permanent, reliable, amateur orchestra can scarcely be developed to the proper extent, or held together if once developed. Such traditions are matters of long and slow growth. But fortunately when once developed within a community, they are as difficult to eradicate as they were to cultivate.

An example of what is possible in the use of a school as a musical center for the community is afforded by the city of Richmond, Indiana. This is a small manufacturing city of less than twenty-five thousand inhabitants, not greatly different from scores of other cities of similar size scattered throughout the Middle West. The city is fortunate in having had a rather slower and more substantial growth than most cities of its size, and in the possession of a number of public-spirited men and women of literary, musical, and artistic tastes and ability.

Its school system is not greatly different from the usual type. It consists of a number of ward-school buildings containing the elementary grades from the first to the sixth. This is followed by the junior high school, as it is called, centrally located, containing all of the seventh- and eighth-grade pupils of the city. At the head of the system is the usual high school. This is housed in a new, modern, fireproof building, located within two blocks of the heart of the city. In the choice of a site for the new high school, consideration was given to the fact that it was to be the chief social center of the community. For this purpose it is provided with an auditorium capable of seating almost a thousand people, and provision has been made for enlarging this auditorium by the removal of partitions whenever the growing need demands it. The auditorium is placed on the first floor at the front of the building, making it easy of access from the street. It is freely open to the public for all sorts of purposes except those of a commercial or partisan nature.

This auditorium is the musical center of the city. It is the meeting-place of four musical bodies: (1) The People's Symphony Orchestra, which meets in this auditorium for four hours' rehearsal and public concert every Sunday afternoon from October until May; (2) The People's Chorus, consisting of some two hundred and fifty voices, which meets regularly one evening per week through the year; (3) The High-School Chorus; (4) The High-School Orchestra, which furnishes the music for the school assembly meetings and for other school gatherings.

The Symphony Orchestra is a local organization of sixty-five members containing all the instruments of the usual, well-developed symphony orchestra. Thirty-five of its members are also members of the High-School Orchestra, or are recent graduates of the high school. This orchestra of sixty-five is a considerably larger body of players than Theodore Thomas had when he made his name famous in the seventies and the eighties. Yet they are young men and women native to the place and educated in its schools. They furnish the city in a voluntary way with a quality of music that is not usually to be found outside of our largest cities where it is usually so commercialized as to be inaccessible to those most in need of development along lines of artistic appreciation.

The larger city orchestra grew out of the high-school orchestra which still continues to be its nucleus, and the leader of which has been the guiding spirit of all of the community, musical movement. The High-School Orchestra consists of fifty-four members with an instrumentation as follows:

10 1st violins	2 basses	2 bassoons	1 timpano
10 2d violins	5 flutes	8 cornets	1 drum
2 violas	2 oboes	2 horns	1 piano
2 cellos	5 clarinets	1 trombone	

Most of the instruments are owned by the students, but a number of the expensive instruments that are of little use except as parts of the orchestra have been purchased for the school by the community. The initiative was taken by the Commercial Club of the city which has been very generous in the support of the movement. Other instruments have been furnished by the Board of Education. This board has been more than usually generous, not only in supplying instruments but also in supplying a teacher qualified to direct and lead in the musical work not only of the schools but also of the larger community. The director of the music is, for example, the most highly paid teacher in the city system, his salary being in fact only a little less than that of the city superintendent of schools. Thus, music in the high school receives as much care as mathematics or science or literature and is credited toward graduation in the same way.

The High-School Orchestra was organized some twelve years

ago. For eight years the high school has been turning graduates out into the community who are trained in skilful execution and in musical appreciation. In this way the school has been developing musical traditions in all ranks of the community.

The feeder for the high-school body of players is the junior high-school orchestra consisting of seventh- and eighth-grade students. This is the place where they try them out for the first time and gather together all of the players of promise, both boys and girls. By the time they reach the high school, they have "found themselves" on some instrument and have already had two years' training in co-operative instrumental exercise. The instrumentation of the junior high-school orchestra of last year shows the nature of its work:

4 1st violins	1 flute	2 cornets	2 drums
4 2d violins	2 clarinets	1 horn	1 piano
1 bass	1 trombone		

With this preliminary two years of training in the junior organization, the fifty-four orchestral members of the high school when they graduate go out into the community having had some six years of systematic, instrumental training. They have reached such a stage of proficiency and appreciation that they naturally feel a desire for continuing their activities after they have left the high school, and have entered upon their vocation. And thus the voluntary adult Symphony Orchestra is the logical result of the work of the schools.

Besides the instrumental work the high school offers four years of vocal music for which due credit is given toward graduation. There is a two-year course in harmony, two years in critical study of music, and chorus practice of an indefinite amount through the four years of the high school. Mr. Earhart, the musical director, in speaking of these courses, says: "The 'critical study' classes have for ten years past been turning into the citizenship of the town a body of young people who are more than usually informed on such facts of musical history, biography, form, and aesthetics as contribute to a sympathetic and discriminating understanding of music. These young people have also learned to sing and to read not only the notes but the quality, mood, or meaning back of the notes. I begin to notice in consequence greater intelligence, quicker grasp, and greater love for the work on the part of the chorus-singers. The addition of chorus singing to the curriculum and the greater number of hours given to the critical study work in the high school will hasten our progress in this direction. And I should not omit mention of the harmony classes. Many of our best chorus-singers and orchestral players owe a large part of their superior efficiency to the thorough musical understanding that two years work in harmony has given them."

The development in Richmond shows what is possible in any city. It also shows the need of slow, substantial growth, and that these things will not grow of themselves. One sees that in the wider use of the school plant where the music is subsidiary only or omitted, this is because it is a form of activity not to be developed in a day or a year. The schools must turn out a community of individuals who are filled with the necessary traditions and appreciation, and who are trained in the confident, skilful execution that can come only with years of steady, systematic training. This is not to be done without a teacher who is willing to work for years till his end is reached, irrespective of the hours consumed by his daily labors; one who is well paid but who does not measure his work by his pay. The teaching must be with the spirit not of the pedagogue but of the artist. And in the undeveloped stage of musical traditions in our country, such teachers are rare.

Such a delevopment is needed for the civic, social centers everywhere. Nothing less will ever be able to offset the attractions of the saloon, the beer-garden, the dance-hall, the low-class music-halls so-called, and other debasing social agencies, all of which use music of some sort as one of the chief sources of attraction. City libraries attract relatively few; public lecture courses reach only certain limited classes. One visits the civic facilities furnished by the small parks system of Chicago, which, by the way, is probably the best of its kind in the world, with distinct feelings of disappointment. The facilities for healthy recreation of many sorts are furnished by these parks and yet the adults of the type that most need them are not there. It is to be noticed, however, that when music is employed as the attractive influence, the park facilities are found inadequate for the demands.

"What our people need," a musician recently said to me, "is to hear music, and to hear music. They must hear it regularly for months and years in order to develop a proper appreciation of proper music. It does not greatly matter what kind they hear in the beginning or what kind they demand. Experience has shown that where people hear music regularly their tastes develop, and they acquire an appreciation for a continually better and better quality. The main thing is that they should hear it." Mr. Earhart told me that he has permitted the members of the high-school orchestra a considerable voice in the choice of compositions to be played, and that while in the beginning there were frequent requests for compositions of the crude, popular order, at the present time the students very rarely care to experiment with anything except music of the better type. And he was of the opinion that when the community has opportunities to hear all kinds of music that it will gradually come to prefer music of the better quality to that of the poorer quality; and standards of appreciation once developed do not deteriorate in the particular individuals in whom developed.

Music is used as a leisure occupation by two classes of persons, the players or singers, and the auditors. The leaving of musical education in our country almost wholly to private initiative has resulted in the musical education of such a relatively small proportion of the population that all or most of the well-trained individuals have been drawn off into professional music; and this has left the community without musical leadership. But the experience of Richmond, in giving in her schools a completer form of musical education than most of our cities, has shown the possibility of developing large and stable, amateur, musical organizations of a superior type. And where such individuals exist in so great numbers one can conceive of no leisure occupation that could be more attractive to them than the exercises and personal associations within such voluntary organizations, furnishing the community at the same time with a superior kind of music as a by-product. In the present agitation for physical education, it ought also to be remembered that there are few forms of in-door, physical exercise so beneficial as the vocal exercises of an enthusiastic People's Chorus.

This high school is not only the community center for music, but also for pictorial art. In the construction of the new high-school building three large rooms on the top floor were set aside as the city's art museum. Art exhibitions are frequent in the city and they are held in these art rooms. A number of valuable pictures have been contributed to the school by various members of the community. The school itself has purchased a number. Public-spirited citizens, the owners of valuable pictures, have hung many of them in the art room of the high school for the sake of aiding in the development of a general appreciation of this form of art. For four years during their most susceptible period, the youth of the community live under the influence of the best art that the city is able to procure. An occasional visit to a city art museum is probably of little value in the development of appreciation where the influences are so tenuous and the individual left so passive. One must live with pictures if his spirit is to be transfused with the spirit of their art. For this reason the method of using the city school as the art museum of the city is incomparably more effective than the method of placing all the pictures in a separate city art museum to be only occasionally visited by the few, and by most of these to a degree wholly insufficient for the development of any considerable degree of appreciation. Richmond believes that her art should be a thing functional in the lives of her people and not merely a thing to be set apart and occasionally admired. So far as an art museum is for the education of artists primarily it is well for the city to possess one. But so far as the city art museum is intended for the education of the community in the appreciation of pictorial art, it would be far better if the pictures and statues of the city art museum were scattered through the various schools of the city. Especially would it be effective if they were scattered among the high schools, since it is during the adolescent period that art has its greatest initial appeal, when the growing individual is most susceptible to its influence, and when his appreciations and attitudes are most modifiable by its presence.

STANDARD SCORES IN ARITHMETIC

S. A. COURTIS
Detroit Home and Day School

For the attainment of efficiency in any manufacturing process three things are necessary: a well-defined, a "standard," product; a knowledge of the properties and possibilities of the material to be acted upon; and a means of measuring the effects produced by the process itself. Given these three, all else is but a matter of trial and selection.

Education, from one point of view at least, is a manufacturing process. The raw material that is sent to a school is molded and shaped by the forces and experiences to which it is subjected. Marked changes are effected and the product has, in a general way, a commercial value that bears some relation to the complexity of the process and the degree of change produced. In a graded system promotion from grade to grade emphasizes the idea of "degree of change," of grade standards. Promotion from the fourth to the fifth grade, for instance, is dependent upon the acquisition of a certain amount of knowledge, the attainment of a certain degree of skill. In an efficient school one does not expect to find children of fourth-grade ability doing eighth-grade work. Each higher grade reached is supposed to mean a correspondingly higher level of ability.

The attempts of the writer to measure the efficiency of the teaching and the growth of the arithmetic classes under his control in the Liggett School have been described in some detail in previous numbers of this Journal. That work gave some knowledge of the nature of the material to be acted upon in school work, and proved that it was possible to measure accurately the changes produced by teaching effort. Clearly defined standards alone were lacking. The present article will deal with an attempt to determine such standards from the measurement of a large number of children.

Because of the complexity of the problem, the scope of the

investigation was limited to the simplest work with whole numbers in the four fundamental operations. The tests used were in all essential particulars like those previously described, and will not be discussed in detail. It is sufficient to say that in their construction the utmost care was taken to eliminate the imperfections of previous tests caused by the inequalities of the units. The subject-matter of the tests, eight in number, was as follows:

Test No. 1. Addition (Combinations, 0–9)
Test No. 2. Subtraction (Combinations, 0–9)
Test No. 3. Multiplication (Combinations, 0–9)
Test No. 4. Division (Combinations, 0–9)
Test No. 5. Copying figures (rate of motor activity)
Test No. 6. Speed reasoning (simple one-step problems)
Test No. 7. Fundamentals (abstract examples in the four operations)
Test No. 8. Reasoning (two-step problems).

The nature of the investigation made it essential that the tests should be given to all grades from the lowest to the highest under identical conditions. To this end detailed instructions for every phase of the work, together with special record sheets, answer cards, etc., were printed in the form of folders to be put into the hands of each examiner or scorer. As experience had shown the most probable source of error to be faulty timing, the time allowances were printed in red. In addition a personal letter of warning was sent with each package of tests. It is realized that no degree of care can prevent either accidental errors, or deliberate fraud, but the testing of many schools tends to eliminate the effects of the first, and the character of the persons who took part in the work makes the second improbable. A few cases of accidental errors were reported, and for these tests either due allowance has been made or the results rejected entirely. The writer believes the precautions taken to have been effective; and that the conditions under which the tests were given were sufficiently uniform for the results to reflect accurately the actual conditions. Check tests of several grades under absolutely uniform conditions and with mechanical timing have yielded similar results.

The co-operation of many persons was secured by letters to personal friends, by circulars, and by editorial notice in this and two other magazines. For the kindness of these notices the writer is very grateful. It not only brought the matter to a wider circle of interested persons than could have been reached without it, but it also gave the investigation a standing it would have been hard to secure in any other way. As a result inquiries were received from many parts of the United States and from several foreign countries. The total of requests and orders for tests exceeded 30,000 copies. Ten thousand sets of tests were distributed free and eight thousand more were sold at the bare cost of printing. Teachers in England and Germany were interested in the work and the tests have been, or are to be, given in those countries also.

From the above it must be evident that the undertaking owes its success to its co-operative features. While the writer alone is responsible for whatever defects there may be in the tests themselves or in the planning of the work, credit is due the many who executed the plans and bore the burden of giving and scoring the papers. The writer is very glad of this opportunity to express his grateful appreciation of the assistance rendered by all those whose generous support and careful work has made this article possible.

Fire, accidents, sickness, and unavoidable delays of many kinds have prevented the completion of the work by many to whom the tests were sent. The tabulations of this article are based upon the returns received from some sixty or seventy schools in ten different states as shown below.

CONTRIBUTORS TO STANDARD SCORES

State	City	Name
New Hampshire	Littleton	D. F. Carpenter, superintendent
Massachusetts	Dorchester	A. R. Winter, sub-master, Mather School
	Fitchburg Leominster	E. A. Kirkpatrick, head of Department of Psychology, State Normal School
New York	New York City	H. C. Pearson, principal of Horace Mann School
		Miss Margaret Eves, acting supervisor of Elementary Mathematics, Ethical Culture School
	Brooklyn	J. C. Bell, Psychology, Training School for Teachers
	Hastings-on-Hudson	W. R. Williams, principal

CONTRIBUTORS TO STANDARD SCORES—*Continued*

State	City	Name
Delaware	Dover	A. Crawford, principal
Maryland	Salisbury	W. J. Holloway, county superintendent
Virginia	Farmville	C. W. Stone, Department of Education, State Normal School
		Miss Mary D. Pierce, supervisor in Practice School
	Williamsburg Toano	H. E. Bennett, professor of education, College of William and Mary
Michigan	Detroit	A. Cotter, principal, Harris School
		W. C. Martindale, superintendent
		Misses Liggett, principals, Liggett School
	Kalamazoo	S. O. Hartwell, superintendent
Indiana	Marion	J. T. Giles, superintendent
	Fort Wayne	Miss Flora Wilber, principal City Normal School
	Bloomington	H. L. Smith, superintendent
Missouri	St. Joseph	Miss Fannie Brennen, principal Garfield School
Kansas	McPherson	G. G. Pinney, superintendent

In the list that follows the number of tests sent to each of the above is given that some idea may be had of the sizes of the different groups of children measured. There is no correspondence, however, between the order of schools in the two lists. The number of actual individual scores returned for tabulation was a little over 9,000 for most of the tests.

Number of tests sent to the individuals in the list above:
2500, 1600, 1400, 1000, 750, 650, 500, 380, 350, 350, 350, 300, 200, 200, 196, 150, 140, 120
Total 12,171

A record sheet for the scores of each individual measured was sent out with each set of tests. These, when completed, were returned and will be used, later in the year, as the basis of tabulations to determine standard scores by age, and the correlation between the abilities measured. For each grade, a copy of the grade record sheet was also returned. Upon this was shown the distribution of the scores of the individuals composing the grade. Tabulations of these distributions are the bases of the tables below.

For instance, returns were received from fifty eighth-grade classes (both A and B). The distributions of the classes having the highest, median, and lowest grade averages are given in Table I; also the total of the distributions of the entire fifty classes. The same facts are shown graphically in Fig. 1.

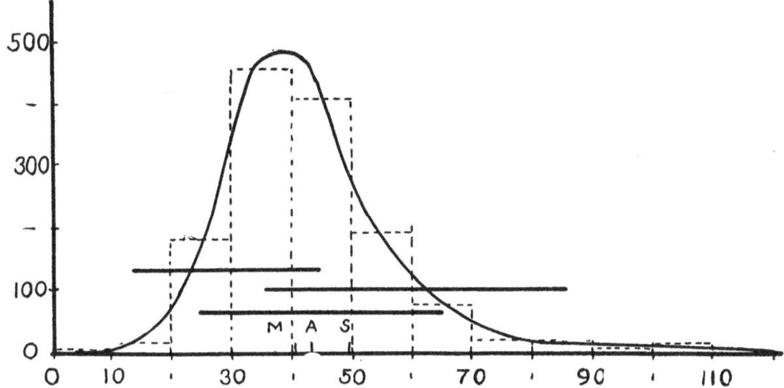

Fig. 1.—Distribution of 1,400 individual eighth-grade scores. Scale at bottom of figure gives number of answers written per minute in test of multiplication tables; scale at left gives frequencies. Solid horizontal lines show range of individual scores in the classes having the lowest, highest, and median grade averages of the fifty classes contributing the individual scores. *M* = median score of the entire group = 41; *A* = average = 43; *S* = score selected as standard for the grade = 49.

In words the meaning of the table is that of 1,401 eighth-grade children measured as to their knowledge of the multiplication tables, 2 could write answers at a rate of but 5 answers a minute,

TABLE I

Distribution of Individual Scores in Speed Test, Multiplication

Three Representative Classes; also Total of Fifty Classes; Eighth Grade

	No. in Class	Scores											
		0–9	10–19	25	35	45	55	65	75	85	95	105	115
Highest	36	...	.....	..	4	5	6	13	4	4	..	...	...
Median	43	...	.....	4	18	16	3	2	..	..	..	...	...
Lowest......	13	...	1	6	5	1	..	..	..	..	..	...	...
Total	1,401	2	17	180	460	410	191	77	26	22	5	10	1

17 at the rate of 15 answers a minute, 180 at 25 per minute, and so on, the average for the entire group being 43.

It is particularly to be noted that the wide range of the distribution is caused not so much by great differences between schools as by great variation in the abilities of individual children. The amount of variation in the grade averages of different schools

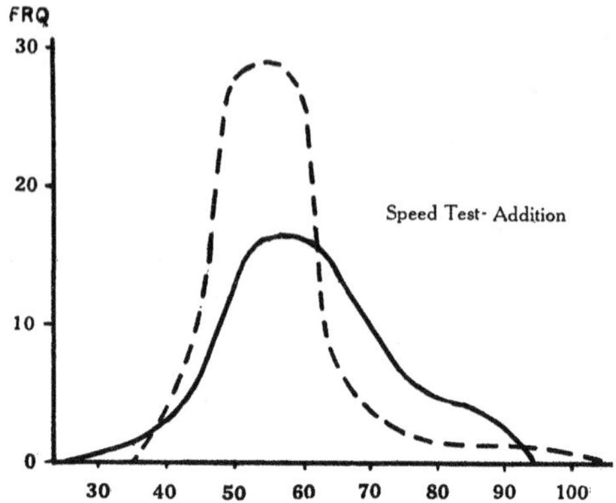

FIG. 2.—Comparison of the distribution of fifty eighth-grade averages with that of forty-seven individual scores in a single eighth-grade class. Solid line, individuals; broken line, classes. The curves show that the individuals in a single class differ more than the grade averages of the fifty schools.

does not equal the variation in the scores of the members of any one class. Table II and Fig. 2 show this plainly. The distribution of an average class of 47 members (selected from the 9 classes of the 51 having a membership of from 42 to 51) is given for comparison with the distribution of the 51 grade averages. The results are from the scores in the addition speed test, for many schools the ability in which the *least* variation was shown.

TABLE II

SPEED TEST, ADDITION: EIGHTH GRADE

Comparison of Distribution of 47 Individual Scores in a Single Class of Average Variability with the Distribution of the Grade Averages of 51 Classes

	No.	Scores						
		30–39	45	55	65	75	85	95
Individuals	47	1	6	16	13	7	4	..
Classes	51	..	11	29	7	2	1	1

The fact shown is a constant feature of the returns for all the tests and grades, and can only mean that the differences in the abilities of individual children are greater factors in determining relative rank in school work than all the differences in abilities of teachers, courses of study, or methods of work combined. The result is that the grades in all the schools overlap to an extent well-nigh incredible, and thus the data from this more extended investigation fully confirms the conclusions reached in a discussion of this point in a previous article, although in that case the data was derived from a single school.

TABLE III

GRADE AVERAGES FROM TOTAL DISTRIBUTIONS

Grade No.	Average of Scores for Each Test	No. 1	No. 2	No. 3	No. 4	No. 5	No. 6		No. 7		No. 8	
							Ats.	Rts.	Ats.	Rts.	Ats.	Rts.
1	55	6	6	..	..	29	...	...	....	....	...	...
2	75	21	12	10	12	51	...	...	....	....	...	...
3	525	26	19	16	11	63	2.8	2.1	5.4	1.7	2.7	0.6
4	1,222	33	25	23	21	70	3.7	2.5	6.6	3.6	2.6	0.8
5	1,177	40	32	30	28	80	4.4	3.4	9.0	5.3	2.8	1.2
6	1,282	46	37	34	35	88	5.1	4.4	10.3	6.9	3.4	1.7
7	1,432	51	40	38	38	98	5.9	5.2	11.5	7.6	3.7	2.2
8	1,370	57	45	43	44	102	6.8	6.1	13.1	8.9	4.1	2.7
9	412	59	47	45	47	108	6.9	6.4	13.7	9.5	4.1	3.1
10	216	57	45	43	46	112	7.2	6.7	14.0	9.5	4.1	3.1
11	151	59	47	44	48	114	7.9	7.4	14.4	9.4	4.5	3.3
12	169	61	48	44	49	112	7.7	7.2	14.9	10.8	4.6	3.6
13	462	71	56	50	56	116	8.6	8.2	16.8	12.6	5.3	4.0
14	131	74	51	58	59	124	9.7	9.1	17.2	11.8	5.4	4.1
	8,679*											

* Certain of the tests were omitted by several schools, thus materially reducing the average. For most of the tests, however, the total number of scores is over 9,000.

From the discussion above it is evident that the average for any grade represents simply a central tendency from which individuals vary widely. Yet in many ways the average scores of each group, given in Table III, and shown graphically in Fig. 3, reveal the character of the development of each of the abilities through the school and show what should be true of the development of the individual. These data, then, in connection with the distributions from which the averages are derived furnish the desired basis for the selection of standard scores.

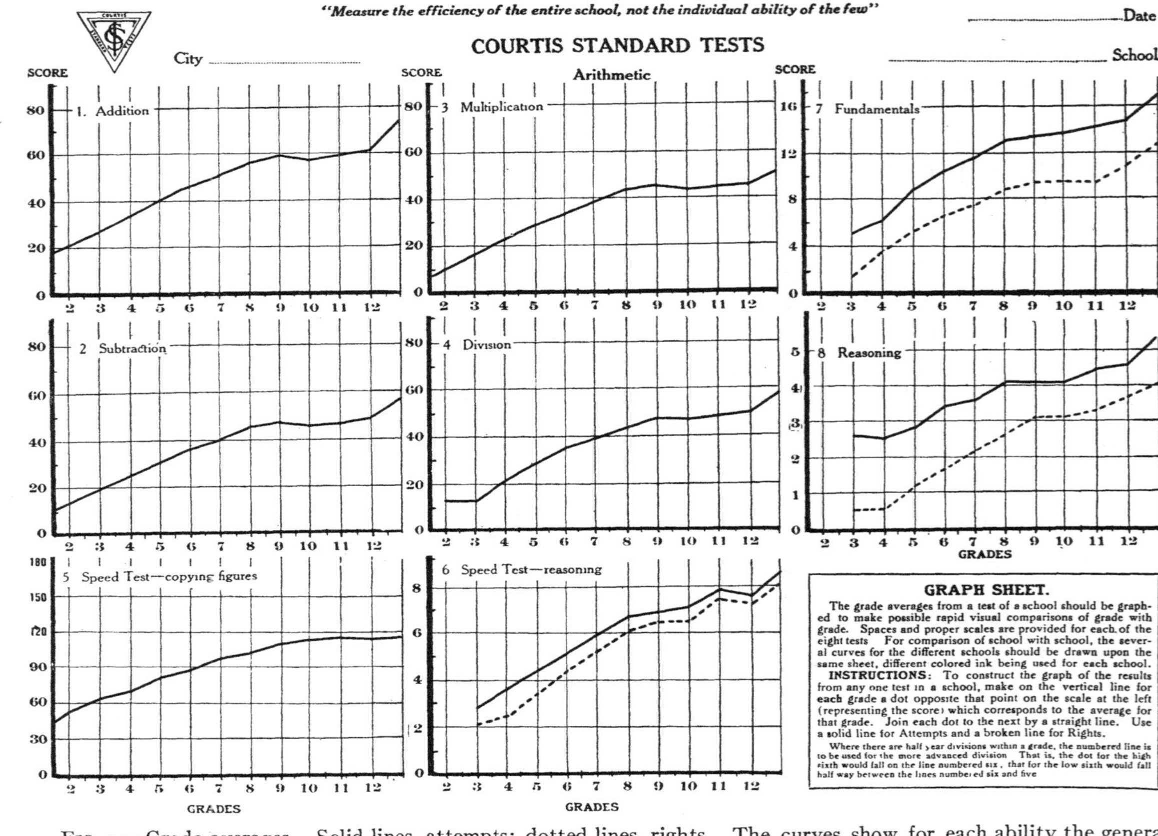

FIG. 3.—Grade averages. Solid lines, attempts; dotted lines, rights. The curves show for each ability the general character of its development through the school. Each curve is based upon approximately 9,000 individual scores.

This table means when put in words that in the third grade, for example, there were 525 individual scores in each test—or about 525. If in some test there were more, as for example, addition, there were enough less in division to make the average number of tests 525. In the addition tests it was found that the standard or average ability was that exhibited by a child who could record 26 in a minute. The standard in subtraction was 19 per minute, and so on.

The writer regrets exceedingly that there is not space to print the distributions in full; for the selection of standard scores must for the present be a matter of individual judgment. Many will be content to use the average scores as standards, and if, indeed, no children in any grade had a lower score than the present average for that grade, the increase in the efficiency of our schools in these abilities would be very great. But the writer feels that a higher score than the average is desirable for a standard and the scores

TABLE IV

STANDARD SCORES

TEST NO.	No. 1	No. 2	NOS. 3 AND 4	No. 5	No. 6		No. 7		No. 8	
					Ats.	Rts.	Ats.	Rts.	Ats.	Rts.
Grade 3	26	19	16	58	2.7	2.1	5.0	2.7	2.0	1.1
Grade 4	34	25	23	72	3.7	3.0	7.0	3.3	2.6	1.7
Grade 5	42	31	30	86	4.8	4.0	9.0	4.9	3.1	2.2
Grade 6	50	38	37	99	5.8	5.0	11.0	6.6	3.7	2.8
Grade 7	58	44	44	110	6.8	6.0	13.0	8.3	4.2	3.4
Grade 8	63	49	49	117	7.8	7.0	14.4	10.0	4.8	4.0
Grade 9	65	50	50	120	8.6	7.8	15.0	11.0	5.0	4.3

given in Table IV were derived as follows: For each test an eighth grade score was selected such that it was equalled or exceeded by thirty per cent of the eighth-grade children measured. This score was plotted and a smooth curve drawn, having the same general form as the average curve and coinciding with it in the lower grades. The scores for each of the other grades were then determined from the graph.

While the results given above were obtained by the use of special tests, and while for exact comparison the reproduction of the identical tests and the identical conditions are necessary, the writer hopes that teachers generally will appreciate the fact that the scores above furnish definite objective standards toward which to work. Accurate measurements are needed twice a year; once at the beginning for purpose of diagnosis, and again at the close of the year to measure the effect produced by the teaching effort. But for general class work, approximate values are all that are required. The scores in Table IV should be translated into words: thus, at the end of a year's work, an eighth-grade child should be able to copy figures in pencil on paper at the rate of 117 figures a minute; to write answers to the multiplication combinations at the rate of 49 answers per minute; to read simple one-step problems of approximately 30 words in length and decide upon the operation to be used in their solution at the rate of 8 examples a minute with an accuracy of 90 per cent; to work abstract examples of approximately 10 figures (twice as many for addition) at the rate of 14.4 examples in 12 minutes with an accuracy of 70 per cent; to solve two-step problems of approximately 10 figures at the rate of 5 in 6 minutes with an accuracy of 75 per cent. At the present time 70 per cent of the eighth-grade children cannot meet these standards. But it must be borne in mind that 3 per cent of the fifth-grade children can, and that experience has shown that individual care and a very little, well-managed drill produces marked changes in the abilities of most children.

A word of caution is necessary for those who use these standards. The writer is well aware of the disfavor into which drill has fallen, and he is heartily in sympathy with the ideas and principles which lead to its disuse. On the other hand, no fair-minded person can consider the wide range of variation in all the classes and not realize that something is wrong. It may well be that the pendulum has swung too far. Inordinate drill is surely harmful. Drill out of place is also harmful. But drill in its proper place—after, and not *before*, understanding control—and in proper amount—enough to insure the minimum ability necessary to effective work but not enough to involve waste of teaching effort—such drill is one of the vital factors in efficient teaching. The scores above, while necessarily tentative only, have been selected with due regard for such critical points in the development of these abilities as have been determined. It is probable that development much beyond the points indicated by the standard scores—and such development is possible—would involve waste of effort and, if not positively harmful, would be useless from the standpoint of efficient, general development. Accurate determination of the proper amount and form of drill required to produce the standard abilities, and similar determinations of standard, yearly growths, are the next problems that will be attacked. For the writer considers that the present investigation has proved that co-operative work on such educational problems is both feasible and of value.

The writer cannot bring this discussion to a close without a plea for both the teacher and the child. When a child's score exceeds the standard for his grade, he will ordinarily need little further attention. The ordinary procedure in grade work furnishes him adequate opportunities and incentives. But when the score is below the standard the case is entirely different. The fault may be in the child. A defective mentality may render the development of a given ability absolutely out of the question. But in such cases it would seem the height of folly and a rank injustice to give a teacher a fourth-grade intellect upon which to work and expect him to secure eighth-grade achievement. Or the child may be normal, but some peculiarity of its mental equipment causes a marked bias in one direction or another. The child that learns addition readily, but falls far below the standard in multiplication, needs special care and special work until the standard ability in multiplication is attained. A balanced, many sided development is the right of all. It is in such cases that standard scores are of the greatest service. On the other hand, the fault may be in the teaching, the course of study, or the methods of work. But here again the number of children who reach, or fail to reach, the standard is the measure of efficiency. From every point of view, therefore, standardization of all school subjects, and the use of standard scores offer a possible escape from present, unsatisfactory conditions.

EDITORIAL NOTES

Attacks on Departments of Education

In the *New York Nation* of September 7, Mr. Warner Fite writes at great length in criticism of teachers of education. He criticizes the professor of education on the ground that he has no special matter to present to students, and on the ground that he has by cunning methods gained recognition in various ways to the disadvantage, as Mr. Fite thinks, of other departments of instruction. Mr. Fite holds that what prospective teachers need is subject-matter and not methods. Students should know how to teach because they have been taught by many instructors each of whom is an example of method. In the *Dial* of October 1, Mr. Fite's remarks are quoted with approval and new adjectives of an opprobrious type are added to those used by Mr. Fite. Both articles are full of bitter personal charges and both are evidently written by writers who have a grievance. It is said for example that the representatives of education as a department are untrained and crude. The science of education is scoffed at without reserve.

The Discussion Shows That the Science of Education Is Known

The appearance of such discussions in journals which address primarily a lay constituency is a matter of great historical interest. Ten years ago there were not enough departments of education in the country to draw the fire of Mr. Fite and the anonymous editorial writer of the *Dial*. The hopes of recognition which were entertained by a few pioneer workers in the science of education seemed very unlikely to be realized. All this has changed. Wherever a university finds itself in real sympathy with the schools it finds more and more reason for training students to study the problems of education. The writer knows of several cases of universities that took on departments of education at first with a great deal of hesitation, but have realized—and that very rapidly—the large service which these departments can render. The fact is, then, that education as a department now has enough standing to bring to it violent attacks of enemies and on the other hand the strong support of friends. That the friends should be eager and hopeful is not, perhaps, a matter deserving special comment. That the enemies of the subject should be so vigorous is interesting and significant.

Attack Based on Lack of Acquaintance

As in most violent criticisms, so in the present articles there is evidence of much ignorance on the part of the enemy of the progress which has been made in the subject criticized. Probably none would attempt to deny that the science of education has shown many symptoms of its youth in the efforts which it has made to become a mature member of academic society. There are papers on educational science which have in them very little significant material. What of it? Is there any subject taught in our graduate classes which could not be ridiculed because of the trivial character of much that has been written in the name of advanced learning? Certainly it is not these negative phases of the effort toward knowledge which constitute the true basis of a sane estimate of any subject. The real question is what are the successes The successes of education as a science are unknown to Mr. Fite and the anonymous writer in the *Dial*. They show that they have never read such a treatise as Meumann's on experimental education. These people have failed to read with appreciation such studies as those which appear from many different sources in this Journal. They write with boldness while they show, as Professor Bowen used to say of the critics of philosophy, that they are like our first parents in the early dawn of the world, "naked but not ashamed."

Will the Critics Succeed?

What will be the practical effect of such criticism? One can hardly forego the pleasure of recalling a bit of history. Years ago an eminent professor of Harvard announced to the waiting world that there is no use of asking the teacher to read psychology. Many teachers said, "Now we are to be free from the necessity of reading more psychology." The indolent teacher took much satisfaction in the saying. The hopeful teacher felt some discouragement. The earnest student of educational psychology felt some regret that a supposed authority in the subject should turn it out of doors. But days passed by and grew into a decade and behold the professor from Harvard wrote a book on psychology especially designed for teachers. Who can tell, perhaps when Mr. Fite is a little older he may come into the fold. He writes a literary style which might serve to rescue the department of education from the accusation that all who contribute to this field are unlettered. His probable skill as a teacher and administrator would furnish suitable material for advice to young pedagogues. At all events the practical outcome of the first attack upon educational psychology was not discouraging and those of us who work in the field are willing to wait until all our enemies, even the bitterest, come over to our side.

Never Were Active Contributions More Numerous

Furthermore, we are not sitting idly by as we wait for Mr. Fite and others to join us. Studies of retardation and elimination are revealing in a new and striking way the problem of the school. The comparative study of grades is doing much to co-ordinate institutions. The methods of writing and reading and number are more economical and productive than they ever were—and what is more, we can prove it. The instruction in modern language is on a sounder basis than instruction in any of the antique and departed languages ever was. School finance is sounder than it ever was because we understand its principles. School promotions are more frequent and more just because the study of the problems involved has been taken up in Indianapolis and elsewhere. So one might go on. We ought to be very grateful to Mr. Fite and the writer in the *Dial* for an opportunity to write editorials and take some partial notice of the bright side of life. They are very generous to give us of their time and examples as a basis for popular consideration of the fact that we are alive.

C. H. J.

BOOK REVIEWS

Experiments in Educational Psychology. By DANIEL STARCH, Doctor of Philosophy, University of Wisconsin. New York: Macmillan, 1911.

The problem of providing experiments for classes in general psychology has been met by the appearance in recent years of several types of books. Some of these books deal with a few selected experiments. Others have attempted to present in an elaborate form all of the different methods of experimentation. Some of the books are intended for use in separate classes, while some of the material has been so organized that it can be used with the general text, the student performing the experiments at the same time that he studies the theoretical material presented in such text.

Mr. Starch's book is the first effort to select material which is peculiarly adapted to the needs of students who are specializing in educational psychology. Some of the experiments are the same as those that are presented in the laboratory books that are to accompany general courses. A number of the experiments, however, are different, but in all cases there is some effort to adapt even the general experiments to the needs of this special group of students. The experiments described by Mr. Starch require very little apparatus. Many exercises are incorporated in the book itself, so that the student can use the printed page as the equipment for the experiment. There are experiments on individual differences, on the different tests for the senses, and for the simpler psychological processes. There are experiments in learning, transfer of training, and fatigue. The selection of experiments is very good, and follows closely the course of study which has been employed at the University of Wisconsin. This course was originally planned by Professor Dearborn, and much of the material contained in the book is borrowed directly from the exercises which he prepared in the course at that institution.

The book will undoubtedly be useful to normal-school teachers of psychology. It is also a book which the individual teacher might with great advantage take up quite apart from any instructor. The difficulty with private experiments has always been that the interpretation of results is usually the most difficult, and at the same time the most productive, part of such an exercise. Unless there is a mature experimenter at hand to give suggestions with regard to the interpretation of results the outcome of individual experimentation is likely to be somewhat confusing. The book contains suggestions of interpretation and if it is used with parallel readings some of the difficulties of interpretation will be met.

Above all, the book illustrates very clearly the advantages of substituting for a mere theoretical text in psychology practical exercises of an experimental type. It will be welcome as a part of the general movement toward the development and establishment of a science of experimental education. C. H. J.

CURRENT EDUCATIONAL LITERATURE IN THE PERIODICALS[1]

IRENE WARREN
Librarian, School of Education, The University of Chicago

ALLEN, J. H. Socialism and the undergraduate. Liv. Age 52:585–92. (2 S. '11.)

ANGELL, JAMES ROWLAND. New requirements for entrance and graduation at the University of Chicago. School R. 19:489–97. (S. '11.)

BAILEY, L. H. The playground in rural communities. Playground 5:181–85. (S. '11.)

BEARD, FREDERICA. The correlation of Bible studies in the Sunday school. Educa. 32:11–15. (S. '11.)

BELLAMY, GEORGE A. Evening recreation. Playground 5:239–44. (O. '11.)

(The) Bible in the schools. Educa. R. 42:109–47. (S. '11.)

BOONE, RICHARD G. The Kindergarten. Its influence upon higher education. Kind. R. 22:69–76. (O. '11.)

BOWDEN, JOSEPHINE HORTON. Learning to read. El. School T. 12:21–33. (S. '11.)

BOWERS, THOMAS. What constitutes preparation for college; a layman's view. Educa. 32:16–19. (S. '11.)

BRADLEY, ERNEST. A rural experiment. Playground 5:190–98. (S. '11.)

BROWN, ELMER ELLSWORTH. The relation of the school to child welfare. Child Wel. Mag. 6:51–55. (O. '11.)

CUBBERLEY, ELLWOOD P. Does the present trend toward vocational training threaten liberal culture? School R. 19:454–65. (S. '11.)

DAUGHERTY, JAMES S. The Illinois State Reformatory School of Sheet Metal Work. Vocat. Educa. 1:22–32. (S. '11.)

DEGROOT, E. B. A practical talk on playground equipment. Playground 5:145–60. (Ag. '11.)

Doctorates conferred by American universities. Science 34:193–202. (18 Ag. '11.)

DYER, WALTER A. A new spirit in college life: "The Amherst idea." Craftsman 20:589–92. (S. '11.)

FAY, E. W. Language study and language psychology. Pop. Sci. Mo. 79:369–84. (O. '11.)

[1] *Abbreviations.*—Atlan., Atlantic Monthly; Cent., Century; Child Wel. Mag., Child Welfare Magazine; Educa., Education; Educa. R., Educational Review; El. School T., Elementary School Teacher; Harp. W., Harper's Weekly; Journ. of Educa. (Lond.), Journal of Education (London); Kind. R., Kindergarten Review; Liv. Age, Living Age; McClure's Mag., McClure's Magazine; Out., Outlook; Pop. Sci. Mo., Popular Science Monthly; Pri. Educa., Primary Education; School R., School Review; Training Mag. (N.J.), Training Magazine (New Jersey); Vocat. Educa., Vocational Education.

FLEXNER, ABRAHAM. Aristocratic and democratic education. Atlan. 108: 386–95. (S. '11.)

FREEMAN, FRANK N. Some issues in the teaching of handwriting. El. School T. 12:1–7. (S. '11.)

French "Flower schools": A new idea in public education. Craftsman 20:563–74. (S. '11.)

HANMER, LEE F. A playground meeting with real play on the program. Playground 5:177–79. (Ag. '11.)

Hard words about pedagogy. Dial 51:239–41. (1 O. '11.)

HARKNESS, MARY LEAL. One view of domestic science. Atlan. 108:474–79. (O. '11.)

HETHERINGTON, CLARK W. Playground directors—sources from which they may be secured. Playground 5:225–30. (O. '11.)

HOFFMAN, HELEN H. To save the babies. Harp. W. 55:12–13. (30 S. '11.)

HUTCHINSON, WOODS. The right of the child to be well born. World's Work 22:14856–58. (S. '11.)

Is our present vacation system a menace to the health and progress of our school children? A word for vacation schools. Craftsman 20:537–44. (S. '11.)

ISRAELS, MRS. CHARLES H. Social dancing. Playground 5:231–36. (O. '11.)

JAMES, EDMUND J. Vocational training and its future. Vocat. Educa. 1:1–9. (S. '11.)

(The) Jacques-Dalcroze rhythmic gymnastics. Journ. of Educa. (Lond.) n.s. 33:603–4. (1 S. '11.)

JASTROW, JOSEPH. The story of the college curriculum. Dial 55:250–51. (1 O. '11).

JOHNSTON, CHARLES. The school republic. Harp. W. 55:13. (23 S. '11.)

JUDD, CHARLES H. Studies of educational principles. El. School. T. 12:34–39. (S. '11.)

KIRBY, GUSTAVUS T. The recreation movement; its possibilities and limitations. Playground 5:217–24. (O. '11.)

LEAVITT, FRANK M. The Cleveland elementary industrial school. Vocat. Educa. 1:10–21. (S. '11.)

LYMAN, ROLLO L. College debating. Cent. 60:937–42. (O. '11.)

MCKEEVER, WILLIAM A. The boy-raising bulletins. World's Work 22: 14924–27. (O. '11.)

MAIN, JOSIAH. Agriculture in the high school. Pop. Sci. Mo. 79:385–95. (O. '11.)

MARKINO, YOSHIO. When I was a child—my mother and I. McClure's Mag. 37:551–58. (S. '11).

MARVIN, WALTER T. A comparison of some mental measurements with the standing of students in two college courses. Training Mag. (N.J.) 9:66–69. (S. '11.)

MASON, GREGORY. College men in practical politics. Out. 99:85–89. (9 S. '11.)

MILES, H. E. To train our craftsmen. Harp. W. 55:19. (23 S. '11.)

MILLINGTON, J. C. Bernard Shaw on education. Journ. of Educa. (Lond.) n.s. 33:601–3. (1 S. '11.)

MOWRY, DON E. Industrial education. Educa. 32:20–25. (S. '11.)

MYERS, G. W. A report on the teaching of secondary mathematics in France. School R. 19:433–53. (S. '11.)

O'SHEA, M. V. School favorites. Pri. Educa. 19:373–75. (S. '11.)

PARKER, S. CHESTER. Pestalozzian industrial education for juvenile reform. El. School T. 12:8–20. (S. '11.)

PERRY, CLARENCE ARTHUR. Social centers. Playground 5:170–75. (Ag. '11.)

PORTER, DAVID R. Football: an impossible intercollegiate sport. Educa. R. 42:162–69. (S. '11.)

PRICE, W. CECIL. The boy scout movement. Liv. Age 52:458–65. (19 Ag. '11.)

REYNOLDS, G. F. English literature in secondary schools. Educa. 32:1–10. (S. '11.)

RIIS, JACOB A. What ails our boys? Craftsman 21:3–10. (O. '11.)

SCUDDER, MYRON T. The rural school as a social center. Playground 5:200–4. (S. '11.)

SEXTON, BERNARD. A little school in the woods. World's Work 22:14808–14. (S. '11.)

SHERMAN, WALDO H. The boy scouts, 300,000 strong. World's Work 22: 14859–72. (S. '11.)

STITT, EDWARD W. Dancing in the social centers of New York City. Playground 5:236–39. (O. '11.)

STORROW, MRS. J. J. Folk dancing. Playground 5:161–68. (Ag. '11.)

THWING, CHARLES F. The American family. Liv. Age 52:451–58. (19 Ag. '11).

VANDEWALKER, NINA C. New fields for the kindergarten: the West. Kind. R. 22:77–85. (O. '11.)

WALTER, HERBERT E. High-school biology and sex hygiene. Educa. 32: 26–34. (S. '11.)

WARD, EDWARD J. Evening recreation center work by a university. Playground 5:206–10. (S. '11.)

WETTER, A. A. Great educators. I. Michael DeMontaigne. Educa. 32:39–42. (S. '11.)

WHITE, FRANK MARSHALL. How a boy was made a thief and the fight to reclaim him. World's Work 22:14843–50. (S. '11.)

WOODS, ROBERT A. Does the present trend toward vocational training threaten liberal culture? School R. 19:466–76. (S. '11.)

VOLUME XII NUMBER 4

THE ELEMENTARY SCHOOL TEACHER

DECEMBER, 1911

A BRIEF SUGGESTIVE LIST OF READING FOR CHILDREN IN THE ELEMENTARY SCHOOL

Compiled by JESSIE BLACK and IRENE WARREN
The School of Education, the University of Chicago

During the last few years a large number of public libraries have published selected lists of the best books for children and have distributed them gratuitously among their patrons. Some excellent lists have also found their way into books on literature for children and are now on sale in the bookstores. Repeated inquiries have come to the School of Education library for lists of books recommended by this institution, both from those who are familiar with the best of these published lists and also from those who seem to be ignorant that any such lists have ever been published.

In the spring of this year the Parents' Association of the Elementary School in the School of Education asked the librarian to have prepared a brief suggestive list of books for children which the parents could use with their children during the long vacation. As many requests have been received for this list from parents, teachers, and librarians, it was thought that it might prove valuable to the readers of the *Elementary School Teacher*. It is offered below with a few additions and some changes. Other selected lists of books for children will be presented in this magazine from time to time.

BRIEF SUGGESTIVE READING LIST—ELEMENTARY GRADES

FOR PARENTS

Bible stories, ed. by MOULTON. Macmillan, 50c.
COUCH, Oxford book of English verse. Clarendon, $1.90.
DANA, How to know the wild flowers. Scribner, $2.00.

DUGMORE, Bird homes. Doubleday, $2.00.
ELSON, Side lights on Amer. history. 2v. in 1. Macmillan, 75c.
HODGE, Nature study and life. Ginn, $1.50.
HOLLAND. Butterfly book. Doubleday, $3.00.
HOWARD, Insect book. Doubleday, $3.00.
JORDAN AND EVERMAN, Amer. food and game fishes. Doubleday, $4.00.
KEELER, Our native trees and how to identify them. Scribner, $2.00.
LYMAN, Story telling. McClurg. $1.00.
SYLVESTER, ed., Journeys through bookland. Bellows, Reeve Co., 10v. $22.50.

PICTURE BOOKS

Book of ships. Dutton, 75c.
BROOKE, Johnny Crowe's garden. Warne, $1.00.
BURGESS, Goops. Stokes, $1.50.
CALDECOTT, Picture book. Warne, $2.50.
CRANE, Beauty and the beast picture book. Lane, $1.25.
FRANCIS, Book of cheerful cats. Century, $1.00.
GREENAWAY, A apple pie. Warne, 75c.
WEATHERLY, Book of gnomes. Dutton, $1.50.

GRADE 1

AESOP, Fables retold by Godolphin. McKay, 50c.
ALEXANDER, Child classics, 1st reader. Bobbs-Merrill, 35c.
BANNERMAN, Story of little black Sambo. Stokes, 50c.
BLAKE AND ALEXANDER, Graded poetry—1 and 2. Merrill and Co., 20c.
Jack and the beanstalk. Longmans, 15c.
POTTER, Tale of Peter Rabbit. Warne, 50c.
Snow drop and other stories. Longmans, 15c.
TREADWELL, Reading literature. Row, Peterson, 40c.

GRADE 2

CALDECOTT, Hey diddle diddle picture book. Warne, $1.25.
COX, Brownies; their book. Century, $1.50.
CRANE, Goody two shoes picture book. Lane, $1.25.
CRUIKSHANK, ed. Fairy book. Putnam, $2.00.
O'SHEA, Old world wonder stories. Heath, 40c.
PERRAULT, Tales of Mother Goose; tr. by Welsh. Heath, 40c.
PYLE, Careless Jane. Dutton, 75c.
SCUDDER, Children's book. Houghton, $2.50.
SMITH, Eskimo stories. Rand McNally, $1.00.
STEVENSON, Child's garden of verses. Rand McNally, 50c.
SUMMERS, Second reader. Beattys, 50c.

GRADE 3

BALDWIN, Fifty famous stories retold. Amer. Book Co., 35c.
CARROLL, Alice's adventures in Wonderland. Macmillan, $1.00.

CARROLL, Through the looking-glass. Macmillan, $1.00.
CRAIK, Adventures of a Brownie. Harper, 60c.
GRIMM, Household stories: tr. by Crane. Cranford ed. Macmillan, $1.50.
JACKSON, Cat stories. Little, $2.00.
JACOBS, English fairy tales. Putnam, $1.25.
LANG, ed., Beauty and the beast and other stories. Longmans, 75c.
LEAR, Nonsense songs. Warne, $2.00.
LORENZINI, Pinocchio. Ginn, 60c.
PEARY, Children of the Arctic. Stokes, $1.20.
RHYS, Fairy Gold. Dutton, $2.50.
SWIFT, Gulliver's travels retold by Baldwin. Amer. Book Co., 35c.
WIGGIN, Posy ring. McClure, $1.25.

GRADE 4

ANDERSEN, Fairy tales; introd. by Hale. Lippincott, $2.00.
Arabian nights' entertainments; ed. by Lang. Longmans, $2.00.
BROOKS, True story of Christopher Columbus. Lothrop, $1.50.
BUNYAN, Pilgrim's progress. Century, $1.50.
CRAIK, Little lame prince. Harper, 60c.
EGGLESTON, Stories of American life and adventure. Amer. Book Co., 50c.
GOULD, Children's Plutarch; tales of the Greeks. Harper, 75c.
GOULD, Children's Plutarch; tales of the Romans. Harper, 75c.
HARRIS, Daddy Jake the runaway, and short stories. Century, $1.25.
JACOBS, Celtic fairy tales. Putnam, $1.25.
KIPLING, Just so stories. Doubleday, $1.20.
LANG, Blue fairy book. Longmans, $2.00.
MACDONALD, Light princess and other fairy tales. Putnam, $1.75.
OTIS, Toby Tyler. Harper, 60c.
SAUNDERS, Beautiful Joe; autobiography of a dog. Amer. Baptist Pub. Soc., 60c.
SEWELL, Black Beauty. Lothrop, $1.00.
STARR, American Indians. Heath, 45c.
STOKES, Ten common trees. Amer. Book Co., 60c.
SPYRI, Moni, the goat boy, and other stories. Ginn, 40c.
SWIFT, Gulliver's travels; il. by Rackham. Dutton, $2.50.
WEED, Seed-travellers. Ginn, 40c.

GRADE 5

ASBJORNSEN, Fairy tales; tr. by Braekstad. Nutt, 6*s*.
BALDWIN, Story of Siegfried. Scribner, $1.50.
BEARD, Jack of all trades. Scribner, $2.00.
BEARD, How to amuse yourself and others, American girls' handy book. Scribner, $2.00.
BURROUGHS, Squirrels and other fur bearers. Houghton, $1.00.
CARPENTER, How the world is fed. Amer. Book Co., 60c.
DEFOE, Life of Robinson Crusoe. Harper, $1.50.

DODGE, Land of pluck. Century, $1.50.
HARRIS, Nights with Uncle Remus. Houghton, $1.50.
INGPEN, One thousand poems for children. Jacobs, $1.25.
MACDONALD, At the back of the north wind. Blackie, *3s 6d.*
MACLEOD, Book of King Arthur and his noble knights. Stokes, $1.50.
MCMURRY, Pioneer history stories of the Mississippi valley. Public School Pub. Co., 50c.
PATTERSON, The spinner family. McClurg, $1.25.
PUTNAM, Children's life of Abraham Lincoln. McClurg, $1.25.
PYLE, Merry adventures of Robin Hood. Scribner, 50c.
RAMÉE, The Nürnberg stove. Lippincott, 50c.
SETON, Krag and Johnny Bear. Scribner, 50c.
SPYRI, Heidi. 2v. in 1. DeWolfe, $1.50.
STOCKTON, Bee-man of Orn, and other tales. Scribner, $1.25.
TAPPAN, Robin Hood and his book. Little, Brown, $1.50.
WILKINS, In colonial times. Lothrop, 50c.

GRADE 6

ALDRICH, Story of a bad boy. Houghton, $1.25.
BAKER, Boys' second book of inventions. McClure, $1.60.
BALDWIN, Conquest of the old Northwest and its settlement by Americans. Amer. Book Co., 60c.
BOYESEN, Boyhood in Norway. Scribner, $1.25.
BROOKS, Boy emigrants. Scribner, $1.25.
CARPENTER, How the world is housed. Amer. Book Co., 60c.
CERVANTES, Don Quixote of the Mancha; retold by Parry. Lane, $1.50.
CLEMENS, Prince and the pauper. Harper, $1.75.
CUSTER, Boy general. Scribner, 50c.
DODGE, Hans Brinker. Century, $1.50.
DU CHAILLU, World of the great forest. Scribner, $2.00.
EGGLESTON, Hoosier school-boy. Scribner, $1.00.
HILL, Fighting a fire. Century, $1.50.
HOMER, Iliad; ed. by Lang, Leaf, & Myers. Macmillan, 80c.
HUGHES, Tom Browne's school days. Cranford ed. Macmillan, $1.50.
JENKS, Boy's book of explorations. Doubleday, $2.00.
KIPLING, Captains courageous. Century, $1.50.
LUCAS, Three hundred games and pastimes; or, What shall we do now? De La More Press, *6s.*
PERCY, The boy's Percy; ed. by Lanier. Scribner, $2.00.
PYLE, Men of iron. Harper, $2.00.
REPPLIER, Book of famous verse. Houghton, 75c.
ST. JOHN, How two boys made their own electrical apparatus. St. John $1.00.
SEAWELL, Twelve naval captains. Scribner, $1.25.

SETON, Biography of a grizzly. Century, $1.50.
THOMPSON, Boys' book of sports. Century, $2.00.
WYSS, Swiss family Robinson; ed. by Kingston. Dutton, $2.50.

GRADE 7

BEARD, Outdoor handy book. Scribner, $2.00.
BEARD, What to do and how to do it; American boys' handy book. Scribner, $2.00.
BENNETT, Master Skylark. Century, $1.50.
BULL, Fridtjof Nansen; tr. by Barnard. Heath, 30c.
BULLEN, Cruise of the Cachalot. Appleton, $1.50.
DAVIS, Stories for boys. Scribner, $1.00.
DU CHAILLU, Country of the dwarfs. Harper, $1.25.
GARLAND, Boy life on the prairie. Macmillan, $1.50.
HALE, Man without a country. Little, 50c.
HOLDER, The ivory king. Scribner, $1.75.
LAUGHTON, Sea fights and adventures. Longmans, $2.00.
MALORY, King Arthur and his knights; ed. by Lathrop. Baker & Taylor, $1.50.
QUILLER-COUCH, Historical tales from Shakespeare. Scribner, $1.50.
ROOSEVELT, Ranch life and the hunting-trail. Century, $2.50.
SCHWATKA, In the land of cave and cliff dwellers. Educ. Pub. Co., $1.25.
ROYDE-SMITH, Una and the Red cross knight, from Spenser's Faerie Queene. Dutton, $2.50.
STEVENSON, Kidnapped. Scribner, $1.50.
THACHER, Listening child. Macmillan, $1.25.
TOLSTOÏ, Where love is, there God is also. Crowell, 35c.

GRADE 8

BUXTON, Stories of Persian heroes. Crowell, $1.50.
CRAIK, John Halifax, Gentleman. Luxembourg ed. Crowell, $1.50.
BLACKMORE, Lorna Doone. Luxembourg ed. Crowell, $1.50.
CUSTER, Boots and saddles. Harper, $1.50.
CUSTER, Tenting on the plains. Harper, $1.50.
DANA, Two years before the mast. Houghton, $1.00.
DARTON, Tales of the Canterbury Pilgrims retold from Chaucer and others. Stokes, $1.50.
HOMER, Odyssey; in English prose by Butcher and Lang. Macmillan, 80c.
JENKS, Boy's book of explorations. Doubleday, $2.00.
KENNAN, Tent life in Siberia. Putnam, $1.25.
KINGSLEY, Westward Ho! Macmillan, $1.00.
LYTTON, Last days of Pompeii. Luxembourg ed. Crowell, $1.50.
MACAULAY, Lays of ancient Rome. Longmans, $1.25.
MANLY, English poetry. 1170–1892. Ginn, $1.50.

NORDHOFF, Whaling and fishing. Dodd, 40c.
PARKMAN, Oregon trail. Little, $2.00.
ROOSEVELT, Wilderness hunter. Putnam, $2.50.
ROTH, First book of forestry. Ginn, 75c.
SAINTINE, Picciola; or, The prison flower. Appleton, $1.50.
SCOTT, Ivanhoe, Dryburgh ed. Macmillan, $1.25.
SCOTT, Kenilworth. Dryburgh ed. Macmillan, $1.25.
STEVENSON, David Balfour. Scribner, $1.50.
WALLACE, Ben-Hur; a tale of the Christ. Harper, $1.50.

SUGGESTIVE READING FOR CHRISTMAS

Compiled by JESSIE BLACK and IRENE WARREN
The School of Education, the University of Chicago

ESSAYS AND SERMONS

BROOKS, Christmas sermon. Century 25:179–183.
STEVENSON, A Christmas sermon (in Across the plains, p. 302).
WALLACE, The boyhood of Christ. Harper 74:3–18.
YONGE, Young folks' Bible history.

MISCELLANY

BEARD, How Christmas cards are made (in Wonderful stories of science).
St. Nicholas Christmas book.
WILTSE, Kindergarten stories and morning talks.

MISCELLANEOUS SELECTIONS IN ST. NICHOLAS

Christmas lights do fade away (picture). 23:177.
Christmas pictures. 34:106.
The mistletoe bough (ballad with living pictures for acting). 2:191.
MOUNT, On Christmas day (song). 19:236.
MURDOCK, A sixteenth century Christmas (drama). 16:145.
One hundred Christmas presents and how to make them. 3:103.
PENNELL, Christmas pantomimes. 15:180.
S. J. D., Christmas eve at Mother Hubbard's (a Christmas play for school or parlor). 25:256.
Santa Claus caught at last (picture). 26:135.

CHRISTMAS IN OTHER LANDS AND TIMES

AMERICA—COLONIAL

COFFIN, First years at Plymouth (in his Old times in the colony, p. 134).
EGGLESTON, Washington's Christmas gift (in his Great Americans for little Americans, p. 61).
HUNTER, A Christmas fox hunt in old Virginia. Outing, 1899. 23:274.
STANTON, Christmas on the Mayflower. St. Nicholas, 1900, 28:122.

ENGLAND

ADAMS, King's feast in Rufus's hall. St. Nicholas, 1884, 12:136.
CHAMBERS, Book of days. 2:733.
CHAMPLIN and BOSTWICK, Christmas sports (in Young folks' encyclopedia of games and sports, p. 190).

Corbin, Middle English nativity. Harper, 1896, 94:4.

Douglas, Ye Christmasse puddinge. St. Nicholas, 1898, 26:158.

Eggleston, St. Nicholas day and the bishops of Salisbury. St. Nicholas, 1877, 4:532.

Irving, Christmas. Christmas eve. (in his Sketch book).

Logsdail, Yuletide in an old English city. New England Mag., 1893, 9:383.

Pennell, London Christmas pantomimes. St. Nicholas, 1888, 15:180.

Reddall, Fact, fancy and fable, p. 125.

Strachey, Christmas eve and Christmas day at an English country house. Atlantic, 1894, 74:729.

Strutt, Sports and pastimes of the people of England. (See index, under Christmas.)

SCOTLAND

Scott, Christmas in the olden time (in his Marmion, Introduction to Canto 6).

Yuletide in Shetland. Living Age, 1882, 152:161.

FRANCE

Janvier, A Provençal Christmas postscript. Century, 1900, 37:179.

———, Christmas Kalends of Provence.

———, Christmas Kalends of Provence. Century, 1896, 31:265.

———, Nöels (in his Provençal Christmas postscript). Century, 1900, 37:183.

Peacock, Christmas customs in central France. Living Age, 1895, 207:813.

Wright, Mistletoe gathering in Normandy. St. Nicholas, 1879, 6:117.

BELGIUM

Belgian Christmas Eve. Living Age, 1887, 172:567.

HOLLAND

Dodge, Hans Brinker.

Kuiper, St. Nicholas day in Holland. St. Nicholas, 1896, 24:253.

GERMANY

Berg, A Christmas eve in Germany. Scribner, 1871, 1:338.

A Christmas in Germany. Harper, 1852, 4:499.

A Christmas in Hamburg. Harper, 1859, 18:359.

Forbes, Christmas-tide with the Germans before Paris. Harper, 1886, 72:263.

Latimer, Legend of St. Nicholas. Harper, 1886, 74:18.

Tutwiler, St. Nicholas day in Germany. St. Nicholas, 1876, 3:97.

SWITZERLAND

Cesaresco, An Alpine Christmas play. Atlantic, 1900, 86:794.

RUSSIA

Christmas in Russia. Review of Reviews, 1904. 29:343.

Thomas, Babousca, a Russia legend of Christmas. St. Nicholas, 1898, 25:233.

SPAIN

Hay, Christmas in Spain. St. Nicholas, 1874, 1:122.

FAR NORTH

(The) King's Christmas, a legend of Norway. Scribner, 1876, 11:385.
LONGFELLOW, King Olaf's Christmas (in Longfellow's Complete poetical works, p. 255).
LONGFELLOW, King Willaf's drinking-horn. Harper, 1857, 16:15.
WOODBURY, Christmas in the Arctic regions. St. Nicholas, 1876, 3:157.

FAR SOUTH AND EAST

FEUDGE, Christmas in the Far East. St. Nicholas, 1876, 3:165.
CUMMING, Christmas in Calcutta. Living Age, 1883, 159:809.
SLADEN, Christmas letter from Australia (Stedman's Victorian anthology, p. 551).

POETRY

ALEXANDER, The adoration of the Wise Men (in Posy Ring, p. 257).
ARNOLD, St. Brandon (in Open sesame 3:47).
BAYLY, The mistletoe bough (in Open sesame 3:354).
BELL, Christmas thim times (dialect). Century 17:319.
BELLAMY and GOODWIN, Open sesame. Christmas selections, 1:212–21; 2:353–66; 3:348–56.
BENNETT, A Christmas song (in Stedman's Victorian anthology, p. 79).
BOWRING, What of the night? (in Stedman's Victorian anthology, p. 173).
BROOKS, Three Christmas chimes. Century 17:224.
BROWNING, R., Christmas eve (in Poetic and dramatic works, v. 4).
Christmas in the olden time (from Scott's Marmion).
BUTTS, The Christmas tree (in Posy ring, p. 265).
Christmas carol (in Open sesame 1:211).
Christmas garlands for American poems. Harper 16:1–18.
COOK, Christmas holly (in Posy ring, p. 273).
DELAND, The Christmas silence (in Posy ring, p. 260).
DODGE, An offertory (in Posy ring, p. 261).
DOMETT, Christmas hymn (old style, 1837, p. 143; new style, 1875, p. 144) (in Stedman's Victorian anthology).
———, Christmas hymn (in Open sesame 2:355).
FIELD, Christmas treasures (in With trumpet and drum, p. 115).
———, The peace of Christmas time (in With trumpet and drum, p. 51).
———, Why do the bells of Christmas ring? (in Posy ring, p. 261).
HENDRICKSON, Songs of Christmas. Century 11:237.
HERBERT, Christmas (in Poetical works, p. 944).
HOLLAND, A Christmas carol (in Stedman's American anthology, p. 235).
"I saw three ships" (in Open sesame 2:362).
"I saw three ships" (in Posy ring, p. 268).
"In excelsis gloria" (in Open sesame 2:364).
JACKSON, The legend of St. Christopher (in her Poems).
KETCHUM, Christmas carillons. Harper 62:1–7.

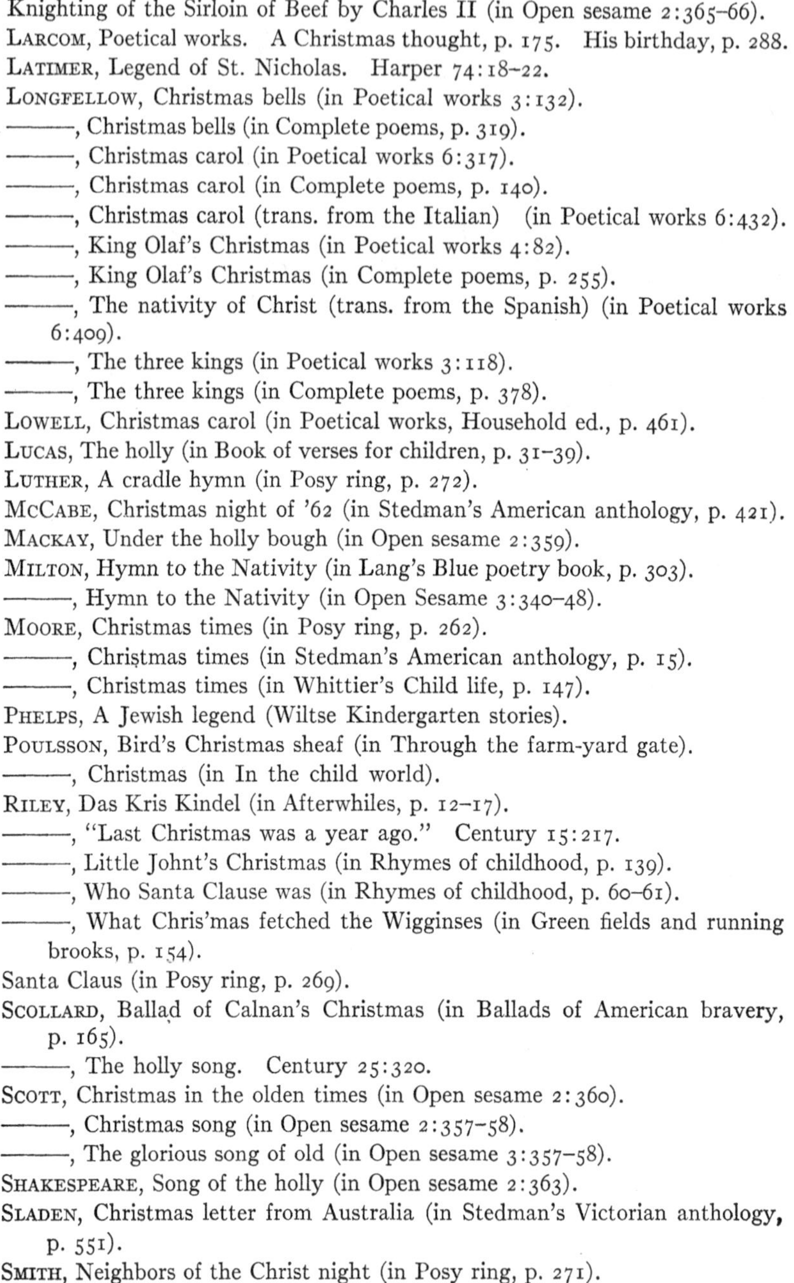

Knighting of the Sirloin of Beef by Charles II (in Open sesame 2:365–66).
Larcom, Poetical works. A Christmas thought, p. 175. His birthday, p. 288.
Latimer, Legend of St. Nicholas. Harper 74:18–22.
Longfellow, Christmas bells (in Poetical works 3:132).
———, Christmas bells (in Complete poems, p. 319).
———, Christmas carol (in Poetical works 6:317).
———, Christmas carol (in Complete poems, p. 140).
———, Christmas carol (trans. from the Italian) (in Poetical works 6:432).
———, King Olaf's Christmas (in Poetical works 4:82).
———, King Olaf's Christmas (in Complete poems, p. 255).
———, The nativity of Christ (trans. from the Spanish) (in Poetical works 6:409).
———, The three kings (in Poetical works 3:118).
———, The three kings (in Complete poems, p. 378).
Lowell, Christmas carol (in Poetical works, Household ed., p. 461).
Lucas, The holly (in Book of verses for children, p. 31–39).
Luther, A cradle hymn (in Posy ring, p. 272).
McCabe, Christmas night of '62 (in Stedman's American anthology, p. 421).
Mackay, Under the holly bough (in Open sesame 2:359).
Milton, Hymn to the Nativity (in Lang's Blue poetry book, p. 303).
———, Hymn to the Nativity (in Open Sesame 3:340–48).
Moore, Christmas times (in Posy ring, p. 262).
———, Christmas times (in Stedman's American anthology, p. 15).
———, Christmas times (in Whittier's Child life, p. 147).
Phelps, A Jewish legend (Wiltse Kindergarten stories).
Poulsson, Bird's Christmas sheaf (in Through the farm-yard gate).
———, Christmas (in In the child world).
Riley, Das Kris Kindel (in Afterwhiles, p. 12–17).
———, "Last Christmas was a year ago." Century 15:217.
———, Little Johnt's Christmas (in Rhymes of childhood, p. 139).
———, Who Santa Clause was (in Rhymes of childhood, p. 60–61).
———, What Chris'mas fetched the Wigginses (in Green fields and running brooks, p. 154).
Santa Claus (in Posy ring, p. 269).
Scollard, Ballad of Calnan's Christmas (in Ballads of American bravery, p. 165).
———, The holly song. Century 25:320.
Scott, Christmas in the olden times (in Open sesame 2:360).
———, Christmas song (in Open sesame 2:357–58).
———, The glorious song of old (in Open sesame 3:357–58).
Shakespeare, Song of the holly (in Open sesame 2:363).
Sladen, Christmas letter from Australia (in Stedman's Victorian anthology, p. 551).
Smith, Neighbors of the Christ night (in Posy ring, p. 271).

SOUTHWELL, New prince, new pomp (in Open sesame 3:252).
SPOFFORD, Christmas peal. Harper 84:14.
STEVENSON, Christmas at sea (in Poems and ballads, p. 365).
SYMONDS, A Christmas lullaby (in Posy ring, p. 267).
TABB, The light of Bethlehem (in Poems, p. 79).
TENNYSON, The birth of Christ (in Open sesame 3:351).
———, Christmas bells (in In Memoriam).
———, Christmas bells (in Open sesame 3:348–49).
———, Christmas bells (in Poetical works, p. 226).
WATTS, Cradle song (in Posy ring, p. 258).
WESLEY, Christmas day (in Open sesame 2:353).
WHITTIER, Christmas carmen, p. 453; Christmas, 1888, p. 467; A star of Bethlehem, p. 417 (in Complete poetical works).
WIGGIN, Golden numbers. Contains: BROOKS, Oh, little town of Bethlehem, p. 648; Christmas carol, Old English, p. 650; DELAND, While shepherds watched their flocks by night, p. 637; DOMETT, A Christmas hymn, p. 646; FIELD, The three kings, p. 644; HEBER, Brightest and best of the sons of the morning, p. 661; HEMANS, Hymns for Christmas, p. 639; HERRICK, Ceremonies for Christmas, p. 658; HERRICK, The star song, p. 638; HOLLAND, A Christmas carol, p. 635; HOWITT, Old Christmas, p. 652; LONGFELLOW, The three kings, p. 641; MORRIS, Minstrels and maids, p. 654; MULOCK, God rest ye, merry gentlemen, p. 653; SCOTT, Christmas in England, p. 659; SOUTHWELL, New prince, new pomp, p. 640; TATE, While shepherds watched their flocks by night, p. 649.

POETRY IN ST. NICHOLAS

ARNOLD, Christmas bells. 21:282.
AUSTIN, The shepherds in Judea. 28:99.
BENJAMIN, Johnny's observations on Christmas eve. 23:204.
BURGESS, Christmas twice a year. 25:131.
BURKE, Santa Claus street in Jingletown. 24:245.
BUSH, Christmas songs of Caedmon. 23:145.
BUTTERWORTH, For Christmas day. 17:186.
Christmas day. 6:168.
Christmas eve. 19:95.
CONE, A Christmas sleigh ride. 21:149.
———, The little Christmas spy. 16:83.
DODGE, The picture (poem). 24:91.
Good news on Christmas morn. 3:177.
HARTLEY, A winter song. 10:81.
HOWE, The knight and the page. 7:99–102.
HUTCHESON, Christmas letter. 17:113.
Jemima. 32:164.
LARCOM, Visiting Santa Claus. 12:82–84.

McCullough, Christmas tree lights. 26:112.
Merry Christmas. 24:193.
Mitchell, Christmas angels. 1:105.
Moses, What does Johnny want? 27:149.
Murphy, Introduction to Santa Claus (a true incident). 28:140.
O Santa San. 31:216.
Paine, Cupid and Santa Claus. 26:253.
Perkins, That little Christmas tree. 27:91.
Perry, Christmas day. 10:92.
Poulsson, The 19th century (as sung by Santa Claus). 24:136.
Raymond, The raid of the Rafferty's, a Christmas legend. 26:193.
Russell, A Christmas song. 4:90.
Sanderson, The best tree. 24:164.
A Southern Christmas eve. 3:83.
Spofford, The Christmas tree. 37:113.
Sterling, A Christmas eve thought. 23:169.
Stone, The pie and the clock. 26:113.
Swett, The Christmas goblin. 24:171.
Thomas, Babouscka (a Russian legend of Christmas). 25:233.
———, Christmas ashes. 37:231.
Trouble in the doll's house by last year's Christmas doll. 32:153.
Turner, The Christmas day. 34:164.
Wells, Christmas gifts. 26:233.
———, The lay of the Lady Lorraine. 25:193.
———, Pompey's Christmas. 27:154.
Wiggin, The tardy Santa Claus. 23:255.

POETRY IN OTHER MAGAZINES

Bearer of glad tidings. Scribner 37:29.
Both-Hendriksen, Songs of Christmas. Century 11:237.
Child Jesus. Harper 110:256.
Christmas folk song. Century 47:298.
Riley, Last Christmas was a year ago. Century 15:217.

JUVENILE STORIES

Alcott, Under the mistletoe (in Eight cousins).
Andersen, The fir tree (in Fairy tales).
Andrews, Christmas on the Rhine (in Seven little sisters).
———, Christmas times again for Louise (in Each and all).
Dodge, Hans Brinker.
Hale, The first Christmas present (in Wiltse Kindergarten stories).
Howells, Christmas every day.
Stockton, Christmas truants (in Fanciful tales).
Walsh, Story of Santa Klaus.
Wiltse, Iddy Bung's April Christmas tree (in Kindergarten stories).

JUVENILE STORIES IN ST. NICHOLAS

ALTON, Children's Christmas club of Washington city. 15:146.
BELLEW, Christmas stars. 13:216.
BURR, A snowbound Christmas. 24:99.
GLADDEN, Santa Claus on a lark. 13:96.
JACKSON, Leon Maturin's Christmas eve. 4:123.
LYALL, How a street car came in a stocking. 23:101.
MOSBY, Santa Claus's pony. 24:132.
SCANNELL, A Christmas legend. 2:141.
TUTWILER, A visit from St. Nicholas. 2:160.
WILSON, The Christmas white elephant. 23:112–84.

STORIES IN MAGAZINES

AUSTIN, The Christmas fiddle. Century 59:239.
CONNOLLY, The Christmas handicap. Scribner 44:683.
GOODLOE, Belated Christmas. Century 47:181.
HAMM, Camel of Jesus. Century 47:245.
LLOYD, A Christmas of Christmases. Scribner 46:693.
LONG, Liebereich's Christmas. Century 47:232.
NICHOLS, Life in a German family the week before Christmas. New England Magazine 41:417.
RICKERT, The Christmas thorn. New England Magazine 41:404.
STUART, A Christmas guest. Century 27:199.
———, Misfit Christmas. Century 47:266.
TOOKER, Kerrigan's Christmas sermon. Century 47:290.
TRAIN, McAllister's Christmas. Scribner 36:655.

ADULT FICTION

DICKENS, Christmas at Fezziwig's warehouse (in Open sesame 3:356).
———, Christmas goose at Cratchit's (in Open sesame 2:366).
FIELD, A little book of profitable tales.
HALE, In His name and other Christmas stories.
STOCKTON, Christmas before last (in The Bee-man of Orn, pp. 87–113).
STUART, A Christmas guest, a monologue. Century 27:198.
VAN DYKE, The first Christmas tree.
WALLACE, Ben Hur.

THE RELATION OF THE PRESENT MOVEMENT FOR VOCATIONAL EDUCATION TO THE TEACHING OF THE MECHANIC ARTS[1]

FRANK M. LEAVITT

It is well-nigh impossible to say anything new on the subject of industrial education. The report of your own state commission on Plans for the Extension of Industrial and Agricultural Training is one of the clearest and most significant statements of the existing situation which has yet appeared, and you are doubtless familiar with that report. If it failed in any particular, it was, perhaps, in neglecting to indicate the very valuable contribution to industrial education which our manual training, or some adequate development of it, might make within the existing school system.

That there is a decided tendency to emphasize the vocational aspects of education, few will deny. This tendency is to be observed in all grades of schools, from the elementary through the university. That we may utilize to the fullest extent, the brief time at our disposal, let us limit our field somewhat by reminding you of the following classification: Vocational education includes professional education, commercial education, agricultural education, household education, and industrial education. We shall confine our discussion to the relation of the teaching of the mechanic arts to industrial education, the education specifically adapted to the needs of the industrial worker.

In the development of things educational, one-third of a century cannot be considered a very long time, yet thirty-three years approximately cover the entire history of what we commonly designate as manual training, or the teaching of the mechanic arts, in this country. There had been earlier experiments in Pestalozzian methods, but these had come to nothing, or at all events, they have no connection with the movement to introduce handwork into the

[1] Read before the Wisconsin Teachers' Association ,November 10, 1911.

schools which took shape shortly after the Philadelphia Exposition in 1876.

It is impossible to understand the present movement for vocational education without a fairly clear conception of the history of manual training. Time will not permit a thoroughgoing analysis of the subject, but I will state, somewhat dogmatically, and as a basis for further discussion, what seem to me to be the significant facts.

Manual training was originally urged as industrial education; that is to say, the purpose of its introduction into the school curriculum was to teach the fundamentals of the trades. The report of a school committee in 1878 is fairly illustrative of the position commonly taken by school boards at that time: "The question of teaching trades in our schools is one of vital importance. If New England would maintain her place as the great industrial center of the country, she must become to the United States what France is to the rest of Europe, the first in taste, the first in design, the first in skilled workmanship. She must accustom her children from early youth to the use of tools, and give them a thorough training in the mechanic arts."

While laymen held this idea, many of the educators did not entirely concur with it. The introduction of manual training was opposed by the conservative educator on the ground that the specific function of the school was to dispense only such education as was broadly cultural, and preparatory for life only in a very general way.

To meet this objection the advocates of manual training claimed that instruction in the mechanic arts provided a very essential element of liberal culture which it was undoubtedly the business of the schools to supply. They said: "Manual training is needful for every individual, irrespective of his calling or professional career. The boy in the grades or in the high school is sent to the school shop, not because he is to be a carpenter. He is sent there though it be already clear that he is to be an attorney or a physician or a clergyman."

The advent of the so-called new psychology with its dependence on physiological phenomena greatly stimulated the introduction of manual training for its general educational values. "Simply as an aid to co-ordination, manual training would justify itself were that the sole point of its educational bearing." "Handwork arouses the initiative, sets in motion the essential activities of the mind, attention, and will, and requires a correct expression of the will. Thus it is an important tool for the development of the intelligence, and the permanent retention of knowledge in the brain." Quotations of this kind could be multiplied indefinitely, but perhaps they are best summed up in the one catch phrase which was very commonly heard fifteen years ago, "Put the whole boy to school."

The rapidity of the early development of manual training and its acceptance by educators throughout the country are to be accounted for almost entirely on the ground that it was considered to be a form of general education, and that it accorded with the prevailing ideals of the schools.

The recent report of the committee of the National Education Association on "The Place of Industries in Public Education" says:

> At the present time, the great majority of manual training high schools—practically all of them notwithstanding the distinction in name—differ in no important educational particular from the other high schools in the United States; they admit pupils of the same general type, of the same age, and of the same preparatory training. These schools aim to develop the same type of intelligence, the same habits of thought, and the same kind of ability as do other high schools; and their graduates are found in the same wide variety of occupations. While the subjects taught are not identical, the manual training schools are, nevertheless, essentially schools of the college-preparatory type in which the instruction, mechanical as well as academic, aims to provide the mental equipment of the kind required by those who would continue by college-preparatory standards. The fundamental aim of these schools is a general training, and specific training for industrial occupation is incidental. . . . .

To understand the new movement for industrial education we must appreciate the fact that while, during the past thirty years, the curricula, the practices, and the appearances of our schools have changed wonderfully, nevertheless their ideals and their conception of the fundamental purposes of education have remained essentially the same.

The new conception of education inherent in the movement for vocational training is that diversified conditions of life and work demand diversified education. It recognizes the fact that all cannot have the same education, that all cannot use, and do not need, and in fact do not want, the same education; that with educational food, as well as with food for the body, "One man's meat is another man's poison." The new ideal of education demands that the schools turn out their graduates as different as God intended them to be, and as their future happiness, success, and satisfaction, in their various vocational and social relations, require that they shall be. The education of the several individuals or groups is to be identical only in this, that the education of each shall be equally adequate, equally respected, and administered with equal intelligence and sympathy.

Thus we see that while manual training, as a part of general education, means a fraction of the education of all children, industrial education, as now conceived, means the complete and adequate education of the industrial worker.

The above statement will almost certainly be met with the objection that this means class education, and that class education or class distinctions of any kind are hateful to the true American. Nevertheless, the strength of the movement for industrial education comes from the belief that our educational machinery is out of harmony with our social and industrial organization.

Some of the more pertinent facts relating to the social organization may well be briefly considered. First of all will be found the wage system itself. As we know, the system places upon the individual the responsibility for his own and for his family's support. It is individualistic, not socialistic. It works well for the fortunate, but for many unfortunate it has worked such evil that it is frequently referred to as "wage slavery." At all events, it has produced two distinct classes with interests apparently widely divergent, if not diametrically opposed—the employers and the employed. We find also that it has led to an exceedingly unequal distribution, not only of wealth, but also of opportunity for securing personal happiness, comfort, and satisfaction in the fundamental experiences of life. Another factor is the factory system of production. Beneficent in many of its results as this system may be, it has, nevertheless, resulted in the degradation of countless individuals by dooming them to the endless repetition of a single process and by its utilization of cheap labor, especially the labor of women and children. By ever increasing the magnitude of the scale of production, it has resulted in a permanency of status of multitudes of wage-earners.

If, with these social and economic conditions in mind, we examine our public-school systems, we are led to conclude that the ideals and machinery of a "leisure-class" education still persist to a very considerable degree. We find that our schools are shaped for those who go to the top. Perhaps there is no better illustration of the saying, "Unto everyone that hath shall be given, but from him that hath not shall be taken away even that which he hath," than that which is afforded by our public schools. They have been so successful in eliminating the unfit, "him that hath not," that probably 50 per cent of our pupils receive only the slightest benefit from the free, public "universal" education which we have fondly believed was the birthright of every child in America.

Furthermore, our schools so monopolize the time and strength of the children who do attend them that we have the spectacle of strong, able-bodied, and able-minded boys reaching seventeen, eighteen, nineteen, or twenty years of age without ever having done an honest day's work in their lives, a spectacle which is, to my mind, quite as disconcerting as the horrors of child labor.

Lest you feel that my arraignment of the public school is entirely unjust, I will remind you of what educators generally consider to be a fact; namely: that the secondary schools are dominated by the universities and by the university spirit. So good an authority as Governor Woodrow Wilson has intimated that the universities, in their turn, are dominated, not by the spirit of social democracy, but by the personality and the ideals of men of large wealth. He says: "Who constitute the trustees of your universities? For the most part, the men of large wealth and of important corporate connections. Do you realize these gentlemen of large wealth and great corporate connections, no matter how honest they are—as those that I have had to do with have been scrupulously honest men—no matter how well disposed toward the progress of education, nevertheless, have a particular point of view with regard to American life that is not the proper point of view for young men of America to be brought up under?"

What is meant by all this is that education is becoming more and more socialistic, and that the desires and needs of all grades and shades and classes of our body politic will soon be taken account of in determining the kind of educational machinery which the public authorities will administer and for which the public will liberally tax itself. The new conception of industrial education is simply this: a publicly supported education which has as much regard for the future success of the industrial workers as it has for that of the professional or managerial classes.

It means that we are coming to look at education from the point of view of the man in the street, as well as from the point of view of the liberally educated. It means that we are to think as carefully and sympathetically about the education of the pupil who can give but eight or ten entire and consecutive years to his schooling as we do about the education of one who can give eighteen or twenty years to that pursuit. It means that the people support the schools, and that they are beginning to feel that they should have something to say about their management. It is, indeed, a part of the general effort of the people to gain control of, and to benefit by, their own institutions.

Whether you agree with the foregoing propositions or not, I am confident that a careful analysis of the present demand for industrial education would lead you inevitably to similar conclusions. This demand comes from four rather distinct sources:

First.—The manufacturing interests desire industrial education because they feel the need of more efficient and intelligent workmen, and because they wish, so far as possible, to avoid increasing the cost of production incident to maintaining apprenticeship systems which, under the existing conditions, are expensive and somewhat unsatisfactory.

Second.—Representatives of organized labor are demanding industrial education partly because they feel the need of the training for the coming generation, and partly because they desire to prevent ill-considered and possibly antagonistic plans for industrial education, which might flood the labor market with cheap and partially trained labor.

Third.—Educators are advocating industrial education because they see the psychological value of the more direct appeal to the vital interests of thousands of our children, and because they believe that in this way the schools will be able successfully to develop a larger percentage of the children intrusted to their care.

Fourth.—Organized society, working for social betterment, is urging industrial education as one of the surest ways to eliminate the most potent causes of crime and unhappiness, unemployed ignorance.

This demand has resulted in the establishment of publicly supported industrial schools and classes in all parts of the country. I think we are justified in saying that they are regarded as "experiment stations," and yet few who know them will have any doubt as to their permanency, their progress, and their ultimate articulation with the public-school systems.

There are no two of these schools exactly alike and they range all the way from the pre-vocational work of the sixth, seventh, and eighth grades of the elementary school, to the thoroughgoing trade school for young men and women, noteworthy examples of which are to be seen right here in Milwaukee, in the Milwaukee School of Trades for Boys and the Milwaukee School of Trades for Girls.

These schools may be roughly classified as (1) pre-vocational or semi-industrial schools; (2) separate or independent industrial schools; (3) vocational high schools; (4) trade schools. The pre-vocational school and the vocational high school illustrate sincere attempts to incorporate real industrial training into our present school system, whereas the separate industrial school and the trade school frankly ignore the present system, at least so far as prerequisite preparation is concerned.

There are also the half-time co-operative schools, and the continuation schools. The first of these provides opportunity for the boy or girl to do gainful work for an employer while pursuing the present school courses. The second is an opportunity offered by the school authorities to boys and girls, or young men and women who have already gone to work, to receive from four to eight hours a week of special education in special public-school classes.

It is impossible at this time to describe in detail the several types of schools, but I will enumerate five of the most distinctive features which are practically common to all types of industrial schools:

1. It is considered better to recognize, stimulate, and guide vocational interest in children of twelve to sixteen years of age than to try to suppress it. The value of the vocational motive in higher education is clearly recognized, and it is believed that industrial workers (who do not come at their life-work by the way of higher education) may equally profit by such incentive.

2. These schools recognize a twofold purpose in industrial education. The first, and perhaps the most important in the more elementary grades, is to prolong the school life of the child; the second is better to equip him for his initial entry into his vocational life. Of the two purposes the one most prominent in the minds of the pupils is the getting of a training which has real economic value, while the one appealing to the teacher is the giving of that benefit which may result from two or three additional years of contact with the ideals of school life.

3. The vocational motive and the vocational work are made paramount and central. Around this center is grouped and correlated all the work of the school, both handwork and bookwork. The bookwork is given with less elaboration, and all superfluous matter is greatly reduced or entirely eliminated.

4. The school day is lengthened to six, seven, or eight hours to provide for participation in, instead of mere instruction about, industrial work. The product system is generally made, therefore, the basis of the handwork.

5. The principle of a proportional subdivision of the time of all pupils is followed. In the broadest professional training the individual's education consists of three rather distinct periods. The first is intended to give a broad general training and extends from the beginning of school to about the third year in high school. The second period is intended to give a broad but somewhat defined or restricted groundwork for the specialty such as is afforded, for example, in the case of the future lawyer, by the study of history, languages, the political and social sciences, etc. This period extends from the middle of the high school to the beginning of senior college

work. The third period consists of relatively narrow and intensively specialized training. The plan of industrial education demands a somewhat similar distribution of the school time of the future industrial worker, the length of each period being proportional to the probable total time to be spent in school. The minimum requirement is as follows: First, a period covering the first six elementary grades. Second, a period covering at least the seventh and eighth grades. The minimum amount of time devoted to the third period should be at least one year. In no case should this period, the period of intensive training for entry into vocational life, be omitted, but where more time is available, both the second and third periods may be materially extended.

This briefly describes the movement for vocational education. As before stated, the report of your own commission discusses it in much greater detail. In stating the problem it has succeeded in giving practically all the pertinent facts, and in excluding a mass of material which is commonly introduced without any other effect than to cloud the issue. This is especially true regarding the statement of the need for industrial education, and the lessons to be learned from the experience of Germany; the analysis of the part-time work of Cincinnati, Fitchburg, and Beverly; the discussion of evening schools; and the insistence on the major necessity of educating the industrial *worker* rather than the officers of industry.

In suggesting solutions of the problem, the report has taken the strongest possible position in regard to administration. It has avoided the mistake of the first Massachusetts commission in demanding "separate" schools, and also the earlier mistake of believing that "general educational valucs," thc cnd sought by the traditional school, will serve effectively the present need. The attitude of the report is most commendable regarding the need of modern apprenticeship laws; the qualifications of teachers; the necessity of adapting methods to local conditions; the importance of advisory boards; the correlation of industry and education; the equity and good policy of treating sympathetically the wishes of organized labor; and the need of liberal financial support.

I have been asked to discuss the relation of this movement to the teaching of the mechanic arts. It seems to me that, if I have succeeded in setting forth the facts with any clearness, the relation which exists *today* must be evident. As a part of the general educational scheme which has proved to be satisfactory for perhaps 15 per cent of our pupils, those who move happily and without retardation through the several grades, the teaching of the mechanic arts is as effective as the instruction which is commonly given in the languages, in mathematics, or in the sciences. As "industrial education" it is as valuable as these subjects but certainly it is not usually more specifically so. Whether, for these pupils, it need to be made so is a debatable question, but the more pertinent question, for us, and indeed for manual-training teachers generally, is this: "Shall we continue to interest ourselves mainly in the education, of the 15 per cent who go well on toward the top, or shall we rather devote our energies to helping on the well-defined movement to greatly increase the efficiency of the education of the 85 per cent?" Frankly, my sympathies are with the latter problem, and my belief in the peculiar fitness of manual-training teachers to help in its solution is strong.

Referring again to the report of your commission, I would say that in only one respect is it disappointing. Throughout the entire discussion, it seemed evident that the commission fully realized the complete failure of the present school system to meet even the smallest needs of a large number of our school children. I refer to those leaving school at fourteen years of age from the fourth, or fifth, or sixth grade. Your commission evidently saw that the remedy, to be effective, must minister to the needs of these children and that, to secure this end, there must be brought about, to use the words of the report, "the betterment of school conditions in general." It does not seem to me, however, that the plans proposed by the commission reach the root of the matter in this particular.

I believe that the introduction of "*pre*-apprentice" or "*pre*-vocational" work in the schools is more important for large numbers of these children than the establishment of industrial, technical, or trade schools. It seems to me that even the continuation school will not benefit largely the boy who has been so hopelessly retarded that his fourteenth birthday finds him in one of the lower grades.

That boy has been a "dead one" for two or three years. Pre-apprentice work for such boys, beginning *before* fourteen, will undoubtedly serve to deter them from leaving school by creating an industrial interest which further training alone will satisfy.

It is in this phase of the new movement that manual-training teachers are peculiarly fitted to give invaluable aid. Here an adequate appreciation of industrial and social realities and of pedagogical principles are alike necessary, and this appreciation is more likely to be possessed by manual-training teachers than by any body of men and women of which I have any knowledge. If manual-training teachers could be empowered by the school authorities to give the right kind of manual training to the right children at the right time and in the right amount, there is no question in my mind that manual training would have a very considerable industrial value. Furthermore, it would be the means of postponing in this part of the country for a generation, and perhaps indefinitely, many of the acute problems which the promoters of industrial education in the East are finding so difficult of solution.

If there is anything certain in the immediate educational future it is this: that radical modifications of existing systems of grading and of courses of study, in both the elementary and the secondary schools, will be effected. It is also probable that the basis of secondary education will be made the subject of scientific study and that the sphere of the secondary school will be considerably extended, both downward and upward. It is clear that these modifications will create new conditions to which manual training, in common with all other subjects in the curriculum, will have to be adjusted. Here is something which all manual-training teachers must meet sooner or later, and, as it involves such widespread educational improvement for the less fortunate members of society, it is a problem which, I believe, should engage their eager and interested co-operation.

THE EFFICIENCY OF THE CONSOLIDATED RURAL SCHOOL

JOHN FRANKLIN BOBBITT
The University of Chicago

The earliest argument in favor of the consolidation of rural schools was its economy. But experience has shown that consolidated schools cost rather more than the one-teacher schools. The more recent argument in their favor is that they are more efficient in securing educational results. This claim is for the most part based upon general appearances rather than upon actual statistical evidence.

The present writer during a visit to Delaware County, Indiana, in which consolidated schools have existed for more than a decade, and in which they are as well developed as in any other county in the country, attempted to secure some statistical data from the records of the county superintendent showing the relative efficiency of the consolidated schools of that county as compared with the ungraded one-teacher schools. The records of the office related only to attendance and scholarship as shown by the eighth-grade examinations given at the end of the school year in both graded and ungraded schools.

Attendance statistics were secured from six graded consolidated schools each having from four to eight teachers. Similar statistics were obtained from thirty-four one-teacher rural schools taken at random having an aggregate attendance about equal to that of the six consolidated schools. The yearly term for most of these schools was one hundred and forty days. Where the length of the term varied slightly from this number, as in a few cases, the figures were reduced to the 140-day basis.

The average number of days attended by each student was, in the consolidated schools, 111.1 days; and in the ungraded rural schools, 107.1 days, a difference in attendance of four days in favor of the consolidated schools. In the latter the pupils attended on an average 79.4 per cent of the time; while in the ungraded schools they attended 76.5 per cent of the time, a difference of 3 per cent in the average record of attendance. If this difference were uniformly distributed through the grades, it would be too slight to be of significance.

The attendance was then studied by grades in order to see whether the consolidated schools tended to hold the pupils better during the latter grades of the elementary school courses. The results are shown by Table I.

TABLE I

ATTENDANCE BY GRADES

Grade	1	2	3	4	5	6	7	8
Average attendance in consolidated schools	98	111	110	113	111	120	123	120
Average attendance in ungraded schools	96	105	110	111	111	115	107	109
Difference in favor of consolidated schools	2	6	0	2	0	5	16	11
Percentage of attendance in consolidated schools	70	79	79	81	79	86	88	86
Percentage of attendance in ungraded schools	68	75	79	79	79	82	76	78
Difference in favor of consolidated schools	2	4	0	2	0	4	12	8

This table shows that the attendance is not appreciably different for the first five grades but that the attendance during the sixth, seventh, and eighth grades is much better in the consolidated schools than in the one-teacher schools. The attendance in the seventh and eighth grades is from 8 to 12 per cent better than in the corresponding grades of the ungraded schools; and, at the same time, it is altogether probable, though we have no figures at hand upon this point, that the consolidated school has also held a larger proportion of its pupils during the seventh and eighth grades. If this is the case, this means a double gain in favor of the consolidated school for the grammar grades. This is significant since one's serious education for adulthood scarcely begins before the seventh grade.

The figures indicate that the consolidated school is more attractive to the students of the grammar grades than is the ungraded school. This is perhaps due to the greater variety of the work that can be offered, which is coming to include manual training, domestic science, elementary agriculture, nature-study, drawing, and music—a series of activities that can be directed very inadequately in the usual one-teacher school. Further, the consolidated schools offer a better stepping-stone for the high school. The township high school is usually in the same building. Naturally the pupils are made familiar with the nature of a high school, a thing not possible in a one-teacher ungraded school.

On the side of scholarship the records of the county superintendent's office showed the result of the final eighth-grade examination given at the end of the school year to those who had finished the work of the elementary school. The questions were prepared in the office of the state superintendent and were therefore uniform for all the schools of the county. The grading was done in the office of the county superintendent and therefore the grading was uniform throughout the county. The examination results are therefore altogether comparable in all the schools.

In grading the papers of the pupils in the superintendent's office, arithmetic was first marked; and if anyone failed in arithmetic the remaining papers were not marked. For this reason the arithmetic series was the only complete series that could be obtained for that county.

The average grade in arithmetic for the candidates from the consolidated schools was 77.7 per cent. The average grade of the candidates from the ungraded one-teacher schools was 76.7 per cent. These figures are for all practical purposes identical. The distribution of the students along the percentage scale in the two classes of schools is also practically identical as shown by Table II.

The figures seem to indicate that in arithmetic, at least for this particular year, the efficiency of the consolidated schools is no greater than that of the ungraded one-teacher schools.

In the consolidated schools 61 students took the final examinations; of these 45 passed and 16 failed. The percentage successful was 73.8 per cent. In the ungraded schools 71 students took the final examinations; of these 52 were successful and 19 failed.

The percentage successful was 73.2. The percentages of successful students in the two classes of schools are the same.

This equality in the percentages of successful students in the uniform eighth-grade examinations in both kinds of schools appears to indicate that what is true for arithmetic is true of every other study covered by the examinations. The scholarship produced by the two types of schools is not appreciably different.

One ought, however, to know the average ages of the pupils. It is not improbable that the graduates of the ungraded schools were considerably more mature than those of the consolidated schools. Also a study of the relative elimination of pupils is necessary; it is possible that the graduates of the ungraded schools were somewhat more of a picked lot than those of the consolidated schools.

TABLE II

FREQUENCIES OF THE DIFFERENT GRADES

Grades	Number of Students		Percentage of Students	
	Consolidated	Ungraded	Consolidated	Ungraded
1— 10	0	0	0.0	0.0
11— 20	2	1	3.7	1.5
21— 30	1	2	1.9	3.1
31— 40	1	2	1.9	3.1
41— 50	1	2	1.9	3.1
51— 60	2	3	3.7	4.4
61— 70	10	12	18.4	18.4
71— 80	8	10	14.9	15.4
81— 90	12	13	22.2	20.0
91—100	17	20	31.4	31.0
	54	65	100.0	100.0

Although the present study is based upon the figures for the greater part of a county, and that a county in which the movement is as well developed as anywhere in the country, yet the quantity of data is insufficient for conclusions. If more extended studies should arrive at the same results, many of the more substantial claims of the defenders of the movement would be nullified. Thus it is urged, for example, in the *Report of the Commissioner of Education of Ohio* for 1908 that, among other things, consolidation "insures a much better average daily attendance, and greatly reduces the cases of tardiness"; "gives an opportunity for better classification of the schools and grading of pupils"; "encourages supervision"; "limits the field of the teacher's work and thus permits better preparation"; "gives few classes to each teacher and longer recitation periods"; and "secures better teachers." These, however, are not ends in themselves, but only means to an end. If they do not secure improved educational results, they do not constitute arguments in favor of consolidation.

The foregoing considerations are presented in no critical spirit. The writer is of the opinion that the many problems of rural education are not to be solved without consolidation, grading, and division of labor. But the argument to be used in promoting the movement must be other than the cost per school child, or the ability of the pupils to pass examinations in arithmetic, geography, and history.

The writer recently visited two agricultural counties, lying side by side and similar in all important respects. In one of these counties a progressive county superintendent had brought about consolidation in half the schools of his county. In the other county, a conservative superintendent had blocked all of the efforts of the advocates of consolidation with two simple arguments: consolidated schools are more expensive per capita; and they produce no greater scholarship as shown by the uniform state examinations. The writer doubted the accuracy of the superintendent's figures; and to test the matter, took the data above mentioned from the records of a county in which consolidation has been looked upon favorably and has been given opportunity to prove its worth. Contrary to expectations, the figures appear on their face to support the contentions of the conservative superintendent.

It is on the basis of such arguments as these that the major portion of our rural population and also the major portion of their school officials oppose the consolidation movement. In many places where the movement has attained considerable growth, it is coming to be looked upon with some disfavor by former supporters, since it seems to be neither cheaper nor more efficient. The argument appears to them to be based upon accurate mathematical considerations, and to be incontestable.

The method of measuring results by examination in the standard subjects, however, and by mere count of individuals, leaves out of consideration a number of essential matters. The examinations referred to above are drawn up to meet the needs of ungraded schools and fail to measure many of the most important results secured by graded schools. In the latter there is 30 to 40 per cent more time given to recitation, discussion, shop and field work under the teacher's immediate direction. In the proportion that a pupil's work with the teacher is better than study periods, to that degree must the graded work secure better results. And yet, the examinations may be so designed that the extra results do not reveal themselves in the percentages received in the textbook subjects.

Social conditions also are demanding many subjects that can be given only in graded schools. All rural schools, for example, should teach agriculture and household science. In order that the teacher have the necessary vocational attitude of mind, there must be a man for the one subject and a woman for the other. While a young lady teacher in an ungraded school might teach textbook agriculture in such a way as to enable her pupils to pass the state examination in proper form, yet the actual results would undoubtedly be far inferior to those secured by a special teacher of agriculture in a consolidated school. The situation would be just reversed in the case of the teaching of household science. Efficient rural education cannot be accomplished without at least two teachers for each school.

Another result not measured by the examination tests is the social education that comes from belonging to a large school community of two hundred children and eight teachers, both men and women, rather than to a small district community of twenty-five children and one teacher. If the "country-life movement" is ever to check the stream of migration from farm to city, it must provide social education and social opportunities of an attractive sort for the rural youth. It must socialize the country; and the consolidated school appears to be a long step in this direction.

Other desirable results not measured by the examination are: (1) the greater number of pupils held through the eighth grade; (2) the greater number directed into the rural high school, a necessary preliminary to the dissemination of agricultural information through the country; (3) the improved health conditions of pupils, due to more sanitary buildings and equipment and better opportunities for efficient medical inspection.

The purpose of this brief sketch is to show the apparent soundness of the argument so frequently used to block the movement for consolidation; and to indicate the ways in which it is essentially unsound because of its leaving out of consideration a number of matters which are probably as important as the intellectual content acquired from textbooks in the so-called standard subjects.

STUDIES IN PRINCIPLES OF EDUCATION

CHARLES H. JUDD
The University of Chicago

III. APPLICATION

One of the most urgent problems of present-day education is that of training pupils to meet the practical issues of life. Knowledge is of no value in the opinion of the ordinary man unless it can be applied. The school is urged to eliminate from the course of study everything which has no bearing on business or health or other practical interests. Our arithmetics must have examples which show the applications of addition and subtraction to buying and selling. We must put into arithmetic more measurement because this can be used. In geography it is the same. We must eliminate the fruitless discussions of boundaries and the long lists of names and study routes of travel and the lines of trade. In the high school we must emphasize science and reduce the attention to literature. In all schools we must give a place to handwork.

This demand for practical applications is no mere academic plea. School boards are calling upon teachers and superintendents to show reasons for this and that type of instruction in the schools. Merchants and manufacturers are devoting time to the discussion of educational problems and are suggesting trade training or the shortening of the course. Parents are withdrawing their children from the schools as early as the law will allow, confident that more valuable training will be gained through contact with the shop or store or farm than from continued schooling. Pupils are restless and inattentive because they do not see what use it is to study that which is offered in the schools.

This extreme emphasis on practical applications is in contrast with the assumption which was formerly the accepted assumption of the school. It used to be regarded as the duty of the school merely to prepare in a somewhat remote way for later life. It was thought that the child should learn to read in school and that later in life he would find uses for reading. So too with number ideas and with geography. These should be cultivated in the school, not as practical arts, but as systems of knowledge. The practical arts were thought of as in some sense different from the knowledge taught in the schools. Indeed, knowledge or theory was often described as wholly different from practical application and skill.

When the urgent demand for practical training encounters the old-time attitude of the school that education is a remote and indirect preparation for later life, some readjustment becomes necessary. The readjustments which are being worked out today are of various types. For purpose of illustration we may refer to three typical efforts along these lines.

First, there is the short-term trade school. This institution goes about the task of making a tradesman of the boy with the greatest possible directness. Here is a boy who would leave school if he were obliged to go on with reading and arithmetic; let us make a carpenter or a mason of him, recognizing that skill in one of these trades will make him a more efficient citizen. Training in a trade is here substituted for book-learning and all the common school subjects. Skill with the saw and hammer is capable of direct application in the urgent practical world where the student must make his living. Substitute skill for knowledge and abandon the effort to make the boy or girl skilful through knowledge.

One cannot consider this first suggestion without realizing that it is based on a deep-seated pessimism regarding the ordinary school course. The ordinary course has an aim which is supposed to be much higher than the mere acquisition of skill. Reading is supposed to give the individual an outlook on the world which will include a correct view of the need and value of skill and industry and will arouse the worker to the highest efforts, but will at the same time give a comprehension of the trade. The short-term trade school says, in effect, the supposition that reading is of value has been overdone. It is better for at least a part of our population that no further emphasis be laid on reading. Their reading is not adequate to guide them in the acquisition of skill. Their reading has not fitted them to make a satisfactory living. Put an end to teaching reading, make a radical change and teach something very different.

If the substitution of pure trade training for our present educational program should become common, it would mean the most radical change in the social treatment of children that has ever been worked out. The most impressive evidence that this would mean an abandonment of our present ideas about the significance of education appears when one considers how little industry stimulates those kinds of intellectual activity which the school aims to cultivate. The ordinary plumber is not stimulated by the experiences which he encounters to study geometry or chemistry or even to read the mechanical journals. The fact is that the more skilful a man becomes, the less likely he is to seek intellectual aids in his work. Trades do not lead workmen to study. The man who reads about the materials which he uses brings the motive for reading into the trade, rather than finds that motive in his practical life.

A second typical suggestion which has been made is the suggestion that certain practical lines of activity be added to the course of study or be substituted for a part of the course. Thus manual training is to take the place of some of the history or a part of the grammar. The use of tools is to be taught while at the same time the essential subjects are kept in their former places in the school program. For the girls cooking is to become a part of school training.

This suggestion conforms more closely to the common notion about what a school ought to do. Some local disputes arise as to how far the new subjects should be allowed to encroach on the old, but in general the new courses and the old are both more or less respected. Yet even this respect for both types of work is colored by a feeling that they are at bottom different. Teachers of the manual arts are looked upon as different in their interests and methods from teachers of reading and grammar and arithmetic. While there is a great deal of discussion about reconciling the two types of work and relating them and deriving motives for one out of the other, the fact remains that no successful fusion has been achieved. Training for knowledge, for reading, and for number work continues to be one kind of training; training for shopwork and cooking is of another type.

Finally, there is the suggestion that there be a frank division of the pupil's time and energy such that he shall spend part of his time in the school and part in some practical work of the world. He shall go into a shop and work in wood or metal, or she shall go into a store and clerk or into a kitchen and cook, but while thus engaged in practical activity, the pupil shall withdraw from the shop or store for a few hours each week and study in some school.

This third suggestion, like the other two, and perhaps more clearly than either of the others, recognizes a difference in character and in spirit between the two types of training. The shop and the store are practical institutions, bent on giving skill as soon as possible. The part-time class in the school supplements the shop with something that the shop cannot give. Together the shop and school cultivate two distinct sides of the child's nature.

This part-time plan differs from the trade-school plan in two essentials. First, this plan does not lay on the school the obligation of doing the practical work. Furthermore, the part-time plan is not wholly pessimistic about the value of the conventional school courses. The part-time plan recognizes schoolwork as fulfilling a function of its own. It limits the amount of schoolwork, to be sure, but admits its value.

As contrasted with the manual-training plan, the part-time plan recognized from the beginning the fundamental and abiding distinction between trade training and schoolwork. It goes so far as to give the supervision of the two types of training to two wholly separate institutions. The hope of the advocates of manual training that handwork will some day be merged into ordinary school work is here abandoned. The school is set off very sharply from the shop and the store. The school is to co-operate with the shop and the store but never to confuse its mission with theirs.

It is not the primary purpose of this paper to advocate or condemn any of the plans above discussed. It is the purpose of this study to discover and evaluate the principles which underlie these various experiments in school organization.

One principle which comes out with perfect clearness in each of the above described suggestions is the principle that practical skill cannot be identified with conventional school courses. Put in specific terms, we may assert that reading can never be identified with shopwork. The manual-training movement has striven faithfully to correlate the two as intimately as possible, but has failed to unite them in any complete way. The part-time school and the short-term trade school recognize the difference without reserve.

The general principle which thus grows out of experience in school organization is that some adjustment must be made between practical applications and theoretical studies other than that which involves the identification of the two. There must be some arrangement of the work in such a sequence as to allow theoretical training to precede practical training or follow it so as to maintain the distinctive advantages of each kind of training.

A concrete example of such a sequence can be described in the case of reading. In the primary grades reading is taught as a process of recognizing words. The children have to learn certain forms of perception, and have to connect with these forms of perception certain articulations. As they progress through the second and third year, it becomes less and less necessary for them to emphasize the formal side of reading. They acquire the mechanics of reading and establish a well-organized habit. As soon as this habit is once established, the pupils grow restless if they are required to go on with more reading of the same type as that which they have taken in the first years. There should be a change in the motive for reading, and there should be a change in the method of instruction. The reading should be employed as a means of introducing the pupil to large bodies of information which will be of some advantage to him in his later practical life.

In such a case as this the relation between theoretical training of the early years and practical applications is such that application of reading follows reading. The term "application" is used in this case in the broad sense, and includes not merely the application of reading to some form of handwork, but also the application of the relatively simple art of reading to higher and more mature forms of experience. It is quite as much an application of reading when we require the pupil to use reading for the sake of acquiring geographical knowledge as it is when we require him to use his reading in understanding directions which are given to him in the shop or in the cooking-class.

In none of these cases, however, is application identical as a mental process with the first intellectual efforts involved in acquiring the ability to read. The acquisition of the ability to read depends upon close attention to the letters and words and to the articulations which are necessary in uttering the words which are seen on the page. The center of attention, therefore, is upon the page; and upon the formal side of the reading process. So limited is the scope of the pupil's attention that there is scant opportunity in the early stage of reading for him to look beyond the printed page and see the significance of the passage. Later, after the art of reading has matured, the child finds it unnecessary to give close attention to the formal side of the process. When he looks at a printed page with its succession of words, he is able immediately to connect with the printed word the appropriate articulation. He is now free to allow his mind to go beyond the printed symbols to the meaning. The extent to which he can apprehend the meaning differs in different stages of the mental development.

In making the transition to application it is important that the instruction begin with simple opportunities to apply reading. Later the application should become more and more complex and more and more intricate.

The school has in the past given too little attention to the special forms of mental activity which are involved in the application of reading. Pupils have been allowed to go out of the elementary schools with the ability to read, but they have never had their attention drawn to the fact that this ability would help them to acquire the information that they need to guide them in the mechanical arts which they take up as a means of livelihood. The fact is that pupils who leave the school at the end of the sixth grade very seldom help themselves in later life by using the power which they have. This is partly due to the fact that they do not know that there is a body of written and printed material which would be of value to them, and it is partly due to the fact that they have never acquired the habit of carrying their reading process beyond the earliest formal stages. The school ought to show them that there is a body of material other than poetry and literary prose. The school ought also to indicate to the children that such reading as they do in poetry and literary prose is not intended to limit them to this type of material, but is intended rather to develop their powers so that in later life they may have independent use of the ability to read. There are certain definite suggestions which can be made along these lines. The writer knows of a case in which the teacher who found it difficult to interest boys in the middle of the elementary school in reading went to a neighboring manufacturing concern and secured copies of their trade catalogues. These catalogues were brought into the school and made the subject of reading. Instantly the boys recognized, as they never had recognized before, that the art of reading had direct relation to practical life. The advantage of such training consisted not merely in the information which they acquired about that particular industry, but also in the habit which they cultivated of using the power of reading to meet all of the practical emergencies of life.

In the same way girls may be introduced to books about kitchen implements and textiles. Either one of these subjects can be made of interest to the girls, and in addition they find in the perusal of this type of material an enlargement of the reading habit which will make them conscious of its value in a way which they are not likely to understand from the study of verse and literary prose alone.

In some cases perhaps the applications which will justify the formal work of the school can be made at the same time that the pupil is acquiring the power to read or use number. There is great danger, however, that we shall make an effort to accomplish something in the way of application before the power to read or the power to use number is sufficiently mature to justify the larger effort to carry it out into practical fields. Thus in an earlier paper, attention was drawn to the impossibility of correlating arithmetic and shopwork before there is any maturity of arithmetical interest. In the same way the pupil who is unable to read for meaning, because his whole attention is absorbed in looking at the words and articulating them, never can acquire a piece of information which calls for attention to the meaning of these words. He must have a sufficiently mature power of reading and of using numbers so that he may have freedom of attention for the higher step of application. For this reason, it is not possible to introduce practical applications too early in the grades. Indeed, there is no necessity in the lowest grades of the elementary school of any large practical motives to encourage the children to acquire reading and writing and number ideas. Children in these lower grades are very docile and willing to take up any kind of material that society sees fit to furnish. During these earlier periods it is advantageous, therefore, that they should be taught to read and use numbers. They are very eager to be introduced to the printed page, and they are very willing to do a large amount of drudgery in the acquisition of number ideas. It is a mistake to surfeit them at this time with outside ideas, and with industrial projects which are too mature for them to comprehend. They should be kept in contact with the social arts which will later make possible some view of the practical world. The practical world will appeal to them very much more as they become mature. Children who have reached the fourth or fifth grade are very likely to leave school just because the practical world makes a strong appeal to them, and they do not see the utility at that time of further lessons in reading and number work. If the earlier grades of the school waste time and energy in the effort to bring to the attention of young children bodies of information for which they are not prepared, and if now in the fourth or fifth grade they are driven to learn something about reading and number in order that they may have a rudimentary possession of these arts, they are likely to become discouraged, and exhibit that discouragement by abandoning the school for practical experience.

The change which should be made in our elementary school in conformity to the principle of application should be made, therefore, in the fourth and fifth years, and from that point onward. The methods of teaching reading and number below this period are well organized and successful. The waste in elementary education appears from the fourth grade on. It is a waste of much of the time of the children who remain in school, and it is also a waste of the community's efforts because the training of the upper grades does not reach as many children as it should.

In the foregoing discussion special emphasis has been laid upon reading. Arithmetic has been mentioned incidentally as a form of training which also should wait for its application. Writing, drawing, and also a direct acquaintance with space through some simple problems in constructive geometry, might properly be recommended under this principle as the best materials for the lower grades of the elementary school.

In an earlier paper the present writer suggested that there is too much haste in the introduction of concrete material into the school. The meaning of that statement in terms of this principle of application is that concrete opportunities to use one's knowledge should not be offered before the child has sufficient mastery of the arts of reading, writing, and number to justify the school in its efforts to deal with concrete material. Children have plenty of concrete ideas when they come to school. The difficulty is to show them how this concrete experience should be worked over and intellectualized. The school should supplement the child's ordinary experience by showing him new methods of dealing with these experiences. The school could never accomplish its purpose by devoting itself exclusively to shop training and handwork. These are essentially concrete forms of experience. Here again it is more important that the child should learn how to plan his work and how to record his plans than that he should be brought merely into contact with the materials of shopwork. The concrete in education has its proper place, but that proper place is at the point of application of powers which have been gained. These powers are essentially intellectual in character, and they need at first relatively very little concrete material on which to work.

The best types of concrete material to use in the early stages of any instruction are materials which are so simple that the attention of the pupil will not be distracted by the material itself. It must be admitted of course that it would be quite impossible to teach practical ideas without having some objects for the pupils to handle. These objects should, however, be very simple objects such as splints for arithmetic, or the immediate objects of the environment for writing and reading. It is quite impossible to expect the pupils to employ number ideas which are altogether immature, and at the same time recall, through imagination, objects that are remote and relatively unfamiliar. There is nothing concrete about an example in interest and percentage to the child who does not understand numbers well enough to spend some mental energy thinking about interest and percentage. Indeed, it may be doubted whether most children in the elementary school have sufficient imagery to make it possible for them to use at any time intelligently such problems as those which are involved in bank transactions. Simple, concrete material as illustrating mental processes may therefore be advocated without leading to the demand that we use at all times in elementary instruction concrete material. Here again a distinction of importance can be drawn between material which illustrates and material which furnishes an opportunity for the application of mature forms of thought. The illustrative material is present for the purpose of cultivating a form of thought. The material to which one applies his powers is introduced for an entirely different purpose, and his mental attitude toward it is entirely different. In the one case the attention is upon the process, and not upon the concrete material, while in the other case, attention is chiefly upon the concrete material itself.

In conclusion, it may be said by way of summary that it has been the purpose of this article to point out the importance of doing more work in the elementary school in the direction of making school-work practical in character. The school must itself discover to the child the possibilities of using the training which he has received; that is, the school should make training in application a special problem to be worked out after the child has cultivated powers which he can apply.

EDITORIAL NOTES

Commissioner Claxton has on several occasions made public announcement of the policy which he expects to adopt during the coming year, for the federal Bureau of Education. His plans are comprehensive, and include many types of research which the bureau has up to this time been unable to undertake because of lack of funds. It will be necessary in order to accomplish what Commissioner Claxton has in mind that Congress be very much more generous in its appropriations to the bureau than at any time in the past. Funds are to be asked for, not merely for the publication of statistical reports, but also for the pursuit of a number of general investigations of the educational activities of the country.

The Aggressive Plans of Commissioner Claxton

There is one difficulty which the aggressive plans of the new commissioner will encounter. A number of agencies in other bureaus, and even in other departments of the federal government, have been placed in charge of educational interests. This subdivision of educational activities has gone so far that there is some danger that the bureau will find its work scattered about in various offices. Thus the general supervision of agricultural education is in the hands of the Department of Agriculture. The promotion of industrial education is rapidly passing over into the hands of the Bureau of Labor of the Department of Commerce and Labor. Mr. Charles H. Winslow, as the special agent of the Bureau of Labor, has recently been engaged in bringing together a large body of valuable material describing the various experiments which are now being made in the country to provide industrial education either in private or in public schools. The Department of Commerce and Labor has also assumed charge of the legislation for the improvement of working conditions among children. This labor legislation may very properly be regarded as a part of the work of the Department of Commerce and Labor. And yet the interests of education are so

Danger of Scattering Educational Activities

intimately bound up in all of the labor legislation which applies to children that there is danger as stated above that the educational interests will become scattered throughout all of the different departments, and thus lack the unity which they should derive from the central control of educational activities through the Bureau of Education. Certainly if this undesirable disintegration of educational interests is to be avoided, it is time that a vigorous policy be adopted both by the Bureau of Education in Washington and by all who are interested in educational organization throughout the country.

Representatives Must Be Personally Interested

It will be quite impossible for the new commissioner to carry through his comprehensive plans without the support of those who are interested in education. It is not enough that this interest should express itself from time to time in formal resolutions passed at gatherings of teachers. There must be active support, and this support must be given in such a way as to be effective in Washington. The difficulty which exists now is that the ordinary representative who goes to Washington has never had it impressed upon him that the Bureau of Education is a matter of large interest to his constituents at home. This same representative knows perfectly well that the interests of the Department of Agriculture are of great importance to his constituents. This fact has been brought home to him by many references during the campaign in which he was elected, to the work of the Department of Agriculture. The teachers of his community, on the other hand, are in very large numbers not voters, and in the second place, they have never taken the pains to draw his attention to the important contributions which are being made by the federal bureau to the general movement of education. Indeed, it may be doubted whether all of the teachers in the public schools of this country are aware of the importance of the bureau as a clearing-house of information, and as a center for the distribution of this information. The new commissioner has a right to ask that school people inform themselves, first, with regard to the service which this bureau has rendered in the past to school organization in this country. He has a right to ask, in the second place, that his plans receive careful consideration from educators in every state;

and finally, that these plans, if approved, be brought to the attention of representatives before they start for the Capitol. The representatives who go up from the different districts will in this way be prepared to act intelligently upon the recommendations of the commissioner, and will realize that these recommendations represent a demand which is as wide as the nation.

Support to Be Effective Must Be Given Now

The first step in this general program of support of the commissioner consists in a clear recognition of the necessity of investigations. It has been pointed out repeatedly in this journal that there are at the present time many very efficient forms of school organization which are little understood by teachers outside of the immediate sphere of influence of these special experiments. There are forms of industrial education, there are methods of dealing with the problem of promotion and with the course of study, which could be made very influential if they could be understood and their results carefully tested. There is great need of some central agency which shall bring together in closer unity the high schools and the elementary schools. There is need of some central investigation of the normal-school problem. All of these larger interests will be properly served only when some agency broader in its interests than the state departments of education concerns itself with the consideration of educational practice and organization. The bureau ought to have in all of these investigations the heartiest support of the school people of the country. The bureau can serve a purpose which no other agency in this country is large enough or comprehensive enough to undertake. The commissioner ought to feel assured that he has the support of the individual members of the national school system. There can be no doubt that the time has arrived in the history of the bureau when it must expand and bring together the educational activities, or its functions will be subdivided among the various other departments of the central government.

BOOK REVIEWS

Spelling Efficiency in Relation to Age, Grade, and Sex, and the Question of Transfer. By J. E. WALLACE WALLIN. Baltimore: Warwick & York, 1911. Pp. 91.

This study, which is published in the series of "Educational Psychology Monographs," is a good contribution to the subject of the method of teaching spelling. The author begins with a description and critical discussion of the two contrasted methods, the incidental method and the method of drill. The incidental method received an impetus from the investigations of Rice and Cornman. This method did not seem to Wallin to be in accordance with the conditions of efficient habit formation. He accordingly arranged a method which should involve the elements of drill, that is, focalization of attention upon the words to be learned, and attentive repetition. The method also included the use of the test words in dictation in order to facilitate their application to the ordinary conditions of the use of words. This method has been used in the public schools of Cleveland.

The results of the method in the spelling efficiency of the Cleveland pupils are compared with the results of the tests given by Kratz, Chancellor, and Rice. The Cleveland averages are from 12.6 per cent to 27 per cent higher than those obtained by the other investigators, with the same sort of test—the word-column method. It was found also that the efficiency reached in the word-column tests carried over into dictated writing or compositions in which the same words were used. This fact meets the objection of the incidentalists that formal drill in spelling does not carry over to connected writing. These results were obtained by devoting to spelling "5.96 per cent of the available time, as compared with 7.22 per cent, the average for a number of the leading cities of the country."

The author also discusses the relation of spelling to age, grade, and sex, but the most important point, which he seems to have made clearly, is that a carefully devised drill has a marked effect in raising spelling efficiency.

FRANK N. FREEMAN

THE UNIVERSITY OF CHICAGO

BOOKS RECEIVED

LAIRD & LEE, CHICAGO

The Standard American Drawing and Lettering Book. The Modern Art of Sign-Writing. Drawn and Arranged by PETER IDARIUS. Pp. 103.

GINN & CO., CHICAGO

Arithmetic. Book I. By GEORGE WENTWORTH AND DAVID EUGENE SMITH. Cloth. Illustrated. Pp. 296. $0.35.

Arithmetic. Book II. By GEORGE WENTWORTH AND DAVID EUGENE SMITH. Cloth. Illustrated. Pp. 296. $0.40.

Arithmetic. Book III. By GEORGE WENTWORTH AND DAVID EUGENE SMITH. Cloth. Illustrated.

Tell It Again Stories. By ELIZABETH THOMPSON DILLINGHAM AND ADELLE POWERS EMERSON. Cloth. Illustrated. Pp. 173. $0.50.

Pinocchio in Africa. Translated from the Italian of Cherubini by ANGELO PATRI. Cloth. Illustrated. Pp. 152. $0.40.

TEACHERS COLLEGE, COLUMBIA UNIVERSITY, NEW YORK

The Social Composition of the Teaching Population. By LOTUS DELTA COFFMAN. Cloth. $1.00.

Progress through the Grades of City Schools. By CHARLES HENRY KEYES. Cloth. $1.00.

A Special Study of the Incidence of Retardation. By LOUIS B. BLAN. Cloth. $1.00.

MENOMINIE PRESS

Paper and Cardboard Construction. By GEORGE FRED BUXTON AND FRED L. CURRAN. Cloth. Illustrated. Pp. 166. $1.50.

AMERICAN BOOK CO., NEW YORK

A Latin Primer. By. H. C NUTTING. Cloth. Illustrated. Pp. 240. $0.50.

First Reader. By JAMES BALDWIN AND IDA C. BENDER. Cloth. Illustrated. Pp. 144. $0.30.

Second Reader. By JAMES BALDWIN AND IDA C. BENDER. Cloth. Illustrated. Pp. 176. $0.35.

Washington's Farewell Address and Webster's First Bunker Hill Oration. By FRANK W. PINE. Cloth. Pp. 117, with portrait. $0.30.

SILVER, BURDETT & CO.

A Mother Goose Reader. By CHARLES W. MICKENS AND LOUISE ROBINSON. Cloth. Illustrated. Pp. 120. $0.36.

HARPER & BROTHERS, NEW YORK

Our Country and Its People. By WILL S. MONROE AND ANNA BUCKBEE. Cloth. Illustrated. Pp. 130. $0.40.

DOUBLEDAY, PAGE & CO., GARDEN CITY, N.Y.

The School of Tomorrow. A Collection of Prize Essays from the *World's Work.* Cloth. Pp. 152.

CHARLES E. MERRILL & CO., NEW YORK

Great Inventions and Discoveries. By WILLIS DUFF PIERCY. Cloth. Illustrated. Pp. 206. $0.40.

AMERICAN BOOK CO., NEW YORK

King's Woodwork and Carpentry. Elements of Construction. By CHARLES A. KING. Cloth. Illustrated. Pp. 181. $0.70.

King's Woodwork and Carpentry. Elements of Woodwork. By CHARLES A. KING. Cloth. Illustrated. Pp. 146. $0.60.

Dramatic Reader for the Lower Grades. By FLORENCE HOLBROOK. Cloth. Illustrated. Pp. 192. $0.40.

White Patch. Bertelli's Italian Story of Ciondolino. Retold by ANGELO PATRI. Cloth. Illustrated. Pp. 216. $0.40.

Shakespeare's Merchant of Venice. Edited by GILBERT SYKES BLAKELY. Cloth. Pp. 112.

Kimball's Elementary English. Books I and II. By LILLIAN G. KIMBALL. Cloth. Pp. 299.

Government in the United States. By JAMES W. GARNER. Cloth. Pp. 416. $1.00.

GINN & CO., CHICAGO

The Seven Champions of Christendom. A Legendary Romance of Chivalry. By AGNES R. MATTHEWS. Cloth. Illustrated. Pp. 161. $0.45.

The Learning Process. By STEPHEN SHELDON COLVIN. Cloth. Pp. 336. $1.25.

A Brief Course in the Teaching Process. By GEORGE DRAYTON STRAYER. Cloth. Pp. 311. $1.25.

D. C. HEATH & CO., BOSTON, MASS.

The Haliburton Primer. By MARGARET W. HALIBURTON. Cloth. Illustrated. Pp. 131. $0.30.

HOUGHTON, MIFFLIN CO., BOSTON, MASS.

The Story of a Bad Boy. By THOMAS BAILEY ALDRICH. Cloth. Illustrated. Pp. 261. $0.50.

Being a Boy. By CHARLES DUDLEY WARNER. Cloth. Illustrated. Pp. 186. $0.40.

Second Reader. By JAMES H. VAN SICKLE and WILHELMINA SEEGMILLER. Cloth. Illustrated. Pp. 192. $0.40.

Third Reader. By JAMES VAN SICKLE and WILHELMINA SEEGMILLER. Cloth. Illustrated. Pp. 256. $0.50.

Old World Hero Stories. By EVA MARCH TAPPAN. Cloth. Illustrated. Pp. 261. $0.70.

The Fall of the Year. By DALLAS LORE SHARP. Cloth. Illustrated. Pp. 126. $0.60.

MACMILLAN CO., NEW YORK

Chemistry. An Elementary Text-Book. By William Conger Morgan and James A. Lyman. Cloth. Illustrated. Pp. 429. $1.25 net.

Introduction to General Science. By Percy E. Rowell. Cloth. Pp. 302. $0.75.

Beginnings in Agriculture. By Albert Russell Mann. Cloth. Illustrated. Pp. 326. $0.75.

Poems Narrative and Lyrical. Edited with Introductions and Notes by Robert P. St. John. Cloth. Pp. 232. $0.25.

The Children's Book of Christmas. Compiled by J. C. Dier. Illustrated. Pp. 111. $1.50.

TEACHERS COLLEGE, COLUMBIA UNIVERSITY, NEW YORK

The Social Factors Affecting Special Supervision in the Public Schools of the United States. By Walter Albert Jessup. Cloth. Pp. 123. $1.00.

UNIVERSITY PRESS, CAMBRIDGE, MASS.

The Cambridge Historical Readers. Introductory. Cloth. Illustrated. Pp. 155. $0.40.

The Cambridge Historical Readers. Primary. Cloth. Illustrated. Pp. 241. $0.40.

The Cambridge Historical Readers. Junior. Cloth. Illustrated. Pp. 284. $0.60.

The Cambridge Historical Readers. Senior. Cloth. Illustrated. Pp. 294. $0.75.

WARWICK & YORK, BALTIMORE, MD.

Psychology and Pedagogy of Writing. By Mary E. Thompson. Cloth. Pp. 128.

Mental Fatigue. By Dr. Max Offner. Translated from the German by Guy Montrose Whipple. Cloth. Pp. 133. $1.25.

WASHINGTON GOVERNMENT PRINTING OFFICE

Age and Grade Census of Schools and Colleges. A Study of Retardation and Elimination. By George Drayton Strayer. Paper. Pp. 144.

Bibliography of Education for 1909–10. Paper. Pp. 166.

Agencies for the Improvement of Teachers in Service. By William Carl Ruediger Paper. Pp. 153.

Bibliography of Child-Study for the Years 1908–1909. By Louis N. Wilson. Paper. Pp. 84.

CURRENT EDUCATIONAL LITERATURE IN THE PERIODICALS[1]

IRENE WARREN
Librarian, School of Education, The University of Chicago

ABBOTT, CHRISTABEL. Dramatic training in the normal schools of New York state. Educa. 32:99–104. (O. '11.)

ARCHIBALD, GEORGE HAMILTON. The aim of religious education. Child 2:35–39. (O. '11.)

ARMSTRONG, EDWARD C. The place of modern languages in American education. School R. 19:596–609. (N. '11.)

BENNETT, CHARLES A. The place of manual arts in education. Educa. R. 42:245–53. (O. '11.)

BENTLIFF, WALTER D. The place of examinations in the primary school. School W. 13:369–70. (O. '11.)

BOBBITT, JOHN FRANKLIN. A city school as a community, art, and musical center. El. School T. 12:119–26. (N. '11.)

BOGGS, ANITA U. A plea for the forward child. Child 2:45–47. (O. '11.)

BOURNE, RANDOLPH S. The college: an undergraduate view. Atlan. 108: 667–74. (N. '11.)

BREDVOLD, LOUIS I. The high-school course in American government. Educa. 32:93–95. (O. '11.)

BRICKER, G. A. A suggestive outline for a one-year course in secondary agriculture for rural and village high schools. Educa. 32:75–76. (O. '11.)

BURGESS, THEODORE C. Athletic relations of Illinois colleges. School R. 19:513–22. (O. '11.)

BURSTALL, SARA A. The place of examinations in education. School W. 13:367–69. (O. '11.)

BUTTENWIESER, ELLEN CLUNE. The obstinate child. Pedagog. Sem. 18: 315–28. (S. '11.)

BYERS, SIR JOHN. Ireland and child hygiene. Child 2:17–24. (O. '11.)

CARTER, RALPH E. Correlation of elementary schools and high schools. El. School T. 2:109–118. (N. '11.)

[1] *Abbreviations.*—Amer. Phys. Educa. Rev., American Physical Education Review; Atlan., Atlantic; Educa., Education; Educa. R., Educational Review; El. School T., Elementary School Teacher; Journ. of Educa. (Bost.), Journal of Education (Boston); Journ. of Educa. Psychol., Journal of Educational Psychology; Kind. M., Kindergarten Magazine; Lit. D., Literary Digest; Liv. Age, Living Age; Out., Outlook; Pedagog. Sem., Pedagogical Seminary; Pop. Educator, Popular Educator; Pop. Sci. Mo., Popular Science Monthly; Psychol. Clinic, Psychological Clinic; R. of Rs., Review of Reviews; School R., School Review; School W., School World; Sci. Amer., Scientific American; Teach. Coll. Rec., Teacher's College Record; Voca. Educa., Vocational Education.

COOLEY, EDWIN G. Organization of the industrial continuation schools of Crefeld. Voca. Educa. 1:65–81. (N. '11.)

COOPER, FRANK IRVING. Schoolhouses and the law. Amer. Phys. Educa. Rev. 16:459–73. (O. '11.)

CRAMPTON, C. WARD. A new system of physical training. Amer. Phys. Educa. Rev. 16:431–38. (O. '11.)

CRAWFORD, CAROLINE. Aesthetic development of children at the kindergarten period. Kind. M. 26:42–44. (O. '11.)

CRICHTON-BROWNE, SIR JAMES. Growth: somatic and cerebral. Child 2:1–16. (O. '11.)

DANA, JOHN COTTON. The study of a city in the schools of that city. Pedagog. Sem. 18:329–35. (S. '11.)

DAVIS, C. O. Reorganization of secondary education. Educa. R. 42:270–301. (O. '11.)

FISH, ELMER H. The commercial school shop. Voca. Educa. 1:82–99. (N. '11.)

FLEMING, PIERCE J. Moving pictures as a factor in education. Pedagog. Sem. 18:336–52. (S. '11.)

FOSTER, W. S. School instruction in matters of sex. Journ. of Educa. Psychol. 2:440–50. (O. '11.)

FREEMAN, FRANK N. Some issues in the teaching of handwriting, II. El. School T. 12:53–59. (O. '11.)

GARDNER, BERTHA LEE. Debating in the high school. School R. 19:534–45. (O. '11.)

GODDARD, HENRY H. The bearing of heredity upon educational problems. Journ. of Educa. Psychol. 2:491–97. (N. '11.)

GOSSETT, J. O. Retardation in the schools of Stockton, California. A study of 300 pedagogical life histories. Psychol. Clinic 5:149–57. (O. '11.)

GREENWOOD, ARTHUR. Juvenile labor problems. Child 2:25–34. (O. '11.)

GREENWOOD, J. M. Educational expansion. Journ. of Educa. (Bost.) 74:397–98. (19 O. '11.)

GULICK, LUTHER H. What our city schools are doing for the health of our children. Amer. Phys. Educa. Rev. 16:447–52. (O. '11.)

HADLEY, ARTHUR TWINING. The college in the service of the nation. Youth's Companion 85:591–92. (2 N. '11.)

Hagenbeck as an educator. R. of Rs. 44:491–92. (O. '11.)

HARTOG, P. J. Examinations. School W. 13:361–64. (O. '11.)

HARTSON, LOUIS D. The psychology of the club; a study in social psychology. Pedagog. Sem. 18:353–414. (S. '11.)

HECHE, ARTHUR. A report on the teaching and practice of hygiene in the public normal schools of the United States. Journ. of Educa. Psychol. 2:429–39. (O. '11.)

Higher education for women in Russia. R. of Rs. 44:502–3. (O. '11.)

HOLLISTER, H. A. Constants and variables in the high-school program of studies. Educa. 32:69–74. (O. '11.)

HOUSE, R. T. An experiment in free tuition. Educa. 32:77–80. (O. '11.)

JUDD, CHARLES H. Studies of educational principles. El. School T. 12:82–90. (O. '11.)

KLATT, WILLIBALD. Changes and innovations in the German school system in the last decade. School R. 19:523–33. (O. '11.)

KUERSTEINER, A. F. The needs of modern-language instruction. School R. 19:555–68. (O. '11.)

LEE, JOSEPH. The two kinds of play. Amer. Phys. Educa. Rev. 16:439–46. (O. '11.)

LINDSEY, BEN B. Juvenile delinquency and employment. Survey 27:1097–1100. (4 N. '11.)

LOWELL, A. LAWRENCE. College studies and professional training. Educa. R. 42:217–33. (O. '11.)

MIDDLETON, RICHARD. *Treasure Island* as a book for boys. Liv. Age 53: 249–51. (28 O. '11.)

MIRICK, GEORGE A. Report on the study of retardation in the schools of Indianapolis, 1908–11. El. School T. 12:60–70. (O. '11.)

MOORE, C. H. Education in England and America. Educa. 32:88–92. (O. '11.)

MURPHY, D. C. American history as a basis of literature. Pop. Educator 29:62–64. (O. '11.)

NOLLEN, JOHN SCHOLTE. Aims of the teaching of modern languages in the secondary school. School R. 19:550–54. (O. '11.)

NUNN, T. PERCY. The influence of examinations upon teaching. School W. 13:364–67. (O. '11.)

PARKER, S. CHESTER. Pestalozzian formalism—degenerate object-teaching. El. School T. 12:97–108. (N. '11.)

PAYNE, I. D. Retardation in the schools of Palo Alto, California. A study of pedagogical life histories. Psychol. Clinic 5:139–48. (O. '11.)

PERRY, CLARENCE ARTHUR. Recreation the basis of association between parents and teachers. Playground 5:262–74. (N. '11.)

PINKHAM, COLBURN. Educate the immigrant. Out. 99:384–87. (14 O. '11.)

PRITCHETT, HENRY S. The moral influence of a university pension system. Pop. Sci. Mo. 79:502–13. (N. '11.)

REAVIS, WILLIAM CLAUDE. Some factors that determine the habits of study of grade pupils. El. School T. 12:71–81. (O. '11.)

SANCTIS, SANTE DE. Mental development and the measurement of the level of intelligence. Journ. of Educa. Psychol. 2:498–507. (N. '11.)

"Scientific management" of colleges. Lit. D. 43:681. (21 O. '11.)

SHAFER, GEORGE H. Health inspection of schools in the United States Pedagog. Sem. 18:273–314. (S. '11.)

SHOREY, PAUL. American scholarship. Educa. R. 42:234–44. (O. '11.)

SMITH, PAYSON. The public school in its relation to civic and social reforms. Journ. of Educa. (Bost.) 74:453–55. (2 N. '11.)

SNEDDEN, DAVID. Problems in the psychology of vocational education. Journ. of Educa. Psychol. 2:481–90. (N. '11.)

STECHER, WILLIAM A. An inquiry into the problem of desks for school children. Amer. Phys. Educa. Rev. 16:453–58. (O. '11.)

STOWE, A. MONROE. The motivation of debate in our secondary schools. School R. 19:546–49. (O. '11.)

SYKES, FREDK. H., and others. Industrial education. Teach. Coll. Rec. 12:1–61. (S. '11.)

(A) symposium on reform in grammatical nomenclature in the study of the languages. School R. 19:610–42. (N. '11.) ROUNDS. The present situation and possible remedies, p. 610; MEADER. The problem from the standpoint of general linguistics, p. 617; KUERSTEINER. The problem from the standpoint of the romance languages: French, p. 618; WAGNER. The problem from the standpoint of the romance languages: Spanish, p. 619; SCOTT. The problem from the standpoint of English, p. 620; DIEKHOFF. Functional change of the subjunctive in German, p. 624; HALE. The closing of the symposium, p. 630.

TAYLOR, CHARLES KEEN. The renaissance of Bob. Psychol. Clinic 5:158–63. (O. '11.)

TAYLOR, JOSEPH S. Quantitive study of reading. Educa. R. 42:254–69. (O. '11.)

VANE, SIR FRANCIS. World scouting and education. Child 2:40–44. (O. '11.)

WADE, HERBERT T. New York's fire college. Sci. Amer. 105:364–65. (21 O. '11.)

WASHBURN, WILLIAM S. The college man in the public service. Science 34:589–93. (3 N. '11.)

WEBB, SALLIE H. The savings bank system in a fifth grade. Pop. Educator 29:61–62. (O. '11.)

WETTER, A. A. Great educators. II. Fénelon. Educa. 32:96–98. (O. '11.)

VOLUME XII NUMBER 5

THE ELEMENTARY SCHOOL TEACHER

JANUARY, 1912

DOMESTIC ARTS COURSES IN PUBLIC SCHOOLS

GEORGE H. WHITCHER
Superintendent of Schools, Berlin, N.H.

For several years our school system at Berlin was manifestly lacking in balance, through failure to provide adequate training for girls who evidently intended to become first of all housekeepers and home-makers. We had provided three courses for boys, namely, a Latin course, a commercial course, and a mechanic arts course; but only two for girls, Latin and commercial. The chief reason why a course parallel to the mechanic arts course was omitted was the honest but mistaken notion that a domestic arts course was by nature expensive beyond our means.

In common with many others, we assumed that the high price of all food materials, when coupled with the pedagogical necessity of cooking on a large enough scale to approximate real home conditions, would make the cooking supplies bear too heavily upon our available general fund for supplies, and so, rather than resort to the all-too-common practice of making jelly by the thimbleful and "rounding out" the course by the making of the simple recipes over and over, we let this gap in our educational chain remain unlinked.

The necessity for the course, however, proved the mother of ways and means for overcoming the obstacle of expense.

Berlin has about 1,200 children in the public schools, and of these 350 are in the high school. We have seven grades in the elementary and four in the secondary course, or eleven years in all from entrance to graduation from the high school. Our plan was to employ the art of cooking as a means of neuro-muscular readjustment during and after the period of upheaval which appears from the eleventh to the thirteenth year. This plan requires that cooking, as well as normal hand sewing, shall be taken in the seventh grade of the elementary school and in the first year of the high school. Moreover, other considerations point to these same activities as educative ends as well as means.

On an average, we have fifty to sixty girls from the seventh grades and fifteen to twenty-five from the high school, who are taking the cooking courses; that is, sixty-five to eighty-five in all.

Our equipment, capable of taking care of groups of sixteen to twenty for both sewing and cooking, cost $257.43. This low initial cost is in part accounted for by the fact that our mechanic arts boys have made all desks, counters, closets, cabinets, and such other pieces of equipment as fell within their capabilities, so that only the cost of the lumber used in these is charged up to equipment. We have added to the original equipment in 1910 to the extent of $21.81 and in 1911 to the extent of $15.95.

Our kitchen and laboratory equipment is ample and satisfactory and the dining-room service abundant for serving luncheons to a maximum of twelve persons.

From the outset the plan has been to commence with plain, wholesome cooking of such everyday substantials as the workingman on an income of $12 a week can afford, and to add to this such semi-luxuries as the modest salary of a dry-goods salesman, or a school superintendent, might permit. Good wheat bread and biscuits, nourishing soups, low-priced meats, well-cooked vegetables, fish, eggs, wholesome cakes and puddings, etc.: these we hope to have selected, prepared and cooked and served in an attractive, wholesome manner.

How to keep down the cost of this department was the one question above all others that had to be solved. Our solution was to "borrow the materials from the neighbors" to cook in such combinations as scientific investigation has shown to be well suited to man's needs, and then after cooking to return the finished product to those who furnished the "raw materials."

This plan has met every demand and no doubt is applicable

everywhere. Each pupil becomes an agent for propagating the plan and collecting food stuffs. Every home wanted bread, cake, cookies, and doughnuts, and gladly sent in flour, milk, eggs, butter, etc., from which to make these substantials. Very soon orders from others than those having pupils in the school came in by note or phone. "Will the domestic arts pupils make a fruit cake for me tomorrow?" "I want a jar of mince-meat. Will your domestic arts classes make it if I send the materials?" Sometimes a very special "hurry-up" call for cake indicates company at home. A roast of beef or pork, lamb or veal croquettes, a roast chicken; indeed, every conceivable dish from Boston baked beans to frozen pudding is on our list of orders cooked. In the canning season grapes, peaches, plums, pears, tomatoes, quinces, blackberries, etc., come by quarts, baskets, and bushels to be made into jelly, conserve, perserve, marmalade, pickles, etc.

In some cases nearly a whole dinner has been cooked for some family, and occasionally a citizen has brought visiting friends to the school dining-room for a luncheon. In all these ways the school has had free materials to work on, while the neighbors have been saved the labor of cooking and have experienced the pleasure of new dishes by new cooks. It may be that in time we shall help to solve the "servant-girl problem" by guaranteeing meals during culinary interregnums.

There are many pedagogical as well as pecuniary advantages in this plan. Pupils are not only interested, but deeply, vitally, and enthusiastically so. If a cake is going to Mrs. X. to be passed upon as the product of the seventh, eighth, or other class, then this cake must be satisfactory. If a group of citizens, the Board of Education, or perhaps the City Council, are to have a luncheon served, then not only must it be well planned and prepared, but the serving must be well done. Responsibility in school as elsewhere brings results.

Given \$200 to \$250 and a room the equivalent in size of an ordinary schoolroom, and given also an enthusiastic young teacher of sewing and cooking, and any school system where there are 500 pupils or more may easily provide for a domestic arts course which will incur an expense for materials and supplies of from twenty cents to thirty cents per pupil in the cooking, or five cents per pupil in the sewing.

Our supply account for the three years is as follows: 1909, $15.23; 1910, $29.15; 1911 (to date), $10.81.

The following detailed statement shows the range of our activities:

KITCHEN WORK

First Term's Work

Date	Item	Disposition
September 7	Canned 30 qts. string beans (picked from school garden)	School use
	Made $1\frac{1}{2}$ pk. tomatoes from school garden into piccallili	School use and 2 orders
	Canned $1\frac{1}{2}$ qts. spiced blackberries	School use and orders
	Canned $2\frac{1}{2}$ qts. plain blackberries	School use and orders
to	$3\frac{1}{4}$ qts. tomato catsup	School use and orders
	$3\frac{1}{2}$ qts. green tomato preserve	School use and orders
	$3\frac{1}{2}$ qts. canned tomatoes	1 order
	2 qts. spiced whole tomatoes	School use
	$1\frac{1}{2}$ qts. chopped pickles	School use
	4 doz. tumblers crab apple jelly	3 orders
	$4\frac{3}{4}$ qts. grape catsup	4 orders
	$1\frac{1}{3}$ qt. grape marmalade	2 orders
	30 tumblers grape jelly	2 orders
October 25	Canned pumpkin	1 order
October 25	Boston favorite loaf cake	5 orders
	Park St. cup cakes	3 orders
	Hermits	5 orders
	Walnut cake	5 orders
	White Mt. cream	3 orders
	Ginger puffs	3 orders
to	Vanilla wafers	6 orders
	Molasses cookies	3 orders
	Salad dressing	2 orders
	Chocolate cake	4 orders
	Patty shells	5 orders
	Gingerbread	3 orders
December 22	Layer cake	1 order

October 25	Ginger snaps	6 orders
	One egg cake	3 orders
	Nut cake	2 orders
	Baking-powder biscuits	2 orders
	Pork croquettes	1 order
	Mince meat	3 orders
	Roast chicken and gravy	1 order
	Molasses doughnuts	2 orders
	Parker House rolls	2 orders
	Frosted birthday cake	2 orders
	Thanksgiving puddings	4 orders
to	Popovers	2 orders
	Raisin cake	1 order
	Twin Mt. muffins	2 orders
	Sponge cake	2 orders
	Bread and rolls	10 orders
	Shamrock rolls	2 orders
	Bow knots	3 orders
	Fruit cake	5 orders
	Christmas puddings	3 orders
	Candy	2 sales
	Fudges	1 order
	Maryland biscuits	1 order
December 22	Dark fruit cake	3 orders

REMARKS.—All material was supplied by people for whom we made orders. Each girl made bread once this first term. Freshman and Sophomore cooking alike. Five times this term we had a thorough house-cleaning lesson.

SECOND TERM'S WORK

January 10	Lemon jelly	1 order
	Snow pudding	
	Fudges	
	Brown bread	2 orders
	Sugar cookies	6 orders
	Molasses doughnuts	3 orders
to	Sponge cake	2 orders
	Nut bread	4 orders
	Entire wheat bread	3 orders
	Stuffed steak	1 order
	Cream soups	
	Stock soups	
	Clear soups	
March 23	Boston favorite cakes	4 orders

January 10	Sugar doughnuts	4 orders
	Cranberry jelly	2 orders
	Veal loaf	1 order
	Molasses tea cakes	2 orders
	Bean pot roast	1 order
	Plain omelet	1 order
	Cheese omelet	
	Foamy omelet	
	Popovers	
to	Molasses cookies	2 orders
	Coffee, tea, cocoa	
	Fish à la rarebit	1 order
	Washington pie	1 order
	Sour cream pie	2 orders
	Gingerbread	
	Patty shells	1 order
	Potato croquettes	1 order
	Scalloped oysters	1 order
	Timbales	
	Vol-au-vents	
	Punch	1 order
March 23	Sandwiches	1 order
	House-cleaning every other week.	

March 23

SEMI-BANQUET

TO

LEGISLATIVE COMMITTEE ON APPROPRIATION FOR NORMAL SCHOOLS

Vol-au-vents of Sweet Breads and Mushrooms

Lobster Timbales Bechamel Sauce

Chicken Salad Potato Balls Saratoga Chips

Shamrock Rolls Bow Knots

Olives Salted Almonds Celery

Cold Sliced Ham

Fruit Salad Wine Dressing

Flowering Ice Cream Lady Fingers

Coffee Punch

Cigars

Third Term's Work

April 4	Bread	54 orders
	Walnut cake	2 orders
	Snow cake	2 orders
	Custards	3 orders
	Cottage cheese	3 orders

April 4
Sugared beets
Shortcake.................................2 orders
Griddle cakes
Gems
Cup cakes.................................2 orders
Tarts
Cinnamon rolls
Cream toast
Dropped egg on toast
Ginger puffs..............................2 orders
Popovers
Potato croquettes.........................1 order
Cereal
Turkish pilaff
Fried mush
Caramel sauce
Macaroni
Molasses doughnuts........................1 order
Cottage pudding...........................1 order
Coffee gelatine
Hermits
Dandelions and potatoes...................1 order
Sugar cookies.............................1 order
Potato salad..............................1 order
Meats
Invalid cookery...........................Hospital

May 19

Practical test every other week on baking-powder biscuits, cake, cookies, doughnuts, gems, bread, and coffee.

Review of foods, beef creature, vegetables, and household accounts.

LUNCHEONS

February 14 (*Red color scheme*)

ST. VALENTINE'S LUNCHEON
TO
BERLIN HIGH SCHOOL ORCHESTRA

Tomato Soup Crisp Crackers
Veal Loaf Mashed Potato String Beans
Bow Knots Nut Bread
Cranberry Jelly
Asparagus on Toast
Vanilla Ice Cream Maraschino Sauce Cake

March 3

LUNCHEON TO LEGISLATIVE COMMITTEE
ON
NORMAL SCHOOLS

Sago Soup Crisp Crackers
Bean Pot Roast Brown Gravy Mashed Potato
Fish à la Rarebit String Beans Piccalilli

Shamrock Rolls Entire Wheat Bread
Spiced Blackberries
Washington Pie Sour Cream Pie
Coffee

March 16

LUNCHEON TO HIGH-SCHOOL FACULTY

Cream of Tomato Soup Crisp Crackers
Stuffed Steak Brown Gravy Potato Croquettes
Chopped Pickles Piccalilli
Baking-Powder Biscuits
Ginger Bread and Whipped Cream Coffee

March 17 (*Green color scheme*)

LUNCHEON TO SOPHOMORE D.A. GIRLS AND TEACHER,
PLANNED WITHOUT ANY ASSISTANCE OR INSTRUCTIONS

Split Pea Soup Croutons
Scalloped Oysters Potato Croquettes
Chopped Pickles Shamrock Rolls
Pistachio Ice Cream Frosted Cake
Coffee

April 8

LUNCHEON TO BATES GLEE AND MANDOLIN CLUB

Soup Croutons
Lamb Croquettes Tomato Sauce Piccalilli
Mashed Potato Sugared Beets
Entire Wheat Bread
Pineapple Shortcake Coffee

April 26

SPRING LUNCHEON TO FRESHMEN D.A. GIRLS AND TEACHER, PLANNED AND PREPARED WITHOUT ANY ASSISTANCE OR INSTRUCTIONS

Vegetable Soup Crisp Crackers
Veal Croquettes Mashed Potato Cucumbers
Nut Bread Shamrock Rolls
Strawberries and Cream Cake
Coffee

May 10

BOARD OF EDUCATION LUNCHEON

Tomato Bisque Crisp Crackers
Roast Beef Brown Gravy Cucumbers
Baking-Powder Biscuits Nut Bread
Cheese Macaroni Timbales
Green Tomato Preserve
Strawberry Short Cake Coffee

May 11

"WARMED OVER" LUNCHEON

Clear Tomato Soup Croutons
Beef and Rice Croquettes Brown Sauce
Baked Cheese Macaroni
Baking-Powder Biscuits
Nut Bread Piccalilli
Sour Cream Pie Coffee

STUDIES IN THE PRINCIPLES OF EDUCATION

CHARLES H. JUDD
The University of Chicago

IV. EDUCATION ACCORDING TO NATURE

Various influences have operated to make very popular the doctrine that education should follow as closely as possible the dictates of nature. This doctrine is advocated first by those who would overcome formalism of all types. Thus, Rousseau advocated a return to nature as a solution of the difficulties which he found in the artificial, stilted schools of his time. Others adopt the formula, "education according to nature," because of their studies in science. Biology has made it clear that human beings, like animals, must progress by the natural processes of evolution. Psychology has made it clear that mental processes, like the processes in the physical world, proceed according to certain definite laws. The experiences of modern life in all directions have shown that conformity to natural law is the only possible basis for successful operation in any line. It would be impossible in this generation, when biology and psychology are accepted as the foundations of educational practice, to advance any such doctrine as that which the Puritans advanced, when they asserted that the child is naturally evil and in need of a change in his nature.

The validity of the general doctrine will hardly be called into question by anyone. Interpretation of the doctrine is, however, difficult. For the purpose of excluding one very common interpretation of the doctrine, let us point out that Rousseau, in many passages, meant by "nature" physical nature, or the objects of the external world. He wished to have the young child brought into contact with the experiences which he encounters in the open fields. Rousseau wished the boy to study astronomy and magnetism and other facts of the physical world. "Nature" as used in this connection, is not the nature of the child, but rather the physical materials for imagery and thought. It would be entirely legitimate to discuss the importance of concrete experiences in education, and undoubtedly Rousseau's teachings have done much to promote the development of concrete education in the modern schools. But this interpretation of the word "nature" is narrow.

The most fundamental doctrine of Rousseau's book is in no wise connected with his frequent references to the physical world. And when the general statement is made that we should follow nature in our educational practices, the ordinary advocate of the doctrine does not mean to lay emphasis on the objects which can be used to promote concrete education, but rather he wishes to call attention to the necessity of conforming to the natural laws of the individual's development and mental activity. We shall discuss, therefore, this general principle, that education should follow the natural laws of individual development, if it is to be successful.

When stated in this form, the doctrine can be illustrated by a number of definite statements that are to be found in all of our modern educational treatises. Perhaps the best single illustration of the application of this principle is to be found in the statement that play is a suitable model upon which to pattern all educational activities.

In the minds of many who make this statement, play is conceived to be a definite form of behavior, which is natural and which gives the child pleasure. Freedom, activity, spontaneity, and concentration are attributes of play which are praised as worthy of emulation. Examples are cited of the natural development of animals, and the fact is brought out that the animals have no other type of education, and yet acquire the highest forms of skill in their activities.

Even a cursory examination of the facts of play makes it clear that the virtues of play cannot be cultivated in individual experience by regarding play as a single act, to be repeated again and again in the same form. Play is a progressive series of developments. Without attempting any exhaustive classsification, one can call attention to the fact that the earliest plays of children are purely individualistic forms of exercise of the organs of sense and of the muscles. Somewhat later there enters the enjoyment of social competitions and associations, when the child begins to feel the pleasure of companionship. This develops in turn into definite forms of group activity, which are characteristic of the adolescent period. Still later these forms of social play evolve into elaborate games, in which conformity to a set of rules and to ideal requirements constitute the real source of enjoyment.

Such a catalogue of the different stages of play shows that the principle of evolution is here in operation, and that no play activity can be regarded as natural which does not change both its content and its purpose. The adult who enjoys a game of chess is certainly not carrying on the same natural activities as the child who enjoys looking at a bright object because of its color and form. The chess game has more intellectual content than any of the simpler activities of the child's life, and it is for this reason that it gives the kind of pleasure which is satisfactory to the adult. Play is therefore not a natural form of activity in any one of its single types. It is natural at different stages of individual development to play in different ways. There is no sense in which it can be said that the same type of play is natural at all stages of individual development.

The most significant fact, therefore, that can be brought out with regard to nature is that nature is always substituting a higher form of activity for a more primitive type of activity. The general principle that we should follow nature gives us no clue as to exactly what is natural at different stages.

The discovery of what is natural at a higher level of development always depends upon a careful scrutiny of that which is preparatory to the stage under discussion. For example, it has been pointed out in many educational discussions, that at a certain age children learn to read or learn to use numbers very rapidly, whereas at an earlier stage they learn with very great difficulty. It has been argued therefore that no effort should be made at the earlier stage to develop these activities, because it is assumed that these activities will come spontaneously at the later age. There is a fundamental fallacy involved in such an argument. The later stage in any such development comes because of a previous development which has been going on. This antecedent development has had some content and it has been brought about by the effort which has been made to master this content. If we should assume that the same degree of maturity would be attained by the pupil without any systematic training, we should find ourselves relying upon nature to do a work which has in all of the observed cases been worked out by nature through the use of some preliminary activity of a lower type, applied to some kind of content. Thus when it is assumed that a child will become interested at a certain age in reading or in number work, we should not forget that this interest is due to his growing contact with people and materials in school. Perhaps the pupil has been getting some training in oral work; he has listened to the reading of stories, and has, through a mastery of these simpler forms of expression, reached a stage where his interest in expression is sufficiently mature so that he will devote himself with concentration to the task of reading. In such a case the ability to concentrate upon reading is the outgrowth of the earlier concentrations upon oral content. If the child had been allowed to dissipate his mental energy upon the indifferent experiences of ordinary life and had never been attracted to expression as a subject of concentrated attention, he might have progressed in a perfectly natural way to a wholly different type of interest. The street gamin and the savage boy are no less natural in their development away from books than is the boy of a civilized family who is interested in books. In the same way the use of numbers can be fostered in a variety of different ways. It is possible to induce a child to be interested in the use of numbers by giving him some occasion to use numbers in shopwork or in other concrete activities. It is possible to train a child to use numbers by giving him the more elementary stages of arithmetic. The question of which is more natural is a difficult if not an impossible question to answer. Certainly the general principle that we should follow nature does not help us in choosing between these two methods of procedure. Both methods have as a matter of fact carried pupils toward that intellectual maturity which makes possible the mastery of later phases of the subject. To assume that the pupil has simply grown up to the point where he can master arithmetic fails to recognize this past history through which he has been developing the maturity that he now employs.

Some educational writers have used the term "nascent period" and have pointed out that there is an analogy between intellectual development and the development of instincts. They have argued that there are certain instincts which mature without any effort on the part of the individual. These instincts begin to express themselves at a certain time in pleasureable forms of activity. In the same fashion they say it would be possible for us to take advantage of the critical periods in the intellectual development of children. Let us wait, they say, for the natural powers to mature; we shall find that through sheer maturity it will become possible for the child to master without any great effort on his own part the later problems in arithmetic or in any other line. Before one relies on this analogy, he should recognize that the nascent period of an instinct is not a period of spontaneous appearance of something for which there has been no preparation in the earlier stages. An instinct matures because specific physical developments have been going forward. The nervous tissues have been maturing and the muscular structures which are involved have reached the stage of growth and power where they can execute the movements that are needed for the life of the animal. There is no nascent period without an antecedent development on the part of the individual. In this same sense we may look for nascent periods in intellectual life. There must be a maturing of the nervous system, and this development of the nervous system undoubtedly involves structural growth. Furthermore, intellectual development also involves the maturing of certain simpler intellectual powers, exactly as the maturing of an instinct involves the development of the muscles which are to act in instinctive performance. These simpler intellectual powers will not appear if they are not cultivated any more than the muscular development essential to the maturing of an instinct would show itself if there had not been some simpler form of muscular behavior antecedent to the instinct under discussion. The nascent period in arithmetic will not appear if there has been no exercise of the simpler intellectual powers which enter into the number ideas. If the simpler intellectual powers are given, there will be a progressive evolution toward the higher form of activity. The mistake which has sometimes been made in the use of the term "nascent period" is the mistake of assuming that this nascent period comes of itself, without definite antecedents and without any effort on the part of the individual or of society. Observation shows how futile is the hope that children will spontaneously grow up into good spellers or good mathematicians. These complex arts are mastered only when progressive development in conformity with psychological laws is provided. Nature does not solve the educational problem unaided by antecedent exercise.

There is another fundamental mistake which is sometimes made when we overlook the progressive character of natural processes. The teacher very frequently gives instruction at a late stage of development in a way which is exactly like that in which instruction is given at an earlier stage. Thus in arithmetic we very frequently call upon children to go through the whole elaborate process, even after they have mastered the process very fully and have repeated it on numerous occasions. When the process of addition is mastered, it tends to become shorter and simpler. Unnecessary steps of the process tend to disappear, and the whole mental activity, if it is properly maturing, reduces itself, as does any habitual performance, to the lowest possible terms. It is a mistake to require of the child who has reached this later stage of maturity the same degree of explicit attention to the operations as that through which he is passing when he first began to add. If we use the analogy of play we are fully aware that we do not require, in playing a game, that the simplest stages of the game be worked out with elaborate detail after one has become an expert. To follow nature in allowing processes to change is very wholesome advice. Nature is progressive to such an extent that the great difficulty in educational activities is to keep pace with nature and understand the stages through which nature carries the developing individual.

The major consideration which grows out of any analysis of play, as an example to be followed by the educator, is that in mature human life play becomes more and more intellectual in character. This fact is paralleled in the animal world by the fact that play disappears in later life, giving way for the most part to the serious engagements of adult activity. That play does not disappear from human life, but develops into art and the other elaborate forms of intellectual enjoyment, ought to make it perfectly clear to the advocates of nature in education that they have no right to ignore the intellectual outgrowths of play in the study of the educational problem. Not only does adult human life exhibit the highest intellectualization of play, but it exhibits also the highest intellectualization of the other activities in which the adult must engage. His work, if he carries it on to the highest development, will be arranged and ordered in terms of motives that are clearly thought out and which represent his highest intellectual development. The preparation for this intellectualization of play and work is to be found in certain forms of training which are in no wise opposed to nature in the earliest stages, but which go beyond that which would be suggested to the individual if he were left to his own immediate devices. Thus there is a sense in which a child would not naturally turn to reading. This is what Rousseau pointed out when he held that reading was unnatural for the young child, that the child should get all of his experiences from direct contact with the physical world. Reading is not the spontaneous form of activity that the child ordinarily exhibits. Rousseau makes the assumption, however, that in later life reading will come naturally. He forgets the street gamin and the savage. He assumes the later development of an ordinary schoolboy without allowing his ideal boy the antecedent experiences which lead this schoolboy to reading.

From the point of view of nature as we have defined it in this paper, the demand that the child mature into a good reader throws an obligation upon the early years of the child's life, namely, the obligation that there be some kind of antecedent activity which will lead up to fluent reading. Education is therefore in such a case as this an anticipation of some of the activities which show themselves to be important at a later stage in the individual's life. Such preparation is in no sense of the word opposed to nature. It is the highest recognition of the possibilities of natural development, in such a case as this, to anticipate later demands by appropriate forms of training.

Indeed, any study of human civilization will show that man

has used nature most effectively by anticipating the demands of nature. Thus in order to make the fullest use of water power man has thrown a dam across the river. It is not unnatural to build a dam across a river, and yet it is wholly out of keeping with that which nature would present to an unintellectual individual. To build a house is not unnatural in any proper sense of the word, and yet to build a house is not in keeping with that which nature spontaneously presents. The building of a dam and the building of a house must both of them be carried on with due recognition of the natural laws of physics, and yet these laws have been utilized in both of these cases for a complete mastery of the environment and for the creation of an environment which is more advantageous to man than that which is presented at the beginning by nature herself. So it is in the development of the individual. We cannot train the child without due recognition of the laws of his own mental life, and yet it is possible so to surround the individual child with advantageous conditions and so to promote his intellectual activities that we shall have a suitable readjustment of his life and a higher advantage to him and to society from a development of nature along directed lines. To direct nature is not unnatural. Slavishly to follow nature from moment to moment is not in keeping with the lesson that one learns as he studies the whole process of evolution, because nature herself progressively modifies the character of every operation. The animal forms have gradually evolved into higher forms. There is no limit in nature upon the changes which may be brought about by evolution. The chief lesson of biology to education is that change should be made as rapidly as it can be made in the direction of more complete adaptation. The whole problem of human education is a problem of accelerated adaptation. To take a child away from his first impulses and give him those forms of reaction which will be advantageous to him in the complex environment of civilized life is natural in the highest degree. It is this direction of his impulses into new channels which constitutes the educational process whereby we supplement nature and bring nature to its highest realization.

When one has thus discussed the principle of education according to nature, he finds that the formula is not very helpful in detail in organizing education, nor is it a suitable weapon with which to criticize any of our current practices. As one reads educational literature he finds that nature has been used as a justification for almost every conceivable practice. We have been told that nature dictates the relatively late teaching of reading. We have been told on the other hand that nature dictates the early training of the child in reading. We have been told that nature calls for a training, first of the large muscles, and we have been told on the other hand that nature calls for a recognition of the finer co-ordinations as necessary even in the early life of the child. The fact is that there is no form of training which is outside of the general domain of nature. Even error is in some sense natural. The problem of discovering what is advantageous is not solved by a superficial inspection of what seems to be natural. The one great lesson which comes to us from biology and psychology is the lesson that we shall make a mistake if we let a child continue for any length of time at the level at which we find him at this moment. What is natural today at the present level of development is utterly unnatural and abnormal tomorrow. Nature is first of all progressive and adaptive. Our problem is to find out the most economical method of promoting change in the direction of adaptation as rapidly as possible.

EXPERIMENTAL SCHOOLS IN GERMANY IN THE EIGHTEENTH CENTURY[1]

S. CHESTER PARKER
The University of Chicago

Experimental schools have influenced educational opinion.—The influence of small schools which have been organized to determine experimentally or to demonstrate practically the best methods of teaching has been an important factor in the history of education. In recent years the most notable example of such a school in America was the small laboratory school conducted by Professor John Dewey in connection with the Department of Philosophy of the University of Chicago, beginning in 1896. The statement of the theory and work of this school in Dewey's *School and Society* has been one of the largest factors in recent years in stimulating a reconstruction of American thought about education. The model and experimental kindergartens conducted by Froebel after 1837 in Germany, and especially the schools of Pestalozzi at Burgdorf (1800–1804) and at Yverdon (1805–25) and of Fellenberg at Hofwyl (1806–1844) in Switzerland are other examples of the widespread influence which practical experimentation on a small scale may have. Before Pestalozzi organized his schools, there was a very important and influential movement organized in Germany to carry out some of the practical reforms in methods of teaching which had been suggested in Rousseau's *Emile*. These reforms were successfully realized in certain experimental schools, one of which (Salzman's) continued in operation for over a century. In this school, methods of instruction in connection with physical education, nature-study, school gardening, geographical and other

[1] In the last two volumes of the *Elementary School Teacher*, a number of articles appeared which were intended to illustrate a method of teaching the history of education by emphasizing school practice in its relation to social conditions. This is the eighth article in this series. A textbook entitled *A History of Modern Elementary Education*, constructed on these principles by the same author, will appear in the near future.

excursions, etc., were organized, probably more effectively than in any school since that time. The initial agitation for this movement, in connection with the work of Basedow, is ordinarily discussed in the histories of education, but its practical culmination in the work of German schools is generally neglected. In view of this fact, a brief description will be presented here, of the whole development which began primarily as a reaction against the narrow, sectarian, religious spirit which dominated the work of German elementary schools.

Agitation for non-sectarian, national education.—Johann Bernard Basedow (1723–90), the leading agitator in this movement, was a relatively mediocre thinker. But moved by fanatical opposition to the narrow-minded sectarianism which prevailed in German thought and education during the eighteenth century, he succeeded in uniting various secular interests by an appeal to public-spirited philanthropists to contribute funds which would furnish the means of opening and conducting schools on a reformed basis.

The same kind of attack as was made by Voltaire and Rousseau in France on the insincerity, the formalism, and other evils of the narrow, sectarian, religious spirit which prevailed, was carried on in Germany by a number of famous university professors. Basedow was one of the minor combatants in this clash of the orthodox and reform religious forces. As professor in a Danish academy he delivered lectures on theology. His lectures and certain publications in which he maintained a sort of natural religion and combated definitely many of the sectarian beliefs, got him into controversies with his colleagues and the public authorities. In the chief cities, Hamburg, Lübeck, and Altona, his writings were condemned in 1764 as containing religious beliefs contrary to the official catechism.

Appeal for subscriptions to provide secular education.—Tiring of religious controversy, and taking advantage of the interest in education which the appearance of Rousseau's *Emile* had created, Basedow issued in 1768 an *Address to Philanthropists and Men of Property on Schools and Studies and Their Influence on the Public Weal.* In this address he appealed for funds to enable him to prepare textbooks and to organize a school which would provide a kind of education quite different from that given in the contemporary schools which were dominated by the orthodox clergy. There were two striking suggestions in this appeal; namely, (1) that the schools should be open to children of all religions, that it should be non-sectarian; (2) that a national council of education should be established which should have charge of all public instruction. In addition to these points, the appeal advocated a type of education including reform proposals taken from many sources; from Locke that education should be practical and playful, from Comenius that it should be based on a study of pictures, from Locke and Rousseau that it should include a large amount of physical exercise, etc.

Model books and an unsuccessful school.—The appeal met with unprecedented success and subscriptions flowed in from Protestants, Catholics, and Jews, from lodges of Free Masons, from the noble, the wealthy, and often the poor of all countries, who were interested primarily in the possibility of an education which would be free from the restrictions of sectarian narrowness. With the aid of these funds Basedow published a book on method, and a manual of information for use in the schools which was accompanied by a volume containing one hundred engraved pictures illustrative of the scientific and practical subjects discussed in the manual. These books enjoyed an astounding and flattering success, and were widely praised. In 1774 Basedow opened his model school, called the Philanthropinum, at Dessau. This was never very large or very successful, owing to Basedow's incompetence, his vicious habits, and his inability to get on with his assistants.

Philanthropinums became an educational fad.—The popularity of Basedow's publications resulted in a fad in Germany for the establishment of Philanthropinums. In the large cities, advertising signs stating "Here is a Philanthropinum" (Allhier ist ein Philanthropinum) were common. Many of these were ridiculous frauds, and were appropriately satirized by contemporary writers. On the other hand, some of these schools, in France and Switzerland as well as in Germany, were serious and successful attempts to carry out Basedow's plans, and they continued their intelligent experimentation down to the time of the influence of Pestalozzi.

A model secular school for children of means: Salzman.—The most successful of these schools conducted on Basedow's plans was that of Christian Salzman (1744–1811) who had been employed by Basedow for a short time. As he could not get along with Basedow, Salzman decided to establish a school of his own, and after careful investigation chose a site at Schnephenthal in Saxe-Gotha where he enjoyed the sympathetic assistance of the reigning family. He secured an ideal location for his school, on a farm near the Thuringian Forest, in a region with a great variety of physiographic features, including mountains, valleys and plains, lakes, and other possibilities for the study of nature and art.

The school was opened in 1784, and the first pupil was Karl Ritter, who later became the founder of modern geography. Salzman restricted the number of pupils, generally below sixty, in order to maintain the spirit of family life. The pupils arose with the sun, spent a few hours in agricultural work, gardening or tending domestic animals; had morning song in the chapel; breakfasted; spent about eight hours of the day in study, at least one in gymnastics, and several in recreation.

Principles of Rousseau successfully followed.—In addition to providing a certain amount of the traditional school work, many of the most important recommendations of Locke and Rousseau were carried out. Among these innovations were the following:

1. *Much physical training.*—A large amount of physical training, including swimming, skating, etc., was provided. Johann Christoph Friedrich Gutsmuths (1759–1839), "the grandfather of German gymnastics," was instructor at the school for many years.

2. *Nature-study and lessons on things.*—The younger children spent three hours a day in the study of natural history and "lessons on things." The instructor said, "Everyday I go with my children into my scientific laboratory and seek what is most worth studying. My laboratory is nature herself."

3. *School gardening and manual training.*—Each child had his own garden plot for which he was responsible, thus giving training in practical agriculture. In his plan for such a school, Salzman announced that he would have workshops for manual training, but

it is not clear from the accounts that I have consulted that these were provided in actual practice.

4. *Many organized excursions.*—Excursions through the surrounding country were very common. Sometimes these were several days in length. On such occasions the pupils were organized as militia into companies with officers. The cavalry went on ahead to prepare quarters, then followed the baggage wagons, and finally came the infantry. The objective point was always of special geographical, industrial, historical, or scenic interest. The children slept at night on straw. On their return each pupil had to give a description of the excursion in which he told about places passed, adventures, plants, animals and minerals, industries and persons that they had noted. Local history was also emphasized. These descriptions were reviewed and corrected by the teachers.

5. *Religion approached via moral stories and nature-study.*—In the religious instruction, theological aspects such as were included in the ordinary catechism for little children were not taught by Salzman until adolescence. Instead, moral tales which had been very carefully selected and prepared were first told the children and discussed with them as a means of developing ideals of worthy behavior. As the children grew older, these were followed by stories from the Bible, including the life of Christ, with emphasis on his character as an ideal man. Observations and discussions of nature supplemented this moral material, and not until the child was about twelve years of age was he introduced to the mysterious phases of religion. Even then such theological problems as are involved in the atonement, etc., were eliminated.

Prospered for over a century.—These phases of the work, namely, physical training, natural history, object teaching, school gardening, manual training, excursions, and non-theological religious training, show how thoroughly the idea of a secular education adapted to the understanding and needs of children had been carried out in practice by Salzman. The institution prospered under his management to his death in 1811, after which it was continued in successful operation by his descendants, and celebrated its one-hundredth anniversary in 1884; an unusual example of an experimental school of long and happy life, surviving the founder. It served as a model of the possibilities of a better education, anticipating in successful practice most of the reforms of Pestalozzi.

Secular schools for peasant children: Rochow.—The secular schools of Basedow and Salzman were intended primarily as boarding-schools for children of means. But it was not long before the reforms which they embodied were attempted to some extent in the ordinary elementary schools or *Volkschulen*. The first experiment in this direction was tried by Baron von Rochow (1734–1805) in schools which he established for the children of the peasants living on his estates in Prussia.

Distress of peasants to be relieved by education.—He had been an officer in the royal Prussian guard, but had retired on account of injuries and devoted his time to the efficient management of his country estates. He pitied the unfortunate peasants who often suffered from failure of crops, from pestilence, disease, and starvation. This was due in a considerable degree to their own stupidity, ignorance, and improvidence, which rendered them incapable of profiting by the assistance which Rochow offered. During a particularly bad winter it suddenly occurred to Rochow that the only way to improve conditions was by a better and more practical elementary education which would be the basis of more intelligent methods of farming and living. He immediately determined to provide such an education and as a first step wrote (1772) a book intended to aid teachers in carrying out his ideas of reform. The title, *A School Book for Country Children, or for Use in Village School*, is misleading, as it was not a book for children but for teachers. Rochow had been captivated by the early publications of Basedow and reproduced many of the latter's ideas.

Famous model schools for peasant children.—The next step was to open a model school on his farm at Reckahn. As teacher he installed a young man who had lived with him as secretary and musician for six years. The school soon had over seventy pupils and the novelty and success of the instruction attracted visitors from Germany and other countries. The Prussian government sent official investigators to examine the work. All reported very favorably. They were particularly impressed with the ease and skill with which the teacher taught lessons on things to a school of seventy-three children. These lessons were conducted by means of Socratic questions which kept up a continual conversation between teacher and class. In all the instruction, every point was made clear and significant to the children, not by wordy explanations, but by connecting it with their real experience and discussing its application in the practical affairs of their lives.

Changed social life resulted from the new education.—Similar schools were opened by Rochow on his other estates and the influence was soon evident in the changed social life of the region. This change is described by Rochow in these words: "Today at Reckahn, the parents have lost their bestial stupidity, thanks to the influence of the children; they believe in the physicians, rather than the sayings of old women. The mortality has diminished on all my estates. Attendance at school, in summer as well as in winter, is now one of the things that the parents most prize and often they thank me with tears in their eyes."

To assist similar schools in other parts of Germany, Rochow prepared two popular reading-books: *The Peasant's Friend* (1773) and *The Children's Friend* (1775). The latter was very successful and was widely used as a textbook even as late as 1850. It consisted mainly of short instructional stories or discussions relating to agriculture, domestic affairs, and good citizenship. It also contained two rhymed prayers for little children.

Christian morality and national regeneration emphasized, not theology.—Although the main emphasis was on training for practical affairs, Rochow's school was not irreligious. He provided training in Christian morality, however, instead of theology, and criticized severely the dull memorizing of the catechism, which constituted the work of the ordinary elementary school. Consequently he aroused the opposition of the ecclesiastics who tried in vain to discredit his work.

Rochow did not rest satisfied with the local results of his endeavors, but published in 1779 a work entitled *The Improvement of the National Character by Means of Popular Schools* (*Volkschulen*) in which he advocated universal education for national reasons instead of merely religious or utilitarian reasons. "Without a national education," he said, "it is imposssible to have a national character, and that is precisely what is lacking in Germany."

One of the most famous of the visitors to Rochow's school, a very influential German professor, wrote: "To admire and praise the worthy founder of this school is not enough either for me or him. His work should be imitated not only in the Mark of Brandenburg, but also in the whole kingdom." How the king and his minister attempted to establish such a system of national secular schools, with special reference to peasant needs, remains to be described.

Rochow's suggestions coincided with king's plans.—The reforms represented by the efforts of Basedow, Salzman, and Rochow coincided in point of time as well as in spirit with the reforms which the Prussian kings were endeavoring to carry into effect especially in the rural schools. The efforts of Frederick the Great in this direction were particularly significant, and from 1771 on were guided to a considerable extent by a special admirer of Basedow and Rochow, namely, the minister Zedlitz, head of the Department of Lutheran Church and School Affairs. In 1763 Frederick issued his General Code of Regulations for Rural Schools, which made attendance of children compulsory from five to thirteen years of age; provided for inspection of the schools; and set up very definite standards for their improvement.

Effective enforcement of law opposed by public opinion.—In many places, this law could not be effectively enforced, owing to the numerous difficulties. There was opposition from existing teachers who were too ignorant to be eligible under the new requirements. There was opposition from the farmers who wished to use their children for work at home. There was opposition from the nobility who viewed the law with alarm, maintaining that "like cattle, the more stupid the peasant, the better will he accept his fate." In spite of this strenuous opposition, the king was very active in his endeavors to enforce the law which he supplemented by additional orders intended to decrease "the great stupidity of the peasant children."

The control of schools transferred from church to national council of education.—Another step in the development of the Prussian system was the creation of the central administrative board or *Oberschulcollegium*, to have direction of all the school affairs of the kingdom. Although this occurred in 1787, after the death of

Frederick the Great, it represented the culmination of the tendencies of his reign as well as the influence of the Basedow tendencies described in the first part of this paper.

Minister Zedlitz reiterated suggestion of Basedow.—The creation of this board was suggested by the king's minister Zedlitz, who had been made head of the Department of Lutheran Church and School Affairs by Frederick the Great in 1717. A similar suggestion for the creation of such a "national council of education" was contained, as we noticed, in Basedow's *Address to Philanthropists* issued in 1768. Zedlitz was an enthusiastic champion of Basedow's ideas and was especially influenced by Rochow's experiments in applying these ideas to the improvement of rural education. Zedlitz kept up an active correspondence with Rochow and consulted with him concerning many of his own (Zedlitz's) plans for national educational reforms. In 1788, Zedlitz wrote:

> It is wrong to let the peasant grow up like an animal, having him memorize only a few things which are never explained to him. His instruction should include, besides religion, reading, writing, and arithmetic, also some experience with mechanics, the study of nature and dietetic rules, and some knowledge of government. Certain industrial activities like spinning and weaving should also be taught in the country schools.

In his suggestions to the king for the establishment of the *Oberschulcollegium*, Zedlitz said that such a board, with some degree of expert permanent membership, would be much more competent wisely to direct school affairs than were the consistories of the church under the direction of a king's minister as was the existing arrangement. Hence the establishment of the *Oberschulcollegium* represents the transition from church administration of the schools under state direction to expert state administration of the schools.

Zedlitz removed through conservative reaction of new king.—Zedlitz was made president of the new board, but he held his place under the new king for only two years. The latter was directly the opposite of Frederick the Great in his general attitudes. Instead of aiming to broaden and secularize the elementary schools, he maintained that their chief function should continue to be the teaching of religion, and that he would do his best to see that they were protected from the influence of rationalism, naturalism, and deism. Owing to this reaction, no further progress was made in elementary education until the reforms at the beginning of the nineteenth century. But one other step in preparation for this latter development was to be taken.

Fundamental Prussian legal code (1794) defined schools as state institutions. Under Frederick the Great was begun the codification of the fundamental Prussian civil law, known as the *Allgemeine Landrecht.* The greatest scholars and jurists of Germany were engaged in this undertaking, the results of which were not published until 1794. Chapter twelve of the code was devoted to education. In it were formulated the culminating principles of the tendencies which had been developing during the century. Of the 129 sections in this chapter the following are especially significant.

1. Schools and universities are state institutions, charged with the instruction of youth in useful information and scientific knowledge.

2. Such institutions may be founded only with the knowledge and consent of the state.

9. All public schools and educational institutions are under the supervision of the state, and are at all times subject to its examination and inspection.

Basedow movement helped develop superior Prussian schools.—Thus a quarter of a century after Basedow issued his famous *Address to Philanthropists*, we find the Prussian schools established on the legal basis which made it possible for them to become the model schools of Europe during the first half of the nineteenth century; schools with which Horace Mann and all other American visitors compared American schools very unfavorably. The superiority of the Prussian schools is often attributed to their adoption of the Pestalozzian methods, and this was, indeed, an important factor. But it must be remembered that long before Pestalozzi's influence was felt, the Prussian kings were actively engaged in developing improved rural schools, and that the agitation conducted by Basedow, and the model schools of Salzman and Rochow, were important factors in showing the possibilities of improved methods, and in developing public sentiment in favor of a broader elementary education to remove the great stupidity and suffering of the peasants.

THE REORGANIZATION OF SCHOOL SYSTEMS

FRANK M. LEAVITT
The University of Chicago

The readjustment of school organization to the present social and economic conditions is worthy of consideration. On every hand additions to the curriculum mark the concessions which are being made to vocational interests. These additions, however, generally leave untouched the common divisions into elementary and secondary schools of eight and four years respectively, and the present practice of grading on averages, and of advancing the pupils by yearly or semiannual promotions based on such grading.

It is not to be doubted, however, that widespread dissatisfaction exists among educators with what are seen to be purely artificial distinctions and inconsequential practices. More clearly formulated *purposes* are determining the selection of subject-matter, the adoption of methods of instruction, and particularly the arrangement of plans of grading and promotion. In all parts of the country this dissatisfaction is to be noted by the thoughtful experiments which are being inaugurated in school management. In the following pages a few of these experiments are briefly described.

All efforts to reduce preventable retardation are worthy of careful study. Wherever "special classes," so called, classes for mental defectives or delinquents, or ungraded classes of any description are organized, this desirable end is brought nearer realization. These classes, however, are so commonly found in school systems today that no detailed mention of them need be made.

The grading system has been quite generally based on the supposition that a certain amount of school work should be accomplished in a definite period, and the *unit* of time has commonly been one year. Under this system, the pupil who is "retarded" usually, albeit with numerous individual exceptions, repeats the entire year's work.

While in many cities promotions are now made semiannually and elements of flexibility are being introduced into school grading generally, it is probably within the facts to consider yearly promotions to be the plan which commonly obtains in the United States. In a few instances only have efforts been made to modify this practice radically. One of these examples is cited herewith.

PORTLAND, OREGON

The systems of promotion which have been in operation in Cambridge, Massachusetts, and St. Louis, Missouri, for so many years are too well known to require more than a passing mention. Less widely known is the plan which is followed in Portland, Oregon. Regarding grading and promotions in the schools in that city, Mr. Frank Rigler, city superintendent of schools, says:

The course of study is divided into fifty-four parts, numbered continuously from one to fifty-four. The time is divided into terms of five months each, promotions taking place regularly at the end of each term. Three terms, or one and one-half years, constitute what we for convenience call a cycle. Classes are permitted to progress at whatever rate is found suitable to their powers. But the two standard rates are three parts per term for second divisions and four parts per term for first divisions.

The normal class interval at the beginning of a cycle is three parts of the course of study, measured not in time but in work. In large schools the class interval is often only two parts of the course. Sometimes in the lower classes only one part of the course.

At the beginning of each cycle, any group of pupils who have reached the same point in the course of study is separated into a first and second division. By the end of the first term, the first divisions will have passed over four parts of the course of study, and the second divisions over only three. By the end of the second term, the first divisions will have passed over eight parts of the course of study and the second divisions over only six. At the end of the third term the first divisions will have advanced twelve parts and the second divisions only nine. It will be seen now that each first division has overtaken the second division next above it. In the new cycle these two divisions are united and again divided. In this redivision, some of the pupils that did first-division work during the preceding cycle are put into a second division, and some who did second-division work are put into a first division.

In every school-room there are two divisions progressing at different rates. Where the more advanced is a first division, the classes are said to be "diverging," i.e., the interval between them is increasing. Early in the cycle this is the condition in most school-rooms, but in the third term of the cycle, we try as far as possible to have first divisions roomed with second divisions which are in advance of them. Such classes are said to be "converging," i.e., the interval between them is diminishing.

In the exigencies of rooming it is sometimes necessary to make up a "division" by taking the stronger members of a first division and classing them with the weaker ones of a second division who are one or one and one-half parts in advance of them. In such cases the division commences its work at the point already reached by its stronger members. The interval of one or one and one-half parts can thus be passed over very rapidly, being review for the weak ones and new work for very strong pupils.

Such emergency divisions, however, do not usually continue more than a term. By that time the strong pupils have outstripped the weak and they are then classed with the strongest members of the same second divisions whose weaker members they have just passed, their place being taken by the middle section of the same division.

An important feature of our system of classification is promotion by subjects instead of by "averages." A pupil may do "first" division work in one subject and "second" division work in another. Sometimes he will have to recite part of his work in one room and part in another, but no inconvenience need result from this. In fact, it is an advantage in rooming, as we can make his headquarters in the less crowded of the two rooms.

Under the Portland plan, a pupil who does first division work during his entire life in the elementary school will be prepared for high-school work in seven years. A pupil who does second division work all the time will require nine years to complete the elementary course. We find that perhaps a third of the pupils require this time and they get it with us, not by failing once or twice and repeating some particular part of the course, but by doing somewhat less work each term for the entire nine years. Our first division proceeds one and one-third times as rapidly as our second division, or one and one-eighth times as rapidly as the normal class in the orthodox eight-grades system.

Fully half of our pupils are able to maintain this rate throughout the course, without detriment to their health and without much home study. A considerable number do part first and second division work, and thus complete the elementary course in seven and one-half, eight, or eight and one-half years.

CHICAGO, ILLINOIS

The vacation period is coming to be regarded as an opportunity for giving such additional attention to retarded children as will permit them to regain their grade and thus to avoid the discouragement of repeating the work of a semester or a year.

Experiments intended to reduce the amount of retardation in both the elementary and the high school were inaugurated in the Chicago public schools in the summer of 1911.

There were administered in connection with three of the vacation schools, although in a measure independently of them, what were styled "Review Schools." Classes were formed for grades five, six, seven, and eight, and were open to children recommended by principals of the elementary schools as being able to profit by such work.

To be eligible for membership in these classes a child must have failed of promotion the preceding year, but at the same time must have shown some ability to recover his grade by the extra work of the summer session. The measure of success was to be determined by an examination given by the principal of the elementary school on the return of the children in September.

Three such review schools were in session for six weeks of the summer vacation on four mornings a week from nine till twelve o'clock.

Summer high-school classes, for pupils who had failed during the preceding year in one or more studies, were organized in the Wendell Phillips High School.

The classes received two lessons a day in each subject, with a study hour between, and were thus enabled, with ten recitations a week, to cover in five weeks the work of a quarter, or what amounted to a complete review of a semester's work.

No pupil was permitted to enter the school for the purpose of doing advanced work.

Partly as an experiment and partly because of financial conditions, a tuition fee of $10 was charged each pupil. This fact is thought to have some bearing on the measure of success attending the venture. Two hundred and ten pupils were registered in these classes and 89 per cent passed in one or more subjects.

The tuition fees practically covered all expenses.

It is expected that the review schools will become an integral part of the Chicago school system.

CLEVELAND, OHIO

Beginning with the summer of 1911, the entire school system of Cleveland was reorganized on a quarterly plan of four terms of approximately three months each, there being only a brief vacation between the quarters.

While this reorganization involves many educational questions, it is of interest in this connection because the schools were open during the first summer quarter only to pupils who were below grade. There were about 10,000 such pupils in the city, about 5,000 of whom enrolled for the summer quarter. This, therefore, may properly be considered another plan for reducing retardation.

BERKELEY, CALIFORNIA

Examples of a more fundamental reorganization of school systems are to be found in the plans of Berkeley, Cal., and Concord, N.H.

The plan of organization described below has been in operation in the Berkeley schools for two years with marked and salutary effect on the retention of pupils.

The units of the school system are three in number instead of the conventional two. The first, the Elementary School, comprises the first six years; the second, the Lower High School, the seventh, eighth, and ninth years; and the third, the Upper High School, the tenth, eleventh, and twelfth years.

While satisfactory completion of the work of the first or second unit confers eligibility for the next higher grade, the main emphasis is not placed on *preparation*, with the higher school as a goal. Instead, the work of each unit is based on the assumption that *all* the children *might* leave school at the end of that particular cycle of work. Mr. Frank F. Bunker, superintendent of city schools, says that he is willing to contend that such a plan results, "not only in the best possible preparation for those who drop out, but likewise the best possible preparation for those who go on from grade to grade, finally entering the university." In a report to the Board of Education recommending the adoption of the plan, Mr. Bunker said:

An examination of this plan will convince one, I think, that the division of the grades into three groups is a much more natural one than the arrangement under which we are now working with a division of the grades into two groups only.

Statistics show that the masses are held in school no longer than through the fifth grade, and that at the close of the fifth grade they drop out in very large numbers, which means, educationally, that whatever is to be taught to the masses must be given in the first five or six years.

In the schools comprising this group of the first six years, I would have the course of study uniform for all children and somewhat narrow in its scope. I would see to it that emphasis is placed on those things which the masses must have if they get on at all. I would see to it that, whether or not anything else were gotten, at least the children learn how to read, how to write, how to use their own language, both orally and in written form, how to perform with facility and accuracy the simple operations of arithmetic and of accounting, and I would also see to it that in these first six years they get somewhat of a sympathetic knowledge of their city, state, and national government, and that they also learn the elementary things about sanitation and health conditions which everybody needs to know, not only to protect themselves as individuals, but to protect society as well. I would select from the corps for work in these first six years teachers who are particularly adapted to handling children of this early age and to inculcating the content which I have just outlined.

In the "Introductory High Schools" there would be congregated the seventh, eighth, and ninth years. These years comprise another natural group, inasmuch as children would enter it at the beginning of the period of adolescence, when by nature they naturally crave an opportunity to dip into a wide range of subjects and activities, which is Nature's way of insuring a freedom of choice in determining occupation and somewhat of intelligence in the same. I would have certain prescribed subjects for this group, but in addition thereto would permit as many electives as possible, thus making it unnecessary, as at present, for every child in the seventh and eighth grades to take exactly the same work as every other child. In contrast to the work of the first six years, I should wish to see the work of this group made exceedingly rich in content and variety, and particularly in human interest. I should hope to see the work of this group relate very closely to life and be as far away as possible from that which is purely academic in education. I should wish much emphasis placed on learning how to study, how to use the library, how to get material from the same with expedition and with judgment. If a child foresees that he wants to take German or Latin in the high school proper, I would wish him to begin these languages when he enters this group and thus have six years of work in the same before he enters college instead of four as according to our present arrangement. I should wish to see the work of this group shaped up to make a more easy transition from the work of the elementary grades to the departmental work of the high school. In line with this I should wish teachers assigned to work in these grades who have a broad culture and wide experience in teaching in the grades.

By an arrangement of this kind it would seem that the work of the high school proper could be made more intensive than it is at the present time with higher standards of scholarship and more rigid requirements than at present obtain, and without working any hardship upon the young people who enter the same, for it would seem that if this work which I have outlined be carefully and efficiently done, that the incoming student will have developed a much more serious attitude toward his work than obtains at the present time; will have oriented himself better, so far as his subjects are concerned, and that the break will not be so great or so discouraging as with the plan under which we are now working.

It is evident that the crucial point of this unique organization is to be found in the Lower High School, and the plan commends itself for the reason that this period of school life coincides very closely with that period of youth which is, perhaps, the most difficult for the teacher to understand and, therefore, the one where the pupils suffer most from misdirected effort on their own part and also on the part of their teachers. In this system of schools the major purpose of the intermediate unit is one of adjustment.

Among other opportunities offered in this "trying out" period is the possibility of selecting studies which appeal to the awakening vocational interests of some of the pupils. Thus far the vocational subjects offered have been commercial rather than industrial, but, in such a community as Berkeley, this is perhaps all that could reasonably be expected in the second year of such an important transition.

CONCORD, NEW HAMPSHIRE

The reorganized school system of Concord consists of three units or groups, which are numbered in the reverse order of the grades or years in school.

Group 3, the elementary group, comprises the first six grades; Group 2, the lower of the secondary groups, comprises the seventh and eighth years, and Group 1, the ninth, tenth, and eleventh years, or the high school proper.

The plan is thus similar to that of Berkeley, with the important difference that, by the Concord plan, an attempt is made to save a year's time. It is believed that this is made possible by eliminating reduplication which so frequently obtains in the last elementary and the first high-school year of the traditional school system.

As carried out, the plan actually provides greater opportunity for differentiation than is found in Berkeley, as will be seen by referring to the following course of study for 1911–12.

ELEMENTARY SCHOOLS—GROUP 3

		Reading	Spelling	Arith-metic	Language	History	Geog-raphy	Hygiene	Penman-ship
6th Yr. 6	L	"	"	"	"	"	"	"	"
	K	"	"	"	"	"	"	"	"
5th Yr. 5	J	"	"	"	"	"	"	"	"
	I	"	"	"	"	"	"	"	"
4th Yr. 4	H	"	"	"	"	"	"	"	"
	G	"	"	"	"	"	"	"	"
3d Yr. 3	F	"	"	"	"	"	"	"	"
	E	"	"	"	"	"	"	"	"
2d Yr. 2	D	"	"	"	*	"	*	"	"
	C	"	"	"	*	"	*	"	"
1st Yr. 1	B	"	*	"	*	"	*	"	"
	A	"	*	"	*	"	*	"	"

* Shows that the subject is not taken in this group.

KINDERGARTEN—ELECTIVE

Manual training—Woodwork, classes K and L—for boys.
Sewing, classes, I, J, K, L—for girls.
Music and drawing—All classes throughout the entire elementary course.
Ethics and nature-study—One period a week for fifteen minutes in *all* classes to K.
Physical exercises—Throughout the entire course.
No pupil below the age of five years can enter class A.
The age of pupils for kindergartens is from four to six years.
Parents are urged to continue children in the Kindergarten until the age of six years, because those pupils entering *class A* at five years of age are usually retarded a year on account of immaturity.
Parents are also urged to continue their children in school through class L, rather than send them to work before completing the elementary-school course.
Promotions—The class letters of each group represent nineteen weeks of school work. At the end of this time promotion to the succeeding class occurs. The figures indicate the years of school work. The years written at the left of each group indicate the number of the year in that group. It is often desirable for pupils to repeat class work of nineteen weeks, and parents are urged to co-operate with the teachers whenever this repetition seems necessary.

HIGH SCHOOL—GROUP 2

			Course I	Course II	Course III
Second Year	8	P	English 5 Algebra 5 Ancient History 5 *Choose One* Latin 5 French 5	English 5 Algebra 5 Commercial History 5 Commercial Geography 4 Penmanship (2) 1	English 5 Algebra 5 Ancient History 5 Mechanical Drawing, boys (4) 2 Free-hand Drawing, girls Advanced Woodworking, Cabinet Making, Turning, boys (8) 4 Domestic Science, Sewing, girls
		O	"	"	"
First Year	7	N	English Literature 5 Algebra 5 Latin 5 U.S. History 5 Manual Training 3	English Literature 5 Algebra 5 English Grammar and Composition 5 U.S. History 5 Penmanship (2) 1 Manual Training—Cooking—Sewing 3	English Literature 5 Algebra 5 English Grammar U.S. History 5 Penmanship 2 Elementary Cabinet Work, boys 3 Sewing, Cooking, girls
		M	English Literature 5 Arithmetic 5 English Grammar and Composition 5 U.S. History 5 Manual Training, Cooking and Sewing (4) 2	English Literature 5 Arithmetic 5 English Grammar and Composition 5 U.S. History 5 Penmanship (2) 1 Manual Training—Cooking—Sewing (4) 2	English Literature 5 Arithmetic 5 English Grammar 5 U.S. History 5 Penmanship (2) 1 Manual Training, boys (4) 2 Sewing, Cooking, girls

Military drill is required twice a week of all the boys in group 1.
Music may be elected one period a week in any course in group 1. Required in all other groups.
Drawing may be elected two periods a week in courses I and II.
Manual training and domestic science may be elected two periods a week in addition to work in courses I and II.
All electives are subject to arrangement of program.
The arrangement of studies in courses is designed to assist students in choosing their subjects so that each may follow out some definite line of work.
Students who intend to enter college should decide before entering class N.

Students are expected to take the full work of one course beginning with class N and thus secure a diploma.

To secure promotion to class N, 10 points are required; to class O, 20 points; to class P, 30; to class Q, 40; to class R, 50; to class S, 60; to class T, 70; to class U, 80; to class V, 90; to graduate, 100 points.

The numerals following subjects in the courses show the number of weekly recitations and the value in points of each study.

HIGH SCHOOL GROUP I

			Course I. Classical and English	Course II. Commercial	Course III. Mechanic Arts
Third Year	11	V	English 4 U.S. History and Civics 4 *Choose Three* Latin 5 Greek 5 French 5 German 5 Review Mathematics 4 Advance Mathematics 4 Chemistry 5	English 4 U.S. History and Civics 4 Bookkeeping ½ yr. 4 Banking ½ yr. Economics ½ yr. 4 Commercial Law ½ yr. *Choose One* French 5 Chemistry 5 Stenography 4 Typewriting (4) 2	English 4 U.S. History and Civics 4 Chemistry 5 Mechanical Drawing, boys (4) 2 Free-Hand Drawing, girls Machine Shop Practice, Advance Mechanics, boys (8) 4 Household Economy, Sewing, girls *Choose One* French 5 Review Mathematics 4
		U	"	"	"
Second Year	10	T	English 5 *Choose Three* Latin 5 Greek 5 French 5 German 5 Physics 5 English History 5	English 5 Bookkeeping 5 *Choose Two* French 5 Physics 5 Stenography 4 Typewriting (4) 2	English 5 Physics 5 Mechanical Drawing, boys (4) 2 Free-hand Drawing, girls Machine Shop Practice, Elementary Mechanics, boys (8) 4 Household Economy, Sewing, girls French 5 English History 5
		S	"	"	"

HIGH SCHOOL GROUP 1—*Continued*

			Course I. Classical and English		Course II. Commercial		Course III. Mechanic Arts	
First Year	9	R	English	5	English	5	English	5
			Geometry	5	Geometry	5	Geometry	5
			Choose Two		Commercial Arithmetic ½ yr.	5	Mechanical Drawing, boys (4)	2
			Latin	5	Bookkeeping ½ yr.		Free-hand Drawing, girls	
			Greek	5	*Choose One*		Pattern-Making, Forging, F'dry Practice, boys (8)	4
			French	5	French	5	Domestic Science, Sewing, girls	
			Mediaeval and Modern History	5	Mediaeval and Modern History	5	*Choose One*	
			Biology	5			French	5
							Mediaeval and Modern History	5
							Biology	5
		Q	"		"		"	

In commenting on the plan Mr. Rundlett, superintendent of schools, says:

Through the first six years of this course the studies remain practically uniform for all pupils, the main idea being to teach them how to read, to write, to use the mother-tongue properly, the essentials of history and geography, how to take care of their bodies and to live in cleanliness and purity—in short, those things which all people should know to make the best use of their lives. Upon completing the work of group 3, the student may take up the work outlined for group 2, making his choice of approved high-school courses or pursuing still farther what are commonly called the three R's.

This change comes at a time in the pupil's life when he seeks variety. If he forecasts a college course he may have five years of study instead of four. If he wishes a more practical course he may choose a commercial or a mechanic-arts course. In these grades emphasis will be placed upon teaching the pupil to become self-reliant, how to study as well as how to recite, and to get material for his work with dispatch and with good judgment. He will be introduced to departmental teaching, handled by teachers who make a study of individual natures, and have the approval of the state department as being qualified for the work, thus securing the benefit of teaching backed by broad culture and by individual grade experience.

In the high school proper, group 1, advantage will be manifest in a decreased enrolment so that the general atmosphere will be relieved of the confusion of numbers.

Eventually, more rigid requirements and better standards of scholarship should result, because entering pupils will have had two years of serious preparation along lines of high-school work.

This scheme is combined with semiannual promotion throughout the entire course.

EDITORIAL NOTES

Eleventh Yearbook of the National Society for the Study of Education

One of the meetings which is held in conjunction with the Department of Superintendence should have the support of all who are interested in the promotion of scientific studies of education. This is the meeting of the National Society for the Study of Education. This society has for a number of years prepared an elaborate yearbook which is made the basis of the discussions at the meeting. The *Eleventh Yearbook*, which will be issued shortly and put into the hands of members of this organization, deals with typical experiments in industrial education, and with agricultural education in secondary schools. It is not the function of this Journal to discuss the second half of this program, although attention may be called in passing to the fact that a number of able contributors have been secured to write on agricultural education in secondary schools. The first half of the *Yearbook*, which deals with industrial education, will describe in detail certain of the current practices in elementary schools which have attempted to solve the problem of industrial education. A section will be devoted to pre-vocational industrial training in the seventh and eighth grades. Superintendent Mirick of Indianapolis will give an account of his observations in this field. Mr. M. W. Murray, director of the Independent Industrial School at Newton, Mass., will give in another section a report on intermediate, independent, or separate industrial schools. Charles F. Perry, superintendent of industrial education at Milwaukee, Wis., will give an account of the trade schools. Meyer Bloomfield, director of the Vocational Bureau of Boston, Mass., will discuss vocational guidance. Other contributors will discuss vocational high schools, the part-time co-operative plan, and continuation schools. The volume promises to give in a definite, concrete way an account of what is going on in different parts of the country, that will supplement the literature already prepared on this general topic in a very important sense. As the secretary of the association points out in his preface, educators in different parts of the country may be acquainted with what is going on in their own immediate surroundings, but they are likely to be ignorant of the experiments that are being tried at remote points. A limitation of the same general type applies to most of the commission reports. A report prepared in the eastern part of the United States is likely to omit consideration of much that is being done in the central part of the country and in the West. The *Yearbook of the National Society* promises to bring together a much wider range of information than is collected in most of the reports on this subject.

The Function and Membership of the Society

The collection of material of this sort is distinctly the business of some society. It is quite impossible for any individual to secure the co-operation of the kind of writers who are willing to contribute to a general report which is to be issued through a society. This *Yearbook* should have a very wide currency, and the meeting itself should attract the interest and attention of all who are seriously engaged in solving this problem. The National Society has had a long and influential history. Its future depends upon the support which can be brought to it by those who are interested in making investigations of the type represented in this *Yearbook*. It is the one organization that has devoted itself regularly to the serious study of a single problem each year. It is made up of practical school people and students of education in college departments and in normal schools, and is therefore one of the most democratic organizations dealing with education. It is smaller than the general Department of Superintendence or the general National Education Association, and consequently can do a type of work which these larger organizations must delegate to sections or even omit entirely because of lack of funds. The National Society has a series of publications which produce enough income to warrant the preparation each year of an elaborate handbook.

Northern Illinois Superintendents' and Principals' Association

The annual meeting of the Northern Illinois Superintendents' and Principals' Association will this year take up for its discussion a report prepared by the Committee of Seven. This organization had as its special subject of discussion last year a program of nature-study courses which had been prepared during the preceding twelve months by the standing Committee of Seven. The committee consists this year of the following members: Chairman,

I. B. Meyers, Francis W. Parker School; Secretary, H. A. Bone, superintendent, Batavia, Illinois; Dr. Charles A. McMurry, DeKalb Normal School; Superintendent C. M. Bardwell, Aurora, Illinois; Dr. O. T. Caldwell, University of Chicago; Dr. D. A. Tear, principal, Gladstone School, Chicago; Superintendent Edward F. Worst, Joliet, Illinois. The Executive Committee has directed the committee for this year to make a study of educational practices in various schools, and to embody their observations in a complete report. The reports will be on history, geography, and science. Each member of the committee is to study at least three schools, and the report will contain the accounts of the practices of the different schools observed. Many of the earlier reports of this organization have been somewhat theoretical in character. This statement may very properly be made with regard to the nature-study course which was proposed last year. The present effort of the committee is to get as much definite information from school experience as can be obtained and to make this the basis for a pointed discussion of the methods and content of instruction in the elementary schools. It is expected that reports of the work of this committee will be printed in the *Elementary School Teacher*.

Chicago Dinner at St. Louis in February

The editors of this journal wish to call the attention of all former students and instructors of the University of Chicago to the dinner which will be held in conjunction with the Department of Superintendence at St. Louis, on the evening of Wednesday, February 28, at the Mercantile Club, corner of Seventh and Locust streets, at 6:30. All who have ever been connected with the University are invited to attend this dinner. Reports will be made by members of the faculty of the work of the year, and it is hoped that the occasion will bring together former members of the institution from all parts of the country. At the Mobile meeting a similar dinner brought together forty former members of University classes.

BOOK REVIEWS

A Cyclopedia of Education. Edited by PAUL MONROE. Volume II. New York: Macmillan, 1911.

The second volume of this important educational work has appeared within nine months after the publication of the first volume. If this rate of production is maintained, the remaining three volumes will appear in a little over two years. This is a creditable degree of promptness in the production of a work of such magnitude.

The second volume has maintained the high standard of excellence which was set by the preceding one and has continued its main features. Among the accounts of national educational systems this volume contains extended articles on education in England and in France. State systems are represented by an article on Connecticut, and city systems by articles on the cities of Cincinnati, Cleveland, Columbus, and others. Among the universities, Columbia and Cornell are given the most space.

Among the more general articles on administration the most important is a group of articles on the different phases of the college. This group of articles covers sixty pages and comprises a very complete and enlightening treatment of the college in its various aspects. This series contains an article on the historical development of the American college; a clear discussion of the principles underlying the college curriculum with a summary of historical and current practice; accounts of the distribution of colleges in the United States, of college attendance in various countries, and of the vocational distribution of college graduates. Another article deals with college-entrance requirements. These examples will serve to indicate the scope of the treatment of this subject.

Another type of article deals with certain specific questions of educational administration. Such topics possess a live interest for educators because of their discussion of current problems. The present volume, for example, contains discussions of coeducation, of consolidation of schools in rural districts, and of evening schools. Another group of articles deals with the education of special classes of children, such as crippled children, the deaf, deaf-blind, and defectives.

The subjects which make up the content of education or which are related to education are fully treated. Among the subjects which appear in this volume are commercial education, education as an academic study, ethics, and forestry education. The social relationships of education are brought out in articles on citizenship and education and on education and crime; the medical and hygienic relationships are treated in articles on contagious diseases and on food and feeding.

Finally two large and important groups of articles deal with the philosophical or psychological questions which have a bearing upon education, and with practical questions which are closely related to these more theoretical disciplines. Here we find, for instance, articles on culture and on the culture-epoch theory; on the emotions and on eye- and ear-mindedness; on examinations and on formal discipline. The wide range of articles which are treated and the evident authoritativeness of a large proportion of them make the cyclopedia indispensable as a work of reference. The bibliographies and cross-references which accompany the articles also makes the work useful as a starting-point for systematic topical study.

As regards balance and distribution of space the present volume is better than the first one and presents few if any glaring irregularities. The ideal is not fully attained, as is illustrated by the fact that the article on ethics occupies eight and one-half pages and the article on experimental education one page, but there appears to be marked improvement. A minor point of criticism may be made of the fact that some of the biographical articles which are accompanied by portraits in another part of the volume do not contain references to these portraits—as for example the articles on Compte and Darwin.

FRANK N. FREEMAN

UNIVERSITY OF CHICAGO

The Social Factors Affecting Special Supervision in the Public Schools of the United States. By WALTER ALBERT JESSUP. New York: Teachers College, Columbia University Contributions to Education, No. 43. Pp. vii+123. $1.00.

This Doctor's dissertation is largely a statement of the historical development of the so-called "special subjects" in American elementary education, with particular reference to the social demands leading to the introduction of each subject. The special subjects discussed are music, drawing, manual training, domestic science, physical education, and penmanship. About three-fourths of the book is of this historical character, and the remaining fourth is devoted to a statistical treatment of the geographical distribution of special supervisors of these subjects, their salaries, sex selection, and division of responsibility. This portion of the dissertation is partially historical since it involves a comparison of the conditions at different periods as shown by the reports of the United States commissioner of education for 1875, 1885, 1893, 1908, etc.

From the point of view of the present reviewer, this dissertation is significant as a relatively unique contribution to the history of American education. In recent years we have become familiar with the idea that the "social point of view" should prevail in the history of education, and that this subject should be treated as "one phase of the history of civilization." Unfortunately, however, many of those who have taken this point of view have made the development of philosophy the fundamental aspect of civilization to which they have related educational developments. At the present time there is a tendency to make economic, industrial, and other more concrete aspects of social life the point of departure. This is illustrated in Carlton's *Economic Influences on Education* (1908) and in Cubberley's little masterpiece entitled *Some Changing Conceptions of Education* (1909) and the several Doctor's dissertations prepared under Professor Paul Monroe which describe the development of the moving school, of local school supervision, of school support, etc., in Masschusetts.

Mr. Jessup's study is one of the first in English to apply this method to the development of the curriculum of the elementary school. The author has endeavored "(*a*) to find sanctions back of the demand for the introduction of these subjects most commonly thought of in connection with special teaching or supervision . . . .; (*b*) to ascertain if possible whether the demand for these subjects came from within the school itself, or whether it came from the [social][1] group outside; (*c*) to point out certain typical ways in which the new subject-matter became a part of the curriculum; (*d*) to determine the effect of the traditions of the school on the interpretation of the subject-matter; (*e*) to determine certain quantitative aspects of the problem. . . . ."

[1] The text reads "school group" but I judge this is a misprint.

As an example of the method of treatment of each subject, chap. iii, which deals with drawing, may be cited. The author takes up certain scattering attempts in teaching drawing before the middle of the nineteenth century; the influence of the reports by Stowe (1839) and Mann (1844) concerning foreign schools; the influence of the London exhibit of 1851 and the Paris exhibit of 1867; the clear-cut industrial basis for the introduction of drawing into the Massachusetts schools in 1870; the impetus given by the Philadelphia Centennial Exposition of 1876; the tendency in the schools to neglect the industrial reasons for which drawing had been introduced and to emphasize its value as a mental discipline.

The mechanics of the structure of the book are good, the liberal use of italicized paragraph headings and their organization in the analytical table of contents being especially helpful.

S. CHESTER PARKER

Progress through the Grades of City Schools, A Study of Acceleration and Arrest. By CHARLES HENRY KEYES, PH.D. New York: Teachers College, Columbia University.

Mr. Keyes has reported in great detail in this book the progress of pupils through the schools of a well-organized district in New England. The tables show the amount of acceleration, as well as the amount of retardation, and the study is especially interesting because it calls attention to acceleration which has commonly been overlooked. The general conclusion which Mr. Keyes emphasizes can be stated in his own words as follows: "Potential accelerates are present in our schools in very large numbers, comprising from one-fourth to one-third of all pupils above the first grade. The average accelerate, under favorable conditions, has the capacity to gain from one year in seven to two years in nine of the traditional city-school course. The number of such pupils is so considerable as to demand that special provision be made in every school system for freeing their progress through the schools. This service, whether it is to be rendered by special teachers or special classes and in a differentiated curriculum is too important for society to neglect. . . . .

"The experience under consideration shows that under the conditions described the middle grades of our schools are places of large opportunity for giving the superior pupil a chance to work up to the healthful limit of his better powers. Less than this is not education in the true sense."

The significance of this study for the general student of school statistics lies in the demonstration which is given of the necessity of a detailed study of the cases under consideration. Ayer's report on Laggards emphasizes only one side of the problem, and offers a method which, as Mr. Keyes has shown, obscures many of the important facts which should be known. Ayer's standard age for admission to schools is certainly too late. All of the studies that have taken up the facts in detail have demonstrated this with regard to Ayer's method, and Mr. Keyes's work is further confirmation of the general conclusion that has been reached in many of these studies.

If such studies as Mr. Keyes here reports could be made by every superintendent in charge of schools, there would be great gain in school organization and in the efficiency of instruction.

C. H. J.

CURRENT EDUCATIONAL LITERATURE IN THE PERIODICALS[1]

IRENE WARREN
Librarian, School of Education, The University of Chicago

ABBOTT, ALDEN H. The New England town school. Educa. 32:153–61. (N. '11.)

ADDAMS, JANE. A new conscience and an ancient evil. McClure 38:232–40. (D. '11.)

BROWN, H. A. A more efficient higher education for the country boy and girl. J. of Educa. (Bost.) 74:563–65. (30 N. '11.)

BROWN, HORACE G. Observance of historic days at school. Educa. 32:147–52. (N. '11.)

CARTER, HENRY. The help that counts. World's Work 23:177–87. (D. '11.)

CURTIS, NATALIE. Value of music school settlements in large cities. Craftsman 21:283–89. (D. '11.)

ELIOT, CHARLES W. Contributions to the history of American teaching (VII). Educa. R. 42:346–66. (N. '11.)

ELLWOOD, CHARLES A. The sociological basis of the science of education. Educa. 32:133–40. (N. '11.)

(A) field school of geology. Science 34:706. (24 N. '11.)

FRESCHI, JOHN J. Parents to the bar! Harp. W. 55:12–13. (2 D. '11.)

Japanese schoolboys on peace. Lit. D. 43:907–8. (18 N. '11.)

LANGDON, WILLIAM CHAUNCY. The pageant of Thetford. Playground 5:302–18. (D. '11.)

LEE, JOSEPH. Play as medicine. Playground 5:289–302. (D. '11.)

LINDSAY, JAMES ALEXANDER. The hygiene of school life in Ireland. Child 2:93–98. (N. '11.)

LOVE, GRACE STANTON. The educational value of literature. Educa. 32:141–46. (N. '11.)

MONKMAN, J. W. Secondary schools and free secondary education. School W. 13:424–25. (N. '11.)

MÜNSTERBERG, HUGO. The Germans at school. Pop. Sci. Mo. 79:602–14. (D. '11.)

[1] Abbreviations.—Educa., Education; Educa. R., Educational Review; Harp. W., Harper's Weekly; J. of Educa. (Bost.), Journal of Education (Boston); Lit. D., Literary Digest; Pop. Sci. Mo., Popular Science Monthly; School Sci. and Math., School Science and Mathematics; School W., School World.

MYERS, G. W. Report on the unification of mathematics in the University High School. School Sci. and Math. 11:777–90. (D. '11.)

MYLECHREEST, WINIFRED BROOKS. The importance of story telling. Child 2:110–14. (N. '11.)

NEYSTROM, PAUL H. Education and money, leadership and morality. World's Work 23:195–202. (D. '11.)

OLDFATHER, W. A. Common sense and the elective system. Educa. R. 42:367–75. (N. '11.)

PATON, STUART. University administration and university ideals. Science 34:693–700. (24 N. '11.)

PRESSLAND, A. J. The teacher of the adolescent. School W. 13:401–3. (N. '11.)

RICHARDS, HERBERT M. Botany in the college course. Educa. R. 42:376–87. (N. '11.)

RIIS, JACOB A. How to save Christmas for the children. Craftsman 21:231–36. (D. '11.)

STRAYER, GEORGE DRAYTON. The Baltimore school situation. Educa. R. 42:325–45. (N. '11.)

TOZIER, JOSEPHINE. The Montessori schools in Rome. McClure 38:123–37. (D. '11.)

VAN WAGNEN, OLIVER. The pedagogy of Jesus. Educa. 32:169–76. (N. '11.)

VOSS, EMILIA V. KANTHACK DE. Child welfare in Germany. Child 2:99–103. (N. '11.)

WETTER, A. A. Great Educators, III. Heinrich Pestalozzi. Educa. 32:165–68. (N. '11.)

WINSHIP, A. E. The elimination of the hoodlum boy element. J. of Educa. (Bost.) 74:509–11. (16 N. '11.)

VOLUME XII NUMBER 6

THE ELEMENTARY SCHOOL TEACHER

FEBRUARY, 1912

MINIMUM GRADE REQUIREMENTS IN ENGLISH AND MATHEMATICS IN THE FRANCIS W. PARKER SCHOOL

FLORA J. COOKE
Principal of the Francis W. Parker School

The following outline gives a brief summary of the formal outcome of the work in English and mathematics, which is expected from pupils in each grade before their promotion to the next higher grade.

These grade standards consist of the necessary knowledge-facts or "tools of expression" which are to be fixed and to be made to function through continued use during the school year. They are given in the form of minimum requirements, and up to these limits the class teachers are responsible for the thorough functioning of the work outlined. Pupils may go beyond these limits, if they can do so and at the same time satisfactorily meet the requirements in their other subjects of study.

There is continual demand for reading and written expression in connection with literature and dramatic representation, geography, and history; and there are mathematical problems constantly arising in connection with the industrial history, science, and handwork. Therefore, the formal work in reading, writing, and number is not isolated in the minds of the children. They see that many drill periods are necessary to overcome the obstacles which they meet in their daily work. Correct spelling, punctuation, capitalization, and facility in the use of mathematical tools are matters of importance and need emphasis and attention.

Therefore, while the regular subjects of study motivate the work, opportunity must be given on the program for definite drill periods. In this way the teacher in each grade may expect that pupils coming to her have been thoroughly taught the foundation facts agreed upon as necessary for that grade.

The requirements as outlined below are wholly for the teacher's consideration. They are the results in each case of at least a year's committee work, which has been checked and discussed by the entire faculty, and some time is spent each year in revising and improving the requirements according to experience and to particular grade conditions. The statements of these minimum requirements here set forth were in use in the school during 1910–11, as the changes made for 1911–12 are minor in character and have not yet been formally acted upon.

MINIMUM REQUIREMENTS IN ENGLISH

(Italicized matter will be functioned in this grade. Matter under other topics expected to be used, but not to be functioned in this grade.)

FIRST GRADE

1. Capitalization—*pronoun I*
   first word in sentence
2. Punctuation—*period at end of sentence*
3. Vocabulary—making of "school dictionary" of words functioned in the grade
4. Spelling—words in "school dictionary"
7. Phonics—games and daily drill

SECOND GRADE

1. Capitalization—*days, months, proper names, words in title*
2. Punctuation—*period after common abbreviations (Mr., Mrs., etc.)*
   question mark after interrogative sentence
3. Vocabulary———— *words in common use added to "school dictionary"*
   quick recognition of either written or printed vocabulary
4. Spelling—*words in most frequent use*
6. Composition—simple sentences

THIRD GRADE

1. Capitalization—geographic names
   interjection O
2. Punctuation—apostrophe in possessives
3. Vocabulary———— *words in common use added to "school dictionary"*
   quick recognition of either written or printed vocabulary

4. Spelling—*words in most frequent use*
5. Use of reference books—selected books referred to for information on special topics

FOURTH GRADE

1. Capitalization—*each verse in poetry*
2. Punctuation—(*a*) *period after all abbreviations*
   (*b*) comma in simpler uses—clauses and phrases
   (*c*) *apostrophe in contractions and possessives*
   (*d*) *hyphen in compound words and in divisions*
   (*e*) *exclamation point after interjections and exclamatory sentences*
3. Vocabulary—(*a*) ———*words in common use added to "school dictionary"*
   (*b*) *quick recognition of printed or written vocabulary*
4. Spelling—*words in most frequent use*
5. Composition and grammar—construction of paragraphs
6. Use of reference books—*unabridged dictionaries*

FIFTH GRADE

1. Capitalization—*proper adjectives*
2. Punctuation—comma (*a*) *in parenthetical expressions,* etc.
   (*b*) *in series*
   (*c*) *after vocative nominative*
3. Vocabulary— ———*words in common use acquired*
4. Spelling—(*a*) oral and written practice
   (*b*) *knowledge of all words in common use*
5. Composition and grammar—*recognition and intelligent use of*
   (*a*) *nouns*— (1) common, (2) proper
   (*b*) *pronouns*—(1) personal, (2) relative, (3) interrogative
   (*c*) *verbs*— (1) regular, (2) auxiliary
6. Use of reference books—dictionaries and encyclopaedias

SIXTH GRADE

1. Capitalization—(*a*) *first word in a direct quotation*
   (*b*) *substantives referring to Deity*
2. Punctuation—(*a*) *comma with direct quotation in a sentence*
   (*b*) *semicolon in compound sentences*
   (*c*) *colon before long quotations*
   (*d*) *quotation marks*—(1) titles of books, plays, and poems
   (2) quotations—prose
   poetry
3. Vocabulary— ———new words in common use acquired
4. Spelling—(*a*) *oral and written practice with all new words*
   (*b*) *accurate knowledge of all words in frequent use*
   (*c*) study of prefixes and suffixes
   (*d*) syllabication (by sound)

5. Composition and grammar—(*a*) *recognition and intelligent use of*
   (1) adjectives—*a*) descriptive
      b) articles
   (2) adverbs—*a*) of time
      b) of place
      c) of manner
      d) of degree
      e) numeral
   (3) conjunctions
   (4) prepositions
   (5) interjections
   (*b*) inflections of—(1) *nouns*—number (regular and irregular)
      (2) *pronouns*—
         a) number
         b) person
         c) gender
      (3) *verbs*—*a*) number
         b) person
   (*c*) Analysis of sentence—first steps (subject and predicate)
   Composition on class subjects—material worked over in class—from outlines furnished; approximately 120 pages of theme paper a year
6. Use of reference books— ——— works of reference

SEVENTH GRADE

1. Capitalization—(*a*) *civil and military titles*
   (*b*) *academic degrees*
   (*c*) *names of organizations and corporations*
2. Punctuation—*comma—special uses*
   - inverted constructions
   - "restrictive" relatives
   - appositives
   - participial phrases, etc.
3. Vocabulary— ——— *new words in common use acquired*
   synonyms sought for
4. Spelling—(*a*) *oral and written drill on all new words*
   (*b*) *accurate knowledge of all common words*
   (*c*) study of word tendencies—final *e* dropped, consonant doubled, etc.
   (*d*) syllabication

6. Composition and grammar—
   (*a*) *recognition and intelligent use of nouns*—(1) *abstract*
   (2) *collective*
   (*b*) inflection of—(1) *nouns*—*a*) gender
   b) case
   (2) *pronouns*—case
   (3) *adjectives*—comparison { regular / irregular }
   (4) *adverbs*—comparison { regular / irregular }
   (5) *verbs*—tense (indicative only)
   (*c*) *sentence analysis*—(1) simple
   (2) compound (complete)
   (3) complex
   (4) clause vs. phrase
   (*d*) composition of business and letter forms
7. Use of reference books—*continued with the needs of the grade*

EIGHTH GRADE

1. Capitalization—(*a*) *names of political parties*
   (*b*) *names of religious sects*
   (*c*) *names of governmental bodies and departments*
2. Punctuation—*dash* (*a*) parenthetical
   (*b*) showing broken construction
3. Vocabulary—(*a*) *careful acquisition of new words*
   (*b*) *synonyms and antonyms gathered*
4. Spelling—(*a*) *oral and written drill on all new words not unusual*
   (*b*) *thorough familiarity with all frequent words*
   (*c*) *formation of word groups*—
   (1) those ending in "able" and "ible"
   (2) those with negative prefixes
   (3) those with regular adjective suffix
   (4) those with regular adverbial suffix, etc.
5. Composition and grammar—
   (*a*) *inflection*—verbs
   (1) subjunctive
   (2) imperative
   (3) infinitive
   (4) participles
   (5) principal parts
   { *a*) regular (weak) / *b*) irregular (strong) }

(*b*) *syntax*—(1) verbs *a*) transitive and intransitive
b) voice
(2) phrases *a*) noun
b) verb
c) adjective } prepositional (form)
d) adverbial }
(3) clauses *a*) noun } use
b) adjective }
c) adverbial }
d) co-ordinate and subordinate (form)
(4) modifiers (*a*) adjective—*a*¹) adjective
*b*¹) adjective phrases
*c*¹) possessives
*d*¹) appositives
*e*¹) adjective clauses
(*b*) adverbial—*a*¹) adverbs
*b*¹) adverbial phrases
*c*¹) adverbial clauses
*d*¹) indirect object
*e*¹) nominative absolute
*f*¹) infinitive
*a*²) complementary
*b*²) of purpose

6. Use of reference books—*extended to meet all needs of the grade*

MINIMUM REQUIREMENTS IN MATHEMATICS

FIRST GRADE

1. Clearness of thought with mathematical ideas used
2. Familiarity with the addition and subtraction combinations of numbers to 12 (not automatic)
3. Fractions—$\frac{1}{2}$ and $\frac{1}{4}$—known and used in measuring and "making" work
4. Standard measures: inch, foot, yard } known and used
cup, pint, quart }

SECOND GRADE

1. All addition and subtraction combinations of numbers to 19 used. Those below 12 automatic
2. Reading of numbers to 1,000
3. Processes: Addition (with carrying) and subtraction (without borrowing) with numbers of three figures, with help of objects; e.g., money
4. Fractions, $\frac{1}{2}$, $\frac{1}{4}$, $\frac{1}{3}$ of objects; $\frac{1}{2}$ of numbers up to 12

5. Standard measures: cent, dime, dollar
   cup, pint, quart, gallon
   inch, foot, yard
6. Geometry: accurate ideas of square and rectangle

THIRD GRADE

1. All addition and subtraction combinations to 19 automatic
2. Reading and writing of numbers to 10,000
3. Mastery of the processes of addition and subtraction of numbers to four places
4. Multiplication facts to 5×12 mastered
5. Meaning of fractions
   Fractional parts of numbers within limits of multiplication table learned
6. Standard measures: automatic—inch, foot, yard
   cent, dime, dollar
   cup, pint, quart, gallon
   square inch
7. Geometry: accurate ideas of squares, rectangle, triangle, areas of rectangles

FOURTH GRADE

1. Multiplication and division tables automatic through 12's
2. Multiplication process complete
3. Division by one figure
4. Rapidity and accuracy in addition and subtraction
5. Fractions: fractional parts of numbers
   multiplication of mixed numbers
6. Bills of goods
7. Standard measures: linear and square measures complete
   the gram—automatic
8. Geometry: accurate ideas of rectangles
   triangles
   circles
   cylinders
   triangular prisms
   areas of rectangles
   volumes of rectangular solids

FIFTH GRADE

1. The four fundamental operations with integers, including long division
2. Multiplication by mixed numbers
3. Use of common fractions in simple combinations
4. Standard measures: dry, liquid, and cubic measures complete
   use of centimeter, cubic centimeter, and gram
5. Bills of goods
6. Geometry: areas of rectangles, parallelograms, triangles, and trapezoids
   volumes of rectangular solids

SIXTH GRADE

1. Fundamental operations with integers reviewed and made automatic
2. All processes with simple, common, and decimal fractions mastered
3. The idea of per cent developed, but no application of percentage to business taught
4. Bills of goods
5. English weights and measures known thoroughly
   Some metric units used
6. Longitude and time, including standard time
7. Geometry: scale work
   areas of rectilinear figures and circles

SEVENTH GRADE

1. Accuracy and efficiency in fundamental operations with integers, common fractions, and decimals
2. Use of metric units mastered
3. Geometry: areas and volumes mastered
   scale work
   constructive geometry
4. Use of equation
5. Proportion as applied in the lever and in geometrical measurements of heights and distances
6. Percentage, with applications to simple industrial problems, and problems in buying and selling
7. Business forms and processes—including accounts
   bills of goods
   commission
   commercial discounts
   depositing and checking at bank
   drafts, bank, postal, and express money orders
   simple interest
   compound interest as applied in savings banks, etc.
   bank discount
   insurance
   partnership

EIGHTH GRADE

1. Accuracy in fundamental operations, common fractions, and decimals
2. Tables of measure
3. Mensuration
4. Review of proportion
5. Use of equation and algebraic formulae
6. Review of percentage, through study of taxes, revenues, stocks

MONTESSORI AND FROEBEL—A COMPARISON

ELLEN YALE STEVENS
Principal of the Brooklyn Heights Seminary

A popular magazine has by a series of very interesting articles introduced the name of Madame Montessori to the American public and created such a widespread interest in her methods of education for young children that there is danger that our proverbial enthusiasm for new ideas may carry this system on a wave of popularity only to swamp it in the end, unless a careful pedagogic study is made and the real basis of truth that it contains made clear.

We have had so many educational fads, or methods so called, widely exploited, loudly hailed, and then left to oblivion, that the question arises: Is Madame Montessori's method of scientific pedagogy to suffer the same fate? I wish that the American edition of her book when it is published, instead of "Method . . . . ," might be named "Principles of Scientific Pedagogy," to avoid the suggestions of the ill-fated name "method."

One sees things here in Rome, where I write these lines, in a long perspective and is taught to look for the fundamental in the evanescent. This great modern city is eager to give its children the best in education as in other things and is erecting new schools everywhere. But it is also very conservative, and so in some of the municipal schools the Montessori method is used in one room and the kindergarten method is another. In other schools such as that in St. Angelo in Pescheria the Montessori method only is used in the two lowest grades, while in still others one finds the kindergarten or *Giardino d'Infanzia* only.

The Association of the Beni Stabili, which has erected in the newer parts of the city where land is cheaper model tenements under the co-operative plan, has in the center of each block of buildings a *Casadei Bambini* or House of Childhood, free to those children of their tenants who are too young to enter the first class of the municipal schools where the Montessori materials and method are used exclusively. Here in Rome, therefore, I can compare the two systems in schools where the type of child is the same, but at home I must see the Montessori method tried with children of a different race and environment. Italian children are at the same time more precocious and less nervous than our own and also more susceptible to impression. In all the schools I have visited I find the Italian children—even the youngest—rhythmic, studious, and naturally graceful. I have yet to find an instance of the monotone singing so prevalent with us.

The kindergarten as seen in Rome is without exception, so far as I have observed, of the strict Froebelian type. The classes are large, sometimes as many as fifty children of five years of age under one teacher; the occupations entirely dictated and the games directed. Yet nowhere have I seen the kindergarten circle; instead the children sit in pairs on a bench in front of a long, narrow, slanting desk. It is the *banco* as thus used that is satirized so severely by Madame Montessori, who has introduced in its place, in the schools under her direction, low, broad, firm tables, where two or at most three children can sit comfortably in little, broad chairs.

But in order properly to compare these two methods, one needs to consider the preparation of their founders, which led in each case to their development.

Maria Montessori has a twofold advantage over Froebel in that she is living at a time when she can make use of the results of the experimental psychology and child-study of the last half-century, and in that her own training and experience have been of the broadest. As a doctor of medicine she early became interested in deficient children, and studied most earnestly the methods of Itard and Séguin with idiots. As a lecturer in the University of Rome on anthropology and hygiene, she extended her researches into the biological foundations of education. When she was placed in charge of one of the hospitals for deficient children in Rome she had six years of observation and experiment, until the results of the education as devised by her brought them on a par, as regards examinations for the municipal schools, with normal children of the same age. This wonderful success turned her attention to the problem of education for the healthy, sane child.

The establishment of the Beni Stabili schools at this time, as they were placed under her charge, gave her the opportunity for experiment and observation which she desired; and for two years she worked with a devotion and enthusiasm few teachers would have shown, without vacation, and from early in the morning until late at night. The results of these years of experience, training, observation, and experiments by a woman whose genius is of the intuitive, inventive order come to us in the fascinating record in her book and in the wonderful series of didactic material invented by her to take the place of the Froebelian gifts, occupations, and games. She is right, I think, in calling her method scientific, for she has based it on scientific principles true to psychology and developed from accurate and painstaking observation and experiment.

Madame Montessori is at this moment engrossed with the problem of the older child. Having revolutionized the education of the child from three to six, she realizes that it must not stop there. A child developed by spontaneous activity in the free atmosphere of a Montessori school, with his senses trained, his muscles co-ordinated, his creative ability stimulated, with a power of self-direction and self-government far beyond that of the usual child of his own age, would be stifled in the ordinary municipal school as found in Rome.

The educational world awaits with keen interest the result of this year of study and research, while it deplores the withdrawal for a time of Maria Montessori from the course of lectures she has given for several years and from the direction of the schools established by her. But a great genius points the way; others must follow in it and make perfect the path. In America we are, I think, ready to take her principles and her educative material into our schools much more readily than they are in Rome, for we are already working in harmony with many of her ideas. Our best teachers have the necessary psychological and pedagogical training, as few in Italy have. I should like to see Madame Montessori the center of a great educational movement, the inspiring force, the creative genius, surrounded by teachers fitted by culture and experience to carry out her methods and in charge of schools properly equipped.

But to return to a comparison of the two systems. As Maria Montessori's preparation was so much broader than that of Froebel, as her genius—creative and intuitive like his—had a severer, more scientific training; so, it seems to me, is the point of view of each essentially different.

Froebel saw the universe in which he wished to interest the child in its unity and yet infinite variety. By means of the gifts, occupations, and games which his genius devised, the child is *led* into the different worlds which make up his environment—the world of sense, that of the family, the social organism in all its occupations, the world of Nature, and finally of the moral and spiritual life. While Froebel sees first the universe, then the child, Montessori's point of view is essentially and wholly that of the child. Frobel said: "Let us live with our children, play with them, direct them into this manifold life of the universe." Madame Montessori says: "Let the child live, free to develop all his powers; let him create his own world." Froebel's teachers are *in front* of their children, leading them, directing them; Montessori's are *behind* theirs, watching them, quietly removing all obstacles to their development, silently placing within their reach all helps to their progress, but leaving the initiative entirely to the children. Conciseness, simplicity, objectivity are their watchwords. The Froebelian training of the senses is too much that of the eye, by it perception is developed, through analysis, not synthesis; too much use is made of the instinct of imitation, not enough that of creation. Froebel's system stimulates too soon the reasoning powers of the child and does not strengthen the nervous system and muscular memory.

Perhaps a comparison of the materials employed in each system will explain this difference. The first exercises in the Montessori system are those of practical life. The child is taught to love cleanliness and order. In one school I visited the children all came up at once to shake hands with me, first showing their hands to me back and front to prove they were clean. In another school I saw a child come back to her table after a game, see a little dust on it, go gently to the closet for a duster, then—without a word from the teacher—clean, not only her own table, but all the others. Children of three learn to button, hook, lace, tie bow knots, so that they are soon dressing and undressing themselves and others. The material for sense-training develops discrimination and exact use of language. Differences in shades of color, weight, and sound of objects are made without a mistake by very young children. For example, a child shakes, with her hand held to her ear, ten cylindrical cardboard boxes—like dice boxes—in which are pebbles or shot graded so as to made a series of five pairs; then deftly places them in order so that there is a perfect gradation from loud to softest sound. Another will take thin blocks of wood two inches square made of wisteria, walnut, and pine, balance each for a moment in his little hand, then place it correctly in a pile of others of like weight when it is impossible for an observer to distinguish any difference. Discrimination in color and tint is developed by means of silks wound on reels, eight colors and eight shades, with very slight gradation, which again trains him for practical life. The material makes the children self-correcting to a marvelous degree. It seems wonderful that the children, after their muscles have been trained and their muscular memory established, by a series of exercises, can write any word they wish on their slates or on the blackboard without a copy, and recognize and quickly correct all mistakes. The gradation from the work of a child of three to that of one of six or seven is perfect, so that our so-called kindergarten and first primary years merge into one. The Montessori teachers realize that a child does not *play* but *works*, and that if his force is guarded and not exhausted in an attempt to follow the thoughts of others, but is allowed free scope, there will be no nervous strain or fatigue. The individual differences of children are seen in this method in their choice of materials and in the time taken by them to master their use. Native bents are observed, natural talents developed. Yet there is much opportunity for group work—children help each other, work things out together. Some children will be seated at one table busily writing, three or four others will be on a square of felt on the floor, using the large, paper-script letters to form words and sentences. Others will be grouped around the series of sticks, from one to ten, which is so valuable for the development of the sense of number. Another group will take their slates, writing sentences for others to read or little problems for others to solve. All is spontaneous activity, yet all are working harmoniously together.

The material invented by Madame Montessori is more practical than that of Froebel, is a means to an end, is exact and accurate, and is scientific because true to psychological and biological laws.

The dangers of this method, as in that of the kindergarten, lie in the teachers employed. Just because in this system the teacher apparently does so little, is her activity really all the greater. I have seen much poor teaching here as well as much fine work, such as that of Madame Galli-Succenti, who has introduced the material and the method into one of the municipal schools, and whose long training and experience make her particularly valuable as a practical exponent of these principles. On the other hand, a teacher with slight pedagogic or psychologic training will get a superficial idea of the principles, and as a result her school will be poorly disciplined and the work in it aimless.

I hope that some great university in America will create a school for the study and practice of the Montessori methods, which are destined, I feel sure, if properly understood and applied, to revolutionize primary education.

ROME, ITALY
December, 1911

THE ELIMINATION OF WASTE IN EDUCATION

JOHN FRANKLIN BOBBITT
The University of Chicago

Six years ago the site where Gary now stands was a region of waste sand-dunes covered here and there with patches of stunted trees. Today there stands upon this site at the southern end of Lake Michigan the most complete system of steel mills west of Pittsburgh, and a rapidly growing city of some twenty-five thousand inhabitants.

The rapid growth of the city has brought to the school department a financial problem of peculiar difficulty. The population consists for the most part of immigrant foreign laborers, possessing but little taxable property. The city having been practically created by the United States Steel Corporation, naturally its plants are undervalued in the assessments for taxation. Still further embarrassment grew out of the fact that according to the laws of the state of Indiana, school revenues for any given year are obtained upon an assessment of property made almost two years before. In a city where the population had been doubling each year, the result was that the revenues for any given year were based upon an assessment made when the population was only about one-quarter as great. Furthermore, the method of distributing the state school revenues failed to recognize the pressing needs of a rapidly growing city. Revenues were apportioned on the basis of an enumeration made the previous April; but the enumeration was increasing 50 per cent between April and September, and another 50 per cent before the end of the school year.

Along with these unusual difficulties in the raising of current revenues there were on the other hand unusual immediate demands. In a city of slow growth, the school plant grows slowly and the yearly increase is no great burden upon the community; but in a new city having no school plant there was the immediate necessity of creating a complete school plant in addition to the annual cost of instruction and maintenance.

There were two ways of meeting the situation. One was to build inferior buildings, omit playgrounds, school gardens, laboratories, workrooms, and assembly halls, to employ cheap teachers, to increase the size of classes, to cut down the yearly term to eight months, or to accommodate two shifts of children in the same building each day by doing half-time work. The other possible method was to create a thoroughly modern school plant, equipped with every modern necessity; then to operate it according to recently developed principles of scientific management, so as to get a maximum of service from a school plant and teaching staff of minimum size.

The majority of cities suffering from a shortage of funds choose some portion of the former alternative. Illustrations are sufficiently numerous, from New York and Chicago on the one hand down to the poorest school district on the other. But the new city was being built by engineers, superintendents, and business managers who were familiar with the principles of scientific management in the steel industry; and when the educational engineer appeared and showed how it was possible to introduce similar principles of management into the operation of the school plant, his words fell upon understanding ears; and Gary, contrary to the usual plan, adopted the latter alternative.

The first principle of scientific management is to use all the plant all the available time.

In a school of the ordinary type, accommodating eight classes, let us say, of forty pupils each, but equipped in the most modern manner possible, there would be eight ordinary classrooms, each capable of seating forty children. In addition, there would be wide corridors, an assembly room, an indoor playroom or gymnasium, bathing and swimming-pool, shops and workrooms, science room, outdoor playground, and school garden. When all of the classrooms were in operation, the rest of the facilities of the plant would be lying idle. To the extent that the other facilities of the plant were actually being used, to that extent the classrooms would be lying idle. The result of such a policy is that half of the plant is idle half the time. In other words, the usual plant, if it is fully equipped is operated during school hours at about 50 per cent of efficiency. The task of the educational engineer at Gary was to formulate a plan of operating his plant during school hours at 100 per cent efficiency.

DAILY PROGRAM NO. I

Time	Regular Studies				Special Activities				Time
	Class-room I	Class-room II	Class-room III	Class-room IV	Basement, Garden, Attic, Auditorium Shops, Work-rooms, Laboratories		Playground		
8:45–10:15....	1A	2A	3A	4A	1B	3B	2B	4B	.... 8:45– 9:30
					2B	4B	1B	3B	.... 9:30–10:15
10:15–11:45....	1B	2B	3B	4B	1A	3A	2A	4A	....10:15–11:00
					2A	4A	1A	3A	....11:00–11:45
1:00– 2:30....	1A	2A	3A	4A	1B	3B	2B	4B	.... 1:00– 1:45
					2B	4B	1B	3B	.... 1:45– 2:30
2:30– 4:00....	1B	2B	3B	4B	1A	3A	2A	4A	.... 2:30– 3:15
					2A	4A	1A	3A	.... 3:15– 4:00

For a group of eight primary classes of forty pupils each he provided a plan of work as shown in Daily Program No. I. For the eight classes only four regular schoolrooms are required. While these classrooms are occupied by four classes, the other four classes are being accommodated half upon the playground and the other half in the workrooms, assembly room, school garden, science laboratory, or science excursions. The program is divided into regular and special studies. The regular studies in the elementary school consist of arithmetic, history, geography, and the formal language studies of reading, writing, spelling, and composition. The special activities are nature study, manual activities, drawing, literature, music, and play. Half the day is given by the pupil to the regular studies, and half the day to the special activities. The regular work consists of two periods of ninety minutes each, one in the forenoon one in the afternoon. The special studies are likewise given a period of ninety minutes in the forenoon and ninety minutes in the afternoon.

The ninety-minute periods devoted to special activities are each divided into two forty-five minute periods as shown in the program. The ninety-minute periods devoted to the regular studies are divided as the teachers see fit. Each teacher has one class that is not divided into sections and a certain portion of the regular studies to be covered in the three hours given to her. She is free to divide the time as seems best. Theoretically she is supposed to divide the time equally between recitation periods and study periods. This gives her an opportunity to train pupils in methods of study, to supervise their study, and to give individual help to those in need of it. During these study periods she is expected to do all the paper work that falls to her for the day, so that when her six hours' schoolroom service is ended, her day's work is done.

DAILY PROGRAM No. II

In actual practice it is found advisable to alternate the manual arts with the music, drawing, and literature so that each may have a ninety-minute period every other day.

Time	Regular Studies				Special Activities				Time
	Class-room V	Class-room VI	Class-room VII	Class-room VIII	Science	Man-ual Arts	Music, Draw-ing, and Litera-ture	Play	
8:45–10:15....	5B	6B	7B	8B	5G	7G	6G	8G	.... 8:45– 9:30
					6G	8G	5G	7G	.... 9:30–10:15
10:15–11:45....	5G	6G	7G	8G	5B	7B	6B	8B	....10:15–11:00
					6B	8B	5B	7B	....11:00–11:45
1:00– 2:30....	5B	6B	7B	8B	5G	7G	6G	8G	.... 1:00– 1:45
					6G	8G	5G	7G	.... 1:45– 2:30
2:30– 4:00....	5G	6G	7G	8G	5B	7B	6B	8B	.... 2:30– 3:15
					6B	8B	5B	7B	.... 3:15– 4:00

The daily program for the four upper grades of the elementary school is shown in Daily Program No. II. Putting the two programs together one has the daily program of a regular elementary school accommodating sixteen classes. This is done, however, with eight regular classrooms used in connection with special rooms and outdoor playgrounds. All the plant is used all the available time. None of it is idle any portion of the school day.

Although operating his plant six hours per day at the very high percentage of efficiency shown, still the educational engineer is not yet satisfied with the percentage of efficiency attained. The six-hour day is not enough. The plant might well be operated continuously from eight o'clock in the morning until six o'clock in the evening. The time once needed for chores at home is no longer used for that purpose in the majority of cases. It becomes "street and alley time," to borrow Superintendent Wirt's expressive phrase and tends toward the undoing of the work that is actually done under school conditions. A start has been made in an informal way toward remedying this lack. The playground teachers have charge of all of the playground facilities for an hour before school, during the noon hour, and for an hour or two after school. Since there is a larger number of playground teachers than usual, it is possible to divide this voluntary work among themselves so as not to require the attendance of any one of them for more than one of these extra periods per day. The plan is to be extended to the early and late use of laboratories and shops as well.

That an expensive plant should lie idle during all of Saturday and Sunday while "street and alley time" is undoing the good work of the schools is a further thorn in the flesh of the clear-sighted educational engineer. That the plant should lie idle is one loss. That work already done should be undone is a further loss. Scientific management demands that the school buildings be in use on Saturdays and Sundays. Gary has made a start in this direction by opening her buildings and placing the entire school plant at the disposal of the city's children for seven hours each Saturday. Attendance is voluntary; yet it amounts to about one-half of the total enrolment. One-half the teachers report for duty on Saturdays and are paid extra for all such voluntary services at the rate of one dollar per hour for those studies that are confining, and seventy-five cents per hour for the active and less exacting portions of the work. The Saturday sessions are proving popular with both teachers and pupils.

There is a further loss of efficiency in the use of the plant by closing the building during the two months of summer. This alone is a loss of some 16 per cent, no small item in the calculations of the efficiency engineer. Several years before, Superintendent Wirt had established the all-year school divided into four quarters, at Bluffton, Indiana. Pupils were required to attend three of the quarters or nine months of the year. They could take as their vacation the quarter that seemed most desirable.

Naturally this feature of scientific management seemed to be a desirable means of economy at Gary; but unfortunately the antiquated legal machinery of the state forbade. All that is permitted them yet is the ten months of regular school, and the two months of voluntary vacation school. Gary will have the all-year school, however, as soon as the state officials see fit to make it legally possible.

A second principle of scientific management is to reduce the number of workers to a minimum by keeping each at the maximum of his working efficiency.

In the usual school system, in a building containing sixteen classes of forty pupils each, there would be sixteen regular classroom teachers. But in addition to these sixteen regular teachers, if the special activities were carried on as fully as modern conditions are demanding, there would be needed the services of additional special teachers of drawing, music, manual activities, elementary science, and organized play; or, if not special teachers, then numerous special supervisors of these subjects to aid the regular teachers.

But Gary does away with the extra expense for extra teachers or the overhead expense of unnecessary supervision by having specialization within the group. According to their system, for every sixteen classes there are needed only sixteen teachers, eight regular and eight special. Both regular and special teachers can be experts in their particular fields, requiring no supervisors other than the regular building principals and the city school superintendent. The plan, if employed in a large city, would probably require the services of a small expert staff of special supervisors. It reduces the number of workers, however, to a minimum.

Maximum working efficiency is brought about here as everywhere by division of labor, special preparation, and the adjustment of the load to the strength and capacity of the worker. The objections to the departmental plan of organization are met by placing the pupils under a classroom teacher for all the regular traditional school work, and by keeping each class intact throughout the day.

Teachers are not expected to do school work of any kind except during the periods of the day for which they are regularly employed. They are to do paper work during study periods and they are not to take books or papers home at night. The highest working efficiency demands certain qualities of personality that are not to be had without normal association with one's fellows, nor without proper and normal leisure occupations. One cannot be a proper teacher if he does not engage in the many varied activities that are normal for every completely developed human creature. Teachers are expected to live like other people, and when their day's work is done to leave it behind them as completely as other classes of workers.

Under present conditions in order to secure even reasonable efficiency, the special activities must usually be taken care of by special teachers. It is argued that if the immature pupil is able to cover the whole range of subjects, that certainly the regular teacher ought to be able to do the same sufficiently for teaching him in his immaturity. But as a matter of fact the special activities require special points of view and special attitudes of mind of such diversity that under present conditions at least it is not possible to secure regular teachers who can assume the different mental attitudes at all adequately. To be a leader in organized play, for example, requires a special type of personality, special attitudes of mind, a special understanding of the needs of the child and of the many directions of individual and social development that have their roots in play. The work requires a special form of dress, a specially developed physique, special training that covers years. Without these things on the part of the teacher, the work will be slighted. It is certain almost to be undervalued by the regular teacher and her valuation of the matter as a school activity is certain unconsciously to be transmitted to the minds of the pupils and to the minds of the parents. The last few years have shown the indispensable nature of a large amount of organized play directed by the playground supervisor. Nobody but the specially trained playground teacher will do the work adequately in the face of the present general undervaluation on the part of the general community. It will never really get into the curriculum if left to the regular teacher.

The manual and industrial activities are in a similar position, as well as music, elementary science, school gardens, practical civic activities, and the like. Left to the regular teacher, they are academicized and devitalized simply because he cannot carry so many points of view. It may be possible for a few highly endowed individuals to see all these matters in so large a way that he can assume the various viewpoints and exchange mental and physical attitudes in passing from one to the other as frequently as required through the day; but it is not this type of individual that is teaching in the elementary grades of our public schools.

The burden must be adapted to the strength and capacity of the worker. To require so much of the elementary teacher of the usual type is to undermine physical vitality and mental integrity. It might well be different, however, if the so-called special studies were matters of the general community consciousness and if the teachers of our day have been effectively trained in all of them from their childhood up. The mental attitudes required by the special activities might then be as much matters of second nature as is the case with the regular studies. But for the immediate present it appears that teaching differentiation is the only practicable solution.

A third principle of efficient management is to eliminate waste. Ayers has given us the figures that measure the waste of retardation. Gulick and others have shown the waste that results from ill-health and lowered vitality. Social workers are pointing out the waste of undoing the pernicious effects of the vicious street and alley influences. Gary attempts to reduce retardation to a minimum by two or three methods. Teachers during the study periods give individual attention to the laggards, teaching them how to study, helping them to overcome difficulties. The voluntary Saturday classes and the summer vacation school classes receive a very large proportion of the backward pupils and aid in keeping them up to grade. Further, if a boy is weak in some particular subject, it is possible to give him double work in that subject. Let us say a 4A boy is weak in arithmetic. It is possible for a time for him to omit some of his special activities and take arithmetic with the 4B class also, thus permitting double time in arithmetic. If he is weak in all of his regular studies it is easy to drop him out of his special activities for a time and permit him to do double work in the regular studies. The special activities are of such a sort that he can return to his classes there without difficulty.

Waste due to ill-health and lowered vitality is in large measure eliminated by employing a large portion of their time in outdoor play under playground teachers specially trained for the work. Pupils of lowered physical vitality are sometimes given double work in the special subjects, the regular studies being wholly omitted until they are sufficiently built up physically. One boy, for example, who was pronounced by the physician wholly unable to attend school, was placed in the special classes for double time and after six months was wholly cured. It was a case of sending a boy to school to make him well rather than the usual situation of taking a child out of school to make him well. The system combines the virtues of the open-air school with those of the regular school.

There is an attempt to eliminate the waste of labor in counteracting the evils of street and alley influences by extending the regular school days, by introducing much healthy play during a portion of the day, and by occupying the pupil for an additional voluntary two hours each day under the regular playground teachers; and for several hours on Saturdays. There is the definite intention of making the school the recreation center for the use of the city. They attempt to gather up in a unitary way in the school system the various influences which in Chicago, for example, are to be found in part in the school system and in part in the small parks recreation centers. They would look upon the introduction of the separate municipal recreation centers such as are being introduced into so many of our cities as a disastrous backward step.

In this connection a statistical comparison, made by Superintendent Wirt, of the uses of the recreational facilities of the Emerson School at Gary with the uses of similar facilities in the recreation centers of the South Park system, which is considered the best of its kind in the world, shows the advantages of a unitary organization of educational facilities. The table shows the Emerson School to be from four to eight times as efficient as the average of these twelve small parks and to be from two to five times as efficient as most efficient of the small parks. This comparison is all the more striking when one remembers that the small parks of South Chicago are located in the most congested portions of. the city whereas Gary has no congested district. And also that the recreation parks of the South Side vary in size from ten to sixty acres whereas the Emerson School plant includes only five acres.

TABLE I

COMPARISON OF THE NUMBER OF USES OF VARIOUS RECREATIONAL FACILITIES OF THE TWELVE SMALL PARKS OF THE CHICAGO SOUTH PARKS SYSTEM WITH THE NUMBER OF USES OF THE CORRESPONDING FACILITIES AT THE EMERSON SCHOOL AT GARY FOR TWELVE MONTHS

	CHICAGO RECREATION PARKS		EMERSON SCHOOL
	Average	Highest	
Outdoor gymnasium	164,314	278,498	1,200,000
Indoor gymnasium	25,750	45,793	330,000
Swimming-pools	60,400	115,542	240,000
Library reading-room	48,940	85,933	300,000

As a means of caring for pupils that come from homes so vicious as to be subversive of all healthy educational influences, the Gary school system owns a farm of one hundred and sixty acres lying twelve miles outside the city. Here boys from twelve to eighteen years of age live in cottages that make up what they call "Boy-town." They attend school during school hours and work about the cottages and upon the farm during out-of-school time. They are paid for their labor at a definite rate, usually fifteen cents per hour; and in turn they are expected to pay their board, at the rate of three dollars per week. The school is neither a parental school, however, nor an orphan home. The boys are neither delinquent nor dependent, and their attendance is voluntary.

The work-cards for two weeks of one of the boys will show the nature of their work outside of school hours. During these two weeks the earnings of the boys ranged from a miminum of $9.30 to a maximum of $18.01. After deducting board for the two weeks, surplus earnings amounted to $3.30 as the lowest and $11.81 as the highest. This out-of-school work is looked upon as an integral portion of their education.

TABLE II

WORK-CARD FOR TWO WEEKS OF ONE OF THE BOYS IN THE FARM SCHOOL

Date	Work Done	Time	Rate	Earned
December 18........	Husking corn.....	2 hrs.	15c	$0.30
December 19........	Shoveling clay....	4 "	15	.60
December 20........	Husking corn.....	3 "	15	.45
December 21........	Mending tent.....	5 "	15	.75
December 22........	Hauling wood.....	5 "	15	.75
December 23........	Husking corn.....	3 "	15	.45
December 25........	No work.........	0 "	15	.00
December 26........	Laying linoleum...	8 "	15	1.20
December 27........	Laying lineolum...	9 "	15	1.35
December 28........	Laying linoleum...	9 "	15	1.35
December 29........	Teaming.........	6 "	15	.90
December 30........	Painting..........	8 "	15	1.20
	Total earned......	....	....	....$9.30
	Board for two weeks	....	....	.... 6.00
	Net earnings......	....	....	....$3.30

A fourth principle of general scientific management is: Work up the raw material into that finished product for which it is best adapted. Applied to education this means: Educate the individual according to his capabilities. This requires that the materials of the curriculum be sufficiently various to meet the needs of every class of individuals in the community; and that the course of training and study be sufficiently flexible that the individual can be given just the things that he needs.

The program as shown above for the elementary grades, and this, by the way, is continued through the high school, appears to go a long way toward meeting both these requirements. If an individual is of the motor type of mind, with his interests lying in the field of manual industry, with neither tastes nor ability for abstract intellection—the type that is prematurely forced out of our schools uneducated and unprepared for his share of the world's work—he can be given a maximum of work in the special activities and a minimum in the academic studies. Upon reaching the age when bookish studies tend to force him out of school, it is possible to give him double work along the line of manual activities and the correlated applied science, omitting the general studies entirely. This is being done at present for certain students who are taking trade courses in the high school. On the other hand, if one is clearly of the intellectualistic type of mind, preparing for a professional career, it may be desirable to give him a maximum of the general studies, and a smaller amount of the concrete activities. There might be periods when all his regular work should be for a time confined to studies of the academic sort, securing his physical exercise during out-of-school hours. The Gary plan is adapted to meet all such contingencies.

There is a very great degree of flexibility. A pupil can take all regular studies, and no special ones; three quarters, regular, and one quarter, special; half regular, and half special; one quarter regular and three quarters special; or all special. The schools are able to make an appeal to every type of student.

There is another aspect of this education according to need that is worthy of attention. The needs of boys are in part different from those of girls along lines of vocation, recreation, civic labors, and personal hygiene. The program of the grammar grades given above shows the separation of boys and girls beginning with the fifth grade. This is based upon no theoretical considerations as to the desirability or undesirability of coeducation. It is simply the practical and more or less unforeseen result of attempting to give to each pupil the thing that he needs.

The organization of classes for play, for gymnasium and swimming-pool, for manual activities, for applied science and mathematics as related to manual activities, brought about the placing of the boys in certain classes and of the girls in others. And further, at this age, it seems advisable that classes be kept together, and not broken up every hour as may be the case with departmental disorganization. The result is that the segregated classes formed for the special activities retain their unisexual character in the regular studies.

This in turn has its effect upon the teaching force. The boys require masculine leadership in many of their activities, and the girls, feminine leadership. These practical demands insure the employment of sufficient proportions of both men and women in the system. Cries of calamity have been arising rather numerously of late on account of the disappearance of men from the profession. But as long as school activities consist of little more than academic matters to be poured into the heads of pupils, a task that can usually be better performed and almost always more gladly performed by women teachers, these Jeremiahs are not likely to accomplish the desired results. But constructive work as at Gary, not even raising the question, is solving the problem in the way in which the country in general is likely to solve it.

Other aspects of the system are reserved for later discussion.

A STUDY OF THE READING VOCABULARY OF CHILDREN[1]

MYRTLE SHOLTY

The problem in this experiment was a study of the reading vocabulary of children who had attended school one and one-half school years, or thirteen and one-half months. When taking up the study of this problem I had five things in mind. I wanted to find out, first, the total number of words in the reading vocabulary of the children; second, the number of words known in context; third, the number of words known out of context when seen on the instant; fourth, the number of words the children could build up when allowed to see the words as long as they wished; and fifth, the number of words they could neither read correctly when seen on the instant through the tachistoscope nor build up when given all the time they wished.

To find out the reading vocabulary of these children, it was necessary to examine all of the readers the children had read since they entered school, and to arrange the vocabularies of these readers in alphabetical order. To find the number of words each child knew in context, I asked each child to read through all of the books he had read and I noted the words he did not know. In order to find the words the children knew out of context when seen on the instant, it was necessary to use the tachistoscope. The words when shown through the tachistoscope were not arranged in alphabetical order. As the words were shown I noted those read correctly on the instant. The words not read correctly on the instant were shown to the children and they were given as much time as they liked to build them up, and I noted the words they could neither build up nor read correctly on the instant.

In choosing the subjects for this experiment I asked the regular reading-teacher of a group of children to select one of the best

[1] From the Laboratory of Experimental Education, the University of Chicago.

readers of the class, one of the poorest, and a medium reader. A was the child selected as the best reader, B as the medium reader, and C as the poorest reader. A and C were each eight years old, while B, the medium reader, was eight and one-half years old.

After the experiment was completed I asked the regular teacher of these children how they stood in their other school work. She reported that A, the best reader, was much below the average in all her other school work, had no initiative, and could never be depended upon to do a piece of work. B, the medium reader, was also below the average but was a good faithful plodder. C, the poor reader, was above the average in all her other school work and always took the initiative.

As the experiment progressed I became anxious to know whether there were more phonetic than sight words in the reading vocabulary of these children, and whether the children read as many phonetic as sight words correctly as wholes. Accordingly I added this question to the original problem.

All the words that could be built up or worked out by sound were called phonetic words. Examples of these words are "finished" and "interesting." All of the words that could not be worked out by phonics were called sight words. Examples of these are "onions" and "cousin."

The reading vocabulary of these children was found to consist of 1,588 words. Of these 834, or 52.5+ per cent, are phonetic words while 754, or 47.4+ per cent, are sight words.

The significant result in Table I is the fact that each child knew a greater percentage of sight words in context than phonetic words. This seems strange when the children had had daily drills in phonics for twelve months. It can probably be accounted for by the facts that the children are interested in the subject-matter and do not want to take the time to work out the words for themselves, and that they have not as yet learned to see the phonetic words as wholes, but depend upon building them up each time.

Table II shows, strangely enough, that B, the child who knew most words in context, knows the fewest words when seen on the instant. It seems still more strange that she read a much smaller percentage of the phonetic than sight words on the instant. C also reads a smaller percentage of phonetic words than sight words on the instant.

TABLE I

THE NUMBER OF WORDS KNOWN IN CONTEXT

	Total No. of Words	No. of Words Known in Context	Percentage of Words Known in Context	Total No. of Phonic Words	Phonetic Words Known in Context	Percentage of Phonetic Words Known in Context	Total No. of Sight Words	Sight Words Known in Context	Percentage of Sight Words Known in Context
A......	1,588	1,392	87.6	834	725	86.9	754	667	88.4
B......	1,588	1,438	90.5	834	704	84.3	754	734	97.3
C......	1,588	1,309	82.4	834	661	79.2	754	648	85.9

TABLE II

THE NUMBER OF WORDS KNOWN WHEN SEEN ON THE INSTANT THROUGH THE TACHISTOSCOPE OUT OF CONTEXT

	Total No. Words	No. Words Known When Seen on the Instant	Percentage of Words Known When Seen on the Instant	Total No. of Phonetic Words	No. of Phonetic Words Known When Seen on the Instant	Percentage of Phonetic Words Known When Seen on the Instant	Total No. Sight Words	No. Sight Words Known When Seen on the Instant	Percentage of Sight Words Known When Seen on the Instant
A......	1,588	977	61.5	834	503	60.3	754	474	62.8
B......	1,588	798	50.2	834	265	31.7	754	532	70.6
C......	1,588	1,009	63.5	834	461	55.2	754	548	72.6

TABLE III

THE NUMBER OF WORDS THE SUBJECTS WERE ABLE TO BUILD UP*

	No. Words Not Known When Seen on the Instant	No. Words Built Up	Percentage of Words Built Up	No. Phonetic Words Not Known When Seen on the Instant	No. Phonetic Words Built Up	Percentage of Phonetic Words Built Up.	No. Sight Words Not Known When Seen on the Instant	No. Sight Words Worked Out	Percentage of Sight Words Worked Out
A......	611	412	67.4	331	232	70.08	280	180	64.28
B......	790	670	84.8	569	525	92.2	221	145	65.61
C......	579	315	56.1	373	254	68.09	206	61	29.61

* These were words they did not know when seen on the instant, but were able to work out when given more time.

Table III shows that B was able to build up a very large percentage of the words, while C was able to build up slightly over half of the words. Although Table II shows that C knew a larger percentage of the words when seen on the instant, Table IV shows that she was the most dependent reader because she could build up fewer words. B knows but half of the words when seen on the instant, but Table III shows that when she is given time she is able

TABLE IV

THE NUMBER OF WORDS THE SUBJECTS COULD NOT READ ON THE INSTANT NOR BUILD UP WHEN GIVEN MORE TIME

	No. Words Not Known When Seen on the Instant	No. Words Not Known	Percentage of Words Not Known	No. Phonetic Words Not Known When Seen on the Instant	No. Phonetic Words Not Known	Percentage of Phonetic Words Not Known	No. Sight Words Not Known When Seen on the Instant	No. Sight Words Worked Out	Percentage of Sight Words Worked Out
A......	611	199	32.6	331	99	29.02	280	100	35.72
B......	790	120	15.2	569	44	7.8	221	76	34.39
C......	519	264	43.9	379	119	31.91	206	145	70.39

TABLE V

RESULTS OF THE READINGS THROUGH THE TACHISTOSCOPE

	Total No. Words	No. Words Read Correctly as Wholes on the Instant	Percentage of Words Read Correctly on the Instant	No. Words Read in Parts	Percentage of Words Read in Parts	No. Words Misread	Percentage of Words Misread	No. Words Not Seen	Percentage of Words Not Seen
A......	1,588	977	61.5	2	0.1	182	11.4	427	26.8
B......	1,588	797	50.2	628	39.5	126	7.9	37	2.3
C......	1,588	1,009	63.5	264	16.6	126	7.9	189	11.9

to work out more words than either of the other children and therefore, though the slowest, she is the most independent reader. A and C are the fastest readers. This probably seems strange when C was given to us as the poorest reader. It can be accounted for by the fact that she made much greater improvement than either of the other children, so that, when the experiment was finished she was the fastest reader of the group.

The results of the readings through the tachistoscope show two types of readers. Messmer[1] calls these two types the objective and

[1] Huey, *Psychology of Reading*, pp. 92.

subjective readers. A is a subjective reader; B and C are of the objective type. While A did not read more words correctly when seen on the instant, she read but two words in parts, and she misread and failed to read more words than the other children. She evidently never had learned to analyze words and always saw the total word form. B and C read a great percentage of the words in

TABLE VI

THE NUMBER OF PHONETIC AND SIGHT WORDS READ IN PARTS

	Total No. Words	No. Words Read in Parts	Percentage of Words Read in Parts	Total No. Phonetic Words	No. Phonetic Words Read in Parts	Percentage of Phonetic Words Read in Parts	Total No. Sight Words	No. Sight Words Read in Parts	Percentage of Sight Words Read in Parts
A......	1,588	2	0.1	834	0	0	754	2	0.2
B......	1,588	628	39.5	834	495	59.2	754	133	17.6
C......	1,588	264	16.6	834	220	26.3	754	44	5.8

TABLE VII

THE NUMBER OF PHONETIC AND SIGHT WORDS MISREAD

	Total No. Words	No. Words Misread	Percentage of Words Misread	Total No. Phonetic Words	No. Phonetic Words Misread	Percentage of Phonetic Words Misread	Total No. Sight Words	No. Sight Words Misread	Percentage of Sight Words Misread
A......	1,588	182	11.4	834	92	11.0	754	90	11.9
B......	1,588	126	7.9	834	57	6.8	754	69	9.1
C......	1,588	126	7.9	834	59	7.0	754	67	8.8

parts. They also misread and failed to read much fewer words than A. B and C depended much more upon phonics than A. Table VI shows that they also read a much larger percentage of the phonetic words in parts than of the sight words. While this is true, we see from Tables VII and VIII that they misread fewer phonetic words than sight words. The children who depended most upon phonics read with fewer errors than the one who read by word wholes.

No conclusions can be drawn from this limited study, yet it seems to me it would be worth while for primary teachers to study the reading of the pupils to find out whether phonics makes more careful as well as more independent readers or whether it leads children to see words in parts and thereby makes slower readers.

The children were taught by the initiative, word, sentence, and phonetic methods. They knew their letters and would often spell a word when trying to work it out.

TABLE VIII

THE NUMBER OF PHONETIC AND SIGHT WORDS NOT SEEN

	Total No. Words	No. Words Not Seen	Percentage of Words Not Seen	Total No. Phonetic Words	No. Phonetic Words Not Seen	Percentage of Phonetic Words Not Seen	Total No. Sight Words	No. Sight Words Not Seen	Percentage of Sight Words Not Seen
A......	1,588	427	26.8	834	.239	28.6	754	188	24.9
B......	1,588	37	2.3	834	17	2.0	754	20	2.6
C......	1,588	189	11.8	834	94	11.2	754	95	12.4

The most significant result in this study is the fact that these children, although taught by the same method, read words differently. I think also that the fact that the two children who depended most upon phonics and read a much greater percentage of the words in parts should be considered. We might conclude that these children had not had enough drill upon recognizing words on the instant; and that it is not enough to teach children how to build up words by means of phonics, but that these words should also have sufficient drill to enable the children to recognize them at sight.

STUDIES IN THE PRINCIPLES OF EDUCATION

CHARES H. JUDD
The University of Chicago

V. SELF-ACTIVITY

In one form or another this principle has been advocated by all of the writers on education in recent times. There is much that can be said in a very convincing way about the importance of arousing a student to activities in which he is naturally interested, and which he will pursue because his own spontaneous desires lead him toward these activities. Indeed, it is axiomatic that one cannot compel intellectual development on the part of another. The teacher can surround the student with all of the incentives to mental activity, but the mental activity must proceed from within.

The doctrine has sometimes been advocated in such an extreme form as to make it appear that it its advocates would leave entirely to the student the determination of what activities are to be undertaken in the school. It has sometimes been said, for example, that the study of Nature may safely be carried on in terms of the objects that children bring into the classroom. Furthermore, it has been said that it would be very much better to allow children to develop their number-work and the other formal types of knowledge through their own discovery of the relation of these types of knowledge to the constructive activities which they themselves initiate. Give a boy the opportunity to work in the shop or a girl the opportunity to deal with textiles, and depend upon these activities to bring in their train a series of questions which will induce the child to exert himself in further study in order that he may arrive at the solution of the questions which he has spontaneously raised.

Certainly when the doctrine is stated in this extreme form, we find ourselves in difficulty in applying it to ordinary school practices. Children undoubtedly exhibit from time to time forms of activity which it is very difficult for the school to utilize. A course commonly adopted in such cases is the suppression of these activities. Furthermore, it does not always follow that the children will bring into the classroom the objects which can most advantageously be studied together, or exhibit in their spontaneous activities just those tendencies which seem to be required for their systematic and economical development. Certain activities need to be suggested by the teacher at a given time in order that the general course may include all of the different phases of training that it is desirable to give the student.

These general statements about suppressing and arousing activities may be made concrete as follows: A child very frequently exhibits certain emotional types of behavior, such as fear or anger, which it is quite impossible for the school to regard as conducive to school activity. One may say in such a case as this that the school should turn the emotion into some other channel, and thereby utilize the energy which would be wasted or perverted if the emotion were allowed to go on without interruption. Such a statement as this is something of an evasion of the real issue. The fact is that the emotion of fear or anger or excitement must be changed, so that it is no longer the type of activity that the child would exhibit spontaneously, and this complete change in the mode of activity shows the importance of a kind of control exercised by the teacher which is superior to that which is supplied by the self-activity of the pupil at the moment and often in opposition to it. An emotion of anger must be checked either by a distracting engagement offered by the teacher, or by a repressive penalty which the teacher uses in order to redirect the child's behavior.

Again, it is very unlikely that a child without some guidance would give attention to certain phases of arithmetic. The teacher may utilize the natural desire of the child to be efficient in what he undertakes to do, but she usually has to carry the child farther in his efforts at exactness than he would naturally go. She calls his attention to the dangers of inexactness and by a comparison of other products with his own shows him the defects into which he has fallen. She thus stimulates in the student a desire to go farther than he naturally would go. She has therefore supplemented his tendencies toward self-guidance by certain social standards which she can present to him as legitimate motives for further behavior. The multiplication table is seldom learned through sheer self-activity.

These examples suggest the desirability of a re-examination of the whole principle of self-activity with a view to determining how far the impulses that children bring into the schools need to be modified on the one hand, or supplemented on the other, in order to make the child's training complete.

Before taking up this discussion of the enlargement of the child's natural activities it may be well to draw a distinction which is of importance in the discussion of this doctrine. Certain writers have emphasized in their discussions of self-activity bodily movements as important in bringing about mental development. All of those who are interested in shopwork and the various forms of constructive activity are likely to regard the principle of self-activity as a principle which emphasizes chiefly bodily movements. There has been a marked tendency in much of the recent reform literature in education to emphasize this phase of the matter. On the other hand, some of the earlier writings, and here and there a passage in the later literature, emphasize the significance of personality and the development of self as important in education. This phase of the doctrine is perhaps most productively set forth in some of the recent discussions which point out how desirable it is that the school should cultivate the ability of pupils to initiate activities without the aid of the teacher or of any of the common devices which are adopted in classroom organization. We sometimes speak of the initiative of the child as the highest characteristic which can be cultivated through education. Activity in this case is not bodily activity—it is rather the expression of mental energy and mental spontaneity. The suggestions which appear in the literature of methodology for the cultivation of initiative on the part of the pupils are relatively few and vague. At the same time some of the recent treatments of the problem of how one should study bring us repeatedly to this problem of the cultivation of independent initiative in attacking studies. The problem of cultivating initiative will be taken up in the next paper; the present paper will devote itself entirely to a discussion of the self-activity in its more obvious and concrete form of bodily activity as exhibited in the school exercises which involve such forms of behavior.

The question with which we shall deal in this paper may briefly be stated as follows: How far do the bodily activities which children exhibit on their own initiative serve as materials for education, and how far must these activities be modified through training? There is no need of reviewing in this connection the extensive literature which exists on instinctive forms of activity. It has been pointed out very fully in all of the studies which have been published by the students of child-study that education must in some sense begin with instinctive forms of behavior. It has also been shown in all of these studies that instincts undergo radical modifications as they develop into habits in mature life. Our problem is to determine how far the educational modifications of instincts may properly be recognized as limiting the validity of the doctrine of self-activity. Furthermore, education very often finds itself struggling with habits, in the effort to change an individual from what he would be through his own initiative into something which society would have him become. Thus when we learn that habit tends to become inflexible by repetition, that the individual has less and less conscious control over his habits the more they are repeated, we come on one of the striking antitheses between the natural evolution of the habit and the necessities of school training. Take for example the development of writing. In the early stages, when writing is a slow and laborious activity, the teacher and the child find themselves in co-operation in the effort to improve the form of the letters written. Without attempting to enter into too great detail as to the motives which prompt the pupil to write, it may be said that at this stage the child's spontaneous efforts to write furnish all of the material which the teacher needs in order to carry on the educational processes. But certainly by the time that the children reach the sixth and seventh grades there comes to be a very marked antagonism between the attitude of the teacher and the natural tendency of the child. The child at this stage in the effort to express himself tries to write as rapidly and fluently as possible, and it has frequently been noted in educational literature that a deterioration in the form of the writing is very noticeable at this stage of school work. The teacher finds that it is necessary to stand in the way of the natural deterioration of the habit of writing. New motives, wholly external to the individual, must be presented for keeping the letters clear and legible in form. This means that the pupil's consciousness must be drawn back time and time again to a certain aspect of his behavior which by nature tends to drop out of sight. Nature must be supplemented in this case and the child's self-activity must be refined in literal opposition to his natural tendencies.

A similar situation appears in drawing. The child is attracted to drawing in the early stages of school life for reasons that are natural enough. He is interested in the expression of the ideas which he has in mind and he enjoys his own products. If he were allowed to go on drawing in a way that would be entirely satisfactory to himself he would fall into certain crude conventions which would be very primitive if not purely personal in their character. There are several stages in the drawings of children and untrained adults which indicate complete though unwarranted satisfaction with the work which they produce. During these periods of self-satisfaction the teacher finds that it is his obligation to arouse in the learner a certain dissatisfaction with his own work. This the teacher must do by bringing to the attention of the student other drawings which are superior to his own. Or the teacher must add through criticisms certain new points of view which would not suggest themselves to the learner who is gradually dropping into a convention. That there is opposition between educational interference and the natural tendencies appears in the fact that a student who is brought to a realization of his defects gives up entirely the cultivation of the art of drawing. This giving up of the drawing habit is nothing more nor less than a reaction to criticism. If the teacher could carry the pupil over the period of discouragement by some external force which acts upon the individual from without just as did the criticism, if he could enforce during this period of discouragement a certain amount of drill and practice which is not in keeping with the child's own desire, there would follow a mastery of drawing at a higher level. Actual school experience shows abundantly that a period of discouragement may ultimately issue in successful behavior, but the later success of the behavior is not due to a natural impulse which has carried the child forward to the highest degree of perfection—it is due rather to a demand which has been imposed upon the child and carried far enough to perfect at a higher level an activity which if carried on merely spontaneously would never have gone to this higher level.

This same type of fact appears in the training of singers. Those who train singers find that their students must be carried beyond the natural stage of spontaneous self-activity in this art. The singing of the young child is undertaken because of the pleasure which he derives from the activity and he is able through his natural impulses to carry this art to a certain degree of perfection. If the educational activities stop with this natural tendency the learner will never reach the higher levels of perfection. Very often in the effort to reach the higher levels of perfection there is an intermediate period of discouragement and deterioration on the part of the pupil. He becomes self-conscious, as we sometimes say, and therefore less able to produce the sound. He becomes discouraged and his whole activity seems to be a failure, because it is no longer suggested by his own natural impulses and it is not yet satisfactory from the point of view of the critical teacher. Everything depends upon the way in which teachers manage a pupil at such a critical period. There is no final solution of this problem to the extreme partisan who would depend entirely on self-activity. One has to face frankly the fact that society is forcing upon the child standards which are external to the individual. Social demands may grow out of the aggregate of individual needs, but social demands are certainly more exacting than the natural tendencies of any individual.

Another example of the same type may be drawn from the experience of the manual-training teacher. Children come into the shops very enthusiastic about certain simple constructive activities which they wish to undertake. These constructive activities do not prove to be as easy as the children had expected. The natural impulse is to throw away the half-finished project or to use it in some imperfect and unsatisfactory form. Children who are left to their own constructive devices very seldom complete an object in any such way as to make it acceptable to the careful critic. If the teacher begins to try to direct these natural constructive impulses with a view merely to self-activity on the part of the child, he will find that he cannot carry the activity forward very far, because he will encounter all of the obstacles that come when activity is felt to be tedious. The teacher therefore has the alternative of accepting very imperfect work and waiting in the hope that these imperfections will be corrected in due course of natural development, or he must take a hand in the process and modify the natural course of the activity by requiring of the pupil certain definite improvements upon his natural activity. These improvements are not suggested to the pupil from within. His attention must be drawn by some outside agency to the desirability of better adjustments in his movements and in his use of tools, and it is only when these external demands for improvement are emphatic that he is aroused to efforts in the direction of perfecting his behavior. To speak of these latter forms of behavior as forms of self-activity is to fail to recognize the educational principle which must be followed in their cultivation. All instruction which leads to higher forms of activity assumes the existence of certain canons of perfection which are external to the individual, and superior to his own natural impulses.

The converse of the educative influence of the group on the individual is shown by those cases of deterioration which result when some member of one of the higher races associates for a time with savage or semi-civilized peoples. Here, again, it is not individual impulses merely which operate to drag the person downward, it is the absence of external influences which are necessary to keep up the high tension of civilized conduct. Life in a highly organized society requires certain forms of effort and certain radical readjustments of conduct which could never have come through self-activity.

Another way of putting the matter is to say that social life creates new problems for which the individual is not prepared by his native equipment, Nowhere is this more clearly shown than in a study of emotions. Emotions are the conscious parallels of certain fundamental instinctive forms of behavior. The emotions were at one time phases of very useful forms of self-activity. But with the development of social life the occasion for both the instinct and the emotion are largely gone. Take, for example, the emotion of anger. If an animal is interfered with in some activity or if he is engaged in combat it may be important for his self-preservation that he be aroused to a high pitch of excitement and to the most desperate struggle. An animal aroused to a state of rage will throw himself into an attitude of attack and will carry out the attack with unlimited vigor and with a use of every possible device of which he is capable. If a man were dependent upon his pure strength and upon his desperation of attack to achieve the ends of life, it would probably be advantageous for him very frequently to go about his activities in a high state of excitement or even anger. But we have come to recognize the fact that in civilized society the most effective action is that which is arranged with calm judgment. The argument seems to run, therefore, in the direction of a complete suppression of the emotion of anger. And yet there are undoubtedly social conditions which call for a much more vigorous attack than the calm, deliberate individual is likely to give them. The natural sort of anger is not useful. If any sort of anger is to be tolerated it must be of a socialized type. In the school we cannot allow the emotion to develop in a purely natural way, and if we try to hold to the principle of self-activity in any immediate and obvious interpretation of this principle we shall have great difficulty in knowing how to meet this situation which Nature has brought to us. If, on the other hand, we accept a higher principle of social guidance of natural activities, we may be able to turn the energy of natural emotional reaction in some new direction. In this case, however, we shall surely carry the individual through a period of suppression of his native, instinctive form of anger.

Another example of the same type appears in children's fears. When a child is afraid of a loud noise he is exhibiting a natural instinct which was of first importance to primitive man, who lived in a simple environment where any unfamilar noise meant the approach of some kind of danger. In the environment in which the civilized child grows up there are a great many noises which would have been terrifying noises in the open forest in which primitive man lived, but are mere indications of the large undertakings of a community life which depends chiefly upon heavy machinery. It is not important that the child should be frightened at these noises. Indeed, we must gradually bring him to a discriminating mode of reaction which is entirely different from that which Nature has provided in his instinctive organization. If fear is to be of any use to the school child it must take on an entirely different form and application. This will require educational interference of some kind with the natural tendency of the individual.

The conclusions of this paper are not different from those which were reached in an earlier discussion of the principle of education according to Nature. Attention was there called to the fact that Nature must be modified and developed in the direction of better social adaptation. The conclusion of this discussion is that a child's activities need very radical modification if the child is to have advantageous forms of reaction upon his environment. In the next paper the present discussion will be continued, and it will be shown that the individual not only should modify his forms of reaction but should also learn to attack situations which are never presented in Nature. Furthermore, he should, by his attack upon these situations, discover new problems. The business of the teacher is to show to the individual the opportunities and requirements of behavior which do not suggest themselves to him in his natural, personal reactions upon his environment. The teacher must very often stimulate types of behavior which never could have had their origin in spontaneous self-activity.

EDITORIAL NOTES

It may not be out of place to comment editorially on the difficulty which such a journal as this experiences in securing the right kind of material to place before its readers. There is educational experience of the greatest value going to waste all over the country because teachers and administrative officers do not know how to report their doings. Here are a few examples. A school superintendent who has worked out an organization for helping pupils to study refuses to report the progress of his organization because it would seem like boasting. There are doubtless others who have the same hesitancy about writing for educational publications. What these people need, and what we all need, is to cultivate the scientific attitude which is exhibited by writers and readers in all of the other technical journals. A physician or a surgeon who has treated a case with success reports the case to his colleagues as a case to be studied and understood. The impersonal attitude of the physician probably grows out of his recognition of the fact that any success he has had depends on his discovery of natural laws and his conformity to these laws. When he reports a case therefore he treats it as a report of natural law, not as a boast of personal achievement. Again, the engineer who has solved a difficult problem sends his plans to a technical journal with comments on his reasons for what he did. This is read with interest by other engineers and by students of engineering as a body of technical, scientific suggestion. The great discoveries of physics and chemistry and physiology are published without hesitation by the scientists who work in these fields. Why should teachers have a different attitude? The answer to this question is probably to be found in the failure of most educators to assume toward their work the scientific attitude.

Educational Discussions Should be Impersonal and Scientific

A second type of difficulty arises because some thoroughly practical men, when they sit down to write, feel that they must make abstract statements and must write about a great many different topics. The editors of this Journal have sought time and time again to get such material as that which was supplied by Superintendent Whitcher

They Should Not be Abstract

in the January number of the *Elementary School Teacher*, and when the material came to hand—if indeed it came at all—it consisted not of a plain statement of details of actual experience, such as Superintendent Whitcher gave, but of abstract general statements about education in general. Or if facts were included with the general comments on education they were stated in such a guarded way that no one could possibly imitate them or profit by their suggestiveness, This type of difficulty is probably to be traced to the fact that most of the books on education are full of theories rather than descriptions of actual practices. The student of the histories of education easily falls into the mistake of believing that in order to make history in this field of activity one must give vent to some speculative platitudes. The fact is, of course, that the real history of the school has consisted in the organization of courses in arithmetic, in new devices for promoting pupils, in new methods of treating grammar. *Barnard's Journal* is of importance to the student of education today because it is full of facts on such topics. No one reads the theoretical articles in that journal. Manuscript after manuscript goes back from the *Elementary School Teacher* because it consists entirely of discussions and has no examples on which the discussion can stand.

Device Material Should be Accompanied by Explanatory Statements

A third type of paper which goes back is that which gives some material which has been used in school and is now offered for publication but without any adequate statement of the purpose for which it was made or the situation into which it fitted. The intelligent appreciation of a dramatic exercise, for example, depends upon some knowledge of the way in which the class was brought up to the exercise presented. Many has been the failure resulting from a hasty effort to use an exercise clipped from an educational publication, with a class trained in a wholly different way from the class which originally succeeded with this same exercise. Indeed, when one becomes critical of the cheap suggestions which are published in journals of methods, his criticism is sometimes justified, not by the material itself, which might be useful if properly placed, but rather by the fact that there is no careful statement of how the material shall be employed. There is here the same danger that would arise from the distribution of a prescription which is not accompanied by a discriminating statement of the uses to which the prescription may be put. From time to time even poems come with the rest of the copy sent to the editor's desk. These purport to be useful to teachers but are usually unaccompanied by any statement as to the particular methods of application.

The Cultivation of a Professional Literature

A fourth difficulty which the editors of this Journal encounter is that people who are efficient in actual school work will not take the time to write. In other words, the claims of the profession are not heeded by these good people. They do not realize that if efficient organizers would only communicate with each other there would be great economy in the long run in the work of each because the experiences of others would be accessible to all. Colleges are making use of an instructor's published material in calling men to new positions. The recognition of the importance of a man's written work is apparent in the German schools today. The time will certainly come when a school board looking for a superintendent will take into account what he has written. The beginnings of this tendency appear at the present time in the disposition to read the annual reports of superintendents.

The Type of Article Which Is Solicited

The purpose of this editorial is to stimulate the creation of more professional educational literature of a high type. The time has come when a hearing can be had for such a literature. Serious educators are calling for something different from the abstract discussions which filled the older treatises. Scientific studies are being made in encouraging number. What is needed now is a general movement throughout the whole teaching profession in the direction of a full impersonal discussion of all current educational activities. This Journal seeks statements of facts from educational workers everywhere. These facts should be set forth with enough detail to be used by others. They should explain difficulties as well as favoring conditions. They should be made the basis of suggestions for new investigations which may carry forward in the spirit of practical application the experience already accumulated.

BOOK REVIEWS

New England Trees in Winter. By A. F. BLAKESLEE and C. D. JARVIS. Pp. 270. Published as Bulletin 69, Agricultural Experiment Station, Storrs, Conn. 1911.

This publication presents one hundred and eleven common New England trees as they appear in their winter condition. Most of these trees are found in other parts of the United States and Canada, which fact will make the book of universal interest. To teachers it is especially helpful to have so good a means of identification of trees at times when, through absence of leaves, identification is difficult to many people.

There is a clear and concise introductory discussion of the nature of a tree, followed by a key to the genera and species. Then each species of tree is presented in two pages, one of which is given to discussion of its habit, bark, twigs, leaf-scars, buds, fruit, comparisons, distribution, and wood. The other page is made up of photographic illustrations showing the form of the whole tree, the characteristics of the bark, twigs, buds; also flowers and fruit in those cases where they are winter characters. The illustrations are strikingly clear and representative. Altogether the presentation of the tree is such that the amateur students should be able to indentify these trees when found.

The book is bound in bulletin form and is sent to residents of Connecticut upon request and "to others who are specially interested in trees."

O. W. C.

The Social Composition of the Teaching Population. By LOTUS DELTA COFFMAN, PH.D. Published by Teachers College, Columbia University.

In this monograph Mr. Coffman reports the results of an inquiry which he made regarding the preliminary training and the experience of typical members of the teaching profession from a number of states. He sent out an inquiry to both rural and city school authorities from New Hampshire to Montana, and from the New England states to Texas. His inquiry does not cover all of the states of the Union, but it is regarded by the author as dealing with cases which are fairly representative of all types of teachers in the United States.

In addition to the questions mentioned above regarding experience and training, Mr. Coffman investigates the salary, the type of certificate now held by the teacher, the kinds of positions which he or she has held, and the home relation in which he grew up. The results of this investigation are presented in elaborate tables which make the material available for anyone who wishes to carry on like studies.

A general summary of the findings is given in a few paragraphs at the end of the volume. The following quotation indicates the scope of the inquiry and something of the results: "The typical American male public-school teacher, assuming that he can be described in terms of the medians previously referred to, but remembering that a median is a point about which individuals vary and that our hypothetical individual is as likely to be below as above it, is twenty-nine years of age, having begun teaching when he was almost twenty years of age after he had received but three or four years of training beyond the elementary school. In the nine years elapsing between the age he began teaching and his present age, he has had seven years of experience, and h s salary at the present time is $489 a year. Both of his parents were living when he entered teaching, and both spoke the English language. They had an annual income from their farm of $700 which they were compelled to use to support themselves and their four or five children.

"His first experience as a teacher was secured in the rural schools, where he remained for two years at a salary of $390 per year. He found it customary for rural-school teachers to have only three years of training beyond the elementary school, but in order for him to advance to a town-school position he had to get an additional year of training. He also found that in case he wished to become a city-school teacher that two more years of training, or six in all, beyond the elementary school were needed.

"His salary increased rather regularly during the first six years of his experience, or until he was about twenty-six years of age. After that he found that age and experience played a rather insignificant part in determining his salary, but that training still afforded him a powerful leverage."

A similar paragraph describes the average characteristics of the woman teacher in American schools.

Such a study as this of the members of the teaching profession does much to indicate the problems that lie before the normal schools and colleges that train teachers, and it also gives a very clear notion of the problems which the superintendent and principal encounter when they attempt to fill their teaching staff. The book is a good illustration of the application of scientific methods to problems of school organization.

C. H. J.

Agencies for the Improvement of Teachers in Service. By WILLIAM CARL RUEDIGER. Washington, D.C.: Government Printing Office.

This monograph, published by the Bureau of Education, calls attention to the many efforts that are being made at the present time to induce teachers to continue their studies after they have become established in school work. School institutes are the agencies most commonly employed for the training of teachers in service. The study made by Mr. Ruediger of these institutes reports for the most part facts regarding their organization and support. The study is very conservative in its criticisms, these being for the most part expressed in quotations from papers written by other authors. One cannot help feeling as he reads the monograph that more emphasis should have been laid upon these criticisms of teachers' institutes. Mr. Ruediger, however, has evidently regarded it as his chief duty to offer examples of what is undertaken and he has given some examples of full programs and announcements.

The other agencies which are employed, particularly in cities where many teachers are brought together, make an encouraging showing, and the summer schools and correspondence schools are discussed at sufficient length to show the value of these means of instruction. There are very interesting reports on teachers' meetings in the monograph, which might very properly serve as suggestive examples for those who are in charge of such meetings.

The monograph calls attention to the large service that the Bureau of Education is rendering in presenting compact statements of the educational agencies in this country. Many of these monographs are of interest to individual teachers, and all of them are helpful to administrators who are organizing school work.

C. H. J.

BOOKS RECEIVED

AMERICAN BOOK CO., CHICAGO

German Epics Retold. By M. Bine Holly. Cloth. Pp. 336. $0.65.

Primary Language Lessons. By Emma Serl. Cloth. Illustrated. Pp. 160. $0.35.

D. APPLETON & CO., NEW YORK

A Reader for the Sixth Grade. By Clarence F. Carroll and Sarah C. Brooks. Cloth. Illustrated. Pp. 288.

A Reader for the Seventh Grade. By Clarence F. Carroll and Sarah C. Brooks. Cloth. Illustrated. Pp. 288.

Stories and Story-Telling. By Angela M. Keyes. Cloth. Illustrated. Pp. 286.

GINN & CO., CHICAGO

Heroes of Everyday Life. A Reader for the Upper Grades. By Fanny E. Coe. Cloth. Illustrated. Pp. 169. $0.40.

D. C. HEATH & CO., BOSTON

Primary Speller. By Edwin S. Richards. Cloth. Pp. 124.

HOUGHTON, MIFFLIN CO., BOSTON

A Handbook of Health. By Woods Hutchinson. Cloth. Illustrated. Pp. 348. $0.65.

MACMILLAN CO., NEW YORK

Third Reader. By Kate F. Oswell and C. B. Gilbert. Cloth. Illustrated. Pp. 244. $0.40.

Syllabus of a Course of Study on the History and Principles of Education. By Paul Monroe. Paper. $0.25.

How to Learn English. By Anna Prior and Anna I. Ryan. Cloth. Illustrated. Pp. 253. $0.55.

JOHN JOS. McVEY, PHILADELPHIA, PA.

Reclaiming a Commonwealth, and other Essays. By President Cheesman A. Herrick. Cloth. $1.00.

OHIO UNIVERSITY PRESS

The Ohio University Bulletin. Souvenir Edition for the Ohio University Summer School of 1911. Paper. Pp. 244.

GOVERNMENT PRINTING OFFICE, WASHINGTON, D.C.

Annual Report of the Board of Regents of the Smithsonian Institution. Cloth. Illustrated. Pp. 674.

Teachers' Certificates Issued under General State Laws and Regulations. By Harlan Updegraff. Paper. Pp. 269.

CURRENT EDUCATIONAL LITERATURE IN THE PERIODICALS[1]

IRENE WARREN
Librarian, School of Education, The University of Chicago

Affleck, G. B. Bibliography of physical training. June–October, 1911. Am. Phys. Educa. R. 16:579–92. (D. '11.)

Allison, Samuel B. Vocational courses and the elementary school. School and Home Educa. 31:155–58. (D. '11.)

Andress, J. Mace. The aims, values, and methods of teaching psychology in a normal school. J. of Educa. Psychol. 2:541–54. (D. '11.)

Bagley, W. C. The outcomes of teaching. School and Home Educa. 31:140–44. (D. '11.)

Baldwin, Charles Sears. Intercollegiate debate. Educa. R. 42:475–85. (D. '11.)

Bardeen, C. W. The monopolizing woman teacher. Educa. R. 43:17–40. (Ja. '12.)

Black, Jessie, and Warren, Irene. A brief suggestive list of reading for children in the elementary school. El. School T. 12:145–50. (D. '11.)

Bobbitt, John Franklin. The efficiency of the consolidated rural school. El. School T. 12:169–75. (D. '11.)

Bourne, Henry Eldridge. The liberation of good will. Univ. of Chic. M. 4:1–13. (N. '11.)

Brown, J. Stanley. The functions of a modern high school in a system of public schools. School and Home Educa. 31:144–47. (D. '11.)

Capen, Samuel P. The supervision of college teaching. Pedagog. Sem. 18:543–50. (D. '11.)

Collins, Joseph V. How to get greater efficiency in arithmetic. Educa. Bi-mo. 6:103–10. (D. '11.)

Conklin, Edmund S. The pedagogy of college ethics. Pedagog. Sem. 18:421–74. (D. '11.)

[1] Abbreviations.—Am. Phys. Educa. R., American Physical Educational Review; Atlan., Atlantic Monthly; Cent., Century Magazine; Educa., Education; Educa. Bi-mo., Educational Bi-monthly; Educa. R., Educational Review; El. School T., Elementary School Teacher; Harp. W., Harper's Weekly; Journ. of Educa. Psychol., Journal of Educational Psychology; New England M., New England Magazine; Pedagog. Sem., Pedagogical Seminary; Pop. Sci. Mo., Popular Science Monthly; School and Home Educa., School and Home Education; School R., School Review; School W., School World; Univ. of Chic. M., University of Chicago Magazine; Voca. Educa., Vocational Education.

COOK, JOHN W. History of education. XV. School and Home Educa. 31:149–55. (D. '11.)

COOLEY, EDWIN G. Pre-apprenticeship schools of London. Voca. Educa. 1:174–83. (Ja. '12.)

COOPER, CLAYTON SEDGWICK. The American undergraduate. Cent. 83: 377–87. (Ja. '12.)

CROCHERON, B. H. A very real country school. World's Work 23:318–26. (Ja. '12.)

DAVENPORT, CHARLES B. The origin and control of mental defectiveness. Pop. Sci. Mo. 80:87–90. (Ja. '12.)

DUFFY, FRANK. How shall the obligation to provide industrial education be met? Voca. Educa. 1:193–95. (Ja. '12.)

EASTMAN, CHARLES A. Education without books. Craftsman 21:372–77. (Ja. '12.)

ELIOT, CHARLES W. The university president in the American commonwealth. Educa. R. 42:433–49. (D. '11.)

FISHBACK, E. H. The supervision of teachers. Educa. 32:234–36. (D. '11.)

GAYLER, G. W. A study of the enrolment by grades of fourteen school systems of central Illinois. School and Home Educa. 31:147–49. (D. '11.)

GRANT, PERCY STICKNEY. A Puritan school. New England M. 45:286–94. (N. '11.)

GRIFFIN, SOLOMON BULKLEY. The political evolution of a college president. Atlan. 109:43–51. (Ja. '12.)

GRUENBERG, BENJAMIN C. Some aspects of the child-welfare problem in the New York high schools. School R. 19:684–88. (D. '11.)

GUSTAFSON, LEWIS. A new task for the public schools. Voca. Educa. 1: 145–58. (Ja. '12.)

HALE, WILLIAM GARDNER. The practical value of humanistic studies. School R. 19:657–79. (D. '11.)

HANDSCHIN, C. H. Problems in the teaching of modern languages. Educa. 32:203–13. (D. '11.)

HEETER, S. L. The school of tomorrow. Educa. R. 42:465–74. (D. '11.)

HOLMES, W. H. Plans of classification in the public schools. Pedagog. Sem. 18:475–522. (D. '11.)

HOLTZ, FREDERICK L. Pedagogical problems in nature-study. Journ. of Educa. Psychol. 2:564–68. (D. '11.)

JACKSON, EDWIN R. Forestry in agriculture. Voca. Educa. 1:184–92. Ja. '12.)

JACKSON, NELSON A. The mission of the private school. Educa. 32:214–19. (D. '11.)

JORDAN, W. H. The function and efficiency of the agricultural college. Science 34:773–85. (8 D. '11.)

JUDD, CHARLES H. Studies in principles of education. El. School T. 12:176–85. (D. '11.)

JUDSON, HARRY PRATT. The idea of research. Univ. of Chic. M. 4:14–18. (N. '11.)

LEAVITT, FRANK M. The David Ranken Jr. school of mechanical trades. Voca. Educa. 1:159–73. (Ja. '12.)

———. The relation of the present movement for vocational education to the teaching of the mechanic arts. El. School T. 12:158–68. (D. '11.)

LURTON, FREEMAN E. The disintegration of a high-school class; a study in elimination. School R. 19:680–83. (D. '11.)

———. A study of retardation in the schools of Minnesota. Science 34:785–89. (8 D. '11.)

MICHELSON, A. A. The American association for the advancement of science: Recent progress in spectroscopic methods. Science 34:893–902. (29 D. '11.)

MUSSEY, H. R. Education and pay of head and hand. Educa. R. 42:450–64. (D. '11.)

NICOLSON, FRANK W. The certificate system in New England. Educa. R. 42:486–503. (D. '11.)

OWEN, WILLIAM BISHOP. Co-operation between home and school. Educa. Bi-mo. 6:95–102. (D. '11.)

RADOSAVLJEVICH, PAUL R. Pedagogy as a science. Pedagog. Sem. 18:551–58. (D. '11.)

REBER, LOUIS E. University extension and the state university. Science 34:825–33. (15 D. '11.)

RITTER, WM. E. The duties to the public of research institutes in pure science. Pop. Sci. Mo. 80:51–57. (Ja. '12.)

SHEPARDSON, FRANCIS WAYLAND. Philippine education. Univ. of Chic. M. 4:19–23. (N. '11.)

SHERWOOD, ADA SIMPSON. An old-time pedagog. Educa. R. 43:41–48 (Ja. '12.)

SMITH, THEODATE L. Dr. Maria Montessori and her houses of childhood. Pedagog. Sem. 18:533–42. (D. '11.)

SNEDDEN, DAVID. What of liberal education? Atlan. 109:111–17. (Ja. '12.)

STEELE, A. G. Training teachers to grade. Pedagog. Sem. 18:523–32. (D. '11.)

STETSON, CUSHING. A school for tars. Harp. W. 55:9–10. (9 D. '11.)

STEVENSON, JOHN J. Small colleges. Pop. Sci. Mo. 80:58–65. (Ja. '12.)

STOCKWELL, S. S. The public-school course of study. Educa. 32:197–202. (D. '11.)

TOZIER, JOSEPHINE. The Montessori apparatus. McClure 38:289–302. (Ja. '12.)

(A) university inaugural. Dial 51:515–16. (16 D. '11).

WALLIS, B. C. Geographical books for the school library. School W. 13: 453–54. (D. '11.)

WEISS, A. P. On methods of mental measurement, especially in school and college. J. of Educa. Psychol. 2:555–63. (D. '11.)

WELLS, FRANCES D. Literature and life. Educa. Bi-mo. 6:170–74. (D. '11.)

WETTER, A. A. Great educators, IV. Rousseau. Educa. 32:220–25. (D. '11.)

WETTSTEIN, CARL T. Schools for defective children in Europe. Educa. R. 43:49–61. (Ja. '12.)

WHITE, W. A. The place of music in public education. Educa. Bi-mo. 6:136–45. (D. '11.)

WILD, LAURA H. Training for social efficiency. Educa. 32:226–33. (D. '11.)

WILM, EMIL C. Colleges and scholarship. Educa. R. 43:62–68. (Ja. '12.)

VOLUME XII NUMBER 7

THE ELEMENTARY SCHOOL TEACHER

MARCH, 1912

CORN[1]

CHARLES A. McMURRY
De Kalb State Normal School

INTRODUCTION (FOR TEACHERS)

The following treatment of the subject of corn is intended as a geography topic for fifth or sixth grade.

Preceding this in the earlier grades a number of lessons have probably been given on the corn topic, both in geography and science, while history and literature have dealt with it also in important ways. These preliminary lessons may be presupposed somewhat as follows.

In primary classes the children have planted corn in window boxes and have watched its growth. Sprouting it between wet blotting papers may have been tried also. In the spring and summer gardens on the campus, the children have planted, cultivated, and harvested the corn. In the fall they may have studied the ripening corn in tassel. This is an excellent lesson on the corn plant as a type of grasses and grains, with which it is compared by bringing specimens of wheat, oats, rye, and the grasses together.

In the third or fourth grade the corn has been studied locally as a geography topic in the prairie region surrounding us in Illinois. Its method of cultivation, its uses on the farm, and its shipment to the Chicago market are worked out.

The pioneer history stories of the prairie states make frequent statements regarding the uses of corn among the Indians and early

[1] This is the first of three papers which constitute the report of the Committee of Seven of the Superintendents and Principals' Association of Northern Illinois.

settlers. In literature and reading, the "Hiawatha" has probably brought to children the beautiful story of Mondamin as told by Longfellow. The children have also seen something of the corn shows and corn testing which are now somewhat common in our schools.

In the present treatment of this topic the children are supposed to have reached the point where they can take up this study from a geographical point of view, and work out the problem of corn production on a large scale in the corn belt, and expand this into a comprehensive survey of its importance for the United States and America.

A brief extension of the idea to other corn- and grain-producing countries may close the treatment with a world survey, though the completion of this phase of the topic may be left to later grades.

The historical thread upon which the treatment is developed is designed to give a concrete and progressive expansion of the thought in close relation to historic facts. This rapid development of the thought may take strong hold upon the minds of children. It interprets the world in a constantly enlarging horizon of thought, bringing in something new and instructive at every step.

OUTLINE ON CORN

1. Corn in the native wild state.
2. Cultivation of corn in Indian villages.
3. The pioneer settlers and their use of corn.
4. The prairie and other farmers of the corn belt.
5. The inventions and machines connected with corn production. Manufacturing plants for agricultural machinery.
6. The cultivation of corn at the agricultural department of the State University. Experiments by scientific experts.
7. Extension of corn cultivation north and south of the corn belt.
8. Other corn-producing countries in America, Europe, Asia, Africa, etc.
9. Corn turned to bad uses—whiskey.
10. Corn compared with other important cereals—wheat and rice.

SUGGESTIONS AS TO METHOD

1. Although geographical in its main purpose this topic is, to a large extent, historical and may be illustrated with pictures from the various periods of history included.

2. Make a collection of the regular products and by-products of corn, as flour, bran, starch, glucose, sugar, oil, breakfast foods, etc. Such bottled collections can be had from some of the manufacturing companies, as The Corn Products Company of Chicago, The American Starch Company, Oswego, N.Y.
3. The later geographies contain maps showing the corn belt in the United States and its extension north and south. Let children also make maps illustrating the corn and grain belts.
4. At the Field Columbian Museum of Chicago is found a large collection of corn and its by-products, well worth visiting with a class.
5. The practical bulletins in regard to corn cultivation and soil treatment, silos, etc., can be had from the State Agricultural Experiment stations, especially for Illinois, Iowa, and other states of the corn belt, and from the government at Washington.
6. A comparison of the corn belt with that for wheat and small grains, and for cotton and other staple products is of much value. Maps showing these areas are in the geographies or can be worked out on outline maps.
7. This topic is one of great interest at the present time in connection with agriculture in the schools and Farmers' Institutes.
8. The supplementary references in geographical readers and in history and literature, as in "Hiawatha," the "Corn Song," etc., are well worth attention.
9. Excursions to corn and grain fields and to experiment stations, and experiments with planting, cultivating, selection, and testing of corn may be carried out to much advantage.
10. A closer inspection of farm machinery at the implement stores and even experience in handling these machines is desirable.
11. Closely related science topics bearing on soils and fertilizers, and experiments on the growth of plants with whatever constructive problems belong to them should be associated with these corn studies.

CORN

1. Corn in its various uses has become one of the great staple products which figure in the large concerns of the world market.

The corn belt in the United States is peculiarly interested in the successful cultivation of corn. In a larger sense corn is produced in nearly all parts of the United States, and is hardly surpassed in importance by any single product.

Originally the corn plant was a wild specimen of the grasses growing in the warm subtropical parts of America, as Mexico. We may suppose that even then it was of some value to the birds and animals feeding on grain, as is the wild rice, the weed seeds, and the nuts and fruits growing wild upon the trees and bushes. The Indians probably found it good relishable food where they could pluck it in the milk or later in the ripened grain.

In the wild state the ears were smaller, as the ground was not cultivated and there was no selection of seed. As in the case of other grains and fruits, it has taken centuries and perhaps thousands of years to develop corn from its primitive wild state, where the stalks were short and the ears small, to the large fruitful stalks and ears of our best varieties of corn, today.

2. The white men, when they first came to the regions of the eastern and southern states, found the Indian women cultivating corn in small fields about their villages. By this time the corn plant had spread northward from the semitropical countries and under cultivation had become a strong, hardy plant producing good large ears. In New England and in Virginia, the early settlers found it a strong necessity to procure corn from the Indians, who stored it away in baskets for the winter supply of food. The first explorers of the Illinois River valley, under LaSalle, found stores of corn in the Indian villages.

Along the valleys of central New York, among the Iroquois, were many villages and quite extensive fields of Indian corn, which gave a settled aspect to the country and brought about the beginnings of social and political life and a stronger organization of society.

The Indians had interesting legends of the corn plant, like that which Longfellow has told in Hiawatha, which expressed their notion of the importance of corn to them as a people. They had not only learned how to plant and cultivate corn, but also interesting modes of cooking and using it in palatable dishes, which were learned by the early settlers and have remained common to this day, as cornmeal mush, hominy, hoe cakes or pone cakes.

In central New York, in the Maumee Valley of Ohio, and in other Indian settlements, the power of the hostile Indians was finally broken by destroying their villages and laying waste their corn fields.

3. The pioneer settlers in Virginia and New England suffered much from hunger and starvation till they had learned from the natives how to plant and raise a corn crop. In Virginia the starving time well-nigh destroyed the colony before they divided up the land into small farms and allowed each man or family to clear the ground for the planting of corn, beans, and pumpkins. But from that time on there was abundance of food.

In pushing westward upon hunting and exploring trips the pioneers carried with them for food a store of parched corn and sometimes they sent forward in the early spring a few men to plant fields of corn for use by the later settlers when they arrived during the summer and fall. This was the case with Robertson, who settled at Nashville.

John Fiske says that on account of corn being more easily raised, harvested, and changed into food than wheat and other grains, it had a great influence upon the rapid settlement and the westward movement of population during pioneer times.

Not only in the hard labors of the pioneers did corn figure, but in their social festivities. The corn-husking frolics were among the chief of social events and the song of the huskers celebrates their festive sports. On Thanksgiving day even till now we gather in the yellow or speckled corn and the tall yellow fodder to decorate our houses and schoolrooms. Popcorn has likewise long held a favorite place at family gatherings and in the fun and frolic of the children.

Throughout the eastern states and far into the Ohio Valley it was necessary to cut down the forests and clear away the brush and logs before a corn crop could be raised. This rendered the early life of the pioneers hard and laborious. Even upon the prairies the tough sod, which had never been disturbed, had to be broken by the heavy breaking plow by one or more yokes of oxen and it required one season to rot the heavy matting of grass roots before the full crops could be secured. But the ground once broken or cleared was rich in vegetable mold and produced surprising crops of corn, melons, vegetables, and other grains, fruits, etc.

4. But the uses of corn in early pioneer days were only the beginning (and a very small beginning) of that vast and profitable farm business of corn-raising which is now carried on in what is known as the *corn belt* of the United States. The few hundreds and thousands of bushels raised in pioneer days have grown into the millions, hundreds of millions, and even billions of our present enormous production. Instead of a few little patches in the river bottoms and around the Indian villages, instead of a number of scattered clearings for corn in the boundless forests of the Ohio Valley, we now find corn fields stretching away field after field over millions of acres.

As the early immigrants moved acrosss the Alleghenies into the Ohio Valley and opened up new farms they soon found that they were raising more corn, grain, and stock than they could use. These new-found lands were so rich that they gave an abundant surplus. The great question in those early days of the nineteenth century was how to find a market in which to dispose of their surplus products. They began to raise pigs, cattle, sheep, and horses, but soon they had too many of these also. Some of these products of the corn belt, they loaded upon flat boats and sent down the river to New Orleans. Recall the story of Lincoln going down the Mississippi River on a flatboat. As soon as the Erie Canal was built, they began to ship their surplus corn, meat, etc., by way of the lakes, Erie Canal, and Hudson to New York. The old National road across the Alleghenies helped them, but much more the Pennsylvania, New York Central, Baltimore & Ohio, and other railroads, which were built to carry the products of the corn country to New York, Philadelphia, and Baltimore. So great were the products of the corn country that they overflowed, beyond New York and Philadelphia, were loaded upon ships for Liverpool, Hamburg, Havre, and other parts of the world.

At the present time the products of the corn belt pour in vast streams eastward over the railroads and by way of the lakes to eastern markets and to Europe.

Corn is the chief product of the corn belt but closely dependent upon it are several other large farm industries, as pork and cattle raising, the dairy and creamery business, the canning of corn, whiskey production in the distilleries, and the great milling industries dependent largely upon corn. In the feeding of stock, as hogs, cattle, and horses, the corn is changed into other farm products of increased value, and the manures so much needed for preserving the fertility of the soils are retained on the farm.

In the silos constructed for feeding dairy cows, not only the ears of corn but the stalks and leaves are converted into a nutritious food of the best kind for producing milk and butter. In recent years many various products of corn have been found serviceable as food for the people, new dishes have been discovered, and it is claimed that corn can be used far more extensively as a nourishing food for human beings. Good corn bread can hardly be surpassed by any kind of warm bread. Hominy and grits are very extensively used in some parts of the country. Corn meal mush and corn flakes are among the best of breakfast foods. Roasting ears in season and canned corn are important food articles in the groceries. From the sale of corn or of corn-fed meats, as of dairy products, the farmers of the corn belt have grown well-to-do, and independent. They have been able from sale of the products of the corn fields to supply themselves with other foods and clothing, fruits, and drinks, as tea, coffee, and chocolate, and the hundreds of manufactured articles of many sorts which are needed by farmers' families. Even the luxuries such as fine china and glassware, tropical fruits, imported silks and laces, pictures and libraries, pianos and automobiles are now very common articles in farmers' homes. Thousands of well-to-do American families of the corn belt are able to send their children to good schools, to put them later through college and university and to train them for any of the higher professions or for a life work in any of the technical and skilled industries. In fact it is from such farmers' families that many of the best educated and most useful men and women of our country are now coming.

5. The rapid development of corn production throughout the corn-growing states has brought about a great improvement in the machines for planting, cultivating, and harvesting of this crop. Among the notable machines invented for these purposes are the following: plows, corn-planters, cultivators, steel-toothed rakes, corn-huskers, corn-shellers, corn-cutters, silos and silage cutters, machines used in canning corn, various forms of corn elevators and roller-mills and other milling machinery.

For the construction of these various machines enormous manufacturing plants have been established at Chicago and in many other cities of the western and even of the eastern states. The general improvement in agricultural machinery and methods of cultivation has been one of the greatest proofs of progress in America and of the inventiveness of our people.

6. The importance of the corn fields to our people is shown in a striking way at the State Universities. In the agricultural department of the University of Illinois experiments have been conducted by scientific experts for

the purpose of increasing the productiveness of Illinois farms. In the cultivation of corn a careful series of experiments has been carried on which has opened the eyes of Illinois farmers. It has been shown that the farmer by careful selection of seed, by proper fertilizing and treating of the soil, and by the best modes of cultivation, can produce nearly three times as much corn per acre as at present. In short our farmers might be twice as rich as they are and could more than double the number of millions of bushels they have to sell or feed. This makes it worth while to study scientifically the best methods of treating the soil and of cultivating corn.

On the University Experiment Farm are many plots of ground where various kinds of field corn are raised and different modes of cultivation tried out, where different fertilizers are tested as to results upon the crops. The selection and development of the best breeds and strains of corn have been worked out with great care. In the Farmers' Institutes all over the state the people are made acquainted with the results of these experiments and the farmers' boys are called in and trained in corn testing. The majority of older farmers go on raising corn in the old way, but in many farm neighborhoods these better, more scientific, methods of corn raising and corn feeding are gradually introduced and worked out to success.

At the University experiment stations, college professors, who have thoroughly studied plant and animal life, who are well posted in physics, chemistry, and biology, who have made a study of soils and fertilizers, are constantly at work applying their knowledge of all these subjects to the raising of corn. For the most successful cultivation of corn depends upon many kinds of scientific knowledge. The corn plant itself in its various stages of growth must be understood. What kind of soil elements are needed and what are the chemical elements in such soils? Some soils are deficient and require the addition of certain definite fertilizers, as potassium or nitrates in order to raise good corn. The soil itself requires, according to its quality different kinds of treatment, with plow and harrow, or tile drainage, or rotation of crops from year to year. Certain insects, as chinch bugs and grubs are destructive to corn crops and it is a scientific problem how to get rid of them.

All these and many other questions have to be experimentally worked out at the University. The proper raising of a corn crop has become a very interesting problem for a large group of scientific experts at the University.

This is the case at many of our state universities because the corn belt includes several great states as Illinois, Indiana, Iowa, Kansas, Minnesota, etc.

7. But the corn-producing region stretches far to the south as well as north of the so-called corn belt. In the Gulf states corn has always been a valuable crop and should become more so. In Minnesota and the Northwest, corn is rapidly becoming an important crop, taking the place largely of the wheat fields. In fact certain varieties of corn have been developed which flourish in northern latitudes. They grow more quickly and ripen more rapidly in the

short, warm northern summers where frost comes early. Corn has been raised and ripened in northwestern Canada as far north as 56° N. latitude. Thus a plant that originated in subtropical lands has gradually modified its nature so as to adapt itself to more northern climates and is now actually cultivated in fields over the greater portion of North America.

Of course, a great variety of field and garden corn has been thus developed, as the white, yellow, and other kinds of field corn, sweet corn and popcorn among garden varieties.

8. Corn was originally a product of the new world of the west and its chief centers of production are in the United States. But it is now cultivated in the temperate regions of South America where the climate and soil conditions are favorable.

In southern Europe corn is produced as an important crop in Hungary, Italy, in the valley of the Po, and other warmer parts of southern Europe. In England and Scotland, in North Germany, Scandinavia, and northern Russia corn is not produced as a crop. Corn requires a summer season of hot warm days and nights with a moderate degree of well distributed moisture. Northern Europe is too chilly for the corn. But wheat, oats, barley, and rye flourish in these cooler places.

In India also and southern Asia, the corn plant has found a home because of favorable soil and conditions of heat and moisture. Parts of southern Australia and Africa are also adapted to corn production.

9. The corn plant is well known to us as one of the few great cereals which are chief among the food plants for the support of the human race. Like all good things it can be turned to bad use. In the manufacture of whiskey in the corn states, millions of bushels of corn are used yearly. Other grains, like rye are also used for whiskey production, but corn is the grain that is chiefly employed. Our great cities like Chicago, Peoria, and St. Louis have distilleries where millions of dollars are invested in the production of whiskey. The large amount of whiskey made is shown by the millions of dollars of taxes collected by the United States government from the distilleries. It is one of the chief sources of revenue to the government, known as excise or internal revenue.

10. Corn is a somewhat new product that has come into use since the discovery of America, and more particularly in the last one hundred years.

The other grains like wheat and rice have been in common use from antiquity. Wheat and rye for bread-making have been in use for thousands of years in Europe, in Egypt and in other eastern countries and later in America. Rice, which is the chief food of the Chinese, is probably as much used for the feeding of the human race as corn, and is now produced in considerable quantity in the southern Atlantic and Gulf States.

It has been claimed that the development of the world in civilization has depended upon the successful cultivation of the great cereals.

LIST OF REFERENCES ON CORN

Corn Plants, Their Uses and Ways of Life. F. L. Sargent. Houghton Mifflin Co.

How the World is Fed. Carpenter. American Book Co.

Geography of Commerce. Trotter. Macmillan.

Encyclopedia Americana on "Corn."

Geography of Commerce and Industry. Rocheleau. Educational Publ. Co.

How We Are Fed. Chamberlain. Macmillan.

Special Method in Elementary Science. (An illustrated science lesson.) Macmillan.

University of Illinois Bulletins on "Corn," Nos. 87, 126, 128, 100, 130, 133, 129.

U. S. Depart. of Agriculture, Farmers Bulletin No. 32.

The American Industry of Corn Products. T. B. Wagner. London: Vacher & Sons.

GROUPED OBJECTS AS A CONCRETE BASIS FOR THE NUMBER IDEA

FRANK N. FREEMAN

The purpose of this article is to give the results of an experimental investigation of number perception in children and adults, and to discuss the bearing of the results of the investigation upon the early development of the number idea in the child.[1] At the outset of the experiment the question to which an answer was sought was the following: What is the difference between the number of objects which may be grasped together in a single act of the attention by an adult and by children of various ages? The question may be illustrated from the field of vision. If there are a number of similar objects in a small group one finds it possible to distribute his attention at a given moment over a certain number of these objects, but if the number is increased he soon finds a limit beyond which it is impossible to grasp all the objects simultaneously. That is, if he attempts to include more in his attention he will find that the collection begins to break up into two or more groups each of which is small enough to be recognized. He then finds an oscillation of attention between groups. The number of objects which can be held simultaneously in a single act of attention by an adult is fairly uniform for different people and averages about five or six. The number of objects which can be grasped in this way is said to determine the scope of attention.

The question with which the experiment was begun, was then: How far do children differ from adults in this elementary capacity called the scope of attention? The assumption which underlay this investigation was that the answer to the question would have some bearing upon the relation between the number perception of

[1] For a detailed account of the experiment and its result see Frank N. Freeman, "Aufmerksamkeitsumfang und Zahlauffassung bei Kindern und Erwachsenen," in *Arbeiten aus dem Institut für Psychologie und experimentelle Pädagogik*, Band I; Alfred Hahn, Leipzig.

children and that of adults. The perception of a series of objects does not necessarily involve number perception, it is true. That is, a person may be able to compare two groups of objects and say that one group contains more objects than the other without definitely counting the number of objects in either group. Again we may test whether or not a person has correctly grasped a group of objects by requiring him to draw them. This might merely be an evidence that he has retained a visual image of the objects and of their arrangement. Although the ability to grasp a series of objects in the attention does not necessarily involve a developed number perception, it does undoubtedly underlie number consciousness: From any point of view, therefore, a study of the scope of attention will throw light on number ideas.

In order to determine the scope of attention in its simplest form it is necessary to present objects which do not have any definite form of grouping. The apprehension of a number of objects simultaneously under these circumstances requires that each object be regarded as a separate unit. If in even this first case one can arrange the objects in a group in his mind he can grasp very many more than the five or six which mark the limit of the scope of attention. In order to measure the scope of attention under relatively very simple conditions without grouping so far as the external objects were concerned, the objects were arranged in a horizontal line with an equal distance between them as in Series I, Fig. 1. Later, in order to test more complex perception, which has a more direct relation to the number idea, the objects were arranged in various kinds of groups. The chief forms of grouping which were used are shown in Fig. 1. The results of tests with these groups showed that greater difference in general exists between the children and adults in the perception of the grouped objects than in the perception of the ungrouped objects.

The method of presenting the objects was to expose upon a large screen and for very brief intervals of time the desired number of circles of light upon a dark background. The room was kept in dim light and the spots of light upon the screen were enough brighter than the background to be clearly seen. The projection apparatus was on the opposite side of the screen from the child and was, therefore, out of sight. It consisted in a stereopticon lantern in which were inserted cards with holes of various numbers and arrangements punched in them. The exposure was made by allowing a pendulum upon which was fixed a large screen having in it an opening of variable size to swing through the beam of light. By adjusting the size of this opening the length of time of the expo-

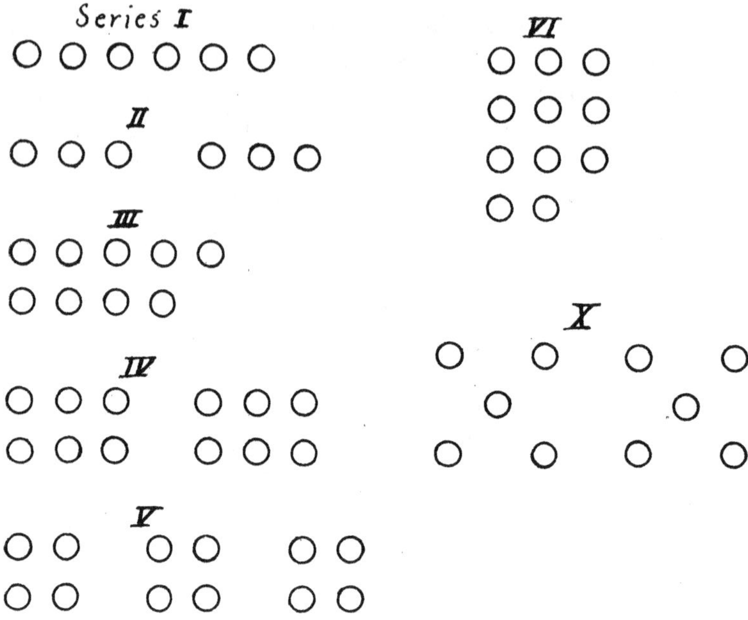

FIG. 1.—Illustrations of forms of grouping used in the experiment

sure could be regulated. The results of the experiment may be summarized as follows.

The persons who served as subjects of the experiment included both children and adults. The ages of the children ranged from six to fourteen years, but the children below the age of eight gave such incomplete and varying results that no positive conclusions could be drawn regarding their perception of number. This was probably due to their inability to grasp the stimulus in the brief time during which it was exposed. The differences which were found between the eight- to ten-year-old and the twelve- to fourteen-year-old children can, however, be extended, without serious danger of error, to the younger children.

The first fact which was brought out was that less difference exists in the scope of attention between adults and children than might be expected. If we place the scope of attention of the adults and older children at about five, that of the younger children would be not less than four. That is, up to and including four objects, the younger children could judge the number as correctly as adults. Later results make it clear that there are differences of a marked character between adults and children; this difference in the number of objects which can be grasped simultaneously may account in some measure for the difference in the capacity of children and adults to deal with number, but it can account for only a small part of the difference between the mature and immature individual. Though there is some difference in this elementary capacity yet the greater part of the difference must be ascribed to the more complex process of organizing the impressions which are received and not to the simple process of grasping the impressions themselves. This was brought out clearly by the fact that as the numbers which were shown increased beyond the limits of the scope of attention, the correctness of judgment of the children fell off very much more rapidly than was the case with adults. This introduces us to the second main result of the experiment.

Though the difference in the scope of attention between adults and children was not great, there was a marked difference in the ability to perceive and correctly judge grouped objects which extended considerably beyond the scope of attention. A marked tendency on the part of adults to organize their perceptions into regular groupings was manifested even in the case of the objects which were in reality ungrouped. That is, an adult was very apt to divide a series of objects equidistant from one another and arranged in a horizontal line into several subgroups of from two to four each. By this process the whole number could be very much more easily managed. This, then, accounts for the fact above mentioned that adults could correctly judge numbers which extended beyond the number which they could grasp directly, even if the number extended much beyond the scope of attention.

When it came to the judgment of objects which were objectively grouped, the same result appeared. Adults and older children nearly always noticed the way in which the objects were arranged. A younger child, on the other hand, was very much slower in seeing that the objects were arranged in the form of a square or in groups of three, five, or six as the case might be, and in many cases the younger children failed entirely to grasp the arrangement. Furthermore, when they did arrange the objects into groups they often put them in a far-fetched and unnatural arrangement. For example, it occurred several times that a child would see two groups of five as in Series X, in the following way: One horizontal row of four, one horizontal row of two, and a second horizontal row of four. Or the groups of four objects, Series V, might be seen as groups of two in horizontal rows. Obviously, then, the younger children were very deficient in the way in which they organized the impressions into regular forms of grouping.

This organization of objects into regular forms is very closely related to number processes, and, as will be shown later, training in this form of perception is one of the best means of giving the child a grasp of the simpler number operations. The child's ordinary experience gives some basis for education in this organization of his impressions into regularly arranged groups. Most of the things with which he has to deal are so arranged. The plates on a table, for example, are symmetrically arranged. The panes in a window have a regular arrangement. The desks in school are arranged in rows with so many in each row. The trees on a street are planted in regular order. Thus his everyday experiences lead the child to the notion of grouping objects and of dealing with them as groups made up of certain numbers of individuals instead of leaving him with the tendency to look at individuals separately. This informal education, however, might very well be supplemented more extensively by formal training in the recognition of grouped objects.

Some of the applications of these general principles to the training of the child in number perception and in the use of number may be made.

The method of using groups of individual objects to illustrate various numbers and their combinations was formerly employed by means of the old-fashioned abacus. This has largely gone out of use in the United States, but its place has been taken in Germany by somewhat more elaborate forms of apparatus. Introductory number work which consists in counting groups of objects has been largely replaced in the United States by the use of measurement as the first stage of arithmetic. This is perhaps due in large measure to the idea that only those units are suitable for illustrating number which are absolutely identical. It is obvious that units of measurement are more nearly identical than separate individual objects. The belief, however, that it is necessary to use identical units is entirely without foundation, and overlooks the fact that number is abstract and is not dependent upon the other characteristics of objects. We may choose to regard any object whatever as a unit and may count it with other units of different concrete nature. In fact it is advantageous at times to use different kinds of objects in order to bring out the fact that the number relations of objects are different from their other relationships. For example, it is perfectly possible to count together twelve chairs and six tables and say we have eighteen pieces of furniture.

The abacus, however, was not especially well suited to this purpose because of the fact that it did not permit of arranging the objects in various forms of grouping. The "reckoning machines" which are used in Germany are so constructed that the objects may be arranged in groups of two, three, four, five, etc. In addition they are so constructed that a group may be made up of two subdivided groups. The subdivision may be made by a line between two subgroups or by having a part of the large group in one color and part in another. Whatever the device used, the aim is conveniently to arrange objects in different groups and subgroups. It is not necessary, however, to have an apparatus for this purpose. The same aim can be attained by the use of the blackboard. The main point to be established is the value of the method.

Other forms of concrete experience are largely used in developing the number idea in the child. Each of these has certain characteristic advantages and disadvantages. The first method by which the child is introduced to the idea of number is ordinarily that of counting. The child learns to count before he comes to school. Some of the forms of counting, however, obviously do not involve any idea of number. The child may say over the number names without applying them to any objects in particular, just as he would say over the A, B, C's. He may even say over the names of the numbers and at the same time point to objects, and still not have a clear idea of the fact that the final number which he reaches refers to the whole group of objects rather than to the last one in the series. That is, his idea may be of the ordinal type, first, second, third, etc., in which the number refers to a position in a series rather than to a whole group. Counting, therefore, serves as an introduction to number, but is not itself self-sufficient for the complete development of the idea. Some form of grouping must be added.

The process of measurement which has been extensively adopted instead of counting differs from counting or the perception of grouped objects in that the unit is not a concrete object but is a fraction of a whole quantity. For example, when we say that a pole is five feet long, or that a pail contains five quarts of water, the individual foot, or the individual quart, is not sharply set off from the other units of the whole quantity. The unit is itself represented, it is true, by a measure which in the illustrations would be a foot rule or a quart measure, but in the recognition of the concrete quantity which represents a multiple of the unit, the unit itself does not appear. Measurement, then, has its particular advantage and its particular disadvantage. The advantage is that the attention is naturally directed to the whole quantity which the number represents, as contrasted, for example, with the tendency in counting to see each element of the group separately. The disadvantage, however, is that the attention is not naturally directed to the units of which the quantity is composed. The illustration may be further developed in connection with the concrete representation of a simple number operation. If we divide an area or a quantity of any sort into two fractional parts, we may easily perceive that the whole quantity is equal to the sum of the two fractional quantities. Our attention is not, however, directed to the actual number relations between the two fractional quantities and the whole, as it is when a group of objects is divided into two subgroups.

It is precisely at this point that the use of objects in various forms of grouping is suited to represent in a concrete way the number operations. If we have a group of five objects we may fix our attention upon this group as a whole, or we may divide the group into two parts and fix our attention upon a group of three objects by itself and upon a group of two objects by itself. This very clearly brings out the numerical fact that a group of five objects may be composed of a smaller group of three and a group of two. We here have combined the view of the whole quantity as represented by the total number and at the same time the thought of the individual units of which the whole group is composed.

In conclusion, we may further illustrate the way in which grouped objects may be used to form the concrete basis for the idea of the fundamental number operations. Suppose that we assume that the child is able to grasp at once four objects. He may then comprehend that a group of four objects may be made up of two groups of two objects each, and when he has grasped this fact he has comprehended the real nature of division. He may not even know the names of the numbers. Of course in order to use this idea in a practical way it is necessary that he have a command of the number names and of the figures which represent them. But the mere manipulation of the figures is not evidence that he grasps the idea, and if he has not grasped the idea the manipulation of the figures is meaningless to him. In the same way subtraction may be grasped by abstracting one object from a group of four and perceiving that the group of three and the group of one are together equivalent to the group of four. The correlative ideas of multiplication and addition are illustrated by reversing the process.

This process of dealing with groups may be extended by using multiples of the groups which are within the child's grasp. That is, if he grasps three separate objects as belonging together he may also grasp together three groups of three objects each. He thus has at his command a much larger number of objects and he can learn to comprehend them in precisely the same manner that adults comprehend numbers which are beyond their grasp. The decimal system is really a means of extending our notion beyond the numbers which we can hold in attention. If the number name *one hundred* means anything to us beyond a name, it means an extension in a certain orderly way of numbers which are beyond our grasp, on the analogy of the extension which may be made within our concrete apprehension. The child may thus be introduced, not merely to the fundamental forms of number operation, but also to the ideas of the larger numbers.

SUPPLEMENTARY REPORT ON THE STUDY OF RETARDATION IN THE SCHOOLS OF INDIANAPOLIS

R. W. HIMELICK
Supervising Principal, Indianapolis Schools

The purpose of this special investigation on retardation was to attempt to throw some light upon questions that arose through a study of the previous report by Superintendent Mirick.[1] There seemed to be a feeling among many teachers that the percentage of retardation was probably low enough; that the agitation had produced a tendency to force the percentage even too low, by causing teachers to feel that they must promote a certain number. At a glance it would seem that it is not difficult to account for the retardation of 4 or 5 per cent. "Lack of attendance," "mental," and "physical" condition of the children are the usual "remarks" as to why children are retarded. There were two fairly well-defined questions that were prominent in this investigation: (1) Have we reached the proper standard for promotion? Should a larger or smaller number be retarded? (2) Are the right ones being retarded?

It seemed that the simplest way to get at this matter would be to ask a number of teachers to put all pupils on trial. If this could be done in different schools the conditions, both as to the nature of the children and the attitude of the teacher herself, would vary enough to make the experiment decisive. This would mean that the success or failure of all promotions would be tested by the ability of the child to do the new work; at present promotion depends on what the pupil had done during the past term. Our promotions have always been made upon the assumption that all school work is perfectly graded and unless the child completes in a satisfactory manner one grade he must not attempt the next

[1] "Report on the Study of Retardation in the Schools of Indianapolis, 1908–11," *Elementary School Teacher*, XII, No. 2, October, 1911, by George A. Mirick, acting superintendent of schools.

higher. Promotions have always been based very largely upon the possession of a definite amount of knowledge rather than real experience. It is a common feeling that a child retrogrades during the summer vacation. In many cases this period of his life is filled with rich experiences. But when he comes into the schoolroom we do not know how to make the best use of these experiences but try to create for him, from books, a new experience.

The individual reports given below are just as they came from the supervisors. Each supervisor made his report in the form best suited to his case. This was done in order to get at the subject from as many viewpoints as possible.

GENERAL STATISTICAL SUMMARY OF THE FOLLOWING REPORTS

1.	Total number of schools included in this report	12
2.	Total number children included in this report	6,270
3.	Number reported for retardation	555
4.	Percentage on trial	.088
5.	Number making good	285
6.	Number retarded	119
7.	Percentage of retardation	.019
8.	Number unaccounted for	150
9.	Percentage of retardation (January, 1911) entire city	.046
10.	Percentage of decrease in retardation for these districts	.027

REPORT FROM THE LUCRETIA MOTT SCHOOL

In the Lucretia Mott School every one of the five hundred pupils was promoted in June, 1911. Those who under ordinary circumstances would have been demoted numbered 27. The certificates of these pupils had a note appended as follows: "John has been promoted to the next grade on a six weeks' trial. If in the fall, he does not make good, he will be retarded at the end of six weeks without further notice." The teachers readily accepted the supervising principal's request that this method be given a trial. We hoped that the physical and perhaps mental development of the child during the summer, as well as the definite consciousness that his standing was not acceptable, might be the means of saving a half-year for him. Teachers were frankly informed by the supervising principal that in the fall they were to make the final decision regarding the promotion or retardation of every child who was on the six weeks' probation list; and that the supervising principal did not wish to have a voice in the last disposal of the cases. I was absolutely unbiased about the final outcome and made an effort to impress this fact upon the teachers.

On November 1 I asked for the judgments of the teachers, with the following results:

Grade	Number on Trial	Number Demoted November 1	Number Not Demoted
8A	2	0	2
8B	3	1	2
7A	4	2	2
7B	3	1	2
6A	3	1	2
6B	2	2	0
5A	2	2	0
5B	1	0	1
4A	2	2	0
4B	1	0	1
3A	1	0	1
3B	2	1	1
2A	1	0	1
2B	0	..	..
1A	0	..	..
1B	0	..	..
Totals	27	12	15

The table shows that 5/9 of the proposed demotions of June, 1911, were, so far, saved a half-year. One of the pupils demoted November 1 has been so thoroughly brought to consciousness that he is now being replaced; thus making the result: 16 pupils out of 27 are able to do better than we expected at the close of school.

LYDIA R. BLAICH
Supervising Principal

REPORT OF MCKINLEY SCHOOL

This is a twelve-room building enrolling five hundred pupils, thirty-six of whom were reported for demotion in June. On the suggestion of the Assistant Superintendent all of these children were placed as trials on the rolls and given promotion cards on which were written statements to the effect that if after from four to six weeks' trial they were unable to do advanced work, they were to fall back into a lower grade.

December's record was as follows: Eleven left the district and we have no report from them, four were demoted, six were reported as doing well, and fifteen were in the advanced grade but were weak in their work. This last class would have been much smaller were it not that many of the children were kept from school four or more weeks on account of diphtheria and also that the classes were too large to enable the teachers to give the individual help necessary to the success of such a plan.

SUMMARY

Reported for demotion	.072
Finally demoted	.008
Doing well	.012
Promoted	.05
A little weak	.03

IDA GEARY
Supervising Principal

REPORT OF SCHOOL NO. 4

Building of 700 pupils, 19 teachers, all grades below the high school. Children for the most part come from homes of working people. They do not have many advantages. School of central interest and importance in the lives of the children.

In the opening of 1911 we were asked to look closely after the matter of irregular promotions. Then came the request that at the June promotion we should send on not only the pupils who we felt had completed their work and were ready to go on, but the others also. In fact every child in the building should go on. This was to serve as an experiment by way of judging to what degree we were correct in our estimate of the ability of the pupils whom we had expected to leave behind. I did not favor the plan, but consented to be open-minded at least and give it a fair trial.

After I had reached this conclusion, I presented the matter to the teachers. No one favored the plan and some strongly opposed it. Knowing that the success of the experiment depended upon the sympathy and co-operation of the teachers I endeavored to convince them that if we undertook it at all we should stand together and give it a faithful trial. Six weeks before the end of the term a number of children whose work was poor were told that they were to have a trial, so instead of settling back and virtually dropping out of the race, they got to work and made considerable headway. Right here is one point in favor of this plan. At the close of the term each teacher marked "promoted" all whom she recommended. Those who she felt were able to make the grade if some pressure was brought to bear were marked "promoted on trial." The others, the hopeless cases, were left blank, and I marked them "special trial." Each "trial" and "special trial" was written up by the teacher, who stated freely whatever she knew that would give light in the case. At the beginning of the new term these trial pupils were looked after and encouraged in every way to keep up their efforts, with the result that a number have done stronger work than the regularly promoted pupils. The plan was to give the "trials" and "special trials" six weeks of the new term in which to prove their worth, but as there was such great absence as a result of the diphtheria epidemic a longer time was needed in some cases to decide. This unusual absence together with the fact that a large number of our children withdrew to attend parochial schools has interfered with making a complete and satisfactory report of the experiment. The figures are as follows:

Total number of children on trial	124
Total number who left the building	29
Total number making good	66
Total number sent to lower grades	29

It is not the intention to ask any teacher to keep any trial pupil beyond the six-weeks period of trial unless his work was satisfactory to his teacher. In a few cases, however, because of crowded conditions some very weak children were obliged to remain in the room as placed at the first of the term. It may be well to mention right here that one drawback in connection with this experiment was this. Parents did not wish to purchase new books for a child who was not sure of making good, and when the books were furnished the parents seemed to feel that such books should be sufficient to make the child's going on unquestionable—that to put the child back after getting his books was a positive injustice. While the conditions in the building have been unfavorable for this experiment the result has thrown valuable light on the subject and proved, so it seems to me, that a larger number of children can be carried over with safety to the higher grades than seemed possible before. I do not believe every child should be promoted at the close of the term, but I am confident that we should be quite generous in this matter of trial promotions.

Lulu Cobleigh Grove
Supervising Principal

REPORT OF GEORGE W. SLOAN SCHOOL

It was decided to try the plan of promoting all of the 968 pupils in the Sloan School at the close of the term in June. No announcement was made of this decision to the teachers, so when the promotion rolls were presented to the supervising principal for approval they showed, as had been the custom, three classes: those who were to be promoted unconditionally, those who were to be passed on trial, and those who should be retarded or kept in the same grade.

In the examination of the rolls, when the name of a pupil who was to be placed upon the retarded list was reached, the teacher was asked, What would be the effect if this pupil were given a trial? The general reply was that he could not do the work of the next grade. However he was passed on trial and given a mark by which he could be distinguished from the other trial pupils mentioned above. After all the rolls had been passed upon it was found that there were 82 such trial pupils.

At the next teachers' meeting they were told that if at the end of six weeks after the opening of school these same children were not doing satisfactory work, they would be demoted without question, having been given a fair trial.

The teachers were unanimous in opinion that the experiment was well worth the trial. Several however predicted that at the end of six weeks most of these children would be demoted.

In making the class lists in September they were distributed through the various rooms, but in case there were two rooms of the same grade they were placed in one room. Nothing was said to the teacher about the particular pupil and as there were several changes in the corps, not much information was received from former teachers. At the beginning of the fifth week of school the teachers were called together and blanks, such as is shown below, were distributed to each of them with instruction to fill out and send to the parent.

GEORGE W. SLOAN SCHOOL
October, 1911

Mr. ....

Your son Arthur is not doing satisfactory work in arithmetic, spelling, etc. Unless there is a marked improvement in his work within the next two weeks he will be put into a lower grade without further notice.

....
Supervising Principal

....
Parent's Signature

An examination of the notices which were sent to parents showed that about 60 per cent of them were for children who had been recommended for retardation in June; the other 40 per cent were those who had been regular trial pupils or were new to the school.

At the opening of the school in September there was diphtheria in the district and at the end of six weeks it had become epidemic. At this time 40 per cent of all the children were out of school, and naturally a large number of these were those whose parents had received the notices of unsatisfactory work. It did not seem practical to carry on the plan at that time. The epidemic continued until the Thanksgiving vacation. Upon investigation after Thanksgiving it was found that to regrade according to teachers' opinions would again disrupt the school, so it was decided to allow the grading to remain as it was and to retard all these children who are reported as unsatisfactory at the end of the term.

Just before the Christmas vacation the teachers were asked for the names of those whose work was unsatisfactory. It was found that 33 of the names were the same as those who were recommended for retardation in June.

SUMMARY

Number enrolled at the close of the term	968
Number recommended for retardation	82
Number recommended for retardation in December (of same list)	33
Number not in this school in December (of same list)	9
Number doing satisfactory work in December (of same list)	40

The conditions have been so extraneous that it is difficult to form conclusions of the results. It however is true that about one-half of those who were recommended for retardation in June have made good in their classes. What the results would have been under favorable circumstances can only be surmised, and whether these same persons continue to be promoted regularly remains to be seen.

DANIEL T. WEIR
Supervising Principal

REPORT FROM SCHOOL NO. 61 AND CALVIN FLETCHER SCHOOL

The plan of promotion herein discussed was presented in detail to the teachers at each building at a meeting early in June. They at once assumed a scientific attitude with regard to it. They were sympathetic toward the children, and on the whole so far as they were a factor the conditions were as favorable as could be desired. They were ready to co-operate in any attempt to get more light on a problem perplexing to them as to the supervising authorities. They were quick to see that the incentive of a trial, new subject-matter, new teachers, the experience and development during the vacation season were factors worth taking advantage of, whose weight could only be determined at some reasonable time within the following term.

At the close of the term in June written statements definitely stating the conditions were sent to the parents in each case. The conditions were also made plain to the children. This was repeated at the opening of schools in September. Only those children about whose success there was serious doubt were taken into account—such children as ordinarily would not have been promoted. All others were promoted clear of conditions.

The Fletcher School is departmental in organization, consisting of 9 teachers, and at that time of approximately 250 pupils of the 7B to 8A grades inclusive. The teachers are of comparatively high grade. Out of this number of children a total of 16 were promoted on trial of six weeks—all others being promoted clear. The distribution by grades and results to date are as follows:

9B grade (first term of high school)......6

Of these the two strongest entered other activities; one withdrew with poor standing; one is probably failing and remains in school only under pressure of parents; and two are doing acceptable work.

8A grade......5

One was returned to the 8B grade; one is doubtful, and three are doing fair work.

8B grade......3

One has a rank of fair, and two have developed into comparatively strong pupils.

7A grade......2

One entered the parochial schools, and one is doing satisfactory work. Out of the total sixteen, three did not re-enter, two have failed, two are doubtful cases, and nine are maintaining acceptable rank.

School No. 61 is a seven-room building with approximately 300 children of the 1B to 6A grades inclusive. The corps of teachers on the whole is a good one. A fact of interest to be noted here is that at the opening of the September term this school was placed under different supervision, and attention to the experiment practically lapsed throughout the term. No six-weeks trial term was thus applied here. This fact, however, does not in any wise impair the results but may be taken into account in their interpretation. Out of the total 300 children 18 were given the trial. The distribution and results are as follows:

7B grade......3

One moved from the city; two were transferred to school No. 8, and are doing fair work.

6A grade......2

One left the city and one is acceptable.

6B grade......2

Both doing satisfactory work.

5B grade......2

Both doubtful of promotion in January.

4A grade......3

One transferred, one is failing, and one is doing well.

4B grade......2

One is failing and one ranks fair.

3A grade......2

One is failing and one is satisfactory.

2B grade......2

One left the city, and the other is succeeding with considerable individual help.

Out of the total eighteen—four were transferred and were dropped out of account, five will probably not be promoted in January, and nine—one-half—are doing acceptable work.

It is not assumed that herein is found the solution of the intricate problem of promotion. In a sense it might appear that the day of reckoning is only deferred to the end of a definite trial period within the term rather than coming at the end of the previous term. There is perhaps never a time when one can be perfectly certain of the wisest course to pursue in many cases. The question of determining in each case between two alternatives the situation in which a particular child may best live and get experience, the conditions in which he may best grow and develop is a question to answer which even to a practical certainty involves a great many factors. This will be true at whatever time the issue is made. As a matter of fact in a good school more or less frequent promotions are made at any time throughout the term. And though it might appear that in this case the time of reckoning is only deferred, it must be granted that by so doing we come to the problem from the consideration of a number of factors, and, with the advantage of a number of facts which otherwise would have been impossible. And as a result it seems fair to assume that 19 children out of a total of 35 were saved the unnecessary repetition of a grade with all the injustice that goes with it, while the 8 who are repeating or will probably repeat the grade next term are quite as well off, so far as can be determined, as they otherwise would have been.

E. R. Ray
Supervising Principal

REPORT FROM SCHOOL NO. 32

In June, 1911, all pupils in School No. 32 were promoted to the next higher grade than the one they were then in. At that time there were 536 pupils besides the 8A's. Twenty of the 536 pupils were considered by the teachers as not ready for promotion. Of the others, 15, including 6 1B's who had been in school less than two months, were weak in one or more subjects and some doubt was expressed as to the wisdom of promotion. In all of these cases the promotion card bore the teacher's statement of the particular weakness of the child and the fact that a trial of six weeks in the advanced grade would be granted the following term.

On the first 20 (the ones poor in all subjects) 4 moved from the city or from the district; 10 are doing the work of the higher grade as well as the average of the class; 5 are still poor in all their work and I fear always will be; 1 out of the twenty was demoted.

Of the other 15 (doubtful in one or more subjects) 6 were the 1B's who had been in school less than two months. They have moved along with their class. Two of the fifteen left school, one has been demoted, and the others are doing as satisfactory work as others in the class.

SUMMARY

536 pupils on the rolls.
20 poor in all subjects.
15 poor in one or more subjects.
The 35 given a trial in higher grade:
2 demotions.
6 left city or district.
5 still poor—but no worse.
22 doing as satisfactory work as others in the class.

Lizzie J. Stearns
Supervising Principal

REPORT FROM SCHOOL NO. 49

In June, 1911, there were 650 pupils, grades 1B to 8A inclusive, enrolled in school No. 49. Of these 97 were marked "on trial." Of this number 45 would not have been promoted under ordinary conditions, and it is upon these 45, consequently, that this experiment was made.

From the start the eighteen teachers in the building were taken into full confidence. Their interest was thus aroused, and was active and scientific throughout. It was realized that their intimate knowledge of the pupils concerned was too valuable to be discarded, or to be used by them "in the dark." Before the promotions in June, the theory and the plan of the experiment were fully explained and discussed in teachers' meetings. Upon the opening of school in September, the conditions were explained to all new members of the corps, and each teacher in the building was asked to keep track of her trial pupils. Reasonable assistance was given, and conferences on individual pupils were often held. New subject-matter, it was thought, was only one of the elements in the possible success of a weak pupil. Intelligent consideration and help by his teacher were thought equally important and equally his due.

At the close of the first six weeks of the term, when the trial period should have expired, the school was in the midst of a diphtheria epidemic. For nearly a month the attendance was about 50 per cent of the enrolment. Naturally enough, most of the trial pupils were numbered among the absentees. This condition in part vitiated the experiment, although the period of trial was considerably extended. A week after the attendance had again become normal, all trial pupils who were evidently failing were carefully investigated and tested. Out of the 45 pupils it was found that 12 had failed "to make good," and that 10 others would possibly be failures at the close of the term. The 23 pupils remaining, however, were found to be doing satisfactory work, some of them, in fact, were stronger than certain pupils who had passed clear in June.

This brief experiment, imperfect and incomplete as it was, has brought up two or three pertinent suggestions.

a) Promotions should be more freely made. Deficient pupils should be given more than the "benefit of a doubt." It is impossible to foresee the effect of a new grade upon such pupils and properly to take into account the growth, mental and physical, which comes to a child from month to month.

b) The success of the 23 pupils who "made good" meant more to them than merely saving a half-year. Undoubtedly the educative process in their cases operated more nearly at the maximum efficiency. Furthermore, on the spiritual side, it would be hard to estimate the value of success, instead of failure, in their tender years.

c) In principle, it is as great an error to promote all pupils as to promote none. The practice of experienced supervisors in making the classification of deficient pupils a study, and each case an individual one, must be followed. The highest discernment and judgment, with all the light available, are none too accurate in placing a pupil where he may be most benefited and work at his maximum efficiency.

J. F. THORNTON
Supervising Principal

REPORT FROM SCHOOLS NOS. 16, 50, AND 52

I feel that the teachers went into this experiment with an open mind. There was no objection on the part of any teacher to the investigation. Many

DEMOTIONS AND SPECIAL PROMOTIONS

School	Enrolment			Demotions			Percentage of Demotion			Special Promotion			Percentage of Promotions			Net Gain or Loss		
	B	G	T	B	G	T	B	G	T	B	G	T	B	G	T	B	G	T
16..........	251	275	526	4	2	6	.016	.007	.011	10	8	18	.04	.028	.034	.024	.027	.023 gain
50..........	273	278	551	7	1	8	.025	.003	.014	6	4	10	.022	.011	.018	.003 loss	.015 gain	.004 gain
52..........	410	429	839	4	2	6	.01	.005	.008	7	4	11	.017	.01	.013	.007	.008	.004 gain
			1,916	15	5	20												

Note:—The above table is presented in order to show the effect which the study of the retardation problem has had upon the bright pupil as well as the retarded one. We have been pulling from both ends. The bright children have been held down to wait upon the slow pupil and the slow ones have been pulled up. Each individual is a standard unto himself.

of the teachers expressed themselves as believing that such a course would help the individual teacher in making a more intelligent classification of her pupils.

TABLE OF RETARDATIONS IN WHITE SCHOOLS GRAPHICALLY REPRESENTED

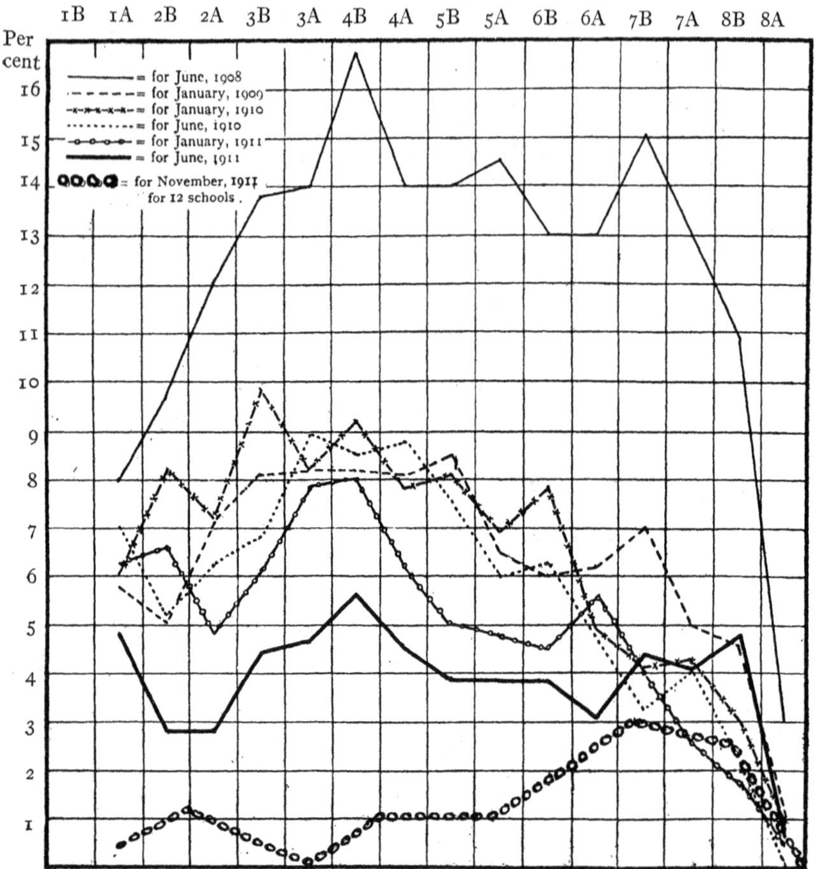

In addition to this work, the teachers were asked to look after the pupils that might be advanced a grade. A study of the chart above will show the results of this experiment. Instead of repeaters there is a net gain in every case. This is not only a gain to the children but a saving to the city.

In a number of cases children recommended for demotion not only made good but did a higher grade of work than some who were passed regularly.

This does not mean that the judgment of the teacher in either case was not good. It does mean that some children grow during the vacation while others retrograde.

Such a plan of promotion seemed to be a relief to both teachers and pupils. Everybody seemed happy, consequently there was a good beginning. Fewer complaints have come from teachers with reference to the grading. The children felt that the responsibility rested with them. It was their business to make good.

A study of the table on retardations, which was given in the previous report, to which is added the retardations for November, 1911, reveals some interesting things. In the first place the crest which had been prominent in the 4B almost disappeared. The crest in the 7B remains. This is due to the fact that teachers feel that these children are near the end of the course and are not prepared to do the traditional high-school work. As a result of this these people are retained in grades 7A and 8B until they quit school. This conclusion has been reached after consulting with teachers who were responsible for retardation of pupils in these grades.

COMMENTS

It should be understood from the beginning that this report is not made to set forth the merits of a method of promotion. The plan as set forth here might not be the best one to follow. But the facts show that some method should be adopted that will not interfere with the progress of the child. The facts also show that we have been "guessing" in matters of promotion.

The fact that more than 50 per cent of those placed in the list of "trials" have made good indicates that we are in need of a new standard. The plan as indicated in this report has had a tendency to put the individual child as the center. The only standard with which a child ought to be judged is whether he is working up to a reasonable limit of his own capacity. A very large percentage of retarded children could be retarded from term to term if a grade standard be maintained. In many cases teachers have said that retarded pupils do poorer work the second term than the first. The fact that it has become an "unwritten" rule that pupils be not retained for more than two terms in any one grade indicates that as a rule these children make little improvement in repeating a grade.

Some teachers have raised the objection that if we are more liberal in our promotions, children will feel that they will be promoted whether they put forth any effort or not. If retardation is simply to serve as a "lash" to whip the children into line, then it is time to search for another motive for work. On the other hand, if children could be made to feel that it is a constant application to duty that is wanted, and that at any time they fail to do the work they are to be retarded, a higher standard would be maintained. Personal comments by many teachers indicate that children do not take advantage of this wholesale advancement. But on the other hand, they feel that they are in the race and must keep up with the others.

Some have said that children may be able to do the work now but will not be able to keep up in one or two years. Such an objection is not very valid. In the first place if our course of study is so constructed that the child may be able to do the work of one grade and fail in some succeeding grade because he was a little slow in a previous grade, it indicates that we should modify the course. In the second place, it would be difficult to say that a weakness in a previous grade is the cause of failure in the advance grade. There are so many changes that may occur in the life of a child in the course of a few years.

It is interesting to note that a large number of pupils who would otherwise have been demoted are doing as good or even a higher grade of work than many who were promoted without question. In a few instances I found that children who would have been retarded were making an average of 80 in all their work, while others, promoted without question, were only making an average of 60.

The individual reports show that no pressure was brought to bear upon the teacher to make her feel that she was under obligation to reduce the number of retarded children. I know that in some cases it was suggested that we should think of both sides. The percentage of retardation had been so materially reduced that probably it had been forced too low. The reduction, as Mr. Mirick stated in the previous report, has come about because of the increase of the number of factors as a basis in making promotions. This increase in the number of factors has been a means of throwing light upon all the children. While special promotions have been mentioned from three buildings only, the same condition exists at all the other buildings.

The general conclusion that may be drawn from such a study is that education must become a science in fact as well as in theory. If any business concern was as indifferent to the kinds of records kept as the average school, it could not possibly thrive. We work on the assumption that in practice, ignorance is the best policy. There is a feeling even yet among many excellent teachers that they do not care to know much of the past record of the children who come to them. We should know everything about the child. His past record should not in any way prejudice the teacher. Promotions must be based upon a knowledge of what the child has done, and how he has acted, in order that we may judge of what he is capable of doing.

The reports indicate that we have judged wrongly in about 50 per cent of the cases of retarded children. It seems evident, therefore, that a larger number of factors, or wholly different factors, should be considered in our promotion. It is also rather plain that one of these new factors should be a trial in the advanced grade.

The stress is often placed upon the number to be promoted rather than the number to be retarded. If, therefore, instead of moving the whole body of students, the few who cannot do the work were changed, the stress might be put at the proper place. It would be far better to have a few pupils pass along who cannot do the work, rather than err in 50 per cent of those who are retarded.

In order to view this whole subject from another angle I have compiled a few statistics from a large number of tests that were given by the teachers and the supervising principal. These tests were given in the following subjects: history, English, arithmetic, and spelling. The two tables that are given below will show the general results of these tests.

The individual report is similar to a large number of others that were handed in by the teachers. In a number of cases the trials were below the others. The differences in percentage, as shown in the general report, are not large enough to mean much. As there are only a few trials in each grade this would have a tendency to lower the average. In almost every case a large number of pupils fell below the trial pupils.

The second table shows that there is a difference of only 9 per cent between the two classes. The most significant thing is that a large number, almost 20 per cent, are below the trial pupils. These children were put on "trial" after carefully considering past records and the nature of the new work.

It seems to be evident that what we need to do is to give all pupils a chance and not the few. When the final judgment is passed it must be based upon what the individual is able to get out of the work, and not how he measures up with his neighbor.

INDIANAPOLIS PUBLIC SCHOOLS

SPECIAL REPORT

1. Number pupils tested 18
2. Class average 59
3. Average of regularly promoted pupils 58
4. Average of trial pupils 64
5. Number who fell below trial pupils 8
6. Grade 7B

GENERAL REPORT

	2B	2A	3B	3A	4B	4A	5B	5A	6B	6A	7B	7A	8B	8A	Totals
1. Number pupils tested	22	26	26	23	37	..	95	103	69	59	56	58	57	45	676
2. Class average	92	100	86	81	82	..	69	71	73	65	69	74	71	69	75
3. Average of those regularly promoted	93	100	85	81	84	..	65	64	79	65	70	78	73	72	76
4. Average of trial pupils	89	100	89	71	76	..	63	57	61	65	72	59	56	40	67
5. Number below trial average	0	0	8	1	7	..	16	19	14	20	20	10	9	4	128

A BRIEF SURVEY OF THE DEVELOPMENT OF COMPULSORY EDUCATION IN THE UNITED STATES

W. A. COOK
Madison, Wisconsin

Just what is the theory upon which rests the right of the state to compel children to take an education? This question has been regarded from very different standpoints at different times and places, and a comparison of current views in our own country, coming from leading educators, would probably afford some interesting material. Very divergent views would doubtless be expressed. The principle has become so generally accepted that it is seldom thought to be necessary to state explicitly the reasons on which the principle rests.

Martin Luther proposed compulsion as a religious duty of the state to its citizens. Everyone should be made to learn to read because he ought to be able to read the Bible for himself. John Calvin also declared for universal education in his ecclesiastical state of Geneva in 1542. John Knox carried the same idea into Scotland. These reformers could hardly have dreamed of the great variation in religious views that would arise from the free reading of the Scriptures. They thought only of the revolt it would spread against Catholicism and not of the differences it would create among the Protestants themselves. With their uncompromising, intolerant attitude it is very likely that these men would have taken a different stand, had they understood the natural results of universal education.

In the sixteenth century French Protestants made a demand for schools in their own country. Holland was liberal in placing educational facilities before all its people, but the principle of action was more the establishment of school than obligatory universal attendance.

Two modern ideas at least may be mentioned, one in the Old World, the other in the New. Compulsory education in England has been regarded as necessary in order to keep the lower classes from wronging themselves; in America the matter has been considered from the social and political point of view instead of from the personal point of view. Americans consider compulsory education as the *sine qua non* of political existence, since the state cannot, for its own sake permit any of its citizens to grow up in ignorance. This little touch of Spartanism is interesting.

Furthermore, one may urge that compulsory education is the natural complement of a system of free schools. If education is so necessary that schools should be supported by public taxation, it must be so invaluable that everyone needs a certain modicum. If the individual will not voluntarily take the free education offered, he should be compelled to accept it, both for his own sake and for that of society as a whole. After providing a proper equipment, after securing a competent teaching force, after defining the work which the schools shall do in order to justify their existence at public expense, it is imperatively necessary to exact the attendance of the children for a sufficient time to accomplish the object in view. Of course, if any parent prefers to educate his child at home or in a private school, no one can object, if this is not a sham and a pretext and if the education so provided is at least equivalent to that which the public requires.

Compulsory legislation began very early in this country, almost as early as the schools themselves. In Massachusetts a law was enacted in 1642 making the education of children and indentured servants necessary, so far as a knowledge of the reading of English and a knowledge of criminal law were concerned. Further legislation was passed from time to time in the same colony and was generally enforced.

It was not until the factory system arose, however, and the flood of illiterate immigration set in that a serious situation arose. The effect of the factory system was to make larger demands on the time and energy of the workingman and to curtail his opportunity to devote himself to preparation for intelligent living. The tendency of immigration was to create a large class without the educational traditions or the helpful home influences of the native New Englander. The laws passed in England about the opening of the nineteenth century were substantially copied in Connecticut and Massachusetts. The responsibility was placed principally upon the employer, less upon the parent. As compulsory legislation the enactments were altogether defective according to present standards, the age limit was low, the prescribed annual term of school attendance was short, and there was no legal machinery competent to enforce penalties, though the penalties written in the statutes sounded somewhat severe.

When the great movement for free public schools began spreading over the country near the middle of the last century, the idea of compulsion followed as a corollary. The Massachusetts law of 1852 was the first to be passed in the new era. Its provisions mark it as a piece of modern legislation in every respect except that of enforcement. Years of experience had demonstrated that special officers are needed for this purpose. This defect in the Massachusetts law has been corrected in later legislation. Later experience has, however, carried us farther. It is becoming evident that an officer of the larger political unit is the best, in order that all idea of local color, or favoritism due to acquaintance or relationship may be eliminated. Officers who are subject to what we term political influences are a failure at this task.

The gradual corrections of the defects in the Massachusetts law have been made with scarcely a backward step. Few states have made so many mistakes or progressed so consistently. The other commonwealths took action later and so were able to avoid some of the blunders of the pioneer in compulsory legislation. New Hampshire, Connecticut, Vermont, and New York all acted from 1867 to 1874. The Connecticut law was from the beginning a practical working measure, though it has repeatedly been amended in important particulars.

In the decade 1880–90 many of the American commonwealths attacked the problem in earnest. Three distinct issues arose in this connection aside from the main point of the law: (1) the restriction of employment of children of school age,[1] (2) provision for very poor children, (3) the supervision of the non-public school. By 1890 laws existed in about thirty of the states. The general age limit was eight to fourteen; six to sixteen was the extreme range and did not occur in any one state. The annual term required

[1] The limitations of this article make it necessary to omit any discussion of factory legislation.

varied from 12 to 20 weeks, except in Massachusetts where 30 was the maximum. Several states provided for the children of needy parents by furnishing free textbooks. Three states excused such from the operation of the law, and two assisted by providing clothing. The penalties were for the most part left to the discretion of courts having jurisdiction. The inferior and superior limits of fines were usually $5 and $20 respectively, but Illinois and New York established a minimum of $1. Labor of those under fourteen was rarely permitted. The attitude toward private and parochial schools was defined in about half of the laws, by prescribing certain branches, but no method of determining conformity to the requirements was specified.

If one were to have traveled overland from Philadelphia to the headwaters of the Ohio, followed that stream to its confluence with the Mississippi, and thence traveled southwest, he would approximately have cut the states having compulsory legislation from those without it.[1] The significance of this general geographical distribution of compulsory statutes is interesting and depends upon a whole group of political, social, and economic factors.

The following is a general summary of the condition in 1910, twenty years later than the time just described. The two decades between 1890 and the present show marked advancement in various ways. Every state now has some sort of a factory law with reference to child labor, but Alabama, Florida, Georgia, Louisiana, Mississippi, South Carolina, and Texas have no law for compulsory education. The extreme age limits affected in any part of the country are seven and eighteen. Idaho and New Jersey stand at the top with ranges of eight to eighteen and seven to seventeen, respectively. The average would seem to be seven to fourteen or seven to fifteen.

Another change appears in the tendency to require attendance for the full term instead of for a limited number of weeks, but in most of the states where the laws are of recent passage 12 or 16 weeks is a common requirement. In states where any discrimination is made between localities, the distinction is made (1) by per-

[1] To be more exact, Missouri, Iowa, Indiana, and Pennsylvania had not yet acted. Those interested in following the movement in detail should consult the Reports of the U.S. Commissioner of Education.

mitting local boards to reduce the annual term of compulsion, and (2) by setting a higher standard in the cities. In general, it is fair to say that the annual period of compulsory attendance varies in length with the annual school term.

Disregard of the law is now a more serious offense than formerly. Many states permit a fine of as high as $50. There is a freer use of imprisonment than a few years ago, especially in default of payment of fines; but some states provide for imprisonment irrespective of the assessment of a fine. Cumulative penalties for repeated offenses are meted out in many states. The penalties in the South, as might be expected, are low.

With private schools there has been much friction in places. The desire of the authorities to maintain a proper standard of instruction in all schools which shall under the law be deemed a substitute for the public school, has caused the management of these private or church enterprises to resent what they considered an infringement of their rights. The cry of religious freedom when raised at this point has at times found listeners. In any case there obviously should be some method of passing on the work of such schools. The authorities, the city, the county, or the state, should inspect the work of all such schools just as the work of public schools is inspected. A superintendent is not willing to judge the work of a teacher as to its passable character by the course of study which that teacher is supposed to teach; and it is safe to assert that no school can be judged rightly by its announcements merely.

A new principle, and an eminently proper one, is coming slowly into operation in enactments dealing with compulsory education. The mental attainments of the child are being recognized as a proper basis upon which to determine whether attendance has been adequate. For instance, the ability or lack of ability to read and write is coming to be recognized as more important than the pupil's age. Most states are still adhering to the old plan of the age limit, but it seems likely that age will be combined with tests of educational efficiency in such a way as to secure a new adjustment. For after all, the theory underlying compulsory education is that there is need of a certain amount of education, and not that one should spend a certain length of time with a book in one's hand.

A THREE-YEAR RETARDATION RECORD

FREEMAN E. LURTON
Superintendent of Schools, Anoka, Minn.

To all who are charged with the administration of school affairs it has long been evident that there are large numbers of children who are behind the schedule set for them, or are "retarded." This is true by whatever method you elect to determine the number or whatever you may believe the causes to be. The undeniable fact is that serious numbers are retarded.

We believe that the amount of retardation is capable of being reduced. Were it otherwise we should face a vast amount of hopeless waste in educating the children.

Probably the most effective way, in the long run, to deal with this question would be wholly to recast the course of study, eliminating that which is irrelevant or non-essential, and adjusting the rest to the actual life-conditions surrounding the children. But that is a work too vast for one man to undertake. The present course of study is the result of the best educational experience of the past. Wide experience and vast educational wisdom would be necessary to attempt a sweeping and constructive revision. Until the man of vision arrives we had better work humbly at the problem of bettering present conditions.

Below, we give a table showing the percentage of retarded pupils, grade by grade, for three years, in the Anoka schools.

	Totals			Grades								Reduction
	Enrolled	Retarded	Percentage	I	II	III	IV	V	VI	VII	VIII	
1908–9...	581	407	70.0	37.8	59.4	57.5	70.8	82.2	85.7	75.3	92.2	...
1909–10..	552	363	65.7	37.3	53.8	62.2	68.7	73.3	87.5	80.3	77.5	4.3
1910–11..	510	317	62.1	42.1	43.5	61.9	65.5	68.0	71.2	76.8	73.4	3.6

The reduction shown in the above table is due to no changes in the course of study. In fact, during the time covered by the report, music was introduced into all the grades and manual training, for the boys, into the seventh and eighth grades. Before 1909–10 pupils were promoted if they had only one major study (arithmetic, geography, history, or grammar) below the required passing mark. Beginning with that year they have been obliged to have *all* studies up to grade to win promotion. So the amount of work required is greater and the standard of passing more severe in the years being discussed.

A friend of mine, eminent in political science, frequently asserts that the moment you convince people that a reform is needed, that moment you have virtually effected it; the rest is merely detail to be worked out. That dictum seems true in this case.

The year 1908–9 shows the high total of 70 per cent of the pupils as being retarded. The average for the state of Minnesota, as determined in an extensive investigation, was 58.9 per cent in 1910. So at the beginning of the year 1909–10 the attention of the teachers was called to the conditions and their sympathy and interest enlisted in an effort to reduce the amount of retardation existing. The data presented here shows that a reduction of 4.3 per cent was effected that first year. In the next year a further reduction of 3.6 per cent was brought about. In the following grades the reduction has been continuous: II, IV, V, VIII; in the others it was variable. But, as said before, this reduction of 7.9 per cent in the number of retarded pupils was not due to any radical changes and certainly to no application of soft pedagogy. The reverse. The attention of the teachers was simply directed to the possible relation between retardation and irregular attendance, tardiness, technicalities in examinations, carelessness in coaching the slower pupils, the marking of examinations, care in assigning lessons, the making-up of lost work, and similar matters that lessen a pupil's grasp upon his work or lower his grades. The exercise of greater care and sympathy, and, in general, a greater concern for the individual, rather than so much concern for the "room," has produced some valuable results in more ways than indicated by the table, for such things cannot be reduced to figures.

The gist of the matter is this, we paid just such attention to the elements of loss and waste that would be paid in a careful business enterprise. To reduce to the minimum the loss in so precious a material as the teacher has to deal with would seem to be worth the best efforts of all whose aim is constructive teaching.

EDITORIAL NOTES

A committee of the National Education Association is considering the general problem of economy of time in elementary education. In the February number of this Journal Dr. Bobbitt gave an account of the efforts which are being made under Superintendent Wirt, of Gary, to economize the time and energy of pupils through a form of school organization which keeps the schools in operation for a longer period each day, and presents the possibilities of many different types of activity. Other students of education have presented with equal emphasis the importance of economizing the time and energy of students through better methods of instruction. It is often suggested that the course of study be modified by the elimination of the unnecessary topics in arithmetic, grammar, and geography, so that only the essentials may be taught. All of these suggestions in the direction of more intensive work on the part of pupils are met by skepticism on the part of some who question whether the forcing process which such intensive methods are supposed to encourage will not be more injurious to the children than the present waste. Some parents urge that children get outside of school quite as much as they get in school, and it is asserted furthermore that the conditions of life are more favorable outside of school. This view is frequently expressed in the statement that children should not be compelled to work too hard, because hard work will injure the child's health. Again, skepticism with regard to the wisdom of plans of economy expresses itself in the question whether children are not losing something of the general culture that came from the slower and less systematic forms of study that prevailed in the older course of study which was not so rigidly administered with a view to economy of time.

A Study of Economy

Certainly there is a problem presented by these various opposing views which it is the business of teachers and superintendents to examine in the light of the broadest possible experience. The committee of the National Education Association ought to have the benefit of the experience of anyone who has succeeded in economizing the time of the elementary school, whatever the direction of the economy

First, Experience Should Be Recorded

achieved. Superintendent H. B. Wilson, of Decatur, Ill., is chairman of the committee and will welcome information from any quarter which will be of assistance to the committee in its work. No contribution should be regarded as trivial if it has been shown in actual school experience to be effective. The teacher who has an economical method of instruction, the principal who has organized a course of study which covers the essentials, and the superintendent who is interested in broader forms of organization, should all be prepared to contribute to the report of the committee by letting their plans be known and by inviting a careful scrutiny of the results brought about through these plans.

Second, Results Should Be Tested

After information has been secured regarding the efforts which are being made to economize time and energy, there still remains a need which the committee ought to be able to meet. This is the need of securing better methods than are now at hand for testing results. There can be no doubt that many plans which are supposed to effect great economy do not succeed in the long run. Children can be induced through special effort to show phenomenal results in certain narrow lines of activity. But it is found impossible to follow up these precocious attainments with anything like a general exhibition of real intellectual maturity. For example, children can learn through the use of blocks and figures to manipulate fractional relations with great facility. When it comes to a mastery of the other forms of number relation, they show no greater ability than pupils who have been taught by other methods. While there should be therefore the largest hospitality for any devices that are suggested in the direction of economy there will never be a solution of the problem of economy until the remoter results of each type of training can be tested and balanced against the results of current practices. The development of methods for testing results goes on very slowly, because new educational methods are usually the results of the enthusiasm of a small group of individuals. No individual can look upon his own efforts in an impartial way. The committee of the National Education Association has, therefore, an excellent opportunity to make a unique contribution to the discussion of this topic, if, in addition to a statement of the various efforts which are now being made, it can contribute some definite evaluations of these efforts.

The Resources of the National Education Association Should Be Used

No greater service could be performed by the National Education Association than to contribute to the support of a general investigation of this type. The Association is in danger during this period, when it devotes itself primarily to the holding of great meetings, of losing the prestige which was gained by its earlier contributions to education. Committee work within the Association has in recent years hardly risen to the level of the great achievements of the earlier committees, which were in possession of the necessary funds to carry on in a large way the complete investigation of the problems committed to them. While the Association spends its time discussing certain petty issues of internal politics, the investigation of large educational problems is taken up here and there by individuals or by institutions of much narrower range of influence than the National Education Association. A permanent fund large enough to give support to many educational investigations is locked up for some mysterious reason and held as an emergency fund for some remote and indefinite future. One can hardly help suggesting that this is in itself a very bad exhibition of economy that savors more of parsimony than of wisdom. Committees ought to have freedom to use the energies of the Association in the investigation of this and other similar large problems.

The Attitude of Educators Should Be Expressed

The answer to the question why these committees are not permitted to go forward in a large way is to be found in the apathy of the members of the National Education Association. If they express themselves with vigor, the policy of that Association would of necessity be changed. The petty politics of which we have heard so much during recent years would be eliminated, and the Association would again become a force in American education. If some such change as this does not take place very shortly, it is altogether probable that other agencies will arise to carry forward educational investigation. The problems are too urgent to be neglected. The agencies for the solution of these problems can be organized without the support of the National Education Association, if that Association fails to recognize the importance of these problems.

BOOK REVIEWS

A Brief Course in the Teaching Process. By GEORGE DRAYTON STRAYER, PH.D. New York: Macmillan, 1911. Pp. xiv+315. $00.

Professor Strayer's book is a concrete, practical discussion of the general principles of method with a wealth of illustrative material drawn from the work of elementary schools. It is the culmination of several years of instruction as a member of the Department of Elementary Education at Teachers College, Columbia University. This fact explains the almost complete omission of discussions of the problems of teaching in high schools. The general organization of the book will be familiar to Professor Strayer's former students and to others who are acquainted with Teachers College syllabi, since it is largely a discussion of the points outlined in the same author's *Syllabus of a Course on the Theory and Practice of Teaching in Elementary Schools* (1909).

The book is intermediate in character between McMurry's *Method of the Recitation* on the one hand and Bagley's *Educative Process* on the other. It is like McMurry's book in the direct practical bearing of most of the points made, in the wealth of concrete illustrations from actual elementary-school practice, and in the ease with which most of it may be understood. The field covered, however, is much broader. It is like Bagley's book in its range of topics, but is unlike the books of Bagley and Colvin in the small number of specific references which it contains to the results of educational and experimental psychology. Perhaps the book that it resembles most is Charters' *Methods of Teaching.*

Seven chapters out of the total of nineteen are devoted to a discussion of different types of lessons, namely, drill, inductive, deductive, appreciation, study, review or examination, and the recitation lesson. The other chapters deal with the aim of education, the factors conditioning the teaching process (largely a discussion of instinct and interest), the teaching process (primarily a discussion of the Titchener-Bagley types of attention), questioning, the social phases of the recitation, the physical welfare of the children, moral training, class management, lesson plans, the teacher in relation to supervision, the teacher in relation to the course of study, and measuring results in education. About two-thirds of the book consists of the author's own text and about one-third of quoted material. The latter includes an appendix of 43 pages, consisting of syllabi on the teaching of English, arithmetic, geography, and history by the heads of the corresponding departments at Teachers College. Forty-eight pages are devoted to sample lesson plans and seventeen pages are quoted from Stone's study of *Arithmetical Abilities.* At the end of each chapter is a list of exercises which involve application by the student of principles learned in the chapter.

The author's point of view is eclectic. The selection and organization of the main points show evidence of the influence of Bagley, Thorndike, McMurry, and Dewey. Of these, perhaps the influence of Dewey is greatest, as shown in the reiteration of the necessity of organizing school work on the basis of a co-operative social situation in which the teaching processes start with the conscious needs of the children.

To those readers who approach the consideration of methods of teaching primarily from the standpoint of educational and experimental psychology, Professor Strayer's book is slightly disappointing. From this point of view it would seem that more definite and frequent references to such material as Professor Colvin summarizes would give the book a more satisfactory and probably more valid scientific character. As it is, one feels that the book might have been written on the basis of an elementary knowledge of such a text as James's *Briefer Course* or Titchener's *Primer*.

On the other hand, it is interesting to note that while much of the material is of the same elementary character as McMurry's *Method of the Recitation*, the content and form of Professor Strayer's book were developed to suit the needs of mature, experienced teachers who were doing senior college or pseudo-graduate work. If the book is really on the plane of such persons, some of our method books which are interpreting teaching in terms of advanced educational psychology are shooting far over the heads of the students for whom they are intended.

S. Chester Parker

Songs of a Little Child's Day. Words by Emilie Poulsson; music by Eleanor Smith. Springfield, Mass.: Milton Bradley Co.

This book is a distinct addition to the simple musical material for the home, the kindergarten, and the first grades of the elementary school, and must be counted as one of the best six books of songs for young children. Here is a collection which realizes the demand which has theoretically been accepted for some time, that songs for little children should be simple in idea, short in expression, attractive in melody and rhythm, and easily learned. The composers have put their ripest products into this volume, and the home and the school are richer for it.

P. W. Dykema

Colonial Carols; Dutch Ditties; A Chinese Child's Day. Three books of children's songs. By Anice Terhune. New York: G. Schirmer. $1.25 each.

It is but faint praise to say that this collection is above the ordinary of those not especially compiled for school use. They are still too much like the usual combination of careful printing, adequate binding, and pretty illustrating bestowed upon mediocre literary and musical material. Some of Mrs. Terhune's words, however, are of real worth. The music, though too often approaching close to a cheap, popular style, and now and then becoming frankly this, forms in a few instances a real contribution to the list of children's songs. It is unfortunate that the composer has, through a serious ignorance or a wilful disregard of the lower limits of the child's voice, for which these songs are obviously intended, made the already small proportion of good songs even smaller. Most of the compositions run below the staff, several down to B, and a few down to G. In each of the three volumes are some bits characteristic of the types discussed. While the books are not to be recommended for general school use, when music descriptive of the children of China, Holland, and our own early colonies is desired these volumes may be resorted to for interesting suggestions.

P. W. Dykema

Child Life in Song and Speech; Tone Plays for Children. By Alice E. Bentley. New York: A. S. Barnes & Co.

These two pamphlets of twenty-four and of twenty-eight pages by the supervisor of music in Washington, D.C., should be in the hands of every teacher or parent of young children. They furnish an inspiring guide to a point of view regarding song which will do much to increase the meaning of music, in fact of all tone, in the life of the child, and will do much for music in the home, and for making music a natural means of expression.

P. W. DYKEMA

Swedish Folk Dances. By NILES W. BERGQUIST. New York: Barnes & Co. $1.50.

This second edition is a decided improvement on the first edition. The introduction by Mr. Crampton gives a brief outline of the causes leading to the present value placed on folk-dancing by educators interested in city problems, and is well worth reading.

The dances are clearly described and the information accurate. The collection is of value to playground teachers or those interested in social centers. There is one disappointment—the pictures are of Americans in America executing Swedish dances in imitation Swedish costumes. One likes the characteristics of a country preserved in as perfect a form as possible when recommending folkwork of any kind to teachers.

Surely the genuine spirit of Swedish dances can best be portrayed by Swedish people in their own country, dressed in national costume. The memory or picture of a Swedish youth on the wharf at Laksend on midsummer's eve, with his long blue coat tails swinging out behind, his white student cap pushed back on his blonde head—dancing as our men cannot, with a lightness and swing and an entire absorption in the joy of the rhythm—is surely worth more as an inspiration or model than any number of imitations given by Americans.

MARY WOOD HINMAN

Morris Dance Tunes. By JOSEPHINE BROWER. New York: H. W. Gray & Co.

The Morris Dance. By JOSEPHINE BROWER. New York: H. W. Gray & Co.

It is a help to all teachers of folkwork to have music and notes condensed, and this has been successfully accomplished by Miss Brower in her two books, *Morris Dance Tunes* and *The Morris Dance.* The dances described are appropriate for playgrounds, social centers, and public schools.

Those who do not possess the English books on morris-dances will find Miss Brower's book valuable. The steps are clearly and accurately described and the music is unabridged. Miss Brower 's introduction to *Morris Dance Tunes* gives a short history of the resurrection of the old morris-dances.

Every book of this kind helps restore to us "our long-lost birthright to recreation which is not manufactured."

MARY WOOD HINMAN

A Leaf Key to the Genera of the Common Wild and Cultivated Deciduous Trees of New Jersey. By MARY F. BARRETT, State Normal School, Upper Montclair, New Jersey. 1911. Pp. 7.

This pamphlet, is designed to use leaf, bark, trunk, and twig characteristics as means of identification. Flowers and fruit are not used, and leaves constitute so nearly all of the features that are called for that it would not be possible to use the key except when leaves are available. Furthermore, the key is so meager that it would seem impossible for general students to use it with any success unless they are constantly assisted by a teacher who has abundant information upon the many points that are omitted. Such a brief key often proves very helpful in the laboratory of the person who devises it, since the teacher may supplement as fully as is necessary, but for accurate identification of plants of any group in any general and independent way, more explicit and comprehensive descriptions are necessary.

O. W. C.

When Should a Child Begin School? By W. H. Winch. Baltimore: Warwick and York, 1911. Pp. 96.

The question put in the title is investigated by comparing the advancement in school of pupils who have entered at different ages. In England, where the study was made, the child may enter school at the age of three and is required by law to enter at the age of five—though some children enter after five because they receive instruction at home or because of neglect. The early years are spent in an infant department. A child is advanced to the grades (or "standards") when he reaches the proper age irrespective of the length of time he has spent in the infant department. The amount of advancement or retardation of a particular child was measured by the number of months by which he was younger or older than the standard for his grade. With this form of measurement it was found that of the children who entered before five years of age there was no difference in the advancement of those who entered early as compared with those who entered later. Those who entered after five were possibly somewhat retarded in comparison with those who entered before five. No difference was found also in the standing in examinations or the deportment or attentiveness of those who entered early or late.

Since this result seemed somewhat surprising (and to the infant-department teachers, discouraging) the author inquired whether it might be due to the fact that children from "poor" homes entered early, in the main, and thus brought down the average of the group of those who entered early. This supposition was not found to be true. We are left with the conclusion, therefore, that entrance before five does not give the child an advantage in his subsequent school career. The investigation seems to have been carefully made and the results justify the author in his conclusion. It is still possible, however, that there is a type of training, different from that given in the infant departments, which would be of advantage to the child in his later school career.

Frank N. Freeman

BOOKS RECEIVED

AMERICAN BOOK CO., CHICAGO

Practical Algebra, Second Course. By JOSEPH V. COLLINS. Cloth. Pp. 303. Price $0.85.

First Lessons in English for Foreigners in Evening Schools. By FREDERICK HOUGHTON. Cloth. Illustrated. Pp. 150. Price $0.40.

Plane Geometry. By C. A. HART and DANIEL D. FELDMAN. Cloth. Pp. 303. Price $0.80.

Second-Year Latin for Sight Reading. By ARTHUR L. JANES. Cloth. Illustrated. Pp. 238. $0.40.

Third-Year Latin for Sight Reading. By J. EDMUND BARSS. Cloth. Pp. 123. $0.40.

Practical Course in Botany. By E. F. ANDREWS. Cloth. Illustrated. Pp. 384. Price $1.25.

THE GORHAM PRESS

Some Fundamental Verities in Education. By M. P. E. GROSZMANN. Cloth. Illustrated. Pp. 118.

Public Education in Germany and in the United States. By L. R. KLEMM. Cloth. Pp. 350. $1.50.

Hassan in Egypt. By ETTA BLAISDELL MCDONALD and JULIA DALRYMPLE. Cloth. Illustrated. Pp. 114. $0.60.

HINES, NOBLE & ELDRIDGE

The Character Building Readers.

First Reader—Part One.	Parental Love.
First Reader—Part Two.	Industry.
Second Reader—Part One.	Helpfulness.
Second Reader—Part Two.	Courage.
Third Year.	Personal Responsibility.
Fourth Year.	Thoughtfulness.
Fifth Year.	Adaptability.
Sixth Year.	Fidelity.
Seventh Year.	Self-Reliance.

By ELLEN E. KENYON-WARNER. Cloth. Illustrated.

THE MACMILLAN COMPANY

In Memoriam. By ALFRED, LORD TENNYSON. Edited, with Introduction and notes, by J. W. PEARCE. Cloth. Pp. 275. $0.25.

The "Iliad" of Homer. Translated by ALEXANDER POPE. Edited by CHARLES ELBERT RHODES. Cloth. Pp. 642. $0.25.

Great Educators of Three Centuries. By FRANK PIERREPONT GRAVES. Cloth. Pp. 289. Price $1.10.

United States History for Schools. By EDMOND S. MEANY. Cloth. Illustrated. Pp. 587. $1.00.

The American School Readers: Fourth Reader. By KATE F. OSWELL and C. B. GILBERT. Cloth. Illustrated. Pp. 322. $0.45.

World Geography. By RALPH S. TARR and FRANK M. MCMURRY. Cloth. Illustrated. Pp. 536. Price $1.25.

CURRENT EDUCATIONAL LITERATURE IN THE PERIODICALS[1]

IRENE WARREN
Librarian, School of Education, The University of Chicago

ADAMS, CYRUS C. Maps and map-making. Harper 124:237–43. (Ja. '12.)

ADDAMS, JANE. A new conscience and an ancient evil. McClure 38:471–78. (Fe. '12.)

AITON, GEORGE B. The small high school of the middle west: a Minnesota type. School R. 20:90–97. (Fe. '12.)

(An) American education for an English peer. Lit. D. 44:205. (3 Fe. '12.)

Arguments advanced for a recreation commission. Playground 5:351–53. (Ja. '12.)

BARDEEN, C. W. The monopolizing woman teacher. Educa. R. 43:17–40. (Ja. '12.)

BEYER, HENRY G. The international hygiene exhibition at Dresden. Pop. Sci. Mo. 80:105–28. (Fe. '12.)

BOYNTON, PERCY H. Suggestions for the English-literature section of a high-school library. School R. 20:111–16. (Fe. '12.)

(The) "boy's own books" of today. Lit. D. 44:211–12. (3 Fe. '12.)

BRICKER, GARLAND A. Problems in the experimental pedagogy of elementary agriculture. J. of Educa. Psychol. 3:29–34. (Ja. '12.)

CAMERON, NORMAN. A new method for determining rate of progress in a small school system. Psychol. Clinic 5:251–64. (Ja. '12.)

CHUBB, PERCIVAL. The menace of pedantry in the teaching of English. School R. 20:34–45. (Ja. '12.)

COOPER, CLAYTON SEDGWICK. The American undergraduate. Cent. 83: 514–23. (Fe. '12.)

(The) cultural and the vocational in the college curriculum. Educa. 32:284–309. (Ja. '12.)

ALLINSON, Culture, the ideal of the college. 284–92.

BIRDSEYE, The college curriculum as a preparation for vocation. 293–309.

[1] *Abbreviations.*—Atlan., Atlantic Monthly; Cent., Century Magazine; Cur. Lit., Current Literature; Educa., Education; Educa. R., Educational Review; El. School T., Elementary School Teacher; Harp. W., Harper's Weekly; J. of Educa. Psychol., Journal of Educational Psychology; Lit. D., Literary Digest; Pop. Sci. Mo., Popular Science Monthly; Psychol. Clinic, Psychological Clinic; R. of Rs., Review of Reviews; School R., School Review; Sci. Am. Sup., Scientific American Supplement; Scrib. M., Scribner's Magazine; Teach. Coll. Rec., Teacher's College Record.

DAVISON, CHARLES. The education of Charles Darwin. Educa. R. 43:125-33. (Fe. '12.)

DRAPER, ANDREW S. Rural supervision in New York. Educa. R. 43:193-98. (Fe. '12.)

Earning-power of young college men. Lit. D. 44:212-13. (3 Fe. '12.)

EASTMAN, CHARLES A. (OHIYESA). Education without books. Craftsman 21:372-76. (Ja. '12.)

FINLAY-JOHNSON, HARRIET. Education dramatized. Atlan. 109:256-64. (Fe. '12.)

FISKE, THOMAS S. The college-entrance examination board. Educa. R. 43:155-67. (Fe. '12.)

HANDSCHIN, C. H. The percentage of women teachers in state colleges and universities. Science 35:55-57. (Ja. '12.)

HILL, ROSCOE CONKLING. Secret societies in high schools. Educa. R. 43: 168-92. (Fe. '12.)

HOSMER, G. W. Mr. Pulitzer's ideals for the Columbia school of journalism. R. of Rs. 45:187-90. (Fe. '12.)

JAMES, EDMUND J. The royal engineering college at Charlottenburg-Berlin. Science 35:172-75. (2 Fe. '12.)

JOHNSON, FRANKLIN W. The high-school boy's morals. School R. 20:81-89. (Fe. '12.)

JUDD, CHARLES H. Studies in the principles of education. El. School T. 12:206-14.

KIRBY, A. H. P. The problem of the feeble-minded child. Child 2:290-98. (Ja. '12.)

LAMBERT, JOHN. Preparations for the prevention of dust in schools. Child 2:279-89. (Ja. '12.)

LEAVITT, FRANK M. The reorganization of school systems. El. School T. 12:225-36. (Ja. '12.)

MCANDREW, WILLIAM. The schoolman's Monday morning. Educa. R. 43:109-24. (Fe. '12.)

MANATT, J. IRVING. The college and the man. R. of Rs. 45:191-93. (Fe. '12.)

MARTY, HENRI. L'Ecole des Roches. School R. 20:27-33. (Ja. '12.)

(Are) memories transmitted from parent to child? Cur. Lit. 52:177-79. (Fe.'12.)

New methods of admission to college. Educa. 32:261-83. (Ja. '12.)

NICOLSON, Recent changes in the rules of the New England college-entrance certificate board. 261-65.

JUDD, Reasons for modifying entrance requirements. 266-77.

KINGSLEY, Plan for college admission proposed by the National Education Association. 278-83.

NEWTON, RICHARD COLE. Narrow jaws and small feet. Pop. Sci. Mo. 80:138-41. (Fe. '12.)

PARKER, S. CHESTER. Experimental schools in Germany in the eighteenth century. El. School T. 12:215–24. (Ja. '12.)

(A) police-court "torchlight." Lit. D. 44:214–15. (3 Fe. '12.)

PRITCHETT, HENRY S. Student ideals in Japan and America. Youth's Companion 86:57. (1 Fe. '12.)

Professor Bergson on the soul. Educa. R. 43:1–16. (Ja. '12.)

Professors and practical men. Sci. Amer. Sup. 73:29–30. (13 Ja. '12.)

ROBERTS, ELMER. The passing of the unskilled in Germany. Scrib. M. 51:199–204. (Fe. '12.)

SHERWOOD, ADA SIMPSON. An old-time pedagog. Educa. R. 43:41–48. (Ja. '12.)

SHOREY, PAUL. An educational culture-bouillon. School R. 20:73–80. (Fe. '12.)

SLOSS, ROBERT. The state and the fool. Harp. W. 56:17. (3 Fe. '12.)

SNEDDEN, DAVID. The opportunity of the small high school. School R. 20: 98–110. (Fe. '12.)

SUZZALLO, HENRY. The teaching of spelling. Teach. Coll. Rec. 12:4–72. (N. '11.)

TOWN, CLARA HARRISON. The Binet-Simon scale and the psychologist. Psychol. Clinic 5:239–44. (Ja. '12.)

UNRICH, FLORA. A year's work in a "superior" class. Psychol. Clinic 5:245–50. (Ja. '12.)

YEAMES, H. H. On teaching Virgil. School R. 20:1–26. (Ja. '12.)

Year book. Playground and Recreation Association of America. Playground 5:325–50. (Ja. '12.)

YERKES, ROBERT M. The class experiment in psychology with advertisements as material. J. of Educa. Psychol. 3:1–17. (Ja. '12.)

WESTGATE, LEWIS G. The efficiency of the college course. Educa. R. 43: 134–54. (Fe. '12.)

WETTSTEIN, CARL T. Schools for defective children in Europe. Educa. R. 43:49–61. (Ja. '12.)

WHITCHER, GEORGE H. Domestic arts courses in public schools. El. School T. 12:197–205. (Ja. '12.)

WILM, EMIL C. Colleges and scholarship. Educa. R. 43:62–68. (Ja. '12.)

WINCH, W. H. Mental fatigue in day-school children as measured by immediate memory, part I. J. of Educa. Psychol. 3:18–28. (Ja. '12.)

VOLUME XII NUMBER 8

THE ELEMENTARY SCHOOL TEACHER

APRIL, 1912

THIRD-GRADE HISTORY WORK IN FRANCIS W. PARKER SCHOOL

PEARL BACKUS CARLEY
Francis W. Parker School, Chicago

The children of the third grade have studied the history of the growth of Chicago. It is most interesting to take up the study of Chicago chronologically, and to place the pupils in the life and movement of the period they are studying. The stories of Indians, fur traders, pioneers, transportation, the early industries, and various simple civic problems having picturesque aspects, appeal to children through a natural interest. These stories become a vital part of the life and experience of each child. The contrasts between the lives of people who lived here fifty to a hundred years ago, and their own, helps them to appreciate their own environment and comforts. Chicago is so young that there are people still living who can tell personal experiences of the early days, and these, with visits to historical spots and museums, make the study more real and vivid. The purpose is not to teach events only, but to show reasons for the beginning of the city; its connection geographically, historically, and commercially with the rest of the country—the interdependence, in general, between the city and the surrounding country. To have children image the landscape, not the map, many excursions to type areas—as the swamps and sand dunes—are necessary. This also enables them to think of conditions around Chicago as they existed long ago. It is essential to make a study of some of the organized civic activities of the present day, to emphasize the beginnings, the growth, and the reasons for instituting them.

The children write their own histories of Chicago. Each child has reprints of thirty or forty pictures which the teacher has collected from every possible source to illustrate this work. Covers are made for the books, and they are simply and artistically bound. The motive of making a book, which is to be both complete and beautiful, appeals very strongly to all of them.

The plan for a series of twenty lessons on Pioneer Transportation, included in this article, was worked out by Miss Beatrice Topping, under Mrs. Carley's supervision. Pictures illustrating this part of the story were drawn by Miss Topping.

The topical outline given below will give some idea of the contents of each child's book. These topics are so closely correlated that it is difficult to classify them under different subject heads. But they have been placed under History, Science, and Geography, according to their significance in the Story of Chicago.

HISTORY

- How Chicago Looked a Hundred Years Ago
- Stories of Indians
  - Indian's Dress
  - Indian Homes
    - Wigwam
    - Summer Home
    - Winter Home
- Indian Village along Creek Where State St. Is Now
  - Industries
    - Basketry
    - Pottery Making
    - Weaving Rush Mats
    - Weaving Blankets
    - Cooking
- How Indians Gather Wild Rice
- Indian Games
- Hunting and Fishing Devices
  - Elk Hunting
  - Buffalo Hunting
  - Hunting Buffalo with Decoys
  - Antelope Hunting
  - Hunting Deer with Decoys

Hunting Bears
Bear Dance
Snow-Shoe Dance
Trapping Animals
Fishing with Soap Root
Fishing with Bow and Arrow
Spearing Fish—Weirs
Picture Writing
Building Canoes
Indians in Lincoln Park
Building Fort Dearborn
Plan of Fort Dearborn
Mr. Kinzie Comes to Chicago
The Kinzie Mansion
Fur Trading
Stories of Trappers
Stories of French Voyageurs
How Chicago Looked in 1812
Tecumseh
Revolutionary War
War of 1812
First Indian Trouble
Massacre of Fort Dearborn
Black Partridge
Captain Wm. W. Wells
After War of 1812
Fort Dearborn Rebuilt
Government Bought Land for Canal
Coming of Settlers; How They Traveled; Traveling with: Ox-Carts; Sledges; Prairie Schooners; Flatboats; Packhorses
Abraham Lincoln Traveling to Illinois; his Trip on Flatboat down Mississippi River
Mr. and Mrs. Kinzie's Traveling Experiences
How Chicago Looked in 1831
Old-fashioned Fireplace: Cooking
River Water
Wells and Sweeps
Selling Water from Cart
Water System: Log Pipes
First City Water Works
Second City Water Works: Tunnel, Crib
The Drainage Canal
Intersecting Sewers
Plan for North Shore Sewers

Street Problems
Lifting Chicago Out of the Mud
The Train of Cars F. W. P. Fast Freight
Playground Plan for F. W. P. Freight Cars

Science

Swamps in Chicago
- Birds in Swamps: Red-winged Black-Bird; Yellow-headed Black-Bird, Kingfisher; Snipe; Turnstone; Heron; Sora Rail; Wild Geese; Wood-Duck, Loon
- Swamp Life
- Plant Life—Animal

Study of Type Trees
- Elm; Pine; Maple; Oak; Willow; Poplar; Uses of Trees; Valuable Sap; Seeds—Dissemination

Stories of Animals Concerned in Fur Trade
- Beaver; Muskrat; Lynx; Badger; Bear; Wolf; Otter; Mink; Skunk; Fox; Marten; Squirrel

Candles
- Dips; Molds; Paraffin; Spermaceti; Wax; Tallow; Bayberry

Making Gas
- How Gas Is Collected
- How It Is Piped to House
- How Made on Large Scale

Experiments with Water
- Water Seeks Its Own Level
- Purification by Distilling

Geography

Excursions to
- Sand Dunes; Swamps; Lake Shore; Ridge; Harbor; on River

Sand and Relief Maps of United States
Sand and Relief Maps of Illinois
Sand and Relief Maps of Great Lakes
Trace Route Traveled by French
Trace Route Traveled by Mr. Kinzie
Trace Route Traveled by Captain Whistler
River Course (see details under "River Excursions" below)
Relation of Chicago River to Des Plaines and Illinois Rivers
Chicago Portage
Illinois and Michigan Canal
Drainage Canal
Harbor Problems
Cutting Channels through Sand Spit
Government Piers

Industries of City
- Tanneries
- Manufacturies
- Stockyards and Packing-Houses

Illinois Tunnel Company

Transportation:
- Primitive and Modern (models of freight cars made by children in shop—coal cars large enough for two children to ride in)
- Imaginary Trips in These Cars to a Texas Cattle Ranch
- To a Coal Mine in Illinois
- East with Refrigerator Car (fresh meat)
- To Minnesota (corn and wheat fields)
- Visit to Flour Mills
- Trip to Michigan for Lumber

Transportation on the Great Lakes:
- Grain; Coal; Ore; Lumber, etc.

River Excursions:
- River Course and Harbor
- Government Piers
- Harbor Lights
- Slips
- Life-saving Station
- Warehouses
- Factories
- Electric Power Houses
- Lake Sand Company
- Tanneries
- Lumber Yards
- Office and Harbor Master
- Fire Boats
- Grain Elevators
- Illinois and Michigan Canal
- Drainage Canal

MAPS: Use large jig-saw map of United States. On the state of Texas, paste pictures of ranch life. On other states paste pictures of farms, wheat and corn fields, etc. Use muslin map of early Chicago to paste on pictures of early homes and buildings. Have large muslin map of modern Chicago to put on pictures of buildings of this period.

SERIES OF TWENTY LESSONS ON PIONEER TRANSPORTATION

I. PURPOSE

1. In a *large sense* to construct as vivid an image as possible of the life, hardihood, and inventiveness of the early pioneer, bringing home throughout the contrast of those early conditions with those of our modern civilization, and

holding up as an example to be admired the courageous, self-sufficient pioneer.

2. In a *smaller sense* to make the following historical points:
   1) Why did people come west?
      a) Because soldiers returning from the War of 1812 brought news of fertile plains and unwooded prairies to their friends in the East
      b) Because of the ever increasing population that demanded an outlet
   2) By what routes did they come west?
      a) Those previously traveled by Indians and hunters
      b) Those which crossed the mountains at the lowest points
   3) How did people travel then?
      a) By side-wheel steamers and by rear-wheel steamers
      b) By Mackinac boats on small streams
      c) By packhorses
      d) By flatboats on the Ohio
      e) By prairie schooners, overland
      f) By ox-carts
      g) By sledges in winter
   4) What did they carry with them?
      a) Salt—why?
      b) Flint and steel—why?
      c) Ax-head—why?
      d) Compass—why?
      e) A few cooking utensils
      f) Blankets—tent

      (*a*–*f*: Essentials)

      g) Such other articles as they had room for—the non-essentials—varying in size and quantity and quality according to individual preferences
   5) What kind of men were they?
      a) Independent
      b) Self-reliant
      c) Courageous—enduring freezing cold weather
      d) Sagacious, able to tell direction when lost
      e) Fearless and strong

II. METHOD

1. In a *large sense* to let objects, rather than words, do the speaking. To substitute memorization of the above facts by an abundance of handwork of numerous varieties and in various mediums, letting the facts thereby gradually take hold through the activities, and the picture grow more clear and more permanent with each successive phase of the child's self-activity.
2. In a *smaller sense* to follow the plan of lessons outlined below.

MATERIALS

Lesson I: Why did people come west?

1. Ask questions and consider carefully each answer.

2. Show pictures of eastern as contrasted with pictures of western farm lands. Let children compare what is seen in each picture and draw their own conclusions as to which they would prefer and why. Which would a farmer prefer, and why?[1]

3. Pass to sand tray to study topographical map. Show New England and the other colonies. Compare area with that of Mississippi plains.[2] Tell of continued immigration from across ocean. Point out fact that more children were being born constantly. Let children decide what would result and next how the congestion could be relieved. Point out horrors of the unexplored mountains, to give some idea of how much harder it was to cross those little humps of sand than they imagine. How could it be accomplished?

4. Return to seats and summarize either verbally or on paper.

Lesson II: How could people cross those mighty mountains that barred their path in every direction?

1. Consider carefully each answer. Ask questions.

2. Pass to sand tray. Ask children if any way looks easier to travel than the rest. Why?

3. Sprinkle white sand along main routes as the children indicate them, letting the sand represent people traveling west.

4. Also sprinkle white sand thickly over eastern portion at that time inhabited.

Lesson III: To fix in minds of children the routes discussed yesterday—

1. Run in slide[3] giving relief map of the United States. Let children, with pointer, follow out same routes as yesterday. Discuss and discard poorer ones.

2. Retain the four main lines of travel. Repeat several times to fix in mind.

3. Take outline maps[4] and mark with red these routes indicating portages by < < < < <, and river travel by — — — — — —.

Lesson IV: Tell first instalment of Mrs. Kinzie's journey from Detroit to Chicago in 1833, as given by herself in "Waubun."

Mrs. Kinzie travels through Lakes Erie and Huron to Mackinac on the "Henry Clay."[5]

Lesson V: To fix yesterday's story—

1. Let children recall story, smoothing out each other's difficulties, as they arise.

---

[1] Sand-map of United States, showing mountains and river valleys.

[2] Pictures of New England and of Illinois farms.

[3] Stereopticon with slide of relief map of United States.

[4] Plain outline map for each child.

[5] Chalk map on board of Great Lakes on which to indicate her progress, using the following pictures: Indian village; Storm; Ox-cart; Steamboat.

2. Take out pads and pencils and write the story to put in their histories of Chicago.

Lesson VI: To revivify images and restock the imagination with fresh material after yesterday's writing—

1. Show slides[1] of early steamers, compare with modern steamers. Show picture of modern steamer to verify comparison.

2. Finish writing stories.

Lesson VII: Tell second instalment of Mrs. Kinzie's journey,[2] taking her from Mackinac to Green Bay in steamer, and from Green Bay to Fort Winnebago in a Mackinac boat rowed by a crew of French Canadians.

Give all the picturesque incidents possible (as taken from *Waubun*) to give scope and variety: enough to fasten something in each child's imagination.

Lesson VIII: To fix yesterday's work—

Write on board as children dictate the story, giving them full scope to criticize one another's mode of presenting the thing.[3]

Lesson IX: Continue yesterday's work. Finish story No. 2.[4]

Lesson X: To clarify images, paint pictures of Mackinac boat and camp fire made on side of river.

Show pictures again. Let children stand in approximate corners of boat to give idea of size.

Lesson XI: Tell the third instalment of the story, taking Mrs. Kinzie from Fort Winnebago to the Fox River Indian Village, where they were lost in a blizzard.

Work out divisions; choose parts.[5]

Lesson XII: To vary scheme, let children divide story into short stories and choose.

Write the parts chosen yesterday.

Lesson XIII: Finish writing stories.

Lesson XIV: Review.

1. Let children tell the story of Mrs. Kinzie's travels as a review, using the return of hitherto absent children as an excuse. Watch to see how much is digested; how much mere repetition.[6]

2. With this as background, tell last instalment of story, bringing her safely to Chicago.

---

[1] Lantern slides of early steamers, both rear and side-wheelers.

[2] Map on board as previously indicated, using following pictures: Camp at night; Rapids in river; and other pictures as given above.

[3] Picture of Mrs. Kinzie in Mackinac boat which men are pulling over strong current.

[4] Picture of Mrs. Kinzie approaching Fort Winnebago.

[5] Map on board as before, leaving portion of journey so far traveled so as to compare distances covered by boat, horse, and Mackinac boat, also time used by each. Add following pictures: Indian trail; Night spent at fur trader's house.

[6] Picture of horses fording streams.

3. Count symbols on map, indicating night encampments. Find that Mrs. Kinzie took eight and a half days to come from region near Madison. How many have been to Madison or Milwaukee? How long did it take?

4. Bring out reasons for length of time; also

(*a*) How to tell directions; (*b*) How foretell a storm; (*c*) How cut their way across frozen streams.

Lesson XV: Let children again divide and choose parts to write.

Lesson XVI: Paint picture of Mrs. Kinzie's party on horseback, going through woods and snow.[1]

Lesson XVII: Give children opportunity to better their pictures if dissatisfied. Bring in clay horse to draw first on trial paper.

Lesson XVIII: Review.

1. Run slides through,[2] letting a child tell the story of each slide.

2. Bring out the various modes of conveyance used by Mrs. Kinzie. Which would children prefer?

3, 4. Work out whole length of journey, and then tell them how many hours it takes today.

Lesson XIX: Various routes.

1. Take out maps of routes and discover other routes of travel besides Hudson River–Great Lakes one.

2. How could men climb mountains?

3. How could men go down the Ohio River on other side? Easier or harder than going up Fox River?

4. Show model of Ohio flatboat.[3] Compare with Mackinac boat. Why the difference?

5. Show slides of Ohio flatboats.[4]

Lesson XX: Prairie schooner as used on Cumberland Gap routes.

1. Trace third route on map. Surmise as to best conveyance after study of other routes.

2. Show prairie schooner slides and model.[5] Why best fitted for that route?

[See outline of "Shop Work" in connection with "Transportation."]

The following story is the outcome of the preceding work. Parts of it were given verbatim from the children's dictation, and parts were rearranged by the practice teacher.

[1] New picture of the Kinzie party on horses lost in wilderness of snow.

[2] Lantern slides of the "Henry Clay" steamer; Ox-cart; Mackinac boat; Pack train.

[3] Model of flatboat made last year.

[4] Slides of flatboat.

[5] Model and slides of prairie schooner.

MR. AND MRS. KINZIE'S TRAVELING EXPERIENCES

The Mr. Kinzie that this story is about is the son of John Kinzie, the fur trader. This story is about him when he is married and grown up. Mr. and Mrs. Kinzie were in Detroit with some friends, and were listening to their stories about men that had been becalmed, and other people that had been caught in a storm. But they only laughed at these stories. They went down to the dock and were glad to see a beautiful boat. That is, to them it was beautiful. Their friends wished them a successful journey. The boat had two cabins. Its name was the "Henry Clay."

One of the cabins was for men, and the other for women. They had a nice journey for a little while, but after a while they struck a storm, and it began to get dark, and the rain began to come down in little streams from the roof in the ladies' cabin. They had to stand in a corner, and then the water began to come down there too. They had to climb in the berth, and for a while it was safe, but soon it began to leak there too. They at last went into the men's cabin. They told Mr. Kinzie and the other men about the awful time they had had, and they had to go into the berth again. There they kept dry. The next day they went on deck. They saw green shores, but no houses. Once in a while they saw an Indian tepee. Finally they got to Mackinac Island. They were happy to get out of the wet boat. The dock was full of Indians that were friendly to Mr. Kinzie. They smiled when they saw him, and said, "Bon jour, Monsieur John."

The Kinzies went from Mackinac Island to Green Bay in the "Henry Clay." It took them several days.

Mr. Kinzie was the agent for the Winnebago Indians. He was going to stop at Fort Winnebago to pay them for the land our government had bought from them. The Kinzies were going to take a Mackinac boat from Green Bay to Fort Winnebago. A Mackinac boat is oblong, and thirty feet long and about seven feet wide. In the middle of the boat a canvas is stretched over little poles. It looks like a little cabin. Mrs. Kinzie's piano was in a box under the canvas. Mrs. Kinzie was a musician, and she wanted to take her piano with her. They put a mattress over it and used it as a couch in the afternoons.

On each side of the boat there were French voyageurs and soldiers rowing, and the voyageurs sang songs to keep time with their oars.

Mr. Kinzie helped to row. He helped a soldier that seemed very weak and looked as if he had run away from home.

They came to many rapids, and the bourgeois would call, "Men overboard!" Then the men would have to jump out and pull the boat up the rapids. They were going against the current all this time, and it was very hard to row.

Sometimes the boat got stuck between two rocks, and the men had to get out and push it through. Sometimes the rapids were so swift that the men had to take everything out of the boat except the piano and carry it around. Sometimes they would have to pull the boat along with ropes.

The first night they stayed at Mr. Grignon's house, at Kakalin. The other nights they camped on the shore.

The Kinzies had one tent and the soldiers another. This was the first time Mrs. Kinzie had ever been west and camped out of doors. They had a fire in front of the camp. Mrs. Kinzie thought it was very beautiful. She sketched a picture of the river, with the sun shining on it.

The French voyageurs cooked ham on sticks over the fire. They ate from tin plates and drank from tin cups. In the morning the bourgeois would call, "How, how, how!" as loud as he could, to wake the people for breakfast. After eight days of such traveling, they came to Fort Winnebago.

Mr. and Mrs. Kinzie lived at Fort Winnebago all that winter. In the spring, they decided to go to Chicago to see their mother and father. First they baked biscuits and boiled ham. They decided to go by packhorse. They took two men. One was named Plante, who was the guide; the other one was named Pierre Roy. Plante was supposed to know the way, but he did not. Mr. and Mrs. Kinzie each had a horse. They also took one packhorse. To the packhorse they tied several bundles of biscuits and their hams. Each one had a tin cup on his saddle bow. The men each had a piece of flint in their pocket, and a piece of steel. They planned to follow some Indian

trails. They took a tent so they could camp. Mrs. Kinzie had a hunting knife hung around her neck.

Behind the fort was a little creek, called Duck Creek. They carried their canoe on an ox cart. When they came to the creek, they took the canoe off the cart and put it in the water. Then they put the trunk into the canoe. Mrs. Kinzie thought it would be best to sit on the trunk, but just as she got into the canoe some dogs jumped into her lap and upset the canoe.

Mrs. Kinzie got all wet. Mr. Kinzie had to carry her over on his shoulder. Mr. Kinzie asked her if she wanted to go back to the fort. She would not go. She rode all day in her wet clothes. It was growing cold, and she had on kid gloves, and her hands were swelling from the cold.

After they had ridden a long way, they found a place to put up their tent. They made a fire by striking flint and steel together. They put Mrs. Kinzie's coat near the fire to let it dry. It froze stiff. It looked like Mrs. Kinzie standing there.

For supper they had ham and biscuits. The biscuits were used as plates.

They cut the ham on the biscuits. They stirred their coffee with their knives.

Before they went to bed they tied their horses' front and back legs together so they could not run away. Then they rolled up in their blankets under the tent and were very comfortable.

While riding they sometimes saw one or two prairie wolves or deer, and the dogs would chase them away. Once in a while they came to an Indian village. The Indians came out and asked Mr. Kinzie for bread. But Mr. Kinzie did not dare give them any, because they hardly had enough for themselves. Mr. Kinzie told them so in their Indian language.

The second night they reached Mr. Morrison's house. They stayed there all night. Before leaving the next morning they asked for more biscuits. They were afraid their supply would run out.

The next day it snowed hard. Mr. and Mrs. Kinzie could hardly see the trail, but they went on. They had been told to keep on until they came to another trail, but they could not find it. Finally they made camp and had their supper and went to bed. It kept snowing. In the night the tent poles broke and the tent fell in on them from the weight of the snow. Mr. Kinzie had to cut new poles. In the morning they went on. Then Mr. Kinzie saw that Plante, the guide, did not know the way, so he took the lead. They did not eat much, because they hadn't much left.

Toward night they saw a fence. They were very happy, because they knew there must be a house near by. They asked what place it was. They found out it was Mr. Hamilton's house, the very place they had meant to reach. This shows what a good woodsman Mr. Kinzie was, and how well he could tell directions.

When they came to the Rock River, there was a ferry boat. It was just a little rowboat. A path was cut in the ice, so that the boat could run. It was sunset as they crossed. The sky was yellow and red, so was the streak of water where the ice was cut away. The horses swam across the river. That night they stayed at Mr. Dixon's house.

The next day they lost their trail. They wandered all day. Toward evening of the second day, Mrs. Kinzie's horse began to kick and jump and didn't want to go farther. Then Mrs. Kinzie knew there were Indians near, because her horse did not like them. Just then a little Indian dog ran out to meet them. Then they went behind the bushes and found two Indian squaws,

who were digging Indian potatoes. Mr. Kinzie asked the squaws where they were, but they did not know. Then Mrs. Kinzie asked where the squaws lived, and they said, "Across the river." Mr. Kinzie was glad, because he knew they must have a canoe there. He asked them if they had a canoe, and they said "Yes, but a very little one." So the squaws paddled them across, one at a time. On the other bank was an Indian village. Here they were able to get something to eat. It was the first they had eaten for two days. The master of the lodges guided them to the nearest cabin on the following morning. From here they knew the trail to Chicago. It took them eight and a half days to make the trip that it takes us only five hours to make.

The following stories, written by individual children, were used as reading lessons to summarize their study of the early methods of transportation.

The Lincoln Family Traveling to Illinois

In a canvas-covered wagon the Lincoln family was traveling from Indiana to Illinois, with all the family possessions. A tall boy, very strong and thin, carried a long whip, which he used to guide four yoke of oxen. None of the people along the road thought he would some day be president. It took them fifteen days to get to Illinois. It was a long, hard trip. They came through muddy forest roads. It was spring, and the streams were high. When they reached Illinois and found a place that suited them, Lincoln and his cousin got to work. They cleared the ground, made a barn, built a cabin, and ploughed the land. When that was done, they split rails and made fences.

Traveling on Packhorses

When all were comfortable, Lincoln left to work for himself. The first thing he did was to build a flatboat and go down the Mississippi River to New Orleans. That is where he saw how the slaves were treated. He had sympathy for them.

G. L.

A family was traveling from the East on packhorses to Chicago. Mr. King was walking in front with his dogs, and carried a rifle. His wife was riding horseback. Behind her on a horse were some pots and dishes and things that were needed for cooking. They did not take any meat with them. They only took salt and cornmeal, because Mr. King expected to get meat by shooting deer or wild turkey in the woods. There was a small path that they were following, which was called an Indian trail. Another horse was tied to the back of Mrs. King's saddle. One packhorse carried a rake, a piece of iron for a plough, and some small farm tools. These things did not have handles, except the hatchet which was used on their way to cut firewood. One horse carried two baskets, one on each side. The baskets were filled with bed clothes, and in a hole in the middle sat the children. Other packhorses carried household goods. The hired man walked behind to see that nothing was lost, and he also kept the cattle together. G. S.

A tired party in two prairie schooners were going slowly along the lake shore on their way to Chicago. They had covered about 500 miles, having come from Buffalo. Three young men walked by the side of the wagon. Their clothes were spattered with mud and they looked as if they had more than once put their shoulders to the wheels. The roads were very bad, it

TRAVELING FROM BUFFALO

seemed as if they had been wading through one mud hole after another all day. The horses looked as if they were pretty well tired out. The lighter of the two wagons was drawn by one horse. The heavier wagon was drawn by two horses. They had just left a tavern and had forty-two miles to go before they could reach another. They were going along the lake shore near the sand. They unhitched two horses from the heavy wagon and had them pull the lighter wagon over to the shore. It was easier to pull there where the sand was hard. It was three o'clock in the afternoon before the large wagon overtook the other. The old horse could go no farther, in spite of all the urging he would not move another step. Then they decided to turn the old horse loose.

A storm was coming up, the sky looked threatening, and they decided to have supper, and camp for the night. They had hardly sat down when a heavy storm broke over their heads. They gathered all the food they could in the short time that they had, and jumped into the prairie schooners. The three young men got into the smaller wagon. They thought they had the best of it, because that wagon carried the mattresses and blankets. But toward morning the cover blew off and they were drenched with rain before they got it back.

In the other schooner the people sat opposite each other and all were holding on to the cover to keep it from blowing away. The next morning they prepared breakfast; it was not easy to get because all the wood was saturated with water. They left the heavy wagon on the beach, with all in it that they could spare, and pressed on with the smaller wagon.

They had written to a friend in Chicago to meet them with some oxen and they were hoping that soon they would have the friend's help. That day the friend did meet them with the oxen. The two horses were almost dead, but

FLATBOATS

they were not so tired but that they could help the oxen. They all reached the tavern.

The next morning the three young men went back with the oxen and horses for the schooner that they had left behind. At night they were among the sand dunes and had to sleep in two inches of snow. They had some pine twigs at their heads and a roaring fire at their feet. They rolled up in blankets and slept soundly. They found the wagon the next night just as they left it. They ate flap-jacks and honey for supper, and altogether had a good time of it.

T. P.

Some of the people built flatboats and keel boats and came down the Ohio River. When they came to a place they liked they stopped. Sometimes they would take their boat to pieces and build their cabin out of it. If they wanted to go up the Mississippi River they took a rope and put it around a tree ahead of them and pulled the boat up to that tree. And they put the rope up the next tree, and so on, up the river. They had to do this because they were going against the current. They would do this until they found a place where they wanted to stop. Sometimes they would go into the woods and cut down trees and build their houses. J. F.

TRAVELING IN A SLEDGE

TRAVELING IN AN OX-CART

Long ago in winter people used to ride in sledges instead of sleighs. Oxen pulled the sledges. M. P.

Mr. Beaubien came from Detroit in an ox-cart. He had an Indian to guide him. He got jolted around because they were following up an Indian trail and the cart didn't have any springs. J. F.

The following is an outline of last year's third-grade shop work in connection with early transportation, under direction of Mr. Leonard W. Wahlstrom.

The struggles of the early pioneers to reach the West from the civilized communities of the East furnished motive for the handwork during part of the year.

Study of pictures and stories of travel furnished a basis for comparison of primitive methods of travel with our own modern means. Simple facts in mechanics and physics were brought out in class discussion of these pictures. The following types of vehicles were studied: prairie schooner, sledge, ox-cart,

flatboat. The following outline shows some of the points brought out in these discussions:

Prairie Schooner

a) High wheels—roll over stones and rough ground better than smaller wheels. Makes possible fording of streams.

b) Wide rims—do not sink into soft ground; cf. coal wagons on city streets, city ordinance requiring wide tires.

c) Hubs—bigger and longer; give more bearing surface on axle causing less wear where it "rubs." "Rubs" = friction. In narrow hub all the wear due to load coming on shorter space on axle; therefore more wear. Trace load from wagon box to ground through axle and wheels. What used to reduce friction? Oil, grease. Is friction a good thing or bad? Sometimes good; cf. brake shoe on wheel, drag shoe and chain. Friction in walking—wears shoes. Why slip when walking on ice? No friction.

Sledges

Wooden runners more friction than steel and iron. Eskimos use walrus bone. Ice less friction than snow. Cf. lumber roads in north sprinkled to make ice. Compare flat iron with round iron on sleds. Which best? Why?

Ox Cart

Compare ox-cart with prairie schooner. Ox-cart=product of primitive community. No shops, few tools, etc. Prairie schooner=product of civilized community. Skilled workers, shops, many tools, etc. Ox-cart wheel, solid, heavy; good only for short distance. Prairie schooner wheel, lighter, stronger; better for long distance. Ox-cart wheel solid; two side braces give strength and greater bearing surface on axle; reduces cutting action on axle but increases friction.

The Wheel

Trace evolution of wheel:

1. Indian drag; two poles tied to horse.
2. Roller; log connecting end of poles.
3. Roller; hollowed out to give two rough wheels; wheels and axle turn together.
4. Separate wheels—sections of log.
5. Wheel built up; hub, spokes, rim, tire.
6. Railway wheel and axle joined in one. A return to primitive roller type. Why?

For a description of another year's work in the Wood Shop in connection with modern transportation, which consisted in the making of a small freight train, see an article in *Elementary School Teacher*, September, 1908. The next year a train consisting of larger cars (4 ft.×1 ft.) was begun. It was intended to use these cars in transporting the crops from the garden. The tops of the refrigerator, box, and furniture cars were on hinges, but the coal cars had seats (two in each car) in which the children might ride. Although the tracks and trucks have not yet been made so that the cars can be of permanent use, still, the children have had sufficient pleasure in making and using them to more than justify their work upon them.

HEAT AS A TOPIC FOR THE EXPERIMENTAL SCIENCE WORK OF THE EIGHTH GRADE[1]

OTIS W. CALDWELL
School of Education, the University of Chicago

The purpose of the present paper[2] is not to give the outlines for the full year's work in the elementary science of the eighth grade, but to present one series of lessons in sufficient detail to show exactly what was done by the pupils, and the conclusions that they made from their experiments. Therefore, but a brief statement is made of the work that has preceded the topic here outlined, and another of the work that follows. Essentially the same method of work was used with the other topics as with that here given.

The topics of the seventh grade which were related to physical phenomena dealt chiefly with electricity and magnetism, the pupils constructing most of the apparatus by means of which they performed their experiments. The work of the eighth grade proceeded in the same manner through experimentation with simple, usually improvised apparatus, construction work, and constant discussion of the significance of the experiments. The experiments are introduced either as outcomes of questions that have arisen from previous experiments or from discussion of common phenomena of the home or environment. While the year's work takes up topics as, heat, sound, light, liquids, gases, and simple machines, and thus seems rather formal from this statement of topics, the treatment is informal, and aims to consider topics as they are illustrated in common phenomena that may be observed by any pupil in his everyday experiences. We do not regard the organization of significant topics as ideal, but the outline represents the present stage of our experiments in organizing this part of the elementary

[1] This is an outline of work as taught by Mr. C. F. Phipps who has assisted in the preparation of this paper.

[2] It is unfortunate that other illustrations intended for this article were defective and could not be used.

science course. No attempt is made to use the organization of topics that would be found in an ordinary course in elementary physics. The topic *heat,* its nature and application, is the first subject of study of the eighth year. The following outline presents the experiments used in the first part of the study. The notes suggest what the pupils observed, what conclusions they reached, and sometimes the chief points of the discussion are added.

I. Heat, Its Nature and Applications as Shown by Experimentation with Common Materials and Through Observation of Common Phenomena.

At the outset the topic of study is announced, and questions are asked regarding what seems to be the importance of the study. Questions are asked that center attention on heat effects in the home, as in boiling water, cooking, maintaining desired temperature of the home by hot air, steam, or hot water, evaporation from surface of water, etc. The pupils are encouraged to suggest as many cases of application of use of heat or its regulation as they can, and all the discussion is finally centered on the question of boiling, it being made certain that some of the questions that are not understood by the class are brought out. In this way the necessity of experiment and trial is clear and as a result there is a problem or several problems that the class attacks by means of experiment. The topics and the experiments follow. It must be understood that while the order of topics and experiments is decided by the teacher, he is always ready to introduce a pertinent experiment that a pupil may present if it is feasible for trial of a point in question.

IA. *Boiling water.*

1. Use tea kettle filled with water and standing above flame. Observe what happens.

(1) The singing of the kettle is noted. Explanations are called for, and various explanations are offered. Pupils cannot explain singing fully —cannot be understood until they know something about bubbles that are coming up in the water in the kettle. Some explanation is given by the teacher, and full explanation is delayed until other facts are noted.

(2) Vapor seen at the spout of the kettle. Thought by the pupils to be steam. No vapor is seen at the end of the spout, but at a little distance from it. Why? Various explanations, the correct one being given by pupils as that the steam turns to vapor.

(3) Cause for the steam turning to vapor. Explained by class as due to condensation of steam when in contact with the cold air.

(4) Relation of the facts just seen to fogs and clouds. Questions and collection of previous observations led to explanation and understanding of relation of vapor to cloud formation.

(5) Tests of vapor to see its nature.

Put flame in it, and see it dissipate. What becomes of it?

Put cold glass plate in it and observe results. Condenses on glass. Because glass is so much colder than the vapor.

Put glass plate in the invisible steam. Same results. Accounted for by class by combining the two previous steps—making steam into vapor and condensing vapor on glass.

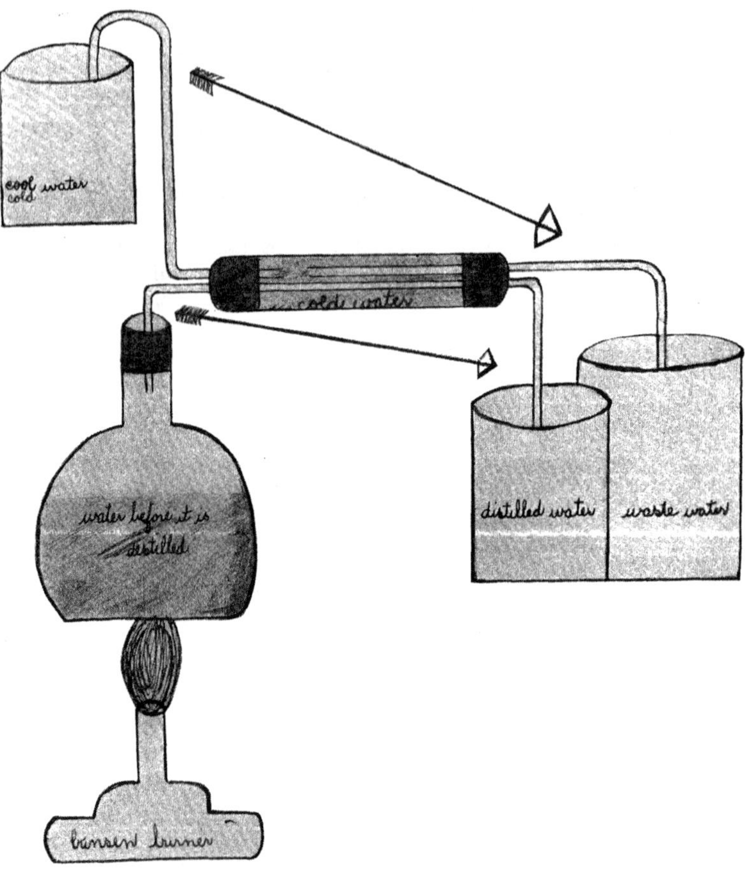

FIG. 1.—A pupil's drawing illustrating his apparatus for distilling water

(6) What will be the effect if we close the spout? How shall it be closed? Why not with hand? Close it with cork stopper.

Steam is found to make the cover rise and fall. Does it rise and fall slowly? At regular intervals? Explain if possible the intermittent rising and falling, and any differences in the rapidity of the rise and the fall.

(7) Experiment with stoppered test tube. Cork the tube and boil the water. Cork is blown out. Explain. Decided that the expansive force of the steam forces the cork out.

(8) Experiment with a glass of water to see if there is air in the water. Put glass of water on radiator, register, or upon stove and leave standing until quite warm. Noted that after a time small bubbles of air gathered on inner surface of glass. The temperature of the room or whatever the glass stood upon caused the air to be forced out of the water, and they gathered on the walls of the glass. Shake the glass and note the rise of the air bubbles through the water. Have pupils repeat this experiment at home under the variety of circumstances that are offered. It will be noted that water from the faucet often appears muddy when first drawn, and soon settles as the bubbles of air rise to the top.

(9) Experiments with individual flasks of water when heated.

- (*a*) Air is driven out in the form of tiny bubbles.
- (*b*) Steam bubbles observed by some as first rising but bursting before reaching the top of the water in the flask.
- (*c*) Larger bubbles of steam rise and burst on surface. The latter is called boiling.
- (*d*) Why do the bubbles rise? They are lighter. Why lighter? Because the air is expanded and steam bubbles are gaseous water, so lighter than water. (Do not follow this further at this time.)
- (*e*) Moisture, then, drops of water noted on neck of flask. The flask is in contact with lower temperature of outside air. Cause? Condensation. Pupils note that enough steam condenses so some drops flow back to the water below.
- (*f*) Insert into mouth of flask a cork with bent glass tube through it, so arranged that steam is passed through the tube.
- (*g*) More moisture and drops noted in the tube. Why? More prolonged exposure to condensing influence of lower temperature. Finally no more steam condenses in neck of flask or in bent tube. Why? Because they have become so hot by the constant passage of steam that they are no longer cold enough to condense steam.
- (*h*) Steam at nozzle, then vapor. Why? Further condensation.

(10) Problem: How hot is water when boiling?

- (*a*) Pupils put thermometer through two-hole cork down into water or hold by string or wire, and test. (Used both Centigrade and Fahrenheit.)

How much higher will thermometer register if allowed to remain in the boiling water a few minutes? Pupils are surprised to find it does not rise above 100° or 212° no matter how long held there while water is boiling over the gas flame. Not wise to explain now that the evaporation surface is increased, when steam bubbles form, to just such an extent that the *loss of heat* because of evaporation exactly equals the heat received from the fire.

(11) Problem: Is the steam that is given off hotter than the water?

(*a*) Hold thermometer in steam just above boiling water. Compare temperatures.

(12) Problem: Do other liquids boil at same temperature as water, and produce steam at same temperature?

(*a*) Try alcohol. Boils at 78°C. Vapor of alcohol also in 78°.

(13) Problem: Would water boil at same temperature if something was dissolved in it.

FIG. 2.—Apparatus made by seventh grade when studying electricity and magnetism.

(*a*) Try salt, first a little, then a larger amount. More heat needed. Found that it boiled at higher temperature with material in solution. Found that it boiled at 103° C. with amount of salt that was used. Would more salt alter the temperature of boiling? Try it. The boiling temperature rises.

(14) Problem: Is it possible to boil water with less heat than 100°C. or 212°F.?

(*a*) Boil water in flask, and while steam is escaping cork up tight, invert the flask and, soon as boiling ceases, pour cold water over flask. Repeat as long as boiling can be made to occur.

(*b*) Discussion as to causes.

Pupils note that the cold water condenses the steam in the flask, and as the air was all driven out by the steam before corking, there must be a partial vacuum. Further discussion brings out the facts that water *not* corked up boils at 100° because it takes that much heat to make bubbles which will lift off the air pressure. In the partial vacuum in the flask, after the cold water condenses the steam, there is very little pressure on the water so it boils easily at reduced temperature.

(*c*) Soon as boiling no longer occurs take temperature of the water. May be 25° or 30°C.

(*d*) Was it hard to get cork out? Why? Partial vacuum within and air pressure on cork pushed it in. Concluded that air pressure affects temperature of boiling.

(*e*) Relation of heat of boiling water to cooking.
Questions and discussion.

(*f*) Would such things as potatoes, beans, etc., cook in the water at last temperature found?
Concluded that potatoes would not cook at that temperature.

(*g*) Do campers find any difficulty in cooking on high mountains? Why?

A few important facts are that:
In Madrid 3,000 feet high, water boils 206°F. = 97 C.
In Quito 11,000 feet high, water boils 194°F. = 90°C.
On Mt. Blanc 15,000 feet high, water boils 180°F. = 82°C.

Again, in the boiler of a steam engine in which the pressure is 100 pounds to square inch the boiling point of water is 155°C.

IB. *Evaporation.*

1. What effect has the sun and dry warm air on bodies of water? General discussion of problem. Pupils say, sun draws water up. What does this mean? Explanation.

2. Can this evaporation be made to occur more rapidly? How? Heating or boiling.

3. Relation of boiling to evaporation. Made clear by discussing previous experiment and general experience.

4. Pupils weigh water in pans and set aside and weigh each day for several days. Causes of less water in pans.

5. Use different sized dishes and solve problem whether same amount is evaporated from each. Found to depend upon amount of surface exposed.

6. Aids to explanations of evaporation. Discussion.

(*a*) Larger the surface, faster evaporation. Why? More heat and air get at the water.

(*b*) Warmer the room, faster evaporation. Why? The more heat, the faster the molecules of water vibrate and the more fly out into the air.

(*c*) What would happen if the pans were fanned all day? Set one pan in air current and compare with one in still air. More rapid evaporation. Why?

(*d*) Why do clothes on the line dry better on a windy day? Saturated air about the clothes is blown away and drier air takes its place and absorbs moisture faster from the clothes.

(*e*) Take same weight of water as in (4) above, boil it for a few minutes and weigh again. In a few minutes as much water evaporated as did in several days when left standing in rooms.

7. Do other liquids evaporate at same rate as water?

Put 3 drops each of water, alcohol, and ether on a piece of glass and time the evaporation of each.

Try again, and fan the drops. Quicker evaporation is noted and same relative periods for each as compared with others.

Pupils raised this question—When the water evaporates from the ocean, does the salt go up with the water? Dissolved salt in a test-tube of water, poured a few drops into a teaspoon on a piece of sheet metal and heated gently. Water evaporated and left the salt behind.

What are the conditions about Great Salt Lake, Utah? Some pupils have seen conditions there and explained the situation.

IC. *Condensation and distillation.*

1. Repeat boiling of water in flask until corked with tube inserted to see steam condense in the glass tube.

2. Put cold object in the steam. Observe condensation on cold object. Why this condensation? Reduction of temperature and condensation.

3. Can the steam be changed to water faster and in larger quantities than in the preceding experiments? Discussion by teacher and class.

4. Have pupils devise and make drawings of apparatus for securing water by condensing. Most of the pupils brought in sketch of plans for condensing and securing water therefrom.

5. Each put his drawings on board and explained. Class criticism of all plans.

6. Best plans were used by pupils in making and setting up apparatus. Water boiled and condensed the steam. Water secured thereby.

7. Can any practical use be made of these processes? Suggestions by class.

8. Try muddy water, colored solutions, salty solutions.

9. What is the process called? Distillation.

10. Application of distilling to industrial life. Discussions by teacher and pupils. Purifying water; making liquors and alcohol; making kerosene, naphtha, etc., from petroleum.

Following these experiments, there were others on topics related to heat as follows: effect of heat on solids, heat and cold by chemical action, effects of heat on liquids, effects of heat on gases, heat conduction in water; then special topics were made of the Thermos bottle, temperature and the thermometer; sources of heat, the application of heating processes, cooling processes, and ice making. This work occupied the time of the class during most of the autumn and winter quarters. In the spring quarter, first there came work with glass tubing; cutting, bending, drawing, sealing, making penfiller and delivery tubes. This work is interesting and instructive in itself and serves well in assisting the pupils to make apparatus to be used later.

Solids, liquids, and gases were taken up by means of experiments; also solutions, crystallization, water pressure, pumps, buoyancy, flotation, specific gravity, air as a gas, air pressure, coal gas, ammonia, carbon dioxid, photography as a means of study of the light, and a few experiments on sound.

ORGANIZING CHILD-STUDY WORK IN A SMALL CITY

VINNIE C. HICKS
Child-Study Laboratory, Oakland Schools

Much of the present interest in child-study is directly due to atypical children. The blindest of us have been forced to see that old-time methods in school did not fit the case of the incorrigible and the imbecile, the deaf mute, the blind, the crippled. All over this country the so-called "special" work for children is starting. This paper aims to show what one small city can accomplish in this line.

Oakland, California, has approximately 20,000 school children, distributed in 27 full eight-grade schools and 13 primary schools, and covering a wide extent of territory. The city is shaped roughly like a long elbow, with the convex side turned toward San Francisco Bay, the concave to the hills and with the center of town at the elbow itself. On the edges of the commercial center and along the water front live the very poor, a large majority of whom are southern Europe immigrants. There is a large oriental population also in this part of town. Except in a few limited districts near the hills there are settlements of all manner of foreigners who came over the bay after the San Francisco fire and stayed. Only three large schools in the city have what may be called a *good* class of children, and many of the others are full to the doors of Italians, Spanish, Portuguese, etc., with a social history which includes for many generations back no adequate schooling.

These were the conditions met by the psychologist who began work in Oakland just a year ago. Superintendent McClymonds before her coming had sent notes to the school principals asking them to consult with their teachers and send in lists of children in their respective schools whom they considered subnormal. The directing psychologist began at once examining these children, so that the first training-room might be opened as soon as possible. Three weeks after the work was begun, the training-room was opened. The dozen children for the class were selected from the first thirty-three examined.

The first mistake often made in serious attempts at special work is to omit expert study of cases before opening a training-room. Take a case in point. In a certain school system observed by the writer a special room was opened. An assistant superintendent placed twenty children in this room. He knew nothing of the children, except that they were reported to him as "off." Four inexperienced or partly experienced teachers tried and failed in the room in rapid succession. The wail arose, "Why is our special room a failure?" The answer to this question is perfectly clear. None of the teachers knew anything about their pupils' mental makeup. There was no psychological diagnosis to fall back on. The inexperienced teacher is as likely to make mistakes as a young interne doctoring a boy for measles who has a broken leg. Furthermore, the teachers put in charge of this special room knew nothing of the pupils' homes, parentage, habits, or physical condition. A clinical examination would have told them all these things. Finally there were twenty children in the room—nearly twice too many. Of these twenty nearly one-half were marked defectives of so serious a type that they should have been institutional cases, a few were bright truants, and a few were the ordinary subnormals for whom these classes are established. Of the conditions of room, yard, work materials, etc., I have not space to tell. They were impossibly bad.

This example is cited to illustrate the need of a well-organized clinic or child-study department before the work of class instruction actually begins. The clinic should have at its service a well-trained psychological diagnostician acquainted with the character and needs of children. The experiment in Oakland is characterized by the organization of a clinic as its first step in the undertaking.

The one classroom opened last February in Oakland has been a success from the beginning, though open only three days a week. Three seemingly hopeless cases, children who had remained in first grade from three to six years, returned months ago to advanced grades in their own schools and are carrying the work. With one exception the children who have remained in the training-room have advanced steadily—in a few cases, rapidly. One could write a volume on the methods used to bring about these happy results, but it is of more importance here to describe other phases of this work in Oakland.

The psychologist in charge of this work has given two days a week to work in the office and to school visiting. Thursday is open clinic day. Children come in from all over Oakland and even from near-by towns and remoter places in the state. Some are children who have never been in school, the nervous, imbecile, etc. After a thorough psychological examination of the child has been made the parents are advised as to the proper course to pursue. Should the child be under the care of a private teacher, the teacher often comes to get help in mapping out studies fitted to a weak mind. If the child is imbecile and the parents can be persuaded, application blanks for the state institution at Eldridge are filled out and the directing psychologist may even go into court to testify if necessary. If the imbecile child is in school, it becomes necessary to show the parents that the child cannot continue to attend ordinary school.

If the subnormal child continues in the regular school classes the work of the child-study department is chiefly advisory. The Department of Medical Inspection deals with the child's physical disabilities. The psychologist describes carefully to the parents any mental helps which they can use with the child at home, and also urges upon them right living for the child in every way. A report is sent to the grade teacher, telling the conditions found, all that has been done or advised, and adding any suggestions which it may be possible for her to carry out in her full schoolroom.

The cost of properly equipped special work for subnormal children includes three kinds of items. The first two are general and will need no duplication. The third belongs to the special room.

I. Salary of the psycho-clinical officers.

II. Fitting out an office:

a) Apparatus for clinical use $115

b) Printed matter for office use 70

c) Office furnishings 100

III. Cost of one training-room, to be added to as finances permit:
- *a*) Teacher's salary $1,200
- *b*) Materials for training-room—initial expense (including piano at $200) 300
- *c*) Materials for training-room—succeeding years 40

The last item in a room for the blind would be considerably increased because of necessary Braille books, machines, etc.; and all subnormal or truant rooms in schools unequipped with manual-training and domestic-science facilities would be far more costly.

The number of rooms ultimately needed will depend on the size of the school system. In Oakland the subnormals approximate closely the 2 per cent to 4 per cent published by other investigators. So far 325 children have been examined. Of these 12 per cent are institutional cases, 4 per cent incorrigible, and 12 per cent so high grade that the ordinary ungraded class can care for them. A close calculation indicates that we shall have at least 550 in all when the schools have reported fully, or about 400 subnormals alone. Dropping one-eighth of these and calling the number 350, we find that it will take 25 rooms of 14 scholars each to accommodate them. It will take $35,000 each year to cover the salaries of psychologist and teachers, and office and room maintenance on this basis.

The school board to whom these figures look large should look at the other side of the budget of expense. Principals and teachers unite in crying for relief from the burden of the atypical. They are the absent, the tardy, the ill-behaved, as well as the stupid. If statements are to be believed, this class of children takes at least 10 per cent of the teachers' time. I have heard the percentage put as high as 90 per cent, but am keeping to the minimum. Now if each teacher devotes one-tenth of her time or one-half an hour a day to these cases especially, she is giving at least 50 cents worth of her time each day. A corps of 400 teachers in a year of 40 weeks will devote $40,000 worth of time. Accounts seem to balance, without taking into consideration the principal's time saved, the better condition in general classes both for pupils and teachers, and the far better results with the subnormals themselves.

A saving of expense can be made in a school system which can correlate its work with a near-by normal school or college. The work in towns and cities has already gone far, far ahead of the supply of specially trained teachers. The demand for teachers in institutions for feeble minded is also far beyond the supply. Some day our training schools and colleges will wake up to the demand, but the day is discouragingly slow in coming, and at present the hardest problem in initiating a child-study department is in finding the psycho-clinicist, and then experienced or trained teachers. It is hoped that this paper may have some influence in opening up this training. If the heads of our normal schools and colleges were more interested in what might be called economic psychology, they would see the need and value of such courses more clearly. They should realize that some who have done good work in general child psychology served their apprenticeship with defective children. The processes of a feeble and erratic mind can be analyzed as those of the more normal and complicated one cannot. One can learn much from these abnormal processes from the idiot who can just barely fixate on an object, past the prehensile stage, through memory, on up to the moron who shows all kinds of brain activity, but all feeble. Every teacher who enters a schoolroom would gain much by studying these subnormal minds, not only to help her to deal with the abnormals she meets in her work, but because of her vastly increased understanding of the mental processes of her normal children.

School men are beginning to realize that from the training-rooms of the atypical come many of the methods which fit the average child. The incorrigible and the imbecile have been the first to be granted the privileges of digging and hammering, of sewing and cooking, of doing things vocational. Because we have been forced to learn what to do with the abnormal, we are learning good educational methods for the normal. The sooner we learn to use wisely psychological information gained from abnormals the better it will be, not only for the weak ones, but for the normal as well.

THE INCEPTION AND DEVELOPMENT OF AN INDUSTRIAL ELEMENTARY SCHOOL

O. P. VOORHES
Principal of Oyler School, Cincinnati, Ohio

In the fall of 1894 the writer was appointed first assistant in one of the public schools of Cincinnati. At that time there was little or no move in public education toward industrial training, so most that was current was given in private or semi-private institutions. At the time our city had two such, namely, the Technical School, now many years out of existence, and the Ohio Mechanics Institute, still one of the prominent schools of its kind in the country.

But it is of the former school I wish to speak in this connection, as the one that helped me, or rather one of my pupils, out of very serious difficulty, and convinced me of the desperate need for industrial training in connection with *public* instruction.

As a member of my class in the school first mentioned I had a boy, we shall call him John, who was nearly sixteen years of age, and had never taken kindly to language or grammar. As his class was the last before the high school, he began to see the seriousness of his neglect along these lines—not all his fault I am sure—and he so expressed himself to me. He engaged my sympathy at once, for I had remembered some difficulties I had encountered along similar lines when I was a boy.

In those days such equipment as his would not permit him to enter any high school, for I am reasonably safe in saying he did not know the difference between a verb and a preposition. But during the lesson in grammar he could make a drawing of the face of the teacher, which was in no sense a caricature. This phase of his ability gave me the cue as to what might be done for him. Knowing both the superintendent and the principal of the technical school previously mentioned, I talked the situation over with them with all the persuasive powers at my command, begging them to take the boy, to forget his shortcomings, and to magnify to him his peculiar talents, which I was sure were along mechanical lines and worth developing. They not only acceded to my request, but did it without money and without price, for John, like many another had neither, but he did have an ambition to make something of himself. He walked three miles back and forth for three years daily, the walk giving him renewed health and strength, and the work he loved giving him an insight into the great world of things.

The sequel is, that for many years John has been superintendent of the lighting plant of a large city; and this incident has always seemed to me a terrible rebuke to the old régime then dominant in high schools, which, in those days, could offer John nothing save a sneer. Today our high schools cater to every educational desire of every ambitious youth, giving him abundant opportunity to magnify his peculiar powers of both mind and body; and he who poses as an educator today, and does not see that the world of things and their manifold combinations developed through the manual side is of equal value with the world of thought developed through the intellectual side only, is truly an object of pity, and one who should scarcely be permitted to run at large.

The facts related above took such a vital hold on me in connection with my school work, and seemed to me to reinforce so fully the further facts that the industrial abilities which I had acquired back on the farm had been and still are of such incalculable value to me that the resolution to promote industrial education became a fixed part of my educational creed. The memory of the above lesson, for it is a lesson in educational equity, kept the need for industrial training constantly in my mind till I had opportunity to give it expression in the school of which I am now the head.

I began the work in 1903 after the following manner. Noting the fact that our district had within it some twenty or more factories of various kinds, and that they were sapping the life of our school, I sent to the heads of these factories, not one of whom lived in the district, a circular letter asking their co-operation in establishing a manual training department in our school. If such a step could be taken I was sure that it would raise the standard of efficiency of the boys and girls the factories were getting from us, it would make these boys and girls more useful to themselves, and must sooner or later, lead to higher standards in the community. Imagine my surprise, when a hearty response to this appeal came in, in the way of checks, till I had in sight almost one thousand dollars. Imagine my further surprise at this time, when a then prominent member of the Board of Education came to me and ordered that I desist, that the board, meaning himself, wanted none of it. I desisted, but for a short time only, for soon there came a new superintendent on the scene who saw these matters much as I did; a new régime was inaugurated, and manual training again raised its voice, this time without the danger of being suppressed.

At first some of the schools of the city were supplied with manual-training centers. Our school had one of the first of these centers through the recommendation of the superintendent, who had but to present to the board a copy of the circular letter referred to, and announce the response thereto. From this time—1905—on, the work was carried on in a more or less conventional manner till the spring of 1911. When I say "conventional," I mean that our boys and girls from the sixth grade up were getting one period per week of manual work, but, to my way of thinking, not enough to establish either habit or efficiency along this line. Also, I noted that I had within my school some 50 boys and girls below the fifth grade who were from two to five years behind the normal grades. That is to say, they were—most of them—of that unfortunate class that had seen more trouble in their short lives than most of us see in a lifetime. I was constantly asking myself, "Where do these folks come in?" "What is our school doing for these that shall help them to function in life?" In order to hold them in school I was keeping the Truant Department and the Juvenile Court busy. In my desperation, and with a constantly growing sympathy for the pupils, I went to the superintendent with a plan for an entirely new organization, one that was really revolutionary in its relation to what had obtained, but one that I was sure would meet the needs of the community, and one upon which I was ready to stake my reputation if I had any.

After thinking it over carefully, the superintendent gave me carte blanche in putting into operation a plan of which the following is a brief description. All pupils of the fifth, sixth, and seventh grades under the new regulations are getting two periods per week of an hour and a half each. The subnormal pupils found in the fourth, third, and second grades are getting three periods per week, the boys in the shop, and the girls all phases of domestic economy, including cooking, the simpler scientific values of foods, sewing, the use of the sewing machine, the simpler forms of cutting, fitting, etc.

They miss much of their regular class work while in the Industrial Department, but this is more than made up to them in the following manner: When the eighth-year pupils go to the Industrial Department, the subnormals leave their regular grade rooms and go to the eighth-year teacher for special work in arithmetic and geography. The work in arithmetic is such as will help them in the Industrial Department. When the pupils of the seventh grades go to the Industrial Department, the subnormals go to these teachers for special work in English, history, etc. Thus through segregation and individual work in which they are treated according to age and not according to grade, these pupils are getting work that is not only highly pleasing to them, but such as many of them would never get under the old régime, for a child aged fifteen in the second or third grade will scarcely reach the upper grades even of the elementary school. What we are trying to do with every student is, to treat him as though each day were his last with us.

The work of the eighth grade is so different from the others as to require special mention. These pupils give one-fifth of their time to industrial work. During this time the boys get twenty lessons in cooking, learning not only the scientific values of foods, but also their preparation into meals necessarily plain but substantial. Along with this they are given instruction in improvising camp equipment, such as the utilization of cast-off cans for cooking utensils, etc. Besides this they will get twenty lessons in the simpler forms of sewing, such as hemming, darning, sewing on of buttons, and the like. The girls in turn are given the same number of lessons in the use of the simpler tools. The work done even thus far would do credit to boys of any grade. What about these pupils when they go to high school? We expect that they will not only be as well prepared, but even better than under the old methods, and if they are not, our whole scheme fails. We are confident however that it will not fail.

In none of our shop work are we doing what is usually seen, the making of set pieces. On the other hand, everything made or done has intrinsic value. To illustrate, this fall—1911—the eighth grade made two dozen book-binding presses for the pupils in the bindery of one of the high schools. The seventh grades made one hundred looms for the salesmanship class of the Continuation School. The sixth grades made thirty botany presses for high-school students. One fifth grade made sixteen window boxes, 42″×10″×8″ for a neighboring school; the other fifth grade made fifty desk book-racks for teachers. The subnormal of the fourth grade, and the subnormals of the third and second grades each made sixty of the book-racks, and to their credit be it said, the work was as good as the best. Besides this more or less formal work, the boys are given opportunity to work on pieces of their own designing, after the plans and specifications have been approved by the master. Also repairing of all sorts is going on all the time, either on things belonging to the school, or on broken furniture or what not brought from the homes. This constitutes another means of uniting more closely the school and the home.

In the conduct of the various classes among the boys, the foreman plan is used, that is, each class is divided into two groups, each under the direction of a foreman selected from their number. It is the business of the foreman to supervise the work as is done in a real shop. This foreman makes his reports to the master, and submits to him all differences that may arise. This method makes possible a much larger range of work, creates a stimulating rivalry, and gives to the boys much that is like the real activities of shop life. To say it holds their attention is putting it mildly.

Above all is the moral effect of all this work, which is most pronounced. I have spoken concerning the Juvenile Court and the Truant Department. The present need for these is about nil. The question of discipline, formerly a difficult one, especially among the subnormals, has nearly eliminated itself. The general school spirit, both among pupils and parents, has become most satisfactory. To be brief, the whole community has become so interested in the school and its work, that the school has become unconsciously a community center around which many of its activities revolve and with it all, good teaching has played a most important part.

EDITORIAL NOTES

Report on Educational Guidance

A very interesting report has been prepared by several members of the Chicago School of Civics and Philanthropy on the subject of vocational guidance for children in the city of Chicago. Especial emphasis is laid in this report upon the vocational guidance of girls. The report is submitted to the Chicago Woman's Club, the Chicago Association of Collegiate Alumnae, and the Woman's City Club. The first paper in the report was prepared by Miss Sophonisba P. Breckinridge and Miss Edith Abbott. It is a statement of some of the experiences which have been encountered by workers in the Chicago School of Civics and Philanthropy who have helped boys and girls to improve their working conditions. The second paper contains a report by Miss Anna S. Davis on the opportunities of employment in Chicago open to girls under sixteen years of age. Three other sections of the report give a brief account of the public care of working children in England and Germany, a list of the technical and trade classes for girls in the city of Chicago, and a bibliography on employment supervision. The report as a whole would be a most excellent document for distribution in women's clubs and other organizations that need to be encouraged to interest themselves in the training of girls. The first two papers are of such interest to teachers that they deserve special comment.

On Occupations for Girls

A statement such as that which Miss Davis has given of the opportunities in the city of Chicago for girls under sixteen would make very suitable material for classroom work in elementary schools throughout the country. Much of the material that Miss Davis has collected could be brought together by older students in any community where the teachers were interested in sending out these pupils to collect information with regard to the trades and industries in the town in which the school is situated. For example, Miss Davis visited eighteen millinery shops, and gives an account of the number of persons who are employed in these shops, the conditions under which they work, their wages and hours, and the seasons during which employment is most abundant. She also indicates the advantages and disadvantages of this particular type of work. The same is done for a score of other kinds of employment. Girls would undoubtedly be interested in writing the results of their investigations with regard to different trades, and the material could thus be used for composition work. They could also discuss with those who have found employment in these various different trades the experiences which they have. At all events, the study in the schools of the opportunities for employment would open to the minds of all of the pupils the large economic and industrial questions which are now too often neglected in elementary-school education. If it does not seem desirable to have the pupils in the grades seek this information themselves, Miss Davis' report would furnish an admirable text to be put into the hands of older pupils. The teacher could undoubtedly supplement this text out of her own investigations of local conditions.

Improvement in Character of Employment

The time is past when any argument needs to be presented in favor of vocational guidance for elementary-school children. The earlier conception of the school, that it was a selective agency which must weed out the mentally deficient, has undergone a rapid change in current thinking and in current practice. We are now seeking in all of the schools to find those forms of training which shall improve every child, and shall make it possible to direct him judiciously to the kind of work which is suited to his capacities and tastes. The community is coming to recognize that the child does not have a sufficiently large view of economic conditions and of his own capacity to make it possible for him to select employment with any intelligence. All who come in contact with working children realize that these children are caught very frequently in a trade which has no future and which does not engage their full ability. The child does not know how to get out of this employment advantageously, and he does not know how to look far enough into the future to see the necessity of learning how to perform a better type of work. The first paper in this report gives some admirable illustrations of what can be done in helping children to find a better and more promising type of work. Thus, one example is given of an Italian boy, fourteen years of age, who was working in a department store as a cash boy for $2.50 a week, and earning an extra $2.00 by working on a milk wagon from 3:00 to 6:00 in the morning. Through the efforts of those who were able to give him vocational guidance, he was placed with an engraving company where the prospects of learning a trade were good, and where his weekly wage from the start was $4.50, that is, quite as much as he was getting from the two unprogressive types of work which he had been pursuing up to that time. Any teacher who reads such an example as this must recognize immediately the importance of drawing attention to a few simple principles of economic life which every child would be able to grasp early in his thinking about society and its organization. Children ought to understand the difference between different types of employment. They ought to realize that some are progressive and others not. They ought to realize that there is an advantage in getting into one of the lines of work which will lead forward, and that this remoter advantage can very properly be balanced against a higher wage at the start in one of the other occupations. At the same time, they ought to be made aware of the meaning and significance of skill as an economic asset. If the work in arithmetic and geography commonly offered in our upper grades is advantageous, then certainly some study, such as this pamphlet represents, of the opportunities for occupation, is equally educative, and immensely more practical in its character.

THE DE KALB MEETING

The annual meeting of the Superintendents and Principals' Association of Northern Illinois will be held at De Kalb, May 3 and 4, 1912.

During the current year the Committee of Seven of this Association has been making a study of practical conditions. The report for the year will consist of three parts: (1) A study of local geography, as worked out by pupils of the third year at the Francis Parker School, Chicago; (2) A study in corn, as worked out in the fourth or fifth grade of the De Kalb schools; (3) A study in elementary science, as carried on in the School of Education, the University of Chicago.

At the De Kalb meeting the discussion of the first paper will be led by Mrs. Pearl Backus Carley, of the Francis Parker School, the second paper by Dr. McMurry of De Kalb, and the third by Dr. Caldwell, of the University of Chicago.

That portion of the report prepared by Dr. McMurry appeared in the March number of this journal. The remainder of the report appears in this issue.

Both the Francis Parker School and the School of Education, propose to exhibit at De Kalb various sorts of projects worked out by the pupils in studying their subjects in the respective schools. The De Kalb school, under the direction of Dr. McMurry, will make a general exhibit of school work. It is believed that these exhibits will add greatly to the interest and value of the meeting. The purpose of the committee is to present to the members of the association some work, as it is actually being carried on, that is in harmony with the general principles for which the committee stands. It is hoped that superintendents, principals, and many teachers will avail themselves of this opportunity to hear a practical discussion of school work and to see something of how the above schools are attempting to realize educational principles in practice.

D. A. Tear

BOOK REVIEWS

Principles of Education Applied to Practice. By W. FRANKLIN JONES, PH.D., Head of the Department of Theory and Practice in the Maryland State Normal School, Baltimore, Maryland. New York: Macmillan, 1911. Pp. xi+293. $1.10.

The author states that he has a threefold aim: namely, "(1) to state the aim of education in a form at once suggestive and tangible to teachers; (2) to work out that aim in terms of actual schoolroom experiences; and (3) to give definite yet simple statements of a group of principles of education and to reveal them as they are to be found in concrete in the schoolroom."

In the aim of education the author recognizes a twofold function, i.e., to make the pupil *willing* and to make him *able* "to realize the ideal values of life." The values of life are defined as the ends that are good for everyone. Subject-matter is divided into experience resulting from contact with things, and experience resulting from contact with persons. Thus the curriculum is divided into (1) nature-studies (nature-study, geography, and the biological studies), (2) social studies (history and literature). A third group, the formal studies (language, grammar, reading, writing, arithmetic, and spelling), is recognized, but only as tools for acquiring and handling experiences and not as ends in themselves. Each of the studies is treated separately and its specific aim defined relative to the general aim of education.

Thus two of the author's purposes are disposed of in the first 75 pages. In the beginning it is pointed out that previous attempts to fix the aim of education have been criticized on the grounds that the definitions are not practical. Although Dr. Jones attempts to meet this criticism, he leaves much to be desired. The functions of the various studies are expressed in terms which convey little meaning to the average teacher. Besides, in the classroom, the teacher is not teaching geography, history, arithmetic, etc., but topics, or even small parts of topics, from the subjects. So that to define the aims of various subjects is only to take the first step toward working out the aim of education in terms of actual teaching experience. The remainder of the book is devoted to the topics of Motivation, Utilization of the Play Impulses, the Teacher as Influence, and Methods.

The immediate basis of interest (motive) is use, the ultimate basis is instinct. A list of 32 human instincts and 21 human reflexes is given. Each of the instincts is discussed, some of them with direct reference to their value in school work. Play is an appropiate and approved tool in teaching (especially in primary grades) so long as it remains an attractive end to the child. The teacher who commands the respect and confidence of her pupils is a very potent factor in their education. In the treatment of method, a distinction is made between methods of dealing with apperception, memory, imagination, reason, and the will, and the form of instruction. The entire chapter lacks concreteness for the average teacher.

The book was evidently written with the elementary school primarily in mind. For this purpose it lacks refinement of treatment. This is especially true of the aims set forth. The relativity of aim to the age and stage of development of the pupil is not considered. Besides, the book contains considerable material which does not pertain directly to the author's aim. Nevertheless Dr. Jones's point of view is commendable, and the book, especially the first chapters, are well worth reading.

WALTER S. MONROE

CURRENT EDUCATIONAL LITERATURE IN THE PERIODICALS[1]

IRENE WARREN
Librarian, School of Education, The University of Chicago

Abandoning night schools. Lit. D., 44:425–26. (2 Mr. '12.)

(The) American School Hygiene Association. Science 35:212–13. (9 Fe. '12.)

ANDERSON, LEWIS F. Industrial education during the Middle Ages. I. Educa. 32:354–59. (Fe. '12.)

———. Some facts regarding vocational training among the ancient Greeks and Romans. School R. 20:191–201. (Mr. '12.)

ANDRESS, J. MACE. The last vestige of Puritanism in the public schools of Massachusetts. School R. 20:161–69. (Mr. '12.)

ANGELL, JAMES R. The combination of certificate and examination systems. School R. 20:145–60. (Mr. '12.)

ASHLEY, M. L. The acquisition of skill. Educa. Bi-mo. 6:225–35. (Fe. '12.)

AYRES, LEONARD P. The relation between entering age and subsequent progress among school children. Educa. 32:325–33. (Fe. '12.)

BAIN, H. FOSTER. The imperial universities of Japan. Pop. Sci. Mo. 80: 246–56. (Mr. '12.)

BARTLETT, A. E. The psychological value of the classics. School R. 20:186–90. (Mr. '12.)

BENNETT, CHARLES A. Vocational training—to what extent justifiable in public schools? Voca. Educa. 1:258–62. (Mr. '12.)

BICKNELL, PERCY F. Mirthful moods of a librarian. Dial 52:83–84. (1 Fe. '12.)

BOBBITT, JOHN FRANKLIN. The elimination of waste in education. El. School T. 12:259–71. (Fe. '12.)

(A) boy's school in Utopia by a Utopian. Atlan. 109:404–11. (Mr. '12.)

BRUÈRE, MARTHA B. The cost of children. Outl. 100:320–24. (10 Fe. '12.)

[1] Abbreviations.—Atlan., Atlantic Monthly; Cent., Century; Educa., Education; Educa. Bimo., Educational Bi-monthly; Educa. R., Educational Review; El. School T., Elementary School Teacher; Harp. W., Harper's Weekly; J. of Educa. (Bost.), Journal of Education (Boston); J. of Educa. Psychol., Journal of Educational Psychology; Lit. D., Literary Digest; Outl., Outlook; Pop. Sci. Mo., Popular Science Monthly; Psychol. Clinic, Psychological Clinic; Relig. Educa., Religious Education; R. of Rs., Review of Reviews; School R., School Review; Sci. Am., Scientific American; Sci. Am. Sup., Scientific American Supplement; Voca. Educa., Vocational Education.

CAMERON, NORMAN. A new method for determining rate of progress in a small school system. Psychol. Clinic 5:279–92. (Fe. '12.)

(The) cinematograph as an educator. Lit. D. 44:264. (10 Fe. '12.)

COOK, W. A. A brief survey of the development of compulsory education in the United States. El. School T. 12:331–35. (Mr. '12.)

COOKE, FLORA J. Minimum grade requirements in English and mathematics in the Francis W. Parker school. El. School T. 12:245–52. (Fe. '12.)

COOLEY, EDWIN G. The Scottish system of continuation schools. Voca. Educa. 1:225–42. (Mr. '12.)

COOPER, CLAYTON SEDGWICK. The American undergraduate. Cent. 83:720–30. (Mr. '12.)

(A) correspondence school for religious school teachers. Relig. Educa. 6:534–36. (Fe. '12.)

Critics of religious garb in Indian schools. Lit. D. 44:428. (2 Mr. '12.)

DAVIS, JESSE B. Vocational guidance. Educa. Bi-mo. 6:206–17. (Fe. '12.)

DRAPER, ANDREW S. Weaknesses in American universities. Educa. R. 43:217–35. (Mr. '12.)

Federal care of children. Lit. D. 44:363–64. (24 Fe. '12.)

FISCHER, EMIL. Recent achievements and problems of chemistry. Educa. R. 43:250–66. (Mr. '12.)

FITZPATRICK, FRANK A. The bookman in his relation to the textbook problem. Educa. R. 43:282–91. (Mr. '12.)

FREEMAN, FRANK N. Grouped objects as basis for number idea. El. School T. 12:306–14. (Mr. '12.)

HANDSCHIN, CHARLES HART. A historical sketch of the Gouin series-system of teaching modern languages and of its use in the United States. School R. 20:170–75. (Mr. '12.)

HAWKES, H. E. Educational values in mathematical teaching. Educa. R. 43:267–73. (Mr. '12.)

HIMELICK, R. W. Supplementary report on the study of retardation in the schools of Indianapolis. El. School T. 12:314–30. (Mr. '12.)

Instinct and education. Lit. D. 44:369. (24 Fe. '12.)

JOHNSON, FRANKLIN WINSLOW. Moral education through school activities. Relig. Educa. 6:493–502. (Fe. '12.)

JUDD, CHARLES H. Studies in the principles of education. El. School T. 12 : 278–86. (Fe. '12.)

KAEMPFFERT, WALDEMAR B. Welfare work in Germany IV. Sci. Am. 106: 193–94. (2 Mr. '12.)

KELSEY, FRANCIS W. The seventeenth Michigan classical conference. School R. 20:176–85. (Mr. '12.)

KENNEDY, JOSEPH. The dam is out! Educa. R. 43:274–81. (Mr. '12.)

LEAVITT, FRANK M. The independent industrial schools of Newton, Massachusetts. Voca. Educa. 1:243–57. (Mr. '12.)

LINDSTROM, E. GEORGE. Trade instruction versus industrial education from the point of view of a practical trade unionist. Voca. Educa. 1:273–78. (Mr. '12.)

LOGIE, ALFRED E. Something worth while but not in the curriculum. Educa. Bi-mo. 6:203–5. (Fe. '12.)

LOPEZ, JOHN S. The school and the show-case. Harp. W. 56:13. (24 Fe. '12.)

LORD, J. COURTENAY. Children's courts. Child 2:392–95. (Fe. '12.)

LURTON, FREEMAN E. A three-year retardation record. El. School T. 12: 336–37. (Mr. '12.)

MCKEEVER, WILLIAM A. Relation of the schools to vocational training. Normal Instructor 21:11. (Mr. '12.)

MCMANIS, JOHN T. Indirect ethical instruction in high school. Educa. Bi-mo. 6:196–202. (Fe. '12.)

MCMURTRIE, DOUGLAS C. The care of crippled children in America. Child 2:378–85. (Fe. '12.)

MACNAUGHTON-JONES, H. Love in the evolution of the child. Child 2:371–77. (Fe. '12.)

MARQUARDT, W. W. Philippine school of arts and trades. Voca. Educa. 1:263–72. (Mr. '12.)

MARRIS, ISABEL D. The making of a hooligan. Child 2:386–91. (Fe. '12.)

MARTIN, GEORGE H. School activities for moral development. Relig. Educa. 6:503–10. (Fe. '12.)

MEYER, FRANK B. Religion and morality in Latin of the high school. Relig. Educa. 6:520–26. (Fe. '12.)

MONROE, HARRIET. The training of Chinese children. Cent. 83:643–52. (Mr. '12.)

MOORE, J. HOWARD. Ethical education. Educa. Bi-mo. 6:189–95. (Fe. '12.)

MOWRY, DUANE. Vocational or cultural education—which? The Amherst idea. Educa. 32:373–76. (Fe. '12.)

Museum extension work in Chicago. Science 35:261–62. (15 Fe. '12.)

(The) newspaper as childhood's enemy. Survey 27:1794–96. (24 Fe. '12.)

PALMER, FRANK HERBERT. Grading an ungraded Sunday school. Educa. 32:334–42. (Fe. '12.)

PROSSER, CHARLES A. The training of the factory worker through industrial education, I. J. of Educa. (Bost.) 75:227–28. (29 Fe. '12.)

RIORDAN, RAYMOND. School activities for moral development. Relig. Educa. 6:511–19. (Fe. '12.)

RITCHIE, JOHN, JR. Shall I give my boy a technical education? Sci. Am. 106:202–3. (2 Mr. '12.)

ROOSEVELT, THEODORE. The court of the children. Outl. 100:490–91. (2 Mr. '12.)

SARGENT, D. A. Coeducational gymnastics in elementary and high school. Educa. Bi-mo. 6:218–24. (Fe. '12.)

SCHULZE, ERNEST. The winning of the Nobel prizes as criterion of the contributions of nations to human progress. Sci. Am. Sup. 73:111. (17 Fe. '12.)

SEASHORE, CARL E. The measure of a singer. Science 35:201–12. (9 Fe. '12.)

SHOLTY, MYRTLE. A study of the reading vocabulary of children. El. School T. 12:272–77. (Fe. '12.)

SIMON, ABRAM. The Jewish child and the American public school. Relig. Educa. 6:527–33. (Fe. '12.)

STEVENS, ELLEN YALE. Montessori and Froebel—a comparison. El. School T. 12:253–58. (Fe. '12.)

STUART, DUANE REED. Latin in the college course. Educa. R. 43:236–49. (Mr. '12.)

STURGES, ANNIS M. Some present methods of dealing with deficient children in a public school. Educa. 32:366–72. (Fe. '12.)

TERMAN, LEWIS M. Professional training for child hygiene. Pop. Sci. Mo. 80:289–97. (Mr. '12.)

———. School clinics for free medical and dental treatment. Psychol. Clinic 5:271–78. (Fe. '12.)

TERMAN, LEWIS M., and CHILDS, H. G. A tentative revision and extension of the Binet-Simon measuring scale of intelligence. J. of Educa. Psychol. 3:61–74. (Fe. '12.)

THURSTON, HENRY F. New methods being tried at Gary, Ind., and many watching the results. Cook County School News 8:1–4. (Fe. '12.)

(A) "welfare" institution on a novel plan. R. of Rs. 45:325–28. (Mr. '12.)

WHITEING, RICHARD. The technical education of kings. Youth's Companion. 86:83. (15 Fe. '12.)

WILD, LAURA H. Training for social efficiency: the relation of efficiency to life. Educa. 32:343–53. (Fe. '12.)

WILM, EMIL C. The moral and religious influence of colleges. Educa. R. 43:292–309. (Mr. '12.)

WINCH, W. H. Mental fatigue in day-school children as measured by immediate memory. II. J. of Educa. Psychol. 3:75–82. (Fe. '12.)

VOLUME XII NUMBER 9

THE ELEMENTARY SCHOOL TEACHER

MAY, 1912

COLONEL FRANCIS W. PARKER

AS INTERPRETED THROUGH THE WORK OF THE FRANCIS W. PARKER SCHOOL[1]

FLORA J. COOKE
Principal of the Francis W. Parker School

Many times in the past nine years I have been asked to speak of Colonel Parker to the parents, and now that you have come here expecting to hear about him, I fear that many of you will go home disappointed—not knowing the things about him that you hoped most to find out. My one comfort is that I believe I should have the approval of Colonel Parker himself in the plan I am going to follow, that of trying to interpret him to you through the work of this school—or, rather, through those parts of the work inspired by him, concerning which there seems to be the most question.

We are moving forward, albeit very slowly, along the path which he blazed with such difficulty. Before us shines the same goal. We shall not reach it—your children will not reach it—nor your children's children. We shall be content if we can clear the path a little for those that follow.

In so far as our work is being well done, we believe that your children can teach you, better than any word of ours can do, what Colonel Parker stood for in education. In this school we are not following his methods or devices—at best these are only suggestive to us—but we are applying, as best we can, the principles which governed his educational work.

[1] Paper read before the Parents' Associations of the Francis W. Parker School and of the School of Education of the University of Chicago.

As nearly as I can interpret it, his working hypotheses were:

The needs of society determine the work of the school.

The supreme need of society is good citizenship.

Ideal citizenship demands of the individual the highest degree of knowledge, power, and skill.

The one purpose of the school is to present conditions for growth into ideal citizenship.

Expressed in the simplest language, the educational principles which Colonel Parker used, and which I have selected as those most needing discussion tonight, are the following:

Self-activity is the law of growth.

The strong, vivid, growing *image* is the most potent factor in the learning process.

The *apperceptive process* is the natural process of widening experience.

Interest is the root law of attention and educative effort.

Habits are the sure result of oft-repeated mental or physical acts.

The *social motive*—the feeling that a certain thing is worth while to an individual, a group, or a community—has been fundamental in all human development.

Social motives generate social interests and result in intelligent social service.

Freedom must be balanced at each step by *responsibility*.

Satisfaction and *joy* in good work are positive essentials in the educative process.

These principles, which later I shall ask you to consider again, did not originate, as you know, with Colonel Parker. He saw what their application would mean in the education of children, and they became his own in a creative sense. It is our hope that they may become ours in the same way.

Before speaking of the work in the school, I wish that I might bring before you the personality of this man, in all his courage and strength—yet I, who loved him as a father, and as a close friend, and who have him before me as a living influence every day, find that I cannot separate him from his work. He was, in a sense, completely lost in it—in his love and enthusiasm for it.

His personal energy was like some impelling, vital force, which accomplished miracles. Teachers worked—yea overworked—gladly under his inspiration. They undertook seemingly impossible burdens, and carried them successfully. They shook off the shackles of years of habit, and self-consciousness, and became free.

They did not do this for Colonel Parker, but because of the feeling of responsibility which he awakened in them. I could give many illustrations of the vigorous means which he used in arousing his associates to action—perhaps you will forgive me for two or three from my personal store:

For instance, I remember when, over twenty years ago, I first began to teach with him in the Normal School. I was young and ignorant, and overawed by the faculty. I went to him and told him that I must resign if I had to speak in the weekly faculty meetings. He said:

"I suppose *you think* that feeling arises from humility and modesty. But it doesn't. It comes from selfish pride—you are not willing to make mistakes."

"But," I said, "surely I cannot say anything that it will be of use for them to hear. Let me wait until I know more."

"No," he said, "probably what you say will not be worth much—but 'out of the mouths of babes and sucklings'—it is only through *expression* that growth comes. Make what you have to say worth while. If you are not willing to do this now and always—*to grow*—you may as well resign now."

At another time, I remember, he came into the schoolroom, and after looking at a piece of work which I considered particularly satisfactory, he said:

"How can you allow children to do that? I wish you would explain it to me."

I went to him, somewhat indignant at the question, and told him what I thought it would mean to children.

He smiled and said, "You have a good partial reason, but there is more to it," and he went on to explain clearly to me the benefits of that type of work.

"Then," I said, "why did you speak about it as you did? Your question made me think that the work must be wrong in your eyes."

"Because," he said, "I want you to learn to be sure enough that what you are doing is right, so that no *mere question*, however stern, can shake your conviction."

In dealing with children, his sense of humor and his habit of emphasizing the positive principle always won their respect and co-operation.

For instance, if the boys on the playground had been rude, or the girls inconsiderate, he might call them together, stand before them for a minute with a shrewd twinkle in his eye, and say: "*Ladies* and *Gentlemen:* Am I *right?*"—and then he would say a few positive words about what true courtesy means in life—and I never saw his counsel fail in its influence upon them.

He had the great gift of making teachers see the glory and the responsibility of teaching children.

To this I can bear abundant evidence. For many years, at Colonel Parker's request, I did each year at least a month's institute work in different parts of the country—in northern Michigan, in the southern states, in California and Rhode Island—and everywhere I was welcomed enthusiastically because I came from Colonel Parker's school—everywhere I found teachers working under heavy handicaps, trying to carry out the ideals which his inspiration had given them. He had the vision of the seer, and the rare power which enabled him to lift the veil for others. The rest followed by natural law, for as Emerson says:

> The lethe of Nature
> Can't trance him again
> Whose soul sees the perfect
> Which his eyes seek in vain.

No one grew conceited or self-righteous under Colonel Parker's searching eye. His keen wit and biting sarcasm were weapons always ready for use. But it was his abiding love for children, personal, genuine, tender, sane, which made us love him. He searched with an eye single in purpose for what was best in them, accepting nothing less than that, making no compromise with expediency, and his intuition concerning them seemed almost divine, so quickly could he scent an influence or tendency harmful to them.

No one yet has written the life of Colonel Parker. We do not know who will do it—but it is written in educational achievement all over the land. It would not trouble him that this work does not bear his name. All the literature that we have pertaining to his life we will gladly share with you, but there is little of it. All that we have in pamphlet form is Mr. Louis J. Mercier's[1] paper given at one of the parents' meetings; a most satisfactory sketch of Colonel Parker's early life, of his boyhood, of his struggles, of the unswerving purpose which governed his life to the end, and it shows us something of his general educational theory.

Mr. Willard S. Bass[2] has outlined, in pamphlet form, a brief story of his life as a soldier. In the Memorial Number of the *Elementary School Teacher*, published soon after his death, we have the points of view of many educational experts—of Dr. G. Stanley Hall, of Dr. John Dewey, of Nicholas Murray Butler, of the great Jewish rabbi, Dr. Hirsch, and the equally well-known Catholic prelate, Bishop Spalding. They speak of him both as a man and as an educator, and they can give you, much better than I do, an idea of his importance in the educational movement in America.

I wish, also, to refer you to an article by Mrs. Emmons Blaine, given in the form of an address at the dedication of the Chicago Normal School. To me, this is the most satisfactory word ever written about Colonel Parker. I wish that she might be prevailed upon to give it to you as a part of this series of discussions upon Colonel Parker's life and work.

And now, after these few words, in which I realize I have failed utterly to add anything of value to your conception of Colonel Parker, I will ask you to consider more in detail some of the things in the theory and practice of this school which have come to it through Colonel Parker's inspiration.

Let us consider the first principle—*self-activity* as the law of growth.

In a school where self-activity is a dominant factor, where it is realized that the active side of education precedes the passive in child-development, much of the routine work, much that is traditional and conventional in school practice, must be excluded. In such a school, children will ask many questions—the work will stimulate them to question.

[1] Mr. Louis J. Mercier, Harvard University; formerly head of French Department, Francis W. Parker School.

[2] Mr. Willard S. Bass, teacher in Chicago Institute under Colonel Parker, and for several years head of Science Department, Francis W. Parker School.

Yet in hundreds of schools, even in this city, a question from a child concerning his work is a quite unheard of thing. It is a matter of course that the teacher will ask the questions. The child is aggrieved if he cannot find the answers ready-made in his book.

A few years ago, in a great school in New York, I watched thousands of children take out their books, open them, and begin to study at the count of "one, two, three." They lifted their slates, poured on the water, erased their work, again to count; they marched to place, stood in line, took position, read, spelled, or repeated the multiplication table, and returned to seats. All worked as smoothly as a high-power machine, and it was the proud boast of the supervisor that she could go into any schoolroom of a given grade at a given hour and find the children working upon exactly the same lesson, using the same methods. This statement is not exaggerated. But this is an exaggerated form of an evil that can be found in many schools today. What outcome could be expected from such routine work for *six hours daily* for *years?*

If *self-activity* is the aim, children may not be herded together for long hours under unnatural conditions. They may not be repressed by authority into continued parroting of answers learned from books. Little children, whose law of growth is action, may not sit with folded hands, always under the eye of a guard.

They must be gotten into contact with Nature and with life materials. They must question and experiment, using all their sense organs freely. They must play and work under good incentives, and grow into habits of initiative and independent thinking. They must reason and measure, judge and select for themselves, means to definite ends. In other words, they must choose, make mistakes, and grow. Results in children's work must be considered *good* only in so far as they represent genuine growth and achievement.

We believe it has been proved that routine methods do not produce the efficient—the socially efficient—human being.

When children had real experience and activity in the home, on the farm, and in the household, it was legitimate to restrict the school activities to drill, but it is not so today, and in the immediate past the docile children, who have submitted to machine methods, whose names have shone on the school "Roll of Honor," have not taken the same high places in the world's list of useful human beings.

Is it not true that the restless ones, the ones who have refused to meet such school conventions placidly, the ones who have broken away from school restrictions, who had initiative and interest outside the school, are the leaders in the world's work today? And I believe that unless there is a change, more and more of our youth will leave school at the eighth grade.

Poor, indeed, are the opportunities which America offers to these boys and girls of fourteen, even to those of eighteen, who do not care to go to college. But that chapter of education does not belong to this discussion.

All of this means, not only radical changes in current school practice, but also in our ideals, as parents, of what activities should go on in our schools.

Children, perhaps, cannot cover ground in reading, writing, and number as rapidly in a school where self-activity is emphasized as in one where all the hours of the day are devoted to one small area of the brain—known as the language center—but we believe there is economy, in the long run, for reading, writing, and number have a vital purpose in their lives from the first day in school onward.

We believe it is necessary to recognize and use all that is good in the old system of education. A child must learn to spell according to the social demand; to memorize pivotal dates; to know where important places and routes of travel are upon the earth; to manipulate figures correctly. These facts and tools deserve and receive much time and attention, but they, in themselves, are not the ends which we seek.

Under this principle, then, the problem of this school is to fill *twelve of the formative years* of the children's lives with types of work demanding *self-activity*. And with only our ideals and what we know of the child to guide us, this is no small undertaking.

Our second principle is that "The strong, vivid, growing *image* is the most potent factor in the learning process."

If mental imagery is to be strong in our children, all the avenues of sense impression and expression must be open and in continual use. This is particularly true in the lower grades, but the principle holds for the older children. It is not well understood by all the parents that we in the Francis W. Parker School hold ourselves responsible to the *child* for his use of all his natural avenues of expression.

Many times, even this year, parents have come to us, and asked to have the children excused from singing, saying that the child had no voice and never could become a singer. In this school no child is excused from singing, unless for exceptional reasons. Why? Because it is the *whole* child that we are interested in—that we are trying to educate. He may never become a singer—if he does become one it will be after years of technical work, which we do not pretend to give him.

But we expect him, in the twelve years here, to get an appreciation of good music; we intend that this key to his higher emotional life shall be turned; that this avenue of his soul shall be kept open. Feeling this responsibility, you will understand that we may not lightly excuse him from singing.

Again, music is one of the great agents of unification, as it is used in morning exercises—one of the chief factors of our community life.

Parents have asked also that children be excused from art—because it is not "practical." It is true that we cannot make artists here, but are we sure that this medium of expression as used in the school is not practical? It is a medium which teaches the child to observe and represent correctly what he sees, and surely this will be valuable to him in almost any phase of his life.

In painting a landscape as it appears at different seasons of the year, the mere holding of the image long enough to paint it allows the color and form and beauty of the landscape to act directly upon the child, and there is almost universal response from the child to such influence. A given landscape, which he has attempted to represent once or twice in each season of the year, gives him unconsciously the mental imagery which enables him to interpret and enjoy other landscapes. He recognizes differences and likenesses and searches for causes—answers to his own self-raised questions. If "*practical*" be defined in terms of "*return for output*," I should say that this form of expression is one of the most practical exercises in the school.

ILLUSTRATION

You have all seen paintings and drawings made by children from the kindergarten through the high school. In the early grades the child draws what he knows, not what he sees. You are familiar with the way a little child draws the inside and the outside of a house at the same time; of how he puts both eyes in a face in profile. He knows that both eyes are there, so he puts them in. Then comes the era of careful observation and study, which belongs to the middle grades, the period of learning to express what he sees, the gaining of skill and technique. With the amount of time we can devote to this work, he cannot get great skill, but he can get a recognition of the principles of correct seeing and representation. In the upper grades he can use his *knowledge* with much the same freedom with which he uses his *fancy* as a little child, and we have such a result of creative imagination as we see in the sketches of high-school pupils.

What the child gets in the elementary study of design, both realistic and conventional, enables him to catch a glimpse of its significance in all relations. He sees its principles applied in the best and most beautiful creations in his environment. It is hoped that his taste, thus aroused, will result practically in later life in civic responsibility, in an effort to get better and more beautiful conditions in life for himself and his associates.

With a few exceptions, however, such as are referred to above, we believe that, on the whole, the parents sympathize with the efforts which the school is making for strong mental imagery; also with its emphasis upon the fact that there is little impression without some form of expression.

This brings us directly to the discussion of the third principle —the *apperceptive process* is the natural process of widening experience.

If we attempt to emphasize in our work the use of the *apperceptive process*, we at once see that a meager experience means stunted growth, since a child can take out of work only a greater measure of what he takes into it. This principle, important as it is, has relative rather than intrinsic value, since to widen and increase uneducative experience is as useless as it is common in school practice. The basis for our emphasis of this principle is therefore that we aim to organize the school so that not only will it give each individual a rich and varied experience, but that in it he will be stimulated daily, through his own efforts, to widen, deepen, and interpret that experience. In it, we believe, he must work along the general constructive lines which have brought civilization into being; he must perform those fundamental types of activities which have made civilization what it is.

Our city homes cannot supply, if they would, a sufficient foundation of actual experience to generate in the child, fully, the sense of duty and responsibility which arises naturally from doing a piece of good work.

Many people believe that the child is living completely in his home, and rest upon the fact that that is the natural form of community life—but the school has left it few hours of the day. We believe that the school should be made a model social unit; that in it, too, the child should live happily and completely—in this larger form of community life, which should represent the social life of the day in simplified form. The school should be linked to the home on one side and to society on the other, so that the child's development shall be one line of continuous growth into citizenship.

Because of this demand for actual experience, as a basis for the widening of experience—for growth—we insist that every member of this school shall attend the school field trips and industrial excursions. During the school year these excursions offer almost the only means of getting the pupil into direct contact with Nature, of questioning it under supervision, so that he may understand the laws and forces which are active in the world.

In this Chicago environment we have typical landscapes which enable the child to interpret the world beyond his sense grasp. We have the sand dunes, the lake shore, the swamp areas, the glaciated regions, and also many industrial processes and institutions. These, together with the child's own manual activity, we believe should precede his book work in connection with them, if they are to be truly educative to him. Second-hand knowledge and memory work concerning things of which he has no *experience* or *imagery* is time wasted.

The fourth principle: *Interest* is the root law of attention and educative effort.

The school owes it to the parents to make its position upon the question of *interest* clear.

In schools where interest is discounted, where children are being "disciplined" for life, do we find interest really lacking, or is it only a different stimulus to interest that we encounter?

It seems to me that the latter is true. There is interest wherever and whenever there is effort. It may be interest in reaching the highest mark at any cost, or it may be interest in escaping punishment, but we venture to say that where we fail in the matter of interest is not in arousing it excessively, but only in directing it wisely. It is only under the stimulus of interest that the child will drudge sufficiently to get the discipline which is rightly deemed so essential.

I cannot resist saying another word upon the native interests of children. We meet much criticism constantly upon this subject. We hear that we are a "play" school; that we simply try to amuse the children—to find out what they want to do and do it. If this were true, the criticism would be just, of course. But no thinking teacher merely follows the native interests of children. She recognizes as far as possible what the native interests of children are —they are symptoms to her of a stage of development; she uses them and brings them to the higher plane of acquired interests.

As you know, among the native interests of children are interest in food, interest in play, interest in sound, in color, in movement, in rhythm, and in counting; and we could name a list which would include some of the natural interests which come later in life, such as the interest in collections, interest in nature, etc. All of these interests are founded upon certain primary needs and instincts of the race. They are the natural responses to given stimuli. These responses in themselves are not educative beyond a certain fixed limit.

A child in the first grade is just as happy pounding nails into a board as he is in using nails to make something. He loves the noise and he is active. This is satisfaction enough for him. The activity is an end in itself at this stage of his development.

But if the teacher is wise enough to use this interest in having him use his nails and his hammer in making a box or a wagon for some real purpose in the school, this interest in mere activity is lifted to an interest in construction, which is upon a higher plane.

In this change from native interests to acquired interests, the truly educative process—the disciplinary process—the control of the will—comes in naturally and rightly.

In pounding the nails there is spontaneous attention, but the child is a prey to the next stronger stimulus. There is no *imaged result* to sustain his attention. On the other hand, when he is making the necessary box, there is an end to accomplish.

This usually means a period of active attention, a time of struggle against the desire to do something else. This holding to the matter in hand by a pure effort of will is against nature, against the tendency to follow the line of least resistance. The skilful teacher knows that this period of active attention must be short at first, but the demand for it should continue systematically and steadily until the child himself sees the value of the results of sustained attention, and learns himself to control it.

It is the teacher's function to see that there is a constant evolution of old interests into new interests upon a higher plane. That is, the pupil sees that the new problem presented is worth struggling for, and attention soon becomes again spontaneous; the child is again absorbed in the idea, and drudgery is willingly undertaken for the sake of the end to be attained.

This secondary stage of spontaneous attention is more educative than the first, because it is more intelligent. The child is learning to subject his impulses and desires to the control of his will, and thus is at the beginning of his training in self-control, which you will agree, I think, is the thing most needed in society today.

The fourth principle states that *habits* are the sure result of oft-repeated mental and physical acts.

The truth of this principle is perfectly obvious, yet I believe that we might profitably discuss for a whole evening the school practice which is based upon the formation of good habits. In the light of this principle, it is clear that routine and machine methods cannot result in habits of initiative and independent thinking. It is equally true that repetition—drill—is the chief factor in habit formation.

The art of teaching lies in the functioning of good habits, and the different types of work—the so-called thought and drill work—must be balanced with reference to that end. Perhaps some ot you may think that this school is not yet quite perfect in this balancing—in the art of teaching.

Be that as it may, if we take a step further and agree that "emotion is the reflex of action," we shall get the significance of school practice in our moral life, namely, good actions repeated will produce good habits, which in turn will induce good emotions.

This seems to me to be the only sure protection which we can give to our children. If we can build up in them a body of good habits, with their corresponding emotions, we need not fear for them when they meet temptation, for *habit*, reinforced by *feeling*, inevitably determines choice of conduct.

The fifth statement of principle is that the *social motive*, the feeling that a certain thing is worth while to an individual, a group, or a community, has been fundamental in all human development.

It is in the application of this principle that the school differs fundamentally from current school practice. To have the work which the child does worth while in his own eyes, because he sees some purpose for it and some value in it, either to the group, or to the community, is a dominating principle in our school which needs full illustration. It does not mean that systematic drill shall be lacking. On the contrary, it means that the child grows to welcome drill as a means of overcoming obstacles which lie between him and his goal. It is the teacher's duty to see that growth is systematic; that there are no gaps in the child's progression from grade to grade to impede his growth.

If we want a child to use all his energy and effort, we must give him ends to work for which seem to him worth while. His goals will not be great ones, perhaps, but they must be of sufficient educational value to be intrinsic parts of the teacher's larger aim.

If a school takes away from children artificial incentives to work, it is responsible for the supply of wholesome natural stimuli to take their places. For example: the school expects *nature-study* to do a certain definite work for children during their school life, but a child cannot understand this general aim of the teacher. He has a right to small concrete ends which give him satisfaction at each step.

ILLUSTRATIONS

First Grade.—Each child in the first grade modeled a clay bowl for his mother's Christmas present. In it was planted a narcissus bulb, which was expected to bloom about Christmas time. While the work was in progress the teacher wrote the child's observations upon the blackboard and edited them for printing—thus making the so-called "First Grade Reading Leaflets," which in this instance state that the child planted several bulbs, some of which he placed in the dark and others in the light; he noticed the growth in each case and tried different conditions of soil and water. Later, he visited an expert in bulb planting, and followed his advice. Finally, after making his bowl in the hand-work periods, he found great satisfaction in this blooming plant. During this process, if he had been asked to tell what he was learning, his probable answer would have been that he was trying to get a plant to bloom by Christmas time. All his experiments were only means to an end which he wanted to reach. The teacher's satisfaction, however, lay entirely in the growth that she found in the child himself as an outcome of this work. She was conscious of all the steps and each had its definite part to perform in using and widening the child's experience.

Another example of working under a social motive is that of making a border of oak leaves upon a curtain for the dressing-room door of the first grade room. The children did little work upon the curtain itself, but much work under its stimulus. They looked at the borders of curtains at home; they went to the park and gathered nuts and berries and arranged them in border patterns; they went to all the trees with which they were becoming acquainted—the maple, oak and willow—and gathered the prettiest leaves. Again the reading leaflet record describes their work, indicating how the patterns were cut, how the colors were chosen, how the leaves were arranged, how Adrian's arrangement of the oak leaf was chosen, how the stencil was cut by sixth grade pupils from the pattern, and, finally, how the actual work of painting, with hot dye, through the stencil upon the curtain, was done. Again *their* satisfaction was found in the finished product as it hung before them daily—a piece of good community work which stimulated them to future efforts and recalled pleasant experiences.

You may ask concerning the children's power to read these leaflet records. I would answer that we may not call the child's effort in this direction "reading" at all, at this stage. He is simply gaining a vocabulary. In connection with each piece of work he functions from ten to twenty words. These are the words which he will use over and over again during the year. For instance, in our last illustration these would be such words as "oak," "maple," "leaf," and the ordinary idiomatic words. These words are placed in his dictionary for reference and use. The first grade reading book is made up of many such centers of work; the lessons are printed in the school print shop, to supplement the work in literature, in science, in industrial history, and in construction. In this way the child should gain a vocabulary of about 300 words during the year. These words he will function; that is, he will not only recognize them, but he will be able to spell and to write them. Moreover, if the work has been rightly presented, he has established a correct attitude toward reading. He believes that books contain all sorts of useful information and good stories and he wants much to learn to read them.

Second Grade.—In this grade the "Industries" chosen for a year might be harvesting and milling, cloth making and lumbering. The children would find significance in the first topic chosen from the fact that they will be harvesting their own school garden crop; in the second, on account of the wide opportunity it offers for satisfactory manual activity, and in the third for the use they can make of such knowledge in the shops. We might select here as our example of a wholesome incentive to work their experiments in cloth making. In this work the children might weave rugs for the doll house in the first grade, or iron holders for their mothers, or they might weave some other article which seemed worth while to them. For this purpose they would card, spin, wash, dye, and weave their own yarn, and while this manual work was in progress they would be told stories of Arab shepherds, and be given descriptions of deserts; they would have stories of Greek shepherds, with descriptions of Greek landscape; they would notice the difference between farm land and grazing land; they would have stories of Hebrew shepherds, and poems about shepherds; they would visit the Hull House Labor Museum, and have experiments in the making and using of dyes, and in the making and using of primitive spindles; they would examine pieces of beautifully woven cloth and have stories of tapestries used in old castles and of oriental rug weaving; they would visit the textile room in the Field Museum, and experiment in printing patterns on cloth, in sewing and cross-stitching bags and other articles; they would observe the characteristics of the hairy coverings of various animals, and give brief consideration to different typical textile materials.

In the "Second Grade Reading Leaflets" they have perhaps thirty reading lessons upon "Shepherd Life" as a background for this work. These seem to me so ideal as types of reading matter for children of this age that I wish you might read every one of them. Some of the titles are: A Shepherd's Life, A Shepherd's Village, A Lost Sheep, The Story of Giotto, A Persian Dyer, A Persian Weaver, A Rug Fair, Navajo Weavers, Navajo Designs. The following is one of these reading leaflets:

A LOST SHEEP

A shepherd stood on the mountain-side.
He was counting his sheep.
One was gone.
Across the valley was another mountain-side.
Here was another shepherd with his sheep.
The first shepherd called across to him.
He had to call very loudly and slowly, because it was far away.
He said, "I have lost a sheep. Is he with you?"
"I will see," called the other shepherd.
He counted his sheep.
There was one too many.
Now, all sheep look very much alike.
How could he tell which one was not his?
The sheep all had their heads down eating.
The shepherd gave his call.
All his sheep knew that call.
They raised their heads.

But one sheep kept on eating.
The shepherd shouted, "Yes, I have one strange sheep."
Then the other shepherd gave his call.
It floated softly across the valley.
The strange sheep heard it and lifted its head.
"He is yours," called the man who was watching.
Then the other shepherd left his dog to guard his herd.
He came across the valley and got his lost sheep.

This illustrates the point that the sentences are short, the imagery vivid, the words not at all difficult. Compare this, if you will, with the ordinary second grade reading lesson. At one time in the primary grade I made a careful classification of the words necessary to function in connection with our work in construction, literature, history and science, and I found there were something over 400 words necessary for the year. I did the same thing with the vocabularies of the Harper's *First Reader* and the Barnes's *Reader.* In each case the vocabularies were less than 500 words. And there was very little difference in these lists, what there was being found in the *nouns* and *adjectives*, and a few verbs which we needed to use on account of the activities of the children, such as "weave," "dye," etc. The point I am endeavoring to make is that the difference in the two types of work lies not in the demand for reading and spelling tools, but in the vast difference, as I see it, in the influence exerted upon the children by actual experience and expression, which we hope our type of work supplies.

Third Grade.—An example under this principle is found in the children's book containing their "History Stories of Early Chicago." This is an ideal center of work for third grade from every standpoint, and especially in its demand for the various kinds of manual activity and in the child's feeling that the work is worth while. Chicago's history is so short that the industrial cycles in it can be traced and understood by children. That is, they can compare through actual experiment or observation the primitive ways of *lighting* with those used at present; the primitive ways used by Chicago people a little over a century ago for getting their *drinking water*, with those used at present; the primitive ways of *transportation* with those now in use.

In this history book made by the third grade pupils, the teacher has for each child not less than one hundred photographs, made by herself, tracing the history of Chicago by pictures and maps from the time it was a swamp through many of these industrial cycles. Compare the work in this book with the kind of language work that children do ordinarily in the third grade; that is, notice carefully what the children have written under the picture of "Chicago as It Looked One Hundred Years Ago," and on the pages showing the various swamp birds that lived here, and on the topics concerning Indian life, or old Fort Dearborn, or the way the Chicago River used to turn, or the way it turns now, and the description of their maps. If you are determined that your children shall learn in school nothing but *reading*, *writing*, and *spelling*, which type of work do you think would produce the best results? Would not the child's interest and his feeling that this book is worth while react upon his attention and effort in such a way that even the formal results must be better? Of course, the spelling will not come by nature, and he will have to have drill upon the words which he uses in this way; he will have to be taught how to capitalize and punctuate his sentences; but I think you will not question the influence of this kind of incentive upon him.

Fourth Grade.—We find our example for this grade in the *Greek History Book*, in which the children have perhaps two dozen good pictures of Greek statuary. The pupils of the seventh grade printed the descriptions of the pictures which go with them. It has been questioned whether the study of Greek life in the fourth grade is not forcing the subject upon the child while he is too young, and whether it does not take the edge from the study of Greek history in the high school, but we venture to say that no parent whose child owns one of these books would be willing to have taken from the child's life the richness which has come to him through this work. The Art Institute is to him a place of joy. His *Poetry Book* is full of references which he understands and appreciates. Certainly there is much in the Greek life, in its strength and beauty and simplicity, which a fourth grade child can make a part of his experience. In fact, this work, as done in the fourth grade in this school, is a good example of what strong mental imagery does for the child and how the apperceptive process naturally widens experience.

I should like to give an illustration from each grade in each subject, but I have selected those in which the point is made most quickly, if not in the best way. The fifth-grade geography work would make an excellent example, but I could not do it justice within the limits of this paper, and I think I must content myself with one more center of work.

Seventh Grade.—I have chosen the seventh grade book on *Mediaeval History*, because it shows the same type of work in an advanced stage. The reasons for the choice of this work itself in seventh grade are given in the school catalogue, and we will not take time for a discussion of that point. The children found but meager data on this subject in our library. They went to other libraries for study, and the teacher brought into the school materials for reference. Each child in his English work wrote upon each topic which the class selected. Among the titles of stories were: "A Day in the Squire's Life," "A Troubadour," etc. When a paper had been made as good as the class could make it, it was printed by the class in the school print shop. Then came the binding and illuminating of the book. Each child made one book for himself and one for the library. I think the work speaks for itself, and you will appreciate the fact that any child who has made a book as beautiful as this one cannot escape the influence of such work; he must through all his life have a keener appreciation of *good work* and of what the *worker* puts into it.

If I have established my point, you have realized that the drill element comes into all of this work; but perhaps one more illustration will make this more clear. Let us take it from *mathematics*.

The children in the first four grades are constantly making articles for use, such as boxes, envelopes, books, furniture, tools. In this work they must use units of measurement in lines, area, volume, weight, and time. Drill comes in upon the *obstacles* which they find in their work. For instance, if a child is making a box and covering it with paper, he may need a margin of a half-inch. Perhaps this is the first time that he has definitely met "*one-half*" in his experience. Right there the teacher stops and drills upon *one-half:* one-half of an apple, one-half of a string, one-half of an inch, until the child understands thoroughly that one-half represents one of the two equal parts of a thing. He then applies his new knowledge—applies it in other relations, until it is fixed. *But when it has been fixed*, and a similar need arises—because the result which the teacher is looking for is not found in the box, outside the child, but in the *child himself* in his knowledge and power and habits—the teacher asks him to use *one-fourth* of an inch as the margin, a smaller amount of paper; and thus he meets a new obstacle, has drill upon it, and overcomes it. And in like manner he gains his knowledge of the different combinations and separations of numbers, and of the elementary processes. He first recognizes a need for them in something he is doing, and then, through teaching, acquires the necessary ability to solve his problem.

You may question, naturally, whether the obstacles which present themselves would be sufficient to give him the necessary foundation in mathematics. We have been facing that question, as a school, in both mathematics and English work. We have a set of "*Minimum Requirements*" which the child must meet in each grade before he passes to the next. Within the limits of these requirements the child is drilled and his knowledge made definite. He may pass beyond these limits if his needs demand it, but the teacher of each grade is *responsible* that his foundation in the fundamentals of arithmetic and English are thorough to the extent which the grade "*Requirements*" demand. Within these limits, the work is motivated by problems arising in science, industrial history, and handwork.

In the third, fourth, and fifth grades the drill is for rapidity and accuracy. Here the child realizes that with the larger numbers he must use different processes and that with the greater number of his problems he needs facility and skill in manipulating figures. These motives for drill he easily understands and appreciates. This is also, physiologically, the best time for drill. It is the period for fixing the multiplication tables and the principles of all the elementary processes and operations.

Many illustrations might be given in this subject showing that the principle underlying drill, which we have used in the lower grades, is applicable in the upper grades also. An excellent example would be the "Business Arithmetic of the Seventh Grade," or the application of mathematics to the eighth-grade civics work. But I believe we have had sufficient examples to show what we mean by natural, wholesome incentives to work, which are wholly within the comprehension of the child. I believe that you can see that in each case the child's goal is a part of the teacher's larger aim. I believe that we have established the fact that the principle of drill used in the school is that of working upon obstacles which come between the child and some end which he wishes to reach, which seems worth while to him, and which, therefore, he is willing to give all his effort to attain. In other words, the teacher and the child work in harmony, whatever the difference in size may be in the point of view or in the motive for work.

Another and different feature of the school which should be discussed under this principle—one which lies at the very center of our school social life and interests—is the *Morning Exercise*. Here, as you know, the entire school, from the kindergarten through the high school, meet together for about a half-hour each day. This year there has not been a single request from parent or child to be excused from the exercises. This may mean only that protest has seemed useless, and that all have resigned themselves to their fate, but I take a more hopeful view of it. Judging from the attitude and attention of the pupils, I believe that its value has come to be better understood.

It is no small thing for high school boys to succeed in making a "Current Events" exercise, through the use of maps and pictures, intelligible to younger children—even if they do not fully succeed in their purpose, the exercise has value. For instance, it happened the other day, in a chemistry exercise, that the boys attempted, through carefully made models, to show the proportion of the different gases that make up common air. Perhaps they did not succeed in making the little children understand all of it, but certainly their expression succeeded in clarifying this work in the minds of the pupils of the chemistry class itself.

> The teaching is to the teacher
> And comes back most to him,

and the little children got out of it the spirit and influence of this serious social effort.

For the little children, the good effect of the morning exercise is perfectly obvious. It is the greatest possible incentive to them for the best expression; the greatest possible opportunity for drill under good motives; the greatest possible means of overcoming self-consciousness and contributing one's self for the community good. It gives a natural opportunity and a normal demand for dramatic work.

Here, in short, the various needs and desires of the entire community are considered. Here the work of the entire school flowers for the benefit of all. What any high-school boy or girl would do in that little half-hour each day in the isolated study of any subject does not seem to me to compare with what is gained in the understanding of the needs, interests, and abilities of his fellows, big and little. It keeps each in sympathy with all.

The reports of our graduates as to what the morning exercises, even as to what the singing together in morning exercises, has done for them, justifies all the effort which it has cost to continue this feature of the school, which unifies all of it, and which Colonel Parker bequeathed to us as a unique educational legacy.

In like manner, were there time, we might illustrate the work which we are trying to do under each principle, but perhaps it would be more useful to turn again for a moment to the general theory which, through Colonel Parker's influence, is actuating the work of the school. On one side is the child, with his inherited instincts, impulses, and tendencies. Some of these are to be inhibited, others, like curiosity and the creative impulse, are to be wisely encouraged and developed. On the other side is the ideal toward which we are all working, the socially efficient man and woman, and each child is to be carried as far as possible toward physical, mental, and moral perfection.

Between the child and this ideal toward which he is to move, lie the rich stores of nature, of social and industrial life. This is the child's rightful inheritance. All that is best in art, literature, science, and industrial development is at the teacher's command as means to this end. And with these must go, *all the way*, the loving sympathy of the friend, the teacher who understands.

From Colonel Parker's point of view, there is in each child a divine spark, whether he be high or low, fortunate or handicapped—a tendency to struggle toward the light, a "love of the best." If this is true, and if our conditions are right, then it will not be necessary to bribe the child by rewards or force him by fear into good work. He will be guided firmly and wisely into an understanding that his birthright and function is service.

The school holds that if children are doing work that is unsatisfactory, the parents should know it, and pressure should be brought to bear upon them strongly and steadily, but it strives, above all, to make its pupils experience the joy and satisfaction which come from doing a piece of good work. If we succeed, no other rewards or prizes will be necessary.

There is one thing which I must say in closing, which I believe this school must do if it would represent Colonel Parker aright. It must be more than a good private school. In fact, it has no right to exist at all as it is at present organized if that is *all* that it is. It must be a laboratory for the public school if it is to carry out Colonel Parker's ideal and hope for it. It must do its work so well that its products will be convincing enough to stimulate the community—even the great public school system—into a demand for like conditions for all pupils. Under that motive, no effort is too great to give to the cause.

The fact that we are small and ignorant is lost in the greatness of our ideal. Perhaps our part is only that of the Roman, Marcus Curtius; if so, we are willing to throw ourselves into the gap, in order that solid ground may be made in the educational forum. Many corps of devoted teachers might well give their lives for such a result.

It is ambitious to hope that in our ten years of effort, this school has made sufficient headway to have its principles received with confidence. It is attempting the difficult task of training human beings into freedom coupled with responsibility. It endeavors to give the child an opportunity of *choice*, of knowing what is right to do. It attempts to form in him ideals of conduct based upon real experience; it seeks to train in him a spirit of democracy, of judging himself and his fellows by what each is and what each does, rather than by what each says or what each has; to lead him to see with tolerance that all are not gifted alike, that there is more than one kind of human worth, and that each is asked to contribute only *his best* to the whole, and that all are needed by each one.

As we see it, then, the immediate problem of this school is to create a school life so wholesome and joyous in spirit, so rich in opportunity for all-around activity and social service, so compelling in its demands for individual initiative, for judgment, self-control, and choice of conduct, so in harmony with the laws of human development, that every child will necessarily respond to its influence and act from good motives and from good habits of thought and action.

Finally, it is our hope that, as we become wiser, every child intrusted to us will move according to his ability to useful, efficient manhood and womanhood; that later, each child, in turn, will take his place in society, trained and ready to carry his full part of the burdens and privileges of citizenship.

To this end, Colonel Parker devoted all his life, all his great energy, and he was more fortunate than most reformers who have broken with tradition. And we, who are allowed to carry on the work which he began, are also fortunate and happy beyond measure. We have had ten years of rare opportunity for unhampered work.

The ideal which inspired him, and which inspires us, shines clearly before us. It reaches far back of Colonel Parker's personal life, and far beyond it. It finds itself personified in the love and in the life of the greatest Teacher in the world.

WARREN COLBURN ON THE TEACHING OF ARITHMETIC TOGETHER WITH AN ANALYSIS OF HIS ARITHMETIC TEXTS[1]

I. THE LIFE OF WARREN COLBURN[2]

WALTER S. MONROE
The University of Chicago

In recent times we have come to recognize Pestalozzi, the humble Swiss philosopher, as the source of certain practices which have been introduced into our elementary schools within the past century. Oral instruction, object-teaching, nature-study, and several minor practices are traceable to Pestalozzi as the first to realize them in practice. The first phase of Pestalozzianism to secure a strong hold on American schools was oral instruction. The introduction of this practice was due primarily to the work of Warren Colburn, although there is reason to believe that Colburn did not owe as much to Pestalozzi as is commonly supposed. But regardless of this question, Colburn must be regarded as a successful exponent of oral instruction and his *First Lessons in Intellectual Arithmetic* achieved almost incredible success as a text.

This alone is sufficient reason to justify a presentation of his life and work. But in addition, a new period in both the organization and the teaching of arithmetic begins with the appearance of his *First Lessons* in 1821. Thus Colburn occupies a place of first importance in the development of American arithmetic and arithmetic teaching.

Finally, his writings and his activities show him to be a man who had an unusual appreciation of the value and importance of education, and to be a man who possessed an insight into the educative process which was far ahead of his time and which we are only now coming to realize.

[1] This is the first of a series of articles on this subject. The next article will consist of Colburn's address on "The Teaching of Arithmetic."

[2] The source of most of the facts of Warren Colburn's life is an account in Barnard's *Journal of American Education*, II, 294.

Warren Colburn was born March 1, 1793, in the part of Dedham (Mass.) called Pond Plain. In 1794 or 1795 the family moved into Clapboardtrees Parish, later to High Rock, and in 1800 or 1801 to Milford. Richard Colburn, his father, was a farmer and the early life of the boy was spent on the farm. Presumably he participated in the usual activities of farm life. At the age of four, Warren attended a summer district school. At Milford, he began to attend the winter district school. From Milford the family moved, about the year 1806, to Uxbridge, where he continued to attend the winter terms of the common school.

It was at this last place that his aptitude and expertness in arithmetic began to attract attention. His father encouraged this aptitude by taking into the family Mr. Gideon Alby, an old schoolmaster who was good at figures. Mr. Alby instructed the boy in "cyphering" during the long winter evenings.

About this time Colburn seems to have developed either a distaste for the farm, or an aptitude for machinery and certain lines of manufacturing. Apparently on his account, the family left the farm about 1810 and moved to Pawtucket, R.I., so that he might have the opportunity to learn something of machinery. During the next five years he worked in factories, and it was not until the summer of 1815 that he began to prepare himself for college. Just why he developed a desire for a college education is not told us, but clearly he possessed a very keen motive for it. Such was his zeal that he prepared for college within twelve months, although apparently he had not studied languages before. For this reason he was ill prepared in all except mathematics when he entered Harvard College in 1816.

Throughout his college course he was recognized as excelling all his classmates in mathematics. It is said that he applied himself with equal faithfulness to the classics, and in spite of his poor preparation he commanded the respect of his instructors and stood well in these classes. In mathematics he mastered the calculus and read through a considerable portion of the great work of Laplace. He graduated in August, 1820.

During his collegiate course he taught during the winter months in Boston, in Leominster, and in Canton. After leaving college he began teaching in a select school in Boston. He continued in this school for about two and a half years. He then gave up school teaching and went to Waltham as superintendent of the Boston Manufacturing Company. In August, 1824, he became superintendent of the Lowell Merrimack Manufacturing Company at Lowell. He continued in this position until his death, September 13, 1833.

In the winter of 1826, Lowell was incorporated as a town, and at the first town meeting Mr. Colburn was chosen a member of the Superintending School Committee. It is said that in order to provide time for proper attention to the affairs of the new school system, the committee often held their meeting at six o'clock in the morning. Mr. Colburn served on this committee for two years and was re-elected in 1831 but was excused at his own request.

He was elected a Fellow of the American Academy of Arts and Science in 1827. Also, for a number of years he was a member of the Examining Committee for Mathematics at Harvard College.

While at Lowell he conceived a scheme for the intellectual improvement of the community by popular lectures on scientific subjects. Throughout the autumn and winter of 1825 he gave illustrated lectures upon natural history, light, the seasons, and electricity. He continued giving popular lectures for several years, varying the content somewhat from year to year. On one occasion he received and accepted an invitation to deliver a series of lectures before the Mechanics' Charitable Association in Boston.

It was while teaching in Boston that he wrote his arithmetics. The *First Lessons in Intellectual Arithmetic* came from the press in the autumn of 1821. The *Sequel to the First Lessons* was published about a year later.[1] In 1825 he published *An Introduction to*

[1] The date of publication of the *Sequel* has been erroneously given as 1824, and one writer has given it as 1826. Neither of these dates is correct for I have in my possession a copy bearing the date of 1822, the date of copyright being October 30.

I have in my possession two other copies of the *Sequel*. One bears the date of 1826 and is a third edition, but retains the copyright date of October 30, 1822. The other bears the date of 1828 and there is a slight change in the title of the book. The first copy bears the title, *Arithmetic; Being a Sequel to First Lessons in Arithmetic*. In the edition of 1828 the title is changed to *Arithmetic upon the Inductive Method of Instruction: Being a Sequel to Intellectual Arithmetic*. The copyright date of this edition is May 25, 1826. This does not appear to be a revision of the original text, except that a few minor changes are made.

Algebra upon the Inductive Method of Instruction. Although the algebra was not published until after he had ceased teaching, it was a part of his originally conceived plan which had its incipiency in his teaching experience.

Mr. Batchelder, of Cambridge, states: "I remember once, in conversing with him with respect to his arithmetic (the *First Lessons*), he remarked that the pupils who were under his tuition made his arithmetic for him: that he had only to give attention to the questions they asked, and the proper answers and explanations to be given, in order to anticipate the doubts and difficulties that would arise in the minds of other pupils; and, the removal of these doubts and difficulties in the simplest manner was the foundation of that system of instruction which his school-books were the means of introducing."

He published about the same time a series of reading books for young children. Each book of the series contained some appropriate instructions in English grammar. It is said that his method of presenting grammar gave results scarcely less admirable than in arithmetic. Before his death he had planned a revision of his *Sequel* which was intended to meet the criticisms which had been made upon it. Unfortunately he had not committed his ideas for the revision to writing and nothing has come down to us of what probably would have been a work of even more merit.

The *First Lessons* was immediately introduced into the schools. It enjoyed greater popularity than any other arithmetic ever published. In 1856 the statement was made that 50,000 copies were used annually in Great Britain and 100,000 annually in the United States. It was even translated into foreign languages. It is still published by Houghton Mifflin Company.

Says Mr. Thomas Sherwin, principal of the high school, Boston: "I regard Mr. Colburn as the great benefactor of his age, with respect to the proper development of the mathematical powers. Pestalozzi, indeed, first conceived the plan; but Mr. Colburn realized the plan, popularized it, and rendered it capable of being applied by the humblest mediocrity. Indeed, I regard the *First Lessons* as the *ne plus ultra* of primary arithmetics.

The *Sequel* is certainly a work of great ingenuity, which shows a great mastery of the principles of education, and which he himself considered a book of more merit and importance than the *First Lessons*. Of the *Sequel*, indeed, it may be said, not only that its true value has not, in general, been sufficiently estimated, but, that its actual influence on the use, the understanding, and popularity of the *First Lessons* has been appreciated only by particular observers.

Colburn received the genuine respect of all who knew him. At college he was liked and respected by all his classmates, although he was not accustomed to participate in the social activities of college life. He was older and more mature than his fellow-students and seems to have taken his college studies quite seriously. He was not brilliant in conversation nor in public speech. Soon after Colburn's death, Dr. Edward G. Davis, a classmate, wrote of him as follows:

> In the constitution of Colburn's mind, many circumstances were peculiar. His mental operations were not rapid, and it was only with great patience and long-continued thought that he achieved his objects. This peculiarity, which was joined with an uncommon power of abstraction, he possessed in common with some of the most gifted minds which the world has produced. Newton, himself, said that it was only by patient reflection that he arrived at his great results, and not by sudden or rapid flights. In Colburn this slowness and patience of investigation were leading traits. It was not his habit, perhaps not within his power, to arrive at rapid conclusions on any subject. . . . . His conclusions, reached slowly and painfully, were established on a solid basis, and the silent progress of time, that great test of truth, has served but to verify and confirm them.

The trend of his mind at the time of leaving college is reflected in his thesis, which was *On the Benefit Accruing to an Individual from a Knowledge of the Physical Sciences.* One paragraph is especially significant:

> The purpose of education is to render a man happy as an individual, and agreeable, useful, and respectable as a member of society. To do this, he ought to cultivate all the powers of his mind, and endeavor to acquire a general knowledge of every department of literature and science, and a general acquaintance with the world by habits of conversation. And this is not inconsistent with the most intense application to a favorite pursuit.

His life after leaving college is an example of the opinion he expresses here. Although engaged as a superintendent of a manufacturing company, a position of responsibility and one which required constant attention, Colburn found time to continue his educational endeavors. His algebra was completed after leaving the schoolroom. He was one of the founders of the American Institute of Instruction, and delivered a masterly address before that body on "The Teaching of Arithmetic."

Dr. Davis, referred to above, says further:

His great and most interesting project, that of improving the system of elementary instruction in mathematical science, appears to have occurred to him during the latter part of his college life, and was the subject of painful thought many years before his first work made its appearance. It required, indeed, no small energy of mind thus to break through the trammels of early education, and strike out a new path; for, Colburn, like others, had been brought up under a system the reverse of that which he now undertook to mature and introduce. . . . . In the course of a few years, the appearance of these little books seemed to have revolutionized the mode of teaching elementary mathematics in the schools of New England. Various modifications have since been introduced into his plan, for which, whether improvements or otherwise, little credit can be claimed on the score of originality; and it may with safety be asserted, that whatever in the present mode of teaching the science of numbers in our schools distinguishes it from that in use twenty years since, is attributed mainly to his publications. . . . .

His *First Lessons* was, unquestionably, the result of his own teaching. He made the book because he needed it, and because such a book was needed in the community. He had read Pestalozzi, probably, while in college. That which suited his taste, that which he deemed practicable and important, he imbibed and made his own. He has been sometimes represented as owing his fame to Pestalozzi. That in reading the account and writings of the Swiss philosopher, he derived aid and confidence in his own investigations of the general principles of education is true. But, his indebtedness to Pestalozzi is believed to have been misunderstood and overrated.

As indicated in this last statement, it is usual to speak of Colburn as one who successfully utilized Pestalozzi's ideas, but, even before I came upon this comment by Dr. Davis, my studies of the works of the two men had caused me to feel that the connection between them was much less than I had supposed. Colburn's work shows much originality, and in any case he went much farther than Pestalozzi. His books contain several important features which do not appear in Pestalozzi's writings.

When we come to give proper recognition to the pioneers in American education, much credit will be attached to Colburn's work. His arithmetic texts and his address on "The Teaching of Arithmetic" can profitably be studied by any teacher. Besides the historical interest which is attached to a significant work, his books contains excellent ideas which we are only now coming to realize. It is my purpose to present in a future article some of the most significant features of his texts.

CURRENT METHODS OF TEACHING HANDWRITING. I

FRANK N. FREEMAN
The University of Chicago

The purpose of this article is to compare critically the typical methods of teaching handwriting which are in extensive use in the United States. The information upon which the article is based was gathered by a questionnaire which was sent to all of the cities of the United States of 50,000 inhabitants or more according to the census of 1900. Seventy-six letters were sent out to which forty-four replies were received. These replies give a sufficiently typical view of the class of school systems which were investigated. This investigation does not, of course, include the rural systems of schools. It cannot, therefore, pretend to be a complete view of the methods of writing in use. The aim, however, was not so much to attain completeness as to determine what the various tendencies of the more enlightened practice are. Probably no important type of instruction is missed by this method. The relative prominence of the different methods is also probably represented with a fair degree of accuracy.

One of the questions which was included in the questionnaire was in regard to the system of writing and the style of copy-book, if any, which was used. On the basis of replies to this question letters were sent to the publishers of the copy-books which were referred to and samples were obtained. A bibliography of the systems of teaching and of the copy-books which were used in the cities from which replies were received is given at the end of the article. These may be referred to in the course of the article by the name of the system.

We may first discuss the replies which were received to the questionnaire regarding some of the more outstanding features of the methods of teaching. The following is a copy of the questionnaire:

QUESTIONNAIRE

What method is used? 1. Vertical———; Slant———. 2. Arm movement: Yes———; No———; Intermediate form——————————. 3. Is any particular system used? If so, what?——————.

Are copy-books used? If so, what kind?——————.

How much time is spent in writing per week? Grade I,———; Grade II,———; Grade III,———; Grade IV,———; Grade V,———; Grade VI, ———; Grade VII, ———; Grade VIII, ———.

In what grade is writing begun? In general?——————. With pen?———.

Is there a writing supervisor? If so, name——————————.

Remarks: ——————————————.

DISCUSSION OF THE REPLIES

The 44 replies which were received have been tabulated and the results are as follows:

Slant of writing.—In the school systems which were studied the vertical system of penmanship is very much in decline. Only 3 cities out of 44 use this system. In 41 some form of slant is used. The variations in slant which are found will be discussed in a later paragraph. The use of vertical writing, however, is clearly an exception in present-day education.

Type of movement.—The prevalence of arm movement is almost as decided as the prevalence of slant in writing. The replies from 38 of the systems which were studied definitely stated that the arm movement was used in the schools, and it is probable that in still others this form of writing is used. A few, to the number of 9, replied that some intermediate or combined form of movement was used. This may mean that finger movement is allowed in the earlier grades or that the attempt is not made entirely to exclude finger movement in the writing of the upper grades; but even in this case some arm movement is emphasized. There is, in fact, scarcely a system which does not to some extent emphasize arm movement. The main difference is in the degree or emphasis which is given to this feature of writing. This forms a sharp contrast to a state of the pedagogy of writing twenty or more years ago. The introduction of the arm movement may be traced to the influence of the business colleges which began this form of writing some time previously. There is no doubt that this is in general a great advance over the older method. The question in regard to the time and manner of its introduction will be touched upon below.

Copy-books.—Another trend in modern teaching of writing is evident in the replies to the question regarding the use of copy-books. In 18 out of 44 cities no form of copy-book is used. The majority of city systems still use the copy-book but these do not include the largest systems. For example New York, Chicago, Philadelphia, and St. Louis have abandoned this method of teaching. It is probable that the rural systems use copy-books very much more prevalently than the city systems. In order to teach writing without a copy-book more skilful supervision and training of teachers is necessary, and the easy method is to put copy-books in the hands of the children and allow them to write without very much direction. The trend in the better systems, however, is decidedly away from this practice.

This trend in the teaching of penmanship is analogous to the change which took place in the teaching of drawing in the latter part of the nineteenth century, and the basis for the change is very much the same in the one case as in the other. The arguments for and against copy-books may briefly be stated. The copy-book is regarded as of advantage in teaching writing, first, because it presents to the child what is regarded as a perfect model for him to imitate. The belief is that the more perfect the model which is set before the child the closer will be his approximation to it. There are several fallacies, however, in this position. In the first place the engraved model is the lifeless result of writing and not the process of writing itself. The child can very much better imitate the process of performing an act than the result of the act after it has been completed. Therefore, the sight of a teacher writing presents to the child in a very much clearer form the process of writing which he has to develop. The whole emphasis of present-day teaching is upon the development of the movement by which the child produces letters and not upon the result as divorced from the movement. Again the copy which is presented in the copy-book is not ordinarily a possible form of writing. It is not produced by writing in the ordinary way, and it does not, therefore, suggest the kind of writing which we wish to develop, but suggests rather the slow drawing process by which it itself was actually produced. An ideal which is impossible of attainment by the method which is to be used is a false ideal and has no advantage above a more imperfect product which was produced by the ordinary writing method. It may be said in reply to this argument that the teacher is ordinarily not capable of setting up a good enough model for the child. If this is the case, however, the teacher is not fit to teach the child properly even with the aid of a copy-book. In every form of teaching which involves skill or dexterity imitation is one of the best means of training, and it is clearly recognized that a person who cannot perform the act himself is not qualified to teach another to do it. To set up as a model the finished result is nowhere else regarded as a satisfactory method of teaching the process. It should no more be regarded as satisfactory in the teaching of handwriting. The remedy for poor writing on the part of the teacher then is not the substitution of the finished product in a copy-book, but is rather an acquisition of skill on the part of the teacher. This is no unreasonable demand of any person who possesses the average degree of manual skill.

A further argument in favor of copy-books is that they present a systematic order of development of the forms of writing and of drills. This is the argument which applies to the use of textbooks in general and is valid so far as it goes. It must be borne in mind, however, that a better method is for the teacher to be so familiar with the principles underlying the development of writing that no such system is necessary. Furthermore, this need could be met by a manual which should give the different stages of development and which could be in the possession of the teacher. It does not require a copy-book with spaces left upon which the pupil may write. A somewhat more elaborate substitute may be found in copy-slips by which the pupil may guide his practice.

A final argument which is introduced in the use of copy-books is that they furnish a means by which the child may keep a permanent record of his attainment at various stages and by which he may be encouraged to produce and keep a neat and clean page. According to this view the copy-book is not used for the main practice of the child but is used after he has gone through his practice period merely to record a sample of his writing at that particular time. In this use of the copy-book one of the fundamental objections to this method of teaching is recognized, namely, the fact that writing can best be taught, not by the labored production of a small amount of writing in the attempt to produce as accurate forms as possible from the start, but rather in abundant writing produced freely and with a gradual approximation to the standard. Under this second method a single page is not at all adequate for the amount of writing which should be done in a period. The practice must in this procedure be done upon other paper, and the copy-book is used merely to record a sample of writing. The difficulty with this use of the copy-book is that there is a tendency to write in a more labored style in the book than upon the practice paper, and the same object may be attained by keeping samples of the child's practice writing at different times.

Time devoted to writing.—The replies which were received to the question regarding the amount of time which is given to penmanship in the grades are presented in Table I. This table shows the number of school systems out of 44 which were investigated which devote various amounts of time to writing in the eight grades. Thus 14 systems devote on the average from 70 to 79 minutes a week in the first grade. The median has been calculated and is shown at the bottom of the table. It will be seen that the amount of time which is spent in the first five grades is fairly constant and that it diminishes in the three upper grades. Some systems devote no time at all in the first and even second grade and some devote no time in the seventh and eighth grades. The greatest emphasis then is placed in the early and middle grades. The amount of time which is devoted is, in general, about fifteen minutes a day, and this also is the amount which is most frequently devoted. A large number of systems spend as much time as twenty minutes a day and over, and no systems spend less than ten to twelve minutes throughout the grades. There is no indication how this time is distributed, since the replies were given in terms of number of minutes a week. If we may draw any conclusion from these facts it is that the general experience has been that at least about fifteen minutes a day is required in order to teach writing successfully.

Time of beginning.—Another feature of the practice in teaching writing upon which the replies give us data is the time at which writing is begun and the time at which the use of the pen is begun. The tabulation of this data is shown in Table II. It will be seen that it is practically the universal practice to begin writing in the first grade, but that writing with the pen is commonly deferred to the second, or still more frequently to the third grade. This practice will be referred to again in the discussion of the various methods and systems of writing.

A final point upon which the replies furnish data is the prevalence of the employment of a supervisor of penmanship. In 18 of the 42 cities from which replies on this point were received a supervisor is employed, while in 24 cities there is no supervisor.

TABLE I

FREQUENCY OF DIFFERENT AMOUNTS OF TIME PER WEEK IN THE DIFFERENT GRADES

Minutes	I	II	III	IV	V	VI	VII	VIII
0– 9	3	1	..	..	..	..	2*	6*
10– 19	..	..	..	..	..	..	1	..
20– 29	1	..	..	..	..	..	1	..
30– 39	1	..	..	..	..	1	1	3
40– 49	..	..	..	..	..	1	3	2
50– 59	1	1	..	1	3	1	2	3
60– 69	4	3	2	4	7	11	10	8
70– 79	14	18	22	18	13	12	6	8
80– 89	..	2	5	4	4	4	5	2
90– 99	3	2	..	..	5	3	2	..
100–109	11	10	8	11	8	7	6	6
110–119	..	..	..	..	..	..	..	..
120–129	1	3	3	3	1	1	..	..
130–139	..	..	..	..	..	..	..	..
140–149	..	..	..	..	..	..	..	..
150–159	1	..	..	..	..	..	..	..
Median	77	78	77	78	77	75	69	66

* Three reports left the columns for Grades VII and VIII blank. If this means that no time was spent these frequencies should be 5 and 9, respectively.

TABLE II

FREQUENCY WITH WHICH WRITING IN GENERAL AND WRITING WITH A PEN IS BEGUN IN THE DIFFERENT GRADES

Grade*	In General	With Pen
I	40	5
II	2	14
III	0	20
IV	0	1

* Where the practice is variable the lower grade is taken.

ANALYSIS OF WRITING SYSTEMS

On the basis of an analysis of the writing systems which were examined in connection with this investigation we may outline the chief methods which are in use at the present time. These methods will then be compared and critically discussed in order to determine, so far as possible, on the basis of psychological analysis, experimental investigation, or practical results, what the more progressive forms of teaching are and in what directions present methods may to advantage be still further modified.

Choice of materials.—The choice of proper materials for writing, such as paper, pens, and ink, while seemingly a trivial matter, is yet of considerable importance if the best results are to be obtained. The various authors of penmanship methods are pretty well agreed upon these points and it is only necessary briefly to summarize the consensus of opinion. The pen should, first of all, be smooth, and so constructed that the ink will flow freely and produce a line without noticeable pressure or scratching. It should not be too fine, especially for the lower grades, and should hold the ink well so that it does not easily drop off and form blots. Where pencils are used they should be large and should contain soft lead, especially for beginners.

The penholder should be about three-eighths of an inch in diameter at the bottom and may be of wood, cork, or rubber. A small penholder, or one which has a smooth surface is very much more difficult to hold firmly without gripping. Especially constructed penholders for the purpose of insuring correct penholding are of doubtful value. Correct pen-holding cannot be secured so well by such mechanical means as by some simple form of drill which insures that the pupil's hand is in a natural position. Differences in the size and proportions of the fingers and thumb make minor differences in the matter of holding the pen essential, and therefore render such mechanical contrivances artificial.

The paper for use with the pencil may be somewhat rough and should be in large sheets which may gradually be reduced in size as the child progresses. For writing with the pen, however, the paper should always be of good quality. The surface should be smooth and at the same time firm, so that the pen does not catch in it and produce a line which is not clean. Economy in practice paper is false economy, since it impairs the development of the habit. For the sake of the pupil's eyes the paper should not have too much gloss.

The question of lines to guide the writing is one in which there is some lack of agreement. The older practice which is represented by the Spencerian system was to divide the paper into spaces which should mark off the heights of the various letters. This practice has been generally given up, though it is still retained by a few of the copy-books which are widely used. It is on the decline, however, and undoubtedly is not in accord with the psychological principles underlying the writing habit. Experiment has determined that the use of restricting lines tends to increase the amount of finger movement and to reduce the freedom of the movement in general. It is better to allow considerable unevenness at first and to work for gradual improvement in the height and alignment of the letters by the development of the control of the movement. The same question arises in regard to the use of a single line to mark the bottom of the single-space letters. The common practice among more advanced teachers of primary writing is to begin with unruled paper, then to use paper with lines an inch or so apart, then a half-inch, and so on, to about three-eighths of an inch. It is a question, however, whether the same reason holds here for not using lines as it does in the case just mentioned. A base line probably does not act as a restriction to the child, but as a guide to his poorly controlled movements. It is probably well then to use a base line from the beginning, but to have the lines far enough apart so that the writing may be large and free.

Posture.—The practice in regard to the posture of the body and to the position of the hand in holding the pen is fairly uniform. The posture which is in widest use is the so-called front position. This posture was resorted to in order to overcome the evils of the side position which formerly was assumed in slant writing.[1] The adoption of vertical writing was primarily a reform in posture and only secondarily a reform in the manner of writing. It was soon discovered, however, that the front position did not necessitate the vertical form of writing, and that the considerations of ease of movement and rapidity of writing required that the paper be tilted toward the left, and that the writing have a slant about equal to the angle through which the paper was tilted. This principle is very generally recognized and the variations in slant or in the positions of the paper are not great.

Pen-holding.—The manner of holding the pen which is recommended in the various systems of teaching is also in general the same. It has been worked out empirically and is based upon the old Spencerian method. Some modifications have been made by allowing for more individuality and flexibility. In order that the hand may be free to move along the line and to move freely in the production of the letters, it is prescribed that the hand should rest only upon the third and fourth fingers. Some require the rest to be entirely upon the finger nails, and others allow the fingers to be folded under and the hand to slide upon the skin of the third and fourth fingers. The old requirement that the hand be turned so that the wrist is level is retained, with allowance for some variation. The purpose of this prescription is to prevent the hand from turning on the side and thus being in a position in which it is not easily moved over the paper. The directions for grasping the pen prescribe that it be held in the natural position between the thumb and first and second finger, in such a way that the thumb and fingers are slightly bent, but not rigid. Emphasis is laid upon the requirement that the pen be grasped lightly. The old requirement that the top of the pen point toward the ear is relaxed somewhat,

[1] For a discussion of the relation of posture to the slant of writing see "Some Issues in the Teaching of Handwriting," *Elementary School Teacher*, XII, 1–7 and 53–59, by the author.

and the usual direction is that it point somewhere between the elbow and the shoulder. The purpose of this prescription is to prevent the hand from turning too far to the side. A final direction is that the pen cross the first finger not back of the third joint, that is, that it be not allowed to fall into the hollow between the thumb and finger. The reason for this prescription probably is that when the pen is allowed to drop behind the third joint it makes a sharp angle with the paper in which position it does not slide over the paper so easily as when it is more nearly vertical. Detailed directions for posture and pen-holding may be found in any complete manual of writing. An elaborate discussion of pen-holding may be found in Vol. I, No. 1, of *The Modern Writing Master*, published by W. A. Whitehouse, Boston. A thorough discussion of posture can be found in The Palmer method.

Bibliography of Systems of Teaching and Copy-Books Used in the Cities from Which Reports Were Received and Consulted in the Preparation of This Survey

1. Barnes' *Natural Slant Penmanship;* American Book Co., New York.
2. M. E. Bennett, *Method in Teaching Writing;* Bennett Publishing Co., Pittsburgh, Pa.
3. Berry's *Writing Books;* B. D. Berry & Co., Chicago.
4. California State Series—*Writing;* Published by the State, Sacramento, Cal.
5. *Economy System of Penmanship;* Laurel Book Co., Chicago.
6. *Gilman Copy-Book;* Thompson-Brown Co., Boston.
7. Houston's *Writing Slips;* Harry Houston, New Haven, Conn.
8. *Medial Writing Books;* Shaylor & Shattuck, Ginn & Co., New York.
9. New Era Series—*Semi-Slant Writing;* Eaton & Co., Chicago.
10. *Palmer Method;* A. N. Palmer Co., Cedar Rapids, Iowa.
11. Philadelphia Public Schools—*Instructions for Teaching Penmanship;* M. G. Brumbaugh, Walther Print., Philadelphia.
12. Platt R. Spencer's Sons, *Practical Writing;* American Book Co., New York.
13. *Standard Free-Hand Writing;* Christopher Sower Co., Philadelphia.
14. Steadman's *Graded Lessons in Writing;* American Book Co., New York.
15. *Whitehouse System of Practical Writing;* Silver, Burdett & Co., New York.
16. J. C. Moody, *Writing Hour;* Chas. E. Merrill & Co., New York.

[*To be continued*]

EDITORIAL NOTES

Rural Schools

A general committee of the National Education Association, under the leadership of Superintendent Fairchild of the state of Kansas, is carrying on an educational campaign to persuade teachers and communities in general of the importance of improving the conditions in rural schools. The facts show that a very large part of the American school population is receiving its elementary training in country schools. It needs very little acquaintance with the conditions in most rural schools to convince even the superficial observer that these schools are not adequate places to prepare for the later obligations of citizenship. The buildings are usually inadequate and unequipped with the materials necessary for the conduct of successful schools. The teachers, even where they are most conscientious in their efforts to do their work, are usually untrained and inexperienced girls, utterly incompetent to give any view of the world into which the children are going to go, or of the knowledge which they ought to possess if they are to deal adequately with their future environments. The periods of schooling are short, and the distractions great. The supervision which is a check upon most of the schools in the large communities is entirely wanting, and the influences that in larger communities operate to make the older members of society aware of the shortcomings of the school are for the most part absent.

Interests of All Involved

This pessimistic picture of the conditions to be found in the great majority of American country schools is significant not merely for the small communities in which these schools are situated, but also for the country as a whole. Many of these children will apply for admission to neighboring high schools, and will be found to be inadequately trained. Most of the children will ultimately find employment in the larger communities and will constitute the working population of the cities to such an extent that their training is a matter of importance to all who come in contact with them.

From the point of view of the state school systems of education, the rural school is the most important single concern. While the city schools can be trusted to take care of themselves to a very large extent, and to equip themselves for educational work, the expenditures of state funds will always relate most largely to the needs of rural districts. In one particular especially the state will have to take up the problem and deal with it. The rural schools cannot prepare teachers; the state must in some fashion meet this demand. The establishment of normal schools has proved to be entirely ineffective in this matter. The normal schools in every state are so few in number that their graduates are absorbed by the neighboring towns, very frequently by the single town in which the normal school is situated, and there is no possibility of sending back to the country districts, where well-trained teachers are needed, the graduates of these state institutions. Various devices, such as training classes in high schools, are being tried, with some degree of success, but the state funds will have to be drawn upon more largely to solve this problem, as well as other problems of the rural school.

Need of a Campaign of Publicity

The problem is one which must appeal to students of education from another point of view. The people in the country districts are not able to raise the standard of rural schools unless they are made acquainted with the deficiencies in their present schools. While the professional teacher in the city is aware of the inadequacies of rural education, he very infrequently expresses his judgment of the inadequacy of this education in such a way as to give assistance to the communities that suffer from the unfortunate conditions known to the professional teacher. There must be a professional condemnation of the existing situation, and a professional movement in the direction of improvement of this condition, if there is to be any large development of better school work in the country districts. The fact that one part of the school system is allowed to drag behind is a sympton of the general lack of professional spirit among educators which has been a frequent subject of comment. If the business of conducting schools in the cities is something more than the mere business of holding classes and organizing educational influences of limited range, then the teachers in the cities should recognize it as their immediate obligation to improve the whole state system, and this includes, as one of its most important elements, the rural schools that surround the city. If the individual teacher recognizes his place in a general system of education, he will see that he suffers by the ineffectiveness of the rural schools, because these schools represent numerically the majority of the educational efforts in the state and in the country at large.

Duty of the National Education Association

In view of all these considerations it is gratifying to note that a Committee of the National Education Association has taken up a serious campaign for the improvement of rural schools. The association could well afford to contribute liberally to the support of the committee. If two thousand to five thousand dollars a year were put at the disposal of this committee it would be an expression of professional spirit, a distinct advantage to the rural schools, and a contribution to the educational interests of the whole country.

BOOK REVIEWS

A History of the United States for Schools. By ANDREW C. McLAUGHLIN and CLAUDE H. VANTYNE. Appleton, 1911. Pp. vi+430.

The authors of this textbook of American history for the higher grammar grades announce in their preface that they are writing a history for "serious study," not for story-book reading, and that consequently only events essential to the understanding of our social, political, and economic institutions have been selected for treatment. The space saved by the sacrifice of unmeaning events is to be utilized for the "fuller explanation and interpretation of really important events." We believe that this is the most useful object that an author can propose to himself in approaching the field of American history, or any other history; for no heavier incubus weighs upon our historical teaching than the accumulated traditions, often trivial, generally inconsequent, which have been hallowed only by long repetition.

The book under discussion is an improvement in this respect over most of the textbooks in American history for the grammar grades. The material is presented in clear, simple language, and in orderly form. Still, there is something to be desired in the emphasis and spacing of the material. Colonial material is picturesque, and perhaps there is greater justification for a relatively full treatment of the Colonial period in a grammar-school book than in a high-school book. Still we feel that 75 pages on the Colonies in a book of 430 pages is a disproportionate amount. The Colonies and the Revolution together occupy one-third of the text of the book. Washington's inauguration is not reached until p. 215—just exactly half-way through the book. It should come not later than one-third of the way. The inevitable result of this disproportionate emphasis on the Colonial period is to prevent the adequate treatment of our later history. Only a few pages are devoted to the years from Reconstruction down to the present. Cleveland's first administration is dismissed with a single page (393) and the tremendous problems of his second administration, which ought to have a chapter, are disposed of in less than three pages (395–97). At the same time over twenty pages are devoted to the military operations of the Civil War. This question of distribution of emphasis is the pressing one for our textbook writers now, and we could wish that the present authors had been more bold and radical than they have been.

Perhaps there is also a little too close adhesion to a chronological sequence in the book. In the treatment of the Revolutionary War, for example, the story of the campaigns is interrupted to insert the account of the Declaration and the Confederation (pp. 161–68), and the operations in the West are sandwiched in between the Atlantic campaigns (pp. 179–82). Probably a topical treatment here would make more impression on the young student than the strictly chronological treatment. The authors have adopted the topical treatment in dealing with slavery (pp. 295–303, 319–28), and it immediately enhances the vividness of their narrative at that point. Only the Missouri Compromise (p. 263) has got isolated from the slavery pages and finds itself among irrelevant matter.

There are a few expressions which we would question. Is "the middle of the earth" a good definition for *Mediterranean*, applied to the sea, (p. 1)? Was Portugal to *keep* Brazil in 1494, seeing that Cabral's voyage did not come till 1500 (p. 28)? Was England at all "exhausted" by the War of the Roses, or were its battles for the most part only ridiculously petty conflicts between a few hundred baronial retainers (p. 36)? Are not the lists of colonies arranged respectively according to social characteristics, political constitution, and local administration, a bit confusing, coming so nearly together as they do (pp. 126, 130, 131)?

The footnotes are perhaps too numerous for a grammar-school book; still, they are illuminating and enlivening. One would not wish this matter out of the book, but probably many of them could be lifted into the text.

David S. Muzzey

Ethical Culture School
New York

Education for Citizenship. By Dr. Georg Kerschensteiner. Rand, McNally & Co., 1911. Pp. xx+133. $0.75.

In his introduction to the above work Mr. Sadler says: "This book will be a landmark in the history of education. . . . . It is a book of ideas which have been realized in practical administration."

The practical situation to which reference is made is the organization of the continuation schools in Munich where Dr. Kerschensteiner is director of the public schools. Chap. v contains a description of the Munich system of continuation schools. In these schools, Dr. Kerschensteiner emphasizes the necessity of making "trade efficiency" the first consideration, but of coupling with this a study of the history of manufacture, of the conditions of workers, of tools and materials, and other subjects which grow out of the trade, and which tend to "humanize" and broaden the workers' point of view. He criticizes the tendency which has prevailed in many continuation schools, to make the instruction too abstract and too general, i.e., not sufficiently related to the worker's special trade.

The organization of continuation schools, however, is only one phase of the problem of training for citizenship which is discussed in the book. The main thesis is an argument for the type of social education which has been represented in America in theory by John Dewey and in practice by Jane Addams. The most important period for training in citizenship according to the author, is from fourteen to twenty. The essential condition of such training is an opportunity to participate in a co-operative social situation in which the youth may develop the point of view and initiate the habits which will apply in his life as a citizen. Apart from the continuation schools, the best opportunities for such activity are found in the clubs and festivals with which we are familiar in this country in connection with the work of the social settlements and the use of school buildings as community centers.

The author treats his problem in a broad and scholarly way, but the language is relatively non-technical and very readable. In these respects it resembles Dewey's *School and Society*. While most of the illustrations are drawn from German conditions, there are many comparisons with English, French, and American conditions. Generally speaking, the book should furnish interesting and profitable study for all who are concerned in the organization of education for boys and girls who have passed beyond the influence of the ordinary schools.

S. C. Parker

How the "Fourth" Was Celebrated in 1911. By LEE F. HANMER. Dept. of Child Hygiene of the Russell Sage Foundation. Pp. 54. Price 10 cents.

This booklet is issued for the purpose of furthering the movement for a "sane Fourth." It is intended to serve as a stimulus and guide to those who desire to work a reform in the celebration of Independence Day in their communities by furnishing information concerning the accomplishments of other communities in the same direction. The booklet includes illustrated descriptions of typical sane celebrations, a list of typical state laws and city ordinances regulating the manufacture, sale, and use of explosives, and a collection of programs and suggestions. A list of other publications on the same subject by the Russell Sage Foundation is given at the end. This timely booklet should prove serviceable in the much-to-be-desired reformation of the dangerous and noisy Fourth.

F. N. F.

Mathematics in the Elementary Schools of the United States. International Commission on the Teaching of Mathematics: The American Report, Committees I and II. United States Bureau of Education, Bulletin, 1911, No. 13. Pp. 182.

The report includes: (*a*) Schematic survey of American educational institutions —their sequence and interrelation; (*b*) General survey of elementary schools:

I. The aim and organization of the elementary schools;
II. The curriculum in mathematics in the elementary schools;
III. Examinations from the point of view of the schools;
IV. Method of instruction in arithmetic;
V. Training and qualification of teachers;
VI. Typical courses of study;

(*c*) Special kinds of elementary schools.

The first five subdivisions under (*b*) above are considered again in more detail, first with respect to grades 1 to 6, and second for grades 7 and 8. The aim of the report is primarily to present present conditions and tendencies.

The standing of the members of the committees and subcommittees is sufficient guaranty of the character of the report. Every teacher and supervisor of elementary mathematics, as well as prospective teachers and supervisors, will find the report especially valuable. The following are of especial interest.

In 50 of the leading cities, 15.26 per cent of all of the school time is devoted to arithmetic. During the past fifteen years the arithmetic course has been curtailed and enriched in 38 per cent of these cities. Supervisors of mathematics are very rare. The possible attitude of the pupil toward arithmetic is being taken into account more than formerly. This is a time of transition from a method of direct instruction (telling) and drill to more rational methods. "The tendency is to reduce the amount of home study except possibly in the upper grades and in the direction of utilizing the class period either for instruction on new topics or for vigorous drill." The detailed discussion of the methods for grades 1 to 6 is by Professor Henry Suzzallo, Teachers College, Columbia University, and is taken from a more extended article which appeared in the *Teachers College Record* for March, 1911.

The following recommendations are made for the preparation of teachers of elementary mathematics:

"1. A foundation in subject matter as a basis for the professional study of mathematics should include a minimum of one-half year of high-school arithmetic, one year of algebra, and one year of geometry.

"2. Exclusive of all courses in psychology, pedagogy, principles of teaching, general method, and history of education, a minimum of one-half year of professional study of arithmetic should be required to include the following:

"A. The teaching of elementary mathematics—'Special Method.'

(*a*) The special pedagogy of arithmetic.

1. The more elementary phases of the psychology of number.
2. Principles of general method applied to teaching arithmetic.
3. Educational values of arithmetic and the place of arithmetic in the general educational scheme.

(*b*) The organization of the general elementary school curriculum in arithmetic.

(*c*) Organization of typical units of subject-matter for presentation to appropriate grades.

(*d*) Development and writing of typical plans for teaching.

(*e*) The utilization of local and general economic studies for number applications.

(*f*) Observation and discussion of typical lessons in the grades showing concrete applications of the principles developed.

(*g*) The place of games and other recreational devices in grade number work.

"B. The historical development of the teaching of arithmetic, and the place and value of certain 'methods,' such as those of Pestalozzi and Grube."

In the report on special kinds of elementary schools there are some very interesting details concerning the actual arithmetic instruction in certain corporation industrial schools.

Walter S. Monroe

BOOKS RECEIVED

AMERICAN BOOK CO., CHICAGO

High-School Geography. Physical and Economic. Parts I and II. By CHARLES R. DRYER. Cloth. Illustrated. Pp. 340. Price $1.20.

Complete Business Arithmetic. By GEORGE H. VAN TUYL. Cloth. Pp. 416. Price $1.00.

Constructive Carpentry. By CHARLES A. KING. Cloth. Illustrated. Pp. 176. Price $0.70.

Our Common Friends and Foes. By EDWIN ARTHUR TURNER. Cloth. Illustrated. Pp. 143. Price $0.30.

Essentials of Health. By JOHN C. WILLIS. Cloth. Illustrated. Pp. 302. Price $0.40.

A First Reader for Foreigners. By MARY F. SHARPE. Cloth. Illustrated. Pp. 170. Price $0.40.

Golden Treasury Third Reader. By CHARLES M. STEBBINS. Cloth. Illustrated. Pp. 256. Price $0.48.

Indian Folk Tales. By MARY F. NIXON-ROULET. Cloth. Illustrated. Pp. 192. Price $0.40.

Little Stories of England. By MAUDE BARROWS DUTTON. Cloth. Illustrated. Pp. 256. Price $0.40.

Selections from Abraham Lincoln. Edited by ANDREW S. DRAPER. Cloth. Pp. 162. Price $0.35.

Lose Blätter. By ERNA M. STOLTZE. Cloth. Pp. 127. Price $0.30.

Cicero, Six Orations. BISHOP-KING-HELM. Cloth. Pp. 109. Price $1.00.

GINN & CO., CHICAGO

The Adventures of Grillo. By ERNEST CANDÈZE. Cloth. Illustrated. Pp. 225. Price $0.45.

HOUGHTON MIFFLIN CO., BOSTON, MASS.

The Boy and His Gang. By J. ADAMS PUFFER. Cloth. Pp. 188. Price $1.00.

Kittens and Cats. A First Reader. By EULALIE OSGOOD GROVER. Cloth. Illustrated. Pp. 84. Price $0.40.

A Child's Reader in Verse. By EMMA L. ELDRIDGE. Cloth. Illustrated. Pp. 112. Price $0.25.

The Dutch Twins. By LUCY FITCH PERKINS. Cloth. Illustrated. Pp. 189. Price $0.50.

Selections from the Riverside Literature Series. For Fifth- and Sixth-Grade Reading.

"Riverside Educational Monographs." Edited by HENRY SUZZALLO:

The Teaching of Primary Arithmetic. By HENRY SUZZALLO. Cloth. Pp. 124.

The Improvement of Rural Schools. By ELLWOOD P. CUBBERLEY. Cloth. Pp. 76.

J. B. LIPPINCOTT CO., PHILADELPHIA, PA.

Lippincott's Second Reader. By HOMER P. LEWIS. Cloth. Illustrated. Pp. 171.

The American Government. By FREDERICK J. HASKIN. Cloth. Illustrated. Pp. 398.

LITTLE, BROWN & CO., BOSTON, MASS.

The Boy's Parkman. By LOUISE S. HASBROUCK. Cloth. Illustrated. Pp. 187. Price $0.60.

Home Economics. By ETTA PROCTOR FLAGG. Cloth. Price $0.75.

THE MACMILLAN CO., NEW YORK

The Century and the School. By FRANK LOUIS SOLDAN. Cloth. Pp. 206. Price $1.25.

Social Aspects of Education. By IRVING KING. Cloth. Pp. 425. Price $1.60.

Outline of a Course in the Philosophy of Education. By JOHN ANGUS MACVANNEL. Cloth. Pp. 207. Price $0.90.

Outlines of the History of Education. By WILLIAM B. ASPINWALL. Cloth. Pp. 195. Price $0.80.

Elementary Biology. By JAMES EDWARD PEABODY and ARTHUR ELLSWORTH HUNT. Cloth. Illustrated. Pp. 199. Price $0.75.

The Continents and Their People. Europe. By JAMES FRANKLIN CHAMBERLAIN. Cloth. Illustrated. Pp. 258. Price $0.55.

The American School Readers. Fifth Reader. By KATE F. OSWELL and C. B. GILBERT. Cloth. Illustrated. Pp. 490. Price $0.50.

Old Time Tales. By KATE FOREST OSWELL. Cloth. Illustrated. Pp. 245. Price $0.40.

THE CLARENDON PRESS, OXFORD

The Clarendon Geography. By F. D. HERBERTSON. Cloth. Illustrated. Pp. 379.

THE A. N. PALMER CO.

A Primer. By WILLIAM ALEXANDER SMITH. Cloth. Illustrated. Pp. 111.

CHARLES SCRIBNER'S SONS, NEW YORK

High-School Education. Edited by CHARLES HUGHES JOHNSTON. Cloth. Pp. 555.

WASHINGTON GOVERNMENT PRINTING OFFICE

Orchestral Music. Prepared under the direction of OSCAR GEORGE THEODORE SONNECK.

Statistics of Railways in the United States. Interstate Commerce Commission. Pp. 898. Cloth.

CURRENT EDUCATIONAL LITERATURE IN THE PERIODICALS[1]

IRENE WARREN
Librarian, School of Education, The University of Chicago

ANDERSON, LEWIS F. Industrial education during the Middle Ages. Educa. 32:423–29. (Mr. '12.)

ANTIN, MARY. The immigrant's portion. Atlan. 109:518–25. (Ap. '12.)

BLISS, D. C. Some results of standard tests. Psychol. Clinic 6:1–12. (Mr. '12.)

BOYCE, ARTHUR CLIFTON. Qualities of merit in secondary school teachers. J. of Educa. Psychol. 3:144–57. (Mr. '12.)

BRECK, EMMA J. A new task for the English teacher. English J. 1:65–71. (Fe. '12.)

BRICKER, G. A. Teachers' extension schools. School R. 20:266–70. (Ap. '12.)

BUTLER, NICHOLAS MURRAY. The international influence of the university. Colum. Univ. Q. 14:146–53. (Mr. '12.)

CAJORI, FLORIAN. A review of three famous attacks upon the study of mathematics as a training of the mind. Pop. Sci. Mo. 80:373–82. (Ap. '12.)

CALDWELL, OTIS W. Heat as a topic for the experimental science work of the eighth grade. El. School T. 12:370–77. (Ap. '12.)

CARLEY, PEARL BACKUS. Third-grade history work in the Francis W. Parker School. El. School T. 12:349–69. (Ap. '12.)

(The) Carnegie foundation for the advancement of teaching. Science 35:477–85. (29 Mr. '12.)

CARPENTER, RHYS. The American at Oxford. Colum. Univ. Q. 14:128–36. (Mr. '12.)

CARPENTER, WILLIAM H. The Association of American Universities. Colum. Univ. Q. 14:168–75. (Mr. '12.)

CHRISTIAN, HENRY A. General examinations in a medical school; plan of examination recently adopted at Harvard. Science 35:485–87. (29 Mr. '12.)

[1] *Abbreviations.*—Atlan., Atlantic Monthly; Colum. Univ. Q., Columbia University Quarterly; Educa., Education; El. School T., Elementary School Teacher; English J., English Journal; J. of Educa. Psychol., Journal of Educational Psychology; Lit. D., Literary Digest; Pedagog. Sem., Pedagogical Seminary; Pop. Sci. Mo., Popular Science Monthly; Psychol. Clinic, Psychological Clinic; R. of Rs., Review of Reviews; School and Home Educa., School and Home Education; School R., School Review; Sci. Am., Scientific American.

DOWNES, FREDERICK E. Seven years with unusually gifted pupils. Psychol. Clinic 6:13–17. (Mr. '12.)

EIKENBERRY, WILLIAM LEWIS. The general-science course in the University High School. School R. 20:217–27. (Ap. '12.)

FISHER, S. CAROLYN. Arithmetic and reasoning in children. Pedagog. Sem. 19:48–77. (Mr. '12.)

HICKS, VINNIE C. Organizing child-study work in a small city. El. School T. 12:378–82. (Ap. '12.)

HULST, CORNELIA STEKETEE. The organization of the course in literature in secondary schools. English J. 1:72–83. (Fe. '12.)

Industrial schools in Germany. Pedagog. Sem. 19:112–15. (Mr. '12.)

Investigations of the Carnegie institution. Science 35:437–44. (22 Mr. '12.)

KERSCHENSTEINER, G. The school of the future, a school of manual work. School and Home Educa. 31:278–86. (Mr. '12.)

LADD, GEORGE T. On the need of administrative changes in the American university. Pop. Sci. Mo. 80:313–25. (Ap. '12.)

(The) Lawrence strike children. Lit. D. 44:471–72. (9 Mr. '12.)

MATTHEWS, BRANDER. The dramatic museum. Colum. Univ. Q. 14:137–45. (Mr. '12.)

MAYER, MARY JOSEPHINE. Vocational training in our public schools. R. of Rs. 45:449–56. (Ap. '12.)

MELVILLE, A. H. An investigation of the function and use of slang. Pedagog. Sem. 19:94–100. (Mr. '12.)

MILLER, W. T. A plan for organized play in a city school. Educa. 32:409–13. (Mr. '12.)

MÜNSTERBERG, HUGO. The German woman. Atlan. 109:457–67. (Ap. '12.)

ORVIS, MARY BURCHARD. A university that goes to the people. R. of Rs. 45:457–65. (Ap. '12.)

OSBORNE, CAROLINE A. The sleep of infancy as related to physical and mental growth. Pedagog. Sem. 19:1–47. (Mr. '12.)

PRESCOTT, SAMUEL C. The teaching of microbiology in colleges of the United States and Canada. Science 35:362–66. (8 Mr. '12.)

PRITCHETT, HENRY S. Education and the nation. Atlan. 109:543–53. (Ap. '12.)

RADOSAVLJEVICH, PAUL R. Social pedagogy. Pedagog. Sem. 19:78–93. (Mr. '12.)

RITCHIE, JOHN, JR. A princely gift for technical education. Sci. Am. 106:289. (30 Mr. '12.)

RUEDIGER, WILLIAM C. Teachers' councils. Educa. 32:397–408. (Mr. '12.)

RYNEARSON, EDWARD. The conference hour in the Pittsburgh high schools. School R. 20:246–53. (Ap. '12.)

SAKAKI, YASUSABURO. Some studies on so-called "abnormally intelligent" pupils. Psychol. Clinic 6:18–25. (Mr. '12.)

SHARP, FRANK CHAPMAN, and NEUMANN, HENRY. A course in moral education for the high school. School R. 20:228–45. (Ap. '12.)

SMITH, THEODATE L. Some European institutions for the protection of motherhood and the prevention of infant mortality. Pedagog. Sem. 19:101–11. (Mr. '12.)

———. Supplement to bibliography of articles relating to the study of childhood and adolescence which have been published in the Pedagogical Seminary and the American Journal of Psychology. Pedagog. Sem. 19:116–22. (Mr. '12.)

TERMAN, LEWIS M., and CHILDS, H. G. A tentative revision and extension of the Binet-Simon measuring scale of intelligence. J. of Educa. Psychol. 3:133–43. (Mr. '12.)

THOMAS, CHARLES SWAIN. The English course in the high school: the New England view. English J. 1:84–94. (Fe. '12.)

TODD, EDWIN S. An economic basis for civics teaching. Educa. 32:436–44. (Mr. '12.)

TREVER, A. A. The status of Greek. School R. 20:254–61. (Ap. '12.)

VOORHES, O. P. The inception and development of an industrial elementary school. El. School T. 12:383–87. (Ap. '12.)

WARREN, HOWARD C. The "house of childhood": a new primary system. J. of Educa. Psychol. 3:122–32. (Mr. '12.)

WEBSTER, EDWARD HARLAN. The teaching of English composition, past and present. Educa. 32:414–22. (Mr. '12.)

WETTER, A. A. Great educators. V. Fredrich Froebel. Educa. 32:430–35. (Mr. '12.)

VOLUME XII NUMBER 10

The Elementary School Teacher

June, 1912

THE BATAVIA PLAN AFTER FOURTEEN YEARS OF TRIAL

SUPERINTENDENT JOHN KENNEDY

In response to the request of the editors of the *Elementary School Teacher* for a special report on the present status of the Batavia plan in Batavia and the observed results of its use, I beg leave to submit the following. I have been very reluctant to speak about our own work. But I feel that such a request should not be disregarded.

The plan is in full operation here, and is well started on its fourteenth year of use. It may therefore be said to have stood the test of time. Its popularity at the outset was instantaneous. The people understood it at once, and applauded it. It never had to to fight its way. It is a reform without martyrs. At present I see no abatement of its popularity, and we know of families that moved into town because of it.

Our plan has the two-teacher phase and the one-teacher phase. In rooms containing more than fifty children we have two teachers, one giving class instruction continuously to classes reciting alternately, and the other giving individual attention all the time to slow and backward children. In rooms containing less than fifty children we have but one teacher. But this teacher gives half her periods of time to the needs of individuals. This phase of the plan permits its extension and use under all conditions. It has furnished the solution for the problem of individualizing the high school. We have a general individual teacher in the high school; and in addition to that each teacher there gives half of his or her periods to individualing. This is the polity at present.

I have observed many and varied results springing from the use of this plan. Some of those results have been surprising, and all have been gratifying. I cannot hope to go into them all; but will mention some.

When a crowd are assembled it is either uplift or crush for the individual. We are confident that our plan has secured the inspiration and warded off the danger.

Where there is inequality of condition the crowd becomes a tangled mass. The attempt to move a tangled mass is overstrain. Overstrain has its inevitable goal in breakdown. Under our plan we believe there is no strain. Our teachers are becoming more vigorous from year to year.

Worry of any kind has its goal in breakdown, if not in death. And few people are aware how contagious a thing nervous debility is. Nerves are responsive to nerves. We feel that worry has been eliminated here, and that our children are calm, composed, safe, and vigorous.

Sanitation should be the first care of school management. Under our plan it seems to me that our schools have become not only sanitary but salubrious. That is, schools properly individualed become conducive to the recovery of impaired or lost health. I have come to feel that the "pale student" is a contradiction in terms. Energy is a red-blooded matter. If a student is becoming pale ask immediately what is the matter with the school?

Interested occupation is preoccupation; and all know that preoccupation in good things is the best safeguard against the approach of evil things. It is my belief that our plan tends toward absorbed preoccupation in the good work of getting an education. This is not only a negative safeguard, but it is also a positive promotive of character by supplying high aims.

I have implied already that our order and discipline have greatly improved. They have greatly improved; and it is the right kind of order; it is the order that not only permits business to proceed; it is the order that is an atmosphere that nourishes the growth of character. Where energy is expended in securing a semblance of order, the same energy must be employed in maintaining it. There is tension that is depleting and depressing all around.

Our individual teaching has enabled us to move our grades. They do not now sink down by their own weight. Our children all move forward and arrive on time. The quick one no longer marks time; he sets the pace for the rest of them; and the rest line up on him. There is no longer any retardation. There is no longer any necessity for skipping grades in order to get on. We always allow an individual to gain a grade where it is to his advantage to do so. But there is a marked difference between *gaining* grades and *skipping* them. The gainer of a grade needs individual attention; and under our plan he gets it. Let no one suppose that the individualing is done only with children of questionable capacity. There are numerous circumstances that send our brightest pupils at times to the individual table.

It is here that we get the benefit of schooling. The child's first incentive is to line up with his fellows. When he gets the war-horse spirit in him his career is made. He works first for his line; then he works because of enjoyment in his work, and at last he works for grand remote aims. When his acquisitive powers are trained, and when he can see the goal of life, he may then work out his own salvation in the solitude of home. The soldier and the war-horse are trained to dress on the standard. And so it should be in schools. The school classes and grades should move forward in lines dressed at right angles to the line of advancement—no obliquity; no dragging; all crowding on the standard; and all champing the bit.

Can this be done? We are told that a Dobbin will never champ the bit, and that a Kentucky thoroughbred will fret himself to death if hitched up beside him. This is true. But it is also true that it is very dangerous to apply to human beings similes, metaphors, and analogies drawn from the brute creation. I have ventured on one such analogy; the analogy of a team, driving ahead, not necessarily at race-horse speed, but driving on a comfortably tightened rein. The Kentuckian does not want always to be driven at the top of his bent; much less does he want to be held down to the sleepy pace of a Dobbin; but one crack of the whip that would incite Dobbin to a more respectable pace is more destructive to the thoroughbred than a dozen races. My experience with children is that they are not Dobbins; that they can be trained to be very good roadsters; and that Kentucky can travel with them without suffering the slightest discomfort or harm. I can remember the time when such a statement sent to me would need to be pretty well supported with data. And I should not now have the temerity to send such a statement unsupported. Under separate cover I have sent you transcripts of the promotion examinations record of every child in our schools.[1]

No child has been promoted here as a favor; no child has been promoted here to get him out of the way and to let him drag upper grades until he can endure the process no longer; we meanwhile nursing the hope that his endurance will not extend to the high school. We have no "dead wood"; we have no *personae non gratae;* we have none on whose absence we could dote; we have nothing to make us inwardly furious; and we have nothing to explain away. Every child here has been promoted because he has shown, under a severe test, that he was ready for promotion.

You will observe that every child has passed the minimum; that nearly all of them have a comfortable margin beyond the minimum; and that most of them are hovering around the maximum. We could not get any such results until we resorted to individualing. We should not have thought such results credible.

It may perhaps strengthen confidence in the integrity and searchingness of the examination to say that the questions for all above the fourth grade come from Albany, and that the examinations are conducted under regulations fixed by the state department. I have many reasons for favoring a strong state department; and not the least is that they make statistics of some value. Without statistics we have a war of words that tends to leave "confusion worse confounded."

One conspicuous result of our individual teaching is that it has enabled us to keep our grades intact. There is not an ungraded

[1] The editors acknowledge the receipt of very full and interesting reports.

school nor an ungraded room in this town, nor is there a grade section. Grade section seems to me the first step toward grade dissection; in other words, the first step toward the ungraded school. Perhaps the ungraded school is needed but I do not think so. I do not think that we need to go back sixty years. The people of sixty years ago were not contented; they struggled for progress, and to some purpose; they gave us the graded school. And in my opinion they gave a contribution nearly as magnificent as Magna Charta.

Since we have been attending to the individual we have seen no necessity for disturbing our annual intervals and annual promotions. There is an advantage, I believe, in having the elementary grades conform to the practice that is universal in the secondary schools, colleges, and universities. The grading of the elementary schools was but an extension downward of the organization that proved so satisfactory in higher education. We are convinced that it obviates much confusion, and that it is better in every way to have a third-year child, for example, mean one thing and not two things. There is something gained, it seems to me, by symmetry and clearness. Furthermore, where the purpose is integration rather than disintegration a semiannual promotion is premature. We need the full year, and the children need the full year, in order to reach the best results.

A very noticeable result of our plan has been the remarkable expansion of our upper grades and high school. In a total enrolment of 1,750 there are over 850 in the upper seven of the twelve grades. In a total enrolment of 1,750 there are 375 in the high school and 125 in the eighth grade. Those eighth-grade pupils are practically high-school students, as they are all studying algebra and other high-school branches; so you may say without much exaggeration that in a total enrolment of 1,750 we have 500 in the high school.

And what those students are doing in the high school I look upon as a result of our plan. Like Plato, we have wanted something for education to hang itself upon. We did not want our education to be spineless or agglutinate, so we have required Plato's educational backbone, geometry. We require geometry and one or two other things. But in the main our high-school course is elective. What our students have elected is quite significant of the workings of our plan. We believe most heartily in industrial education and have made ample provision for it. Every boy in this town has to put on the apron and every girl in this town has to put on the cooking cap and the thimble. We have, moreover, a very finely equipped commercial department; and we have a course in mechanical drawing and a class in agriculture. Our young people become very expert in their several lines of industry. I should be very sorry to see them satisfied with their industrial expertness. We all concede that it is incumbent upon the school to make the children good earners and providers. But the highest authority on vocational education in this country has formulated the matter thus: "Culture without industrialism is helplessness; industrialism without culture is brutality." Therefore I believe that industrialism should be taught only in the atmosphere of culture. A proper education implies immediate aims and remote aims. They should never in my opinion be divorced. Two kinds of schools are likely to generate two kinds of people, and two kinds of people are two armed camps. Civil order and peace would seem to require common ideals and a homogeneous training.

I do not say that those who choose remote aims always choose wisely; but I do say without fear of challenge that the mere fact that they have chosen remote aims is the highest possible compliment to them and to their teacher. The election in our high school has compelled us to provide extensively for cultural as well as practical work. And this is as it should be. The one makes the other virile and available; the other humanizes, refines, and ennobles the one.

It is only a corollary of the foregoing to say that our students are going to college in larger numbers and seeking the benefits of higher education. We have about fifty students in the colleges at present. And I mean the college of liberal culture as distinguished from the technical and professional schools. We have other numbers in those schools; and they all make quite a colony, or even a community on their home-comings. We have in college those who are in easy circumstances; and we have in college those to whom a dollar has always been a large matter. We have sixty students in the graduating class of our high school this year We have brought this phenomenal number to the threshold of the college; and I expect to see a large percentage of them enter in.

The school register is a good index of the efficiency and success of the school. A school must take hold in order to tend toward a maximum of registration and a maximum of average daily attendance. Our registers have shown a gratifying response to our plan. Whatever expands the aggregate registration and average attendance tends to reduce the per capita cost of education. We have been reducing the per capita cost since the introduction of the Batavia plan. But we have also been reducing the aggregate and actual cost by reducing the number of buildings, the number of janitors, the number of separate equipments, and other items. The reduction of expense has never been a motive with us. But it will be of interest to those who would like to compare the costs of different plans.

Our plan tends to the reduction of expense in another way. It has taught us the desirability of large classes. A large class under proper conditions is a powerful educational factor. There is a point of course at which a class will break down by its own weight. But the ordinary school cannot easily reach that point. The trouble with an ordinary school is that it has to have many classes that are too small. It seems to me a great pedagogical mistake to make small classes deliberately.

An efficient school has a tendency to approach the condition of a balanced school as to the sexes. Ineffective school work tends to make boys cheap. I like to see something like a boy-famine in a town; I like to see the owners of delivery wagons and other petty jobs concerned as to their sources of supply. I never did think much of the man-hunt that we read about in history; I think even less of the boy-hunt. The cheap boy sags down in school and he eventually sags out. It would be well for him if no one worse than the greengrocer got hold of him. When the hoodlum swarms in the street and infests public places it shows that boys are very cheap. The school is the Noah's ark for the immature boy. Of course I mean this with a proviso. I can readily see how a school itself can cheapen boys. But this regulates itself automatically; the cheap boys will drop from its register.

We have not a balanced school as to the sexes; but I believe that we are tending that way. In an aggregate enrolment of 1,750 we have 850 boys; and 160 of those boys are in the high school. Last June we got out of balance the other way; in a graduating class of 32 in the high school 19 of them were boys. Now we would not intimate that the girls are of less consequence than the boys. But the girls are like the pounds—they are able to take care of themselves; the boys are like the pennies—they must be cared for.

I trust that no one looks upon the Batavia plan as a labor-saving device; it is rather a labor-making device. Our teachers and pupils are very busy; they have much to do to meet on time all the demands made upon them. But such is the law of the matter. There is no royal road to a generous and sustaining education. Work and sustained diligence are the price of education. Indeed, work and diligence are education in its best aspect. Let no one have any fears of work and diligence. If force, and strain, and unkindness, and bitterness, and cross-purpose are eliminated you cannot impose too much work and diligence; the well will get sick on worry; the sick will get well on and work diligence.

You will naturally ask what our experience has been with reference to atypical, defective, and subnormal children. I do not see any reason why we should not have our share of all kinds of unfortunates. I believe that we do have our full share of them. I refer you again to the promotion reports. If those were selected children the data would be worth nothing. Those are *all* our children. It must be acknowledged that many children are handicapped at the outset in many ways by mental and physical troubles. For such children there is no chance at all in the school that teaches only *en masse;* they are foredoomed. As to what can be done with them in the school that singles out the individual to deal with him according to his need, I must cite again the reports. To debate such a question academically and affirmatively would be a truly fiery ordeal. I am convinced that you will find some who were very seriously handicapped among those whose records are by no means the lowest.

Any intelligent attempt at cure implies diagnosis. The mere calling of a lagging and backward child leads at once to a diagnosis of his case. It is often found that the mere calling was all that he needed. He was too far away; he did not see well, or he did not hear well. By the side of the teacher he both hears and sees; and he looms at once in his power. He is thereafter seated with reference to his infirmity; and his case is solved. With some it is a wandering and unmanageable attention that needs to be controlled and trained. With others it is a distressing nervous timidity which has been their undoing. Some have that woeful passivity and inertness so likely to mislead and discourage the inexperienced teacher; so likely to cause her to pronounce that fatal phrase, "born short," and to go on with the "go-on-ers." But we have seen the giant roused too often to permit ourselves to yield to discouragement. We have "learned to labor and to wait." And, by the way, we never have to wake a giant twice; when he once has realized his brawniness he never thereafter forgets it; he is never again a pygmy in his own estimation. Some are late arrivals in the room and need much adjustment. Others have been absent by reason of illness and have gotten out of touch with the work. Some are trying to make an extra grade. But whatever the cause may be, the teacher has become expert in detecting it, and has adapted the cure to the case. Cure in the grade is our plan. We are of the opinion that segregation should never be thought of. Possibly we might modify this view somewhat if we had upon us the full weight of life in the larger cities. But the very principle of segregation seems to me fraught with possibilities that are truly dire.

But would I not segregate the feeble minded and the incorrigibles? Yes, I would consent to the segregation of the feeble minded. But they segregate themselves; the number of hopeless defectives that present themselves for registration in a public school does not amount to more than a fraction of 1 per cent. That is not enough to constitute a problem in a town of only twelve thousand inhabitants. When one of those unfortunates presents himself we register him and give him our best possible attention. And it does him good to mingle with normal children. He even learns something. No one will question the wisdom of segregating the totally blind and the totally deaf. But we have advanced stages of defective sight and hearing that are doing very well.

I am not quite ready to concede the segregation of the incorrigible. I am not quite sure that a school system needs something like a lock-up. I am quite sure that it would be very wicked to "run in" to that institution children who have never offended, children who have only suffered. The "bitter bread of banishment" was never designed for the innocent. And I need some further evidence to convince me that a strong grade is not the best place for an incorrigible.

The immediate goal of the individual teaching is to put the pupil into a condition to react against the sweep of the class, and to enable him to appropriate the benefits of class-membership and class instruction. Knowledge is not the aim at the individual table; it is power, initiative, vigor. It is not a taking of him off his feet; it is a putting of him on his feet. He cannot get his lessons at the individual table; he can only get his power there; so there is no coaching. This means, of course, that the pupil cannot offer himself as a subject for individual attention. Every pupil knows that he must recite on his own preparation. If he does not recite well his case receives such attention as it merits. A plan that aims at vigor puts no premium on laziness or cowardice.

Our individual teacher does nothing but ask questions. It is no refuge for an evader to run up against a questioner. No one is rendered weak or dependent by being asked a question. The question meets the needy one at a crisis of his life, and proves his salvation. The question picks him from in front of the car of Juggernaut; the question saves him from being a victim offered up to Moloch.

Justice is defined as the giving unto each human being his right. The rights of an individual are exactly coextensive with his needs. Needs, rights, and duties are correlative terms, covering the same exact subject or object-matter. Duty is what is *due* from us, and what we *ought* to do is what we *owe* to do. If anyone suffers any restriction of his right someone is delinquent in the discharge of his duty. Someone is either *insolvent*, or he is disregardful of his obligations. Children have many debtors because they have many needs; but there are few on whom they have as great and as sacred claims as on their teacher.

My own convictions after fourteen years' experience with this plan are a result that may possibly be of interest. I offer them for what they are worth. I like our children as they are. I believe that they are susceptible of a fine education if we subject them to the dual process of individual attention and class stimulus. I believe that either of these processes will break down without the sustaining aid of the other. But in due combination I think they are invincible. But the combination, like other wholesome compounds, must have its quantitative formula. The combination of individual and class instruction that gives a potency is the proportion of one to one. It is a formula easily remembered. It is *HO* without any subscribed exponents or indices whatever. By *HO* combined in due proportion we live; by either taken separately we die. Believing as I do in the feasibility of universal education, I feel confident that our republic can endure, and that free institutions will remain the blessed possession of men.

THE GREGG SCHOLARSHIPS OF THE INDIANAPOLIS PUBLIC SCHOOLS

LYDIA R. BLAICH
Supervising Principal in the Indianapolis Schools

The public-school system of Indianapolis has a scholarship fund, whose income is devoted to advanced professional training of a limited number of teachers each year. The conditions under which the scholarships are conferred are as follows:

Only teachers who have had at least three years of successful experience in the public schools of Indianapolis are entitled to such scholarships, and no person is entitled to more than one in any one year nor more than two in successive years.

Teachers who receive and accept the Gregg Scholarships enter into a contract provided by the Board of School Commissioners in order that the Indianapolis public schools may receive the benefit of the special training given. Beneficiaries must return to Indianapolis and teach in the public schools for a specified number of years agreed upon (from one to five years in proportion to the size of the scholarship). They are not entitled to any advantage as to position or salary, but are in all things subject to the rules of the board for their appointments and salaries when they return.

The special committee by whom the scholarship recipients are selected consists of the President of the School Board, the Trustee of the Gregg Fund, the Superintendent of Schools, the Assistant Superintendents, and the Principal of the Normal Training School. It is known as the Gregg Bequest Committee. In addition to selecting the teachers who are to receive the scholarships, it designates the school or institution in which such persons are to study.

The names of such teachers are placed upon the list of teachers regularly appointed at the annual meeting for the appointment of teachers. They are assigned to work under the Gregg Scholarship contract, which means that during their absence for study they are absolutely in the employment of the board.

The first scholarships were granted in 1894. Since that time about 200 have been given. The sums have varied from $25 to $1,000. They range from a three or six weeks' summer term in a university or school of education to five months during the regular school year. Three teachers have each been given a year's scholarship. Two of these studied in foreign educational institutions in Germany, namely at the Froebel-Pestalozzi School in Berlin and the University of Jena under Dr. Rein. The third spent the year in studying leading schools in the United States. She took courses in the Chicago Kindergarten College, the Cook County Normal, and the Boston School of Sloyd. In addition she visited and reported upon the Oswego Normal, and the public schools of Chicago, Boston, Washington, Providence, Springfield (Mass.), and Brookline. These ten months' scholarships which were granted in 1894–95–96 brought to Indianapolis a general survey of educational aims and ambitions of Germany and America.

Since then quite as much stress has been laid on cultural scholarship as on the specific study of educational methods, and no one has had more than a five months' leave of absence for such study. Among the institutions selected for the beneficiaries are the following: Harvard University, Yale University, Columbia University, Chautauqua Summer School, Clark University, Hampton Institute (Va.), Tomlin School of Music, Earlham College (Richmond, Ind.), Stout Training School (Menomonie, Wis.), Bradley Polytechnic Institute, and the universities of Indiana, Chicago, Wisconsin, Cornell, and Berkeley (Cal.).

The Gregg Fund is the outcome of Iowa lands bequeathed to the school city of Indianapolis by a pioneer teacher, Mr. Thomas D. Gregg, who died in 1876. After making provisions for various heirs, the part of the will which pertains to the school bequest reads as follows:

> All the rest, residue and remainder of my estate, of every description, real, personal, and mixed, I give, devise, and bequeath to the city of Indianapolis, in the state of Indiana to be and remain a perpetual fund for the advancement and promotion of free schools in said city, hereby authorizing and directing the legal authorities of said city to invest said bequest in productive stocks, or put the same out on interest, and the income or interest thereon only to be expended annually for the benefit and advancement of said free schools.

This will left the school authorities absolutely unhampered concerning the use to which the money is to be put, aside from the general one of the "benefit of the free schools."

The net returns of this bequest were $12,850, which were placed in the hands of Mr. George Merritt as trustee. Under his careful management the funds increased to $22,000 by 1894. At that time through the wise planning of Mr. Merritt, the Board of School Commissioners, Mr. L. H. Jones (Superintendent), and Miss Cropsey (Assistant Superintendent), arrangements were made to devote the interest of the fund in whole or in part to special training of teachers along lines most needed by the schools. The plan has worked admirably and great good has come to the schools by virtue of this modest bequest which has now accumulated to a sum of $37,500. Eight or ten teachers are annually benefited by the interest from this fund. While no one knows exactly what the gain has been to the children, 30,000 of them and more have through it become the lifelong heirs of Thomas D. Gregg.

WARREN COLBURN ON THE TEACHING OF ARITHMETIC TOGETHER WITH AN ANALYSIS OF HIS ARITHMETIC TEXTS[1]

WALTER S. MONROE
The University of Chicago

II. TEACHING OF ARITHMETIC[2]

By Warren Colburn

I have been requested to address the convention on the subject of teaching arithmetic. I have accepted the invitation with extreme diffidence, believing there would be many gentlemen present much more competent to this task than myself. The subject is certainly an important one in every point of view, whether we consider its application to the affairs of life, or its effect as a discipline of the mind, or the time which is usually devoted to it.

With regard to its application, there are very few persons, either male or female, arrived at years of discretion, who have not occasions daily to make use of arithmetic in some form or other in the ordinary routine of business. And the person the most ready in calculation is much the most likely to succeed in business of any kind. As our country becomes more thickly peopled, and competition in the various branches of business becomes greater, and further progress is made in the arts, and new arts are discovered, knowledge of all kinds is brought into requisition; and none more so than that of arithmetic, and the higher branches of mathematics, of which arithmetic is the foundation.

Arithmetic, when properly taught, is acknowledged by all to be very important as a discipline of the mind; so much so that even if it had no practical application which should render it valuable on its own account, it would still be well worth while to bestow a considerable portion of time on it for this purpose alone. This is a

[1] This is the second article of a series. The third will appear in an early issue of this journal.

[2] This is an address delivered by Warren Colburn before the American Institute of Instruction in Boston, August, 1830. It was published in the proceedings of that society and is reprinted here by permission.

very important consideration, though a secondary one compared with its practical utility.

The fact that the study of arithmetic is allowed to occupy so large a portion of time in all our schools shows sufficiently the degree of importance attached to the subject by all classes of people. And that it does occupy so large a portion of time is another very strong reason for attention to the mode of teaching it, that the time may be employed to the best advantage. As the demand for all kinds of knowledge is increasing, and new branches of learning are almost daily brought within the compass of the ordinary means of education, it becomes highly important that those kinds which require considerable labor for their acquirement should be made to occupy as little time as may be consistently without sacrificing the advantage of learning them well.

It may not seem improper here to introduce a few remarks concerning the relative advantages of the old and new systems of teaching arithmetic. For though most teachers at the present time prefer the new system, and the majority of the community are decidedly in favor of it, yet there are persons, and some whose opinions are entitled to high respect, who strongly object to the new system and give a decided preference to the old. To such we ought at least to be able to give a reason why we prefer the new system.

For this we shall appeal to facts; they are stubborn things, and the side which they favor must prevail. It must be allowed by all that previous to the introduction of the new system fewer persons learned arithmetic than at present. At least, fewer made any considerable progress in it. Very few females pretended to study it at all, and the number of either sex that advanced much beyond the four primary rules was very inconsiderable. And the learner was very seldom found who could give a satisfactory reason for any operation which he performed. The study of it used to be put off to a very late period. Scholars under twelve or thirteen years of age were not considered capable of learning it, and generally they were not capable. Many persons were obliged to leave school before they were old enough to commence the study of it.

At present the study of arithmetic is very general with both sexes and among all classes. It is taught to advantage even to the very youngest scholars in school and made to fill a portion of time which used to be left unoccupied. And most scholars now have a thorough knowledge of arithmetic at an earlier age than it used formerly to be commenced. And scholars who cannot give a satisfactory reason for their operations are now as rare as were formerly those who could.

But perhaps the advocate for the old system will say, "I grant that it was a little more difficult, and on that very account it was a better exercise for the mind, and when it was learned, it was learned more thoroughly." But in this we shall again find the facts on our side. It cannot be pretended that those who did not study it at all had their minds exercised by it; nor can much more be claimed for those who pretended to learn it. In those two classes, we have seen, was comprehended a very large proportion of the scholars. And with regard to the remainder, a very little observation will show that the advantage is in favor of the new system. I believe most teachers who have understood and taught well the new system will give it as their opinion that most scholars who have studied arithmetic well have learned more of other things, and learned them better, than they would have done if they had not studied arithmetic at all or had studied it the old way. And in this class of teachers we shall find a great number who have been successful both on the old and new systems. It will pass for no argument at all, at the present time, for a man, however well skilled in arithmetic he may be himself, to come forward and say, "I have tried your system, and could not succeed with it at all; therefore it is good for nothing." The reply to such a one is, "You have not taken the trouble to understand the system; therefore you have not given it a fair trial." And we are sure that a sufficient number of successful teachers on the new system can be produced to justify such an answer. Those who do not believe that pupils taught by the new system are as ready and expert in the use of figures and in calculation generally as those taught in the old way have only to go into the best schools taught on the two systems and examine for themselves. Unless they will do this, they will not be convinced; and if they do, we do not fear for the result.

We believe also that we have reason on our side as well as facts. By the old system the learner was presented with a rule which told him how to perform certain operations on figures, and when these were done he would have the proper result. But no reason was given for a single step. His first application of his rule was on a set of abstract numbers, so large that he could not reason on them if he had been disposed to do so. And when he had got through and obtained the result, he understood neither what it was nor the use of it. Neither did he know that it was the proper result, but was obliged to rely wholly on the book, or more frequently on the teacher. As he began in the dark, so he continued; and the results of his calculation seemed to be obtained by some magical operation rather than by the inductions of reason.

By the new system the learner commences with practical examples on which the numbers are so small that he can easily reason upon them. And the reference to sensible objects gives him an idea at once of the kind of result which he ought to produce and suggests to him the method of proceeding necessary to obtain it. By this he is thrown immediately upon his own resources, and is compelled to exert his own powers. At the same time he meets with no greater difficulty than he feels himself confident to overcome. In this way every step is accompanied with complete demonstration. Every new example increases his powers and his confidence. And most scholars soon acquire such a habit of thinking and reasoning for themselves that they will not be satisfied with anything which they do not understand in any of their studies.

Instead of studying rules in the book, the reason of which he does not understand, the scholar makes his own rules; and his rules are a generalization of his own reasoning, and in a way agreeable to his own associations.

We conclude, then, that the new system is preferable to the old. We now come to the question, What is the best mode of teaching the new system? This is a question frequently asked and frequently discussed. In the way that the question is usually considered, it does not admit of an answer. It may be briefly stated to be his who teaches the best. But then it will be found to be the best only in his hands. For any other teacher, another method would be better; so that the method must be suited to the teacher; and the teacher again, to be successful, must adapt his method to the scholar. For until mankind are all made to think alike, and act alike, and look alike, it will be worse than useless—it will be absolutely injurious—to endeavor to make them teach alike or learn alike: I mean in the detail. For there are a few general principles, some of which I shall endeavor by and by to explain, which are applicable to all and must be attended to by all who wish to be successful in teaching. The best method for any particular instructor is that by which he can teach the best. It is that which is suited to his particular mode of thinking, to his manners, to his temper and disposition; and generally, also, it will be modified by the character of his school. So that if I am to give an instructor particular directions with regard to teaching, I must see him in his school and see him teach. Then my instructions would not tend to change his manner, but to improve it if it were faulty.

Teachers are very apt to pride themselves upon some plan which they have discovered for keeping up the attention of the scholars, or of directing their attention to some important point, or of making them remember certain things, or of explaining certain difficult subjects, or of exciting emulation among their pupils, and many other things of the like kind—which, they suppose, if it were generally known and adopted, would be a great improvement, not being aware that the thing is peculiarly adapted to themselves, and to themselves only, and that if another person were to attempt the same thing he would fail. Many have felt so much confidence in improvements of this kind, mistaking a particular case in which they have been successful for a general principle, that they have been at the pains to prepare books adapted to those particular modes, with the greatest expectations of success. But such books always fail of general success, not because the methods were not good and successful in the authors' hands, but because others cannot enter into the spirit of them. Such books, if they are not used in precisely the way that the authors intended, cannot be used at all.

By these remarks, however, I would by no means discourage any teacher from communicating his method to others. On the contrary, I would encourage everyone to do it, whatever his methods may be. For though others should not think proper to adopt them exactly, yet they may frequently draw hints from them to improve their own. And the very fact of a teacher's giving so much attention to his own methods as to be able to explain them to others will be very useful to himself, and often the cause of improvement in them. But no one should feel disappointed because others do not adopt his plans; neither should he despise the plans of others, though he does not choose to adopt them himself.

Without giving any very particular directions with regard to modes of teaching, I will state a few general principles that will apply to almost all modes; and whoever will pursue his own mode according to them, will teach successfully. Most of them are applicable to all other subjects as well as to arithmetic. And, if in the course of the lectures, you may have heard them from others, or may hear them hereafter—which I dare say will be the case—they will not be injured by the repetition.

The first precept which I shall enjoin upon you is to teach but one thing at a time. This is a grand point in arithmetic and in all other branches. Select the principle which you intend to teach the pupil, and apply yourself strictly and exclusively to that, until he is master of it. For as certainly as you endeavor to fix upon his mind two or more things at once, you distract his attention and blend the things together in his mind, so that he does not get a distinct idea of either; and neither of them will be learned well. In teaching any one point, therefore, all others should be kept entirely out of sight, except those which he already knows. These may be referred to at any time for illustration, or for showing the connection. Be sure that the pupil is master of the principle before he is allowed to leave it, let it require what time it will, unless he becomes weary of it and his mind gets confused; in which case, leave it entirely for the present, and take it up afresh at some other time. If the learner is allowed to pass from one point to another when the first is but partially learned, he soon acquires a habit of learning things imperfectly, which it is very difficult afterward to break up. It begets habits of inattention, of thinking loosely and carelessly, and of not fixing anything in his mind as it should be.

And if the teacher thinks to remedy this evil by constantly calling up those things which have been poorly learned, he will find himself disappointed; for he will only confirm the habit instead of curing it.

Almost every instructor succeeds in teaching some things, and almost everyone partially fails in some things; that is, there are some things which he does not teach to his own satisfaction. If he will refer to them, he will perceive that in those things in which he does succeed, his scholars are made thorough as they proceed; and that he is in the habit of seizing the important points, and keeping them distinct, both in his own mind and in the minds of his pupils. But in those things in which he does not succeed, he lets them pass from step to step, without becoming perfect in any of them, and he is probably endeavoring to make up the deficiency by a constant repetition of the things which they have so passed. With many teachers, English grammar would be a familiar illustration of the latter mode of proceeding. The old method of teaching grammar was very faulty in this respect. The learner was first required to commit the grammar to memory, without understanding it at all, or being expected to understand it. And then he was put to parsing all parts of speech at once. Of the success of that mode many of you, I dare say, are able to judge from experience in learning, if not in teaching by it. Many persons still find the subject a difficult one to teach, and the difficulty will generally be found to arise chiefly from the fault I have been speaking of; that is, of endeavoring to teach too many things at once.

In arithmetic this difficulty does not happen exactly in the same way, though in this it is very likely to happen. In grammar, teachers frequently endeavor purposely to teach several things at once; but in arithmetic they do not do it intentionally. They endeavor to teach only one thing at a time; but they are in too great haste to get along, and they do not make their scholars perfect in one thing before they let them pass to another. Hence there is necessarily a reference to what is past while what is past is still imperfectly understood, and the scholar is kept in continual confusion.

I repeat, therefore, Teach but one thing at a time, and be sure that that one thing be learned before another is attempted. If by mistake the scholar is found to have passed some essential point without learning it, he should be put back to it again and be made to learn it; but on no account should he try to learn it by reference. When such a case has taken place, the scholar will show it by failing to get his lessons, by getting into difficulties too often, and requiring too many explanations. If it cannot readily be discovered what it is that he has neglected, he should be examined backward, until a place is found where he meets with no difficulty, and then let him proceed from that. But it is by far the best way that the scholar should be made thorough as he goes, and it is the only way to be successful. It is also the easiest and most expeditious.

By teaching one thing at a time I would not be understood to mean that the scholar should not study different subjects on the same day. It is necessary for most scholars to be attending to several subjects at the same time; for young persons cannot well be made to apply themselves to the same thing long at a time. A change, therefore, is necessary as a relief to the mind, and a judicious teacher will not keep his pupils upon any one exercise longer than he can keep their attention upon it.

Whatever subject you are teaching, keep this precept in view: to teach only one point of it at once, and apply yourself strictly to that, until the learner is master of it, and then give him another. Be careful, in the selection, to choose the easiest first, and then the next easiest, and so on. And where one thing depends on another, make them follow each other as much as possible in the order of dependence. You cannot always decide, by your own judgment, what is the easiest. This must be discovered by trial on the scholars. It will often be found that the thing which one scholar will learn the easiest first will not be the same for another. Also, what is easiest with one teacher will not always be so with another. Each teacher should satisfy himself, by experiment, what order he succeeds best with, and then pursue it as nearly as he can, varying only when the learner requires it. It is not always necessary to pursue the precise order of the textbook. The order of the book should be followed in preference to any other, unless the teacher feels very sure that some other order succeeds better with him.

The learner should never be told directly how to perform any operation in arithmetic. Much less should he have the operation performed for him. I know it is generally much easier for the teacher, when a scholar finds a question a little too difficult and comes for assistance, either to solve the question for him, or tell him directly how to do it. In the old method this generally was done. Not infrequently the teacher took the question and solved it at home in the evening if he could and gave the scholar the solution the next day to copy into his book. Now by this generally no effect was produced on the scholar, except admiration of the *master's* skill in *ciphering*. He himself was none the wiser for it.

If the learner meets with a difficulty, the teacher, instead of telling him directly how to go on, should examine him and endeavor to discover in what the difficulty consists; and then, if possible, remove it. Perhaps he does not fully understand the question. Then it should be explained to him. Perhaps it depends on some former principle which he has learned but does not readily call to mind. Then he should be put in mind of it. Perhaps it is a little too difficult. Then it should be simplified. This may be done by substituting smaller numbers, or by separating it into parts and making a distinct question of each of the parts. Suppose the question were this: *If 8 men can do a piece of work in 12 days, how long would it take 15 men to do it?* It might be simplified by putting in smaller numbers, thus: *If 2 men can do a piece of work in 3 days, how long would it take 5 men to do it?* If this should still be found too difficult, say, *If 2 men can do a piece of work in 3 days, how long will it take 1 man to do it?* This being answered, say, *If 1 man will do it in 6 days, how long will it take 3 men to do it? In what time would 4 men do it? In what time would five men do it?* By degrees, in some such way as this, lead him to the original question. Some mode of this kind should always be practiced; and by no means should the learner be told directly how to do it, for then the question is lost to him. For when the question is thus solved for him, he is perfectly satisfied with it, and he will give himself no further trouble about the mode in which it is done.

When the learner begins to require assistance too often, it is an indication that something has not been learned thoroughly. He should then go back to some place that he does perfectly understand, and review.

All illustrations should be given by practical examples having reference to sensible objects. Most people use the reverse of this principle and think to simplify practical examples by means of abstract ones. For instance, if you propose to a child this simple question: *George had five cents, and his father gave him three more, how many had he then?* I have found that most persons think to simplify such practical examples by putting them into an abstract form and saying, *How many are five and three?* But this question is already in the simplest form that it can be. The only way that it can be made easier is to put it in smaller numbers. If the child can count, this will hardly be necessary. No explanation more simple than the question itself can be given, and none is required. The reference to sensible objects, and to the action of giving, assists the mind of the child in thinking of it, and suggests immediately what operation he must perform; and he sets himself to calculate it. He has not yet learned what the sum of those two numbers is; he is therefore obliged to calculate it in order to answer the question; and he will require some little time to do it. Most persons, when such a question is proposed, do not observe the process going on in the child's mind; but because he does not answer immediately, they think that he does not understand it, and they begin to assist him, as they suppose, and say, How many are five and three? Cannot you tell how many five and three are? Now this latter question is very much more difficult for the child than the original one. Besides, the child would not probably perceive any connection between them. He can very easily understand, and the question itself suggests it to him better than any explanation, that the five cents and three cents are to be counted together; but he does not easily perceive what the abstract numbers five and three have to do with it. This is a process of generalization which it takes children some time to learn.

In all cases, then, especially in the early stages, it will be perplexing and rather injurious to refer the learner from a practical to an abstract question for the purpose of explanation. And it is still worse to tell him the result, and not make him find it himself. If the question is sufficiently simple, he will solve it. And he should be allowed time to do it and not be perplexed with questions or interruptions until he has done it. But if he does not solve the question, it will be because he does not fully comprehend it. And if he cannot be made to comprehend it, the question should be varied, either by varying the numbers, or the objects, or both, until a question is made that he can answer. One being found that he can answer, another should be made a little varied, and then another, and so on, till he is brought back to the one first proposed. It will be better that the question remain unanswered than that the child be told the answer, or assisted in the operation any further than may be necessary to make him fully understand the question.

Some children, when a question is proposed, instead of thinking of it, and trying to solve it, will endeavor to guess at the result. This should be checked immediately.

It has often been asked whether the plates which sometimes accompany Colburn's *Intellectual Arithmetic,* or anything else of a similar nature, are of any use to the learner. I think myself that they have very little effect upon his progress. At first, before he is familiar with the addition and multiplication tables, some kind of counters seem to be necessary; but it is not important what they are. The plates are very convenient, but I believe the fingers do about as well as anything. If the scholar is allowed any helps of this kind, he should be left to manage them entirely by himself, and in his own way. Any helps by which the work is partly done for the scholar are certainly injurious. It is by his own efforts, that a child is to learn if he learns at all. The teacher cannot learn for him. Neither will he labor himself, if the teacher will endeavor to do the work for him. You might, with as much propriety, expect that his muscles would be strengthened by seeing others exercise in the gymnasium as to expect a child's mind to be strengthened and improved when the teacher does the work for him. The teacher may assist him in understanding the question, but not in the operation—not even in arranging his counters; for to do this, is to do for him the most important part of the solution.

It is best that the learner should be exercised for some time in solving practical questions involving addition and multiplication before he commits to memory the addition and multiplication tables. He should understand the use of them, and be able to make them, before he is required to learn them, and then he should be made to learn them thoroughly. It is not well for a child to commit anything to memory that he does not understand, for he thereby acquires a habit of repeating it without attending to the sense; and it is more difficult to make him attend to the sense afterward, when he repeats it, than if he had not seen it before. At least, this is generally the case. There may be exceptions. I might refer again to the subject of grammar as furnishing the most familiar instance of this. For example, it is very easy for a scholar, when properly taught, to learn the distinction of cases in the pronouns. And yet I have had scholars who had learned their grammar before they came under my care, so as to repeat it by heart, in parsing the word *him*, call it in the nominative case; and still persist in calling it so, after being required to decline it five or six times in succession. Arithmetic, or any other subject, would furnish examples enough of the difficulty of making the scholars attend to the sense sufficiently to understand a rule or principle when they have first committed it without understanding it. But grammar, perhaps, affords the most striking instances of it.

I shall now endeavor to explain a principle which I consider to be a very important one. It is one less generally understood than any that I have mentioned or shall mention. Many teachers have practiced upon it very well without having particularly thought of it. Many of you, I presume, have both thought of it and practiced upon it. But there are many who do not observe it, either in theory or practice. This principle depends on the association of ideas. I shall not enter here into a discussion of the principle of association. I leave it to the metaphysician to determine whether there are any general laws which regulate it or not. I shall confine myself to one simple matter of fact concerning it and the practical consequences to be derived from it.

The fact is this, that two persons never have exactly the same associations of ideas. I mean, they never associate their ideas in exactly the same order. The consequence is that no two persons think of the same proposition alike. Hence a proposition expressed in certain terms may be very clear and intelligible to one person and very obscure or altogether unintelligible to another. And perhaps, with a very slight change of terms, the case would be entirely changed. It would be intelligible to the latter and unintelligible to the former. An explanation which is very clear and lucid to one will often convey no idea at all to another. When a proposition is made for two persons to reason upon, they will often take it up and manage it very differently in their minds. When the subject is such as to admit of demonstration, as is the case with mathematics, they will generally come to the same conclusions. But on other subjects their conclusions will sometimes agree and sometimes not.

There are several practical results to be derived from this. First, it is very important that a teacher should be able readily to trace, not only his own associations, but those of all his pupils, when he hears them recite their lessons. When a proposition or question is made to a scholar, he ought to be able to discover at once whether the scholar understands it or not. If he does not understand it, the teacher should be able to discover the reason why, and then he can apply the remedy. This is to be done only by questioning the scholar, and tracing his associations, and finding what he is thinking about, and how he is thinking about it. Without doing this, the teacher is as likely to perplex the scholar as to assist him by his explanations. And it is a very common thing to see scholars perplexed in this way.

Secondly, when the scholar does not understand the question or proposition, he should be allowed to reason upon it in his own way, and agreeably to his own associations. Whether his way is the best or not, on the whole, it is the best way for him at first, and he ought by no means to be interrupted in it or forced out of it. The judicious teacher will leave him to manage it entirely by himself, and in his own way, if he can. Or if he meets with a little difficulty, but is still in a way that will lead to a proper result, he will apply his aid so as to keep him in his own way. When the scholar has been through the process in his own way, he should be made to explain how he has done it; and if he has not proceeded by the best way, he should be led by degrees into the best way. Many teachers seem not to know that there is more than one way to do a thing, or think of a thing; and if they find a scholar pursuing a method different from their own, they suppose of course he must be wrong, and they check him at once, and endeavor to force him into their way, whether he understands it or not. If such teachers would have patience to listen to their scholars and examine their operations, they would frequently discover very good ways that had never occurred to them before. Nothing is more discouraging to scholars than to interrupt them when they are proceeding by a method which they perfectly comprehend, and which they know to be right; and to endeavor to force them into one which they do not understand, and which is not agreeable to their way of thinking. And nothing gives scholars so much confidence in their own powers and stimulates them so much to use their own efforts as to allow them to pursue their own methods and to encourage them in them.

It is very important for teachers to lead their scholars into the habit of attending to the process going on in their own minds while solving questions, and of explaining how they solve them. Unless the teacher possesses the faculty of tracing the associations of others, he cannot make them do it effectually. But the teacher who does possess this faculty perfectly will get an explanation out of anybody that has any thoughts and can be made to speak on the subject upon which he is questioned. He can take one of his scholars, or any other person, and make him trace out and explain a process of reasoning which has passed in his mind, but of which he was not at all aware, and concerning which, if left to himself, he could give no account. He seems to have the thoughts of his scholars under his control. He will not only find out *what* they are thinking about, and *how* they are thinking of it, but he is able to turn their thoughts into almost any channel he pleases. And it is next to impossible for one person to direct the current of another's thoughts on any subject, unless he knows the channel in which they are already flowing.

This subject also suggests a hint with regard to making books, and especially those for children. The author should endeavor to instruct, by furnishing the learner with occasions for thinking and exercising his own reasoning powers, and he should not endeavor to think and reason for him. It is often very well that there should be a regular course of reasoning in the book on the subject taught; but the learner ought not to be compelled to pursue it, if it can possibly be avoided, until he has examined the subject and come to a conclusion in his own way. Then it is well for him to follow the reasoning of others, and see how they think of it.

I will now say a few words concerning recitations. They are of very great importance in instruction in a great many points of view; and it is very essential that they be well conducted. They are the principal means which the teacher has to know what progress the scholars are making. It is chiefly at recitations that one scholar can compare himself with another; consequently they furnish the most effectual means of promoting emulation. They are an excellent exercise for the scholar, for forming the habit of expressing his ideas properly and readily. The scholar will be likely to learn his lesson more thoroughly when he knows he shall be called upon to explain it. They give him an opportunity to discover whether he understands his subject fully or not, which he will not always be sure of, until he is called upon to give an account of it. Recitations in arithmetic, when properly conducted, produce a habit of quick and ready reckoning on the spur of the occasion, which can be produced in no other way except in the business of life; and then only when the business is of a kind to require constant practice. They are therefore a great help in preparing scholars for business.

Directions concerning recitations must be general. Each teacher must manage the detail of them in his own way.

In the first place, the scholar should be thoroughly prepared before he attempts to recite. No lessons should be received by the teacher that are not well learned. If this is not insisted on, the scholar will soon become careless and inattentive.

It is best that the recitations, both in intellectual and written arithmetic, should be in classes, when practicable. It is best that they should be without the book, and that the scholar should perform the examples from hearing them read by the teacher. Questions that are put out to be solved at the recitation should be solved at the recitation, and not answered from memory. The scholars should frequently be required to explain fully and clearly the steps by which they solve a question and the reasons for them. Recitations should be conducted briskly and not suffered to lag and become dull. The attention of every scholar should be kept on the subject, if possible, so that all shall hear everything that is said. For this it is necessary that the questions pass around quickly, and that no scholar be allowed a longer time to think than is absolutely necessary. If the lesson is prepared as it should be, it will not take the scholar long to give his answer. It is not well to ask one scholar too many questions at a time; for by that there is danger of losing the attention of the rest. It is a good plan, when practicable, so to manage the recitation that every scholar shall endeavor to solve each question that is proposed for solution at the time of recitation. This may sometimes be done by proposing the question without letting it be known who is to answer it until all have had time to solve it, and then calling upon someone for the answer. No further time should be allowed for the solution; but if the scholar so called on is not ready, the question should be immediately put to another in the same manner.

There is one point more which I shall urge, and it is one which I consider the most important of all. It is to make the scholars study. I can give no directions how to do it. Each teacher must do it in his own way, if he does it at all. He who succeeds in making his scholars study will succeed in making them learn, whether he does it by punishing, or hiring, or persuading, or by exciting emulation, or by making the studies so interesting that they do it for the love of it. It is useless for me to say which will produce the best effects upon the scholars; each of you may judge of that for yourselves. But this I say, that he who makes his scholars study will make them learn; and he who does not will not make them learn much or well. There never has been found a royal road to learning of any kind, and I presume there never will be. Or if there should be, I may venture to say that learning so obtained will not be worth the having. It is a law of our nature, and a wise one too, that nothing truly valuable can be obtained without labor.

There are some facilities for learning at the present day, perhaps, which were not formerly known. These serve to render study less irksome, but they do not render it less necessary. They enable the scholar to obtain more knowledge with an equal quantity of labor, but they do not enable him to obtain any valuable knowledge without labor. If scholars were to learn wholly by the assistance of the teacher, without any efforts of their own, they would acquire habits of idleness and inactivity which would be more injurious to them than their learning would be beneficial; and they would be little able to make any progress in learning after leaving school. But the scholar who is made to apply himself closely, and to learn by his own efforts, acquires habits of diligence and perseverance which will be useful to him through life. And he learns (which is of more advantage than the immediate subject of his studies) how to learn by his own efforts, without the aid of a teacher.

I have now briefly noticed what I consider the essential points to be attended to in teaching arithmetic. Many of them, as I observed before, are not peculiar to arithmetic but apply equally to all subjects. And I dare say you will hear some of them much more ably discussed during the course. But there are many essential points of a good instructor that cannot be taught by lecture. This I will not undertake to describe. One point more, however, I will remark: that to teach a subject well, it is necessary for the teacher to understand it well himself, and to take an interest in it; otherwise he will not make it interesting to his scholars.

Allow me to close with a few remarks, expressing, though imperfectly, the interest I feel in the occasion that has brought us together. There have been, in every age, a few persons who have felt the importance of the subject of education. But generally the numbers have been few. The business of teaching, except in great seminaries, has not been considered as one of the most honorable occupations, but rather degraded; so that few persons of talents would engage in it. Even in our own country and age, it has been too much the case that persons with a little learning, and unwilling to work and unfit for anything else, have turned schoolmasters, and have been encouraged in it. They have been encouraged in it because the pay of school teachers, in most instances, has been just sufficient to obtain that class of persons, and no other but one, which, with few exceptions, is not much better. I mean such as engage in the business of teaching for a short time, in order to discharge a few debts previous to entering on a profession.

But a new era, I trust, is now opened upon us. The community at large is beginning to feel the importance of the subject, and to show an interest in it. The fact of there being so many persons, both teachers and others, and many of them from distant parts of the country, collected here on this occasion, is a sufficient proof that the interest is neither small nor confined to one section of the country. A few years ago it would have been impossible to assemble such a number of persons for such a purpose. It seems now to be generally agreed that the business of teaching ought to be considered as a profession; and that the persons engaging in it ought to be instructed expressly for it, as for a profession. And institutions are getting up for that purpose. Your assembling here in this way, for mutual instruction on this important subject, though it will not supply the place of regular institutions for it, will greatly promote the general object and hasten on the period of their adoption. I rejoice, therefore, to see this meeting. Though at present engaged in a pursuit very different from yours, I cheerfully accepted the proposals to deliver a lecture before you; not because I felt that I could do the subject justice, but because I was glad of the opportunity of contributing my mite, however small, to the promotion of so great a cause. I hope, therefore, that you will improve the opportunity you now have of receiving and communicating information, and that you will lay the foundation of a great work of which not only your own immediate neighborhoods, but our country at large, and not our country only, but the whole world, shall feel the influence.

CURRENT METHODS OF TEACHING HANDWRITING

FRANK N. FREEMAN
The University of Chicago

II

This article continues the analysis of the chief methods of teaching writing in use in the United States, which was begun in the May number of this Journal.

Slant.—The slant of writing, as indicated in the previous paragraph, is closely related to the position of the paper upon the desk. The down strokes of writing tend to take a direction perpendicular to the edge of the desk, and, therefore, deviate from the vertical by the same amount that the bottom of the paper deviates from

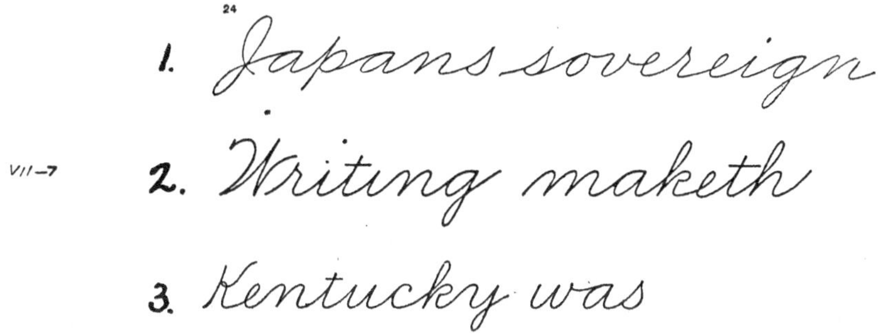

1. Japans sovereign

2. Writing maketh

3. Kentucky was

FIG. 1.—Illustrations of three different slants: 1. Standard Free Hand. 2. Economy System. 3. Medial Writing. (Reproduced with the permission of the publishers.)

the horizontal. We may divide the slants which are commonly employed into several classes. In the first class belong the old Spencerian writing and, among the systems which are in present use, the Standard Freehand writing and the Palmer method (see Fig. 1). These have a slant of 52 and 55 degrees respectively. In the next group belong most of the methods which emphasize rapid and free writing. The writing has a slant of about 60 degrees. This type of writing is represented by the California series, the Economy system, the Gilman method, the Houston copy-slips, and Spencer's Practical writing. In the next group belong the so-called Medial and Semi-slant styles of writing, in which is included the Whitehouse method, which have a slant of 65 degrees or more. Finally there is the Inter-medial system in which a slant of 75 degrees is used. The time is past when there is much splitting of hairs in regard to fine differences of slant, and very few systems lay stress upon this point. It is to be noted, however, that the systems in general which lay stress upon freedom and rapidity of movement naturally fall into a slant of about 60 degrees. It would seem to be reasonable, therefore, to expect a difference in slant in the different school grades, provided a difference in method is used. That is, if in the lower grades a slower movement and one which involves more finger movement is allowed, the paper may very well be placed more nearly in a vertical position and the writing be more nearly vertical than when the arm movement with rest is required. In general, however, the slant is not a matter of primary importance, but is dependent upon the other conditions of the writing and will settle itself naturally in accordance with the way in which these other conditions are determined.

Analytic v. *synthetic method.*—We turn now to a more detailed study of the methods by which the writing habit is developed. A contrast which immediately strikes our attention has been described in a previous article above referred to as a distinction between the analytic and synthetic method. In the analytic method the pupil begins from the start to write whole words or sentences, whereas in the synthetic method he begins with separate letters or the constituent strokes of which the letters are composed. Both of these extremes are represented in the systems which are under discussion. In the Barnes, Berry, California, Medial, New Era, Spencer's Practical, Standard Freehand, and the Writing Hour systems the analytic method in general is followed, whereas in the Bennett, Economy, Gilman, Houston, Palmer, and Steadman systems the synthetic method is followed. If we characterize these two groups of systems in a general way we should say that the first group, which begins with words or sentences, lays relatively more stress upon the acquisition of form, whereas the second group lays relatively more stress upon the development of correct writing movement. This, of course, is only a rough characterization, but, in general, it brings out a distinction which is valid. The only qualification which needs to be made is that some of the systems represent an intermediate position, in that they begin with the use of whole words or sentences, but build up the writing forms synthetically in a later grade, or in a separate form of drill in the earlier grades. The first of these exceptions is represented by the Berry method which begins the synthetic development of the letters in the fifth grade. The method of separating the writing of words from a drill upon the letters while carrying them along in parallel lines is represented by the Whitehouse system. In this system each copy-book is furnished with the ordinary list of words and sentences as copies, and in addition with a number of detachable slips which contain letters and drill forms.

We may conclude from this survey that the motive for the synthetic development of the letters is largely based upon the demands of movement control rather than upon the demands of form perception. The latter may be sufficiently developed by the use of complete words, but the former demands a more systematic and progressive drill upon the separate letters. If we regard the purpose of the teaching of writing in the primary grades to be mainly development of the perception of the forms of the letters and of the ability to produce them with a limited degree of freedom and accuracy, the analytic method is the one which is suitable for this period of the child's development. If, then, we aim in the intermediate grades to develop greater skill in writing, the drill upon the individual letter forms should be introduced. This procedure seems to the writer to be one which will produce the best development with the least unnecessary waste of time and energy.

Order of development of letters.—In the development of the letters synthetically it immediately becomes evident that there is opportunity to classify them and to develop them systematically. The order of development of the letters, then, becomes important. The degree to which this problem of arrangement has been worked out varies in the different systems. In some cases very little systematic arrangement is apparent, whereas in others the order has been worked out with care.

The basis of classification, when such classification is made, is the type of movement in general which is utilized in the formation of the various letters. Among the systems which have paid most attention to this matter may be mentioned the Bennett, the Berry, the Economy, the New Era, and the Steadman systems. The classification used in the Economy system may be taken as typical, as it is apparently most consciously worked out. In this system the small letters are divided into six groups, as follows (see Fig. 2): first, *i*, *u*, and *w*, which are based upon the direct oval; second, *n*, *m*, *v*, and *x*, which are based upon the reverse oval;

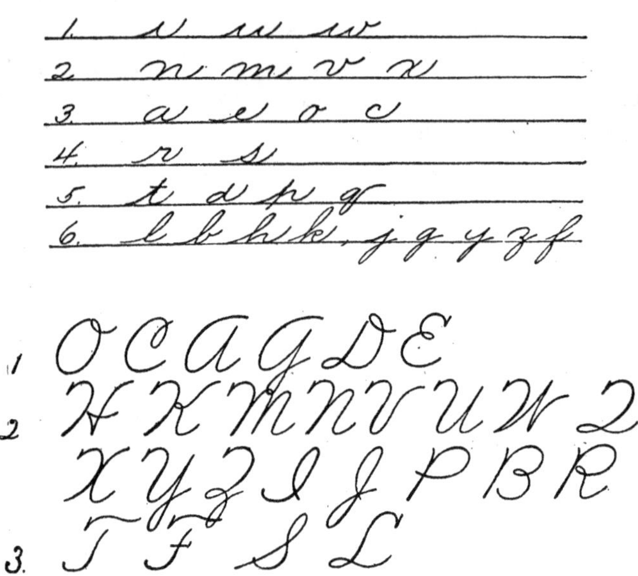

FIG. 2.—Classification and order of development of letters in the Economy system. (*Teacher's Manual*, p. 18. Reproduced with the permission of the publishers, The Laurel Book Co., Chicago.)

third, *a*, *e*, *o*, and *c*, which are also based upon the direct oval but are regarded as more complex than the first group; fourth, *r*, and *s*, which are miscellaneous letters; fifth, *t*, *d*, *p*, and *q*, which have in common the straight up-and-down line; and sixth, *l*, *b*, *h*, *k*, *j*, *g*, *y*, *z*, and *f*, which have the upper or the lower loop in common. The first and third groups might very well be placed together since they are based upon the same type of movement. This, of course, is not the only possible classification. For example, *a*, *d*, *q*, and *g* might be classed together on the basis of the similar movement which is used in making the parts which are common between these letters. Similarly *n*, *m*, *p*, and *h*, might be grouped together. The purpose of any such classification is not to make the grouping rigid but to classify the letters for a particular purpose, that is, to secure systematic and consecutive practice. In the course of the development similarities which are not represented in the main classification may very well be brought out and made the subject of drill. Some such classification as is here suggested is to be highly recommended for the purpose of introducing system and consecutiveness to the drill.

The capital letters may also be grouped according to the similarity of the movement by which they are written. The classification will depend to some extent upon the type of letters which are chosen, but the broad lines of grouping may be illustrated again from the Economy system. The first group, which is based upon the direct oval, is composed of *O*, *C*, *A*, *G*, *D*, and *E*. The second group, which is related to the reverse oval is composed of *H*, *K*, *N*, *M*, *V*, *U*, *W*, *Q*, *X*, *Y*, *Z*, *I*, *J*, *P*, *B*, and *R*. The third group is composed of the complex letters *T*, *F*, *S*, and *L*.

With this system of development of the letters the order of development in the Bennett method and the Steadman system may be compared. In the Bennett method the letters are divided into three general groups and the treatment of each group forms one part in the system. Thus the first part includes the letters which are based upon the "*i*" as the basic form (see Fig. 3). In this group are included the *i*, *u*, *w*, *e*, *l*, *b*, and *t*. The second group is based upon the "*n*," and includes all of the small letters which are not included in the first group, and the capital letters *P*, *B*, *H*, *K*, *E*, *O*, *C*, *D*, *A*, *W*, *X*, *Q*, *I*, and *J*. The third part includes the connections between letters which involve a complex curve, that is, a curve which includes the curve at the bottom of the "*i*" at the beginning, and the top of the "*n*" at the end. Such a connection is found in the connection between the "*i*" and "*n*," the "*i*" and "*a*," etc. In this part the capital letters *N*, *M*, *V*, *U*, *Y*, *T*, *S*, *L*, *G*, and *R* are included. It will be seen that this grouping is not altogether consistent. That is, certain letters are included in the second group which are not at all obviously related to the "*n*" form. The difficulty here appears to arise from the fact that too few type forms are chosen as the basis for the letters.

The Steadman system begins with somewhat the same type form but adds others to them. The small letters are taken first. The first group is based upon the "*i*" form and includes *i*, *n*, and *u*. The second group is based upon the "*n*" form and includes the other one-space letters. The third group is based upon the "*t*" and includes the letters which have a straight stem, the *t*, *d*, *p*, and *q*. Next come the upper loops, then the lower loops, and finally the

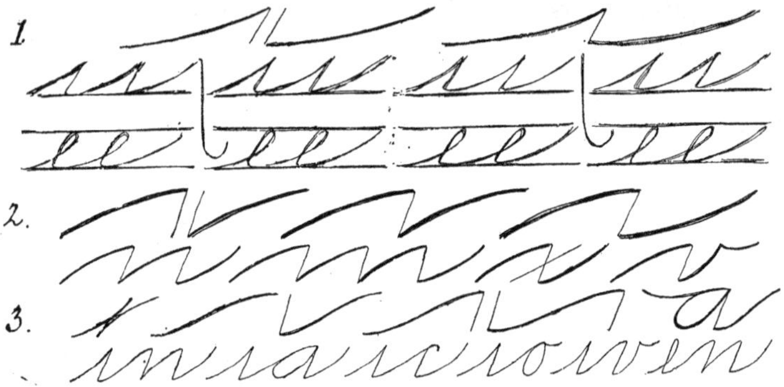

FIG. 3.—Illustration of the three stages of development of letters as given in the Bennett system. Reduced to one-half original size. (Reproduced with the permission of the publisher from M. E. Bennett, *Method in Teaching Writing*.)

"*f*." The capital letters are grouped in very much the same way as in the Economy system. These examples will be sufficient to illustrate the possible methods of grouping letters according to the similarity of type forms, or more fundamentally according to the type of movement which is chiefly involved in forming them.

Form and movement.—We have already touched upon the relation between the development of form perception and the development of the writing movement. The various systems fall into groups according as they treat of the relation between these two aims of the teaching of writing. In some methods the development of the correct recognition of form is tacitly or explicitly regarded as the primary purpose, and the development of freedom of movement is regarded as secondary to this. The extreme of this position is, however, on the decline, if we may judge from the relative frequency with which it is expressed. It is rarely stated openly but is usually implied merely in the mode of procedure. The copy-book method of teaching in general has laid stress upon this feature of teaching. The representatives of this method, however, usually modify their methods, at least to the extent of furnishing movement exercises upon the back page of the copy-book. This attitude may be illustrated by a quotation from the teachers' manual for the New Era system:

> The New Era copy-books provide a complete course in writing, but in deference to the wishes of a few teachers who think pupils in the upper grades should be drilled on movement exercises in addition to copy-book work we present herewith several movement drills properly graded for such supplementary practice. This, however, is an optional matter and is not necessarily an integral part of the New Era System (p. 13).

This illustrates the attitude of the representatives of the copy-book method who have recognized and yielded to a certain extent to the demand for formal drill in the writing movement.

The contrasted point of view is much more explicitly and emphatically stated in the Bennett method as may be seen from the following quotation:

> . . . . Teaching form before movement is uneducational—there is no go-ahead in it. Form should grow out of movement—be a picture of movement. . . . . In the true teaching of writing forms impress themselves upon the minds of children without special effort on the part of the teacher (Bennett, p. 6).

This position is, in general, held by A. N. Palmer and A. H. Steadman, and in general by those who emphasize arm movement. An intermediate position which is represented in the Economy system is that both form and movement should be acquired simultaneously. According to the directions of this method part of the time of each period from the beginning of instruction in writing should be spent upon movement drills and part of the time in the development of correct form.

Here again an intermediate position consists in adopting a different aim in the primary and intermediate grades. In the primary grades the chief aim may be to develop correct recognition of form, and in the intermediate grades to introduce the development of rapidity and ease of movement while at the same time continuing the development of form. This method of procedure is adopted for instance in the Berry system. In this system great stress is laid in the primary grades upon visualization and writing from memory, in order to fix the form of the writing in the child's mind. In the fifth grade the customary movement exercises are introduced for the first time.

Direction of attention in learning.—This issue raises a psychological question which has been touched upon frequently in experiments upon the learning process. The question which is there considered is: Where is the attention directed in learning, toward the process of manipulation, or toward the result which is to be attained? So far as experiments have shown it appears that the attention is toward the objective result to be attained rather than toward the movement which produces it. At any rate this is the condition which is attained when skill has been acquired. It may be necessary temporarily to direct the attention toward the movement, especially when this consists in an adjustment which can easily be produced voluntarily. But where the adjustment is one which must be acquired by a considerable period of practice in which success is attained by trial and error, the uniform conclusion is that the result is reached most efficiently by directing the attention upon the end to be attained. Applied to handwriting this principle would lead to the conclusion that the better type of procedure is to direct attention chiefly to the form of the writing. This, of course, refers to the attention of the pupil and not to that of the teacher. The teacher may introduce exercises which will require the pupil to use the desired movements. But the position that the best procedure is to make the movement prominent in the consciousness of the learner is clearly out of harmony with the results of investigations of learning. The method of improvement consists in a general adjustment of the hand in a way which experience has shown to be the most profitable, and then the gradual development of the co-ordination through repeated trial with the attention directed upon the result of the trials. If the movement is uppermost in the attention the form is in great danger of being neglected. Certain characteristics of form it is true will tend to take care of themselves if the correct movement is used. Such characteristics are slant and general uniformity of alignment, etc. But it is absurd to conclude that the details of the letters will be produced automatically without attention to them.

Accuracy v. *speed.*—An issue which is connected with the relation between form and movement concerns the question whether the aim should be to develop accuracy first or speed first. That is, should the pupil be urged to form the letters correctly at the beginning and then gradually write them more rapidly, or should he be required to maintain a fairly rapid speed from the beginning and gradually develop accuracy? Some systems hold to the former alternative to the extent of requiring the same speed of writing in all of the different grades. A standard speed is chosen which is taken to represent the natural rate of writing, and this is introduced from the start. A speed of 200 simple strokes a minute is the one ordinarily chosen. This seems to the writer to be clearly an artificial form of procedure which should be modified in adapting writing method to the stage of development of the child. The general question, however, remains. In order to throw light upon this question the general analogy of other forms of development of skill may be drawn. In similar cases a speed of movement is usually chosen which is sufficient to insure that the various elements of the movement shall be united into a single co-ordination, instead of taking place one after the other. The movement, however, is not made so rapid that the learner will not be able to organize it and direct it toward the purpose desired. The beginner is not expected to make a movement which is either so rapid or so accurate as the movement of the expert. And there seems no reason why the same principle should not be applied to the development of the writing movement. We should, then, not expect great rapidity or extreme accuracy at the beginning, but a gradual development in both these characteristics.

Development of form.—One extreme type of attitude toward the development of form has been referred to in the discussion of the relation of form and movement. In this view little attention needs to be paid to the form directly, but the assumption is that correct form will be produced as a consequence of the correct movement. In general, however, it is believed that in order to develop form advantageously more explicit attention must be paid to it. This problem has been given special attention in several of the systems which are under consideration. In these special methods two types of treatment may be distinguished. In the first type the effort is made to develop correct ideas of form by calling the child's attention more closely to the copy. The assumption underlying this procedure is that the child will naturally imitate those forms which are directly before his eyes. In order to keep the copy before the child the Economy system and the Gilman system have special devices. In the former system the copies are printed upon separate slips which are so attached to the top of a card that they may be turned over and successively brought to view. The practice paper is placed under these slips and may be shifted up as each line is written in order to bring the succeeding line directly under the copy. The purpose of this device is to prevent the child from copying his own writing rather than the copy which is set before him. A somewhat similar method is used in the Gilman "Optically Adjustable Copy." This device consists in slips which are inserted in the book between the copy sheets, so that instead of lying flat upon the desk they may be held at such an angle that they are easily seen.

The opposing method is brought out most clearly in the Berry system, not so much in any particular device as in the recommendation which is given for the manner of using the copy. Emphasis is here laid not upon following the copy, but upon fixing the form in mind in such a way that it may be reproduced from memory. The purpose of this method is to lead to the visualization of the word or sentence as a whole rather than to the following of the letters part by part.

This raises the whole question of the place and function of the copy. If the letter or word is to be written as a whole instead of as a collection of isolated parts the second method above referred to is the one which is justified upon psychological principles. The copy in this view is to be used not as a guide during the process of writing but rather as a model to be referred to in analyzing and criticizing one's own production. The pupil is more apt to repeat his errors if his attention is not called to errors in his own writing than if his writing is withdrawn from view and his attention is again turned to the copy. Psychological experiments have suggested that errors in reproduction of form are better corrected by an analysis of the form which has been drawn with the standard in mind than by merely referring again to the standard without comparing with one's own drawing. The attempt to emphasize the copy in the mind of the child fails then in two respects: first, in the unification of the writing process; and second, in the direction of the attention toward an analysis of the pupil's own production.

Content of the copies.—In respect to the content of the copies which are set before the child there have been some attempts toward improvement. We may here compare the method of teaching writing with the teaching of reading. Reading-books have justly been criticized because of the disconnectedness and lack of interest of the subject-matter, and the same criticism may be directed toward the majority of copy-books. They ordinarily begin with isolated words, then toward the end of the first book, or in the second book, they introduce short phrases and disconnected sentences. In succeeding books, proverbs or disconnected statements of fact are commonly used, and finally in the last two books, business forms and social forms are introduced. Several of the systems of teaching have attempted to improve upon this uninteresting type of subject-matter by making it somewhat more connected and systematic and by using interesting illustrations. This is worked out with some completeness in the California series and the Whitehouse method, but the most elaborate and successful attempt in this direction has been made in the Berry system (see Fig. 4). Great care has been taken in these books to secure subject-matter which is interesting to the child at the various stages of his development and at the same time possess literary excellence. The subject-matter is largely chosen from jingles, nursery rhymes, proverbs, quotations, etc., which have become standard as literature for children. The illustrations have been drawn by some of the best children's artists and are very attractive. If one is to use copy-

FIG. 4.—Illustrations from (1) the *Whitehouse Copybooks*, Book I, and (2) the *Berry Copybooks*, Book II. (Reproduced with the permission of the publishers.) The reproduction from the *Berry Copybooks* loses something by not being printed in color, as it is in the original.

books these probably represent the best development which has yet been attained in this direction.

It may be pointed out in this connection, however, that writing should be closely related with the reading, spelling, and other subjects of the elementary curriculum. If this correlation is carefully worked out the subject-matter may be made interesting without organizing a special set of material for writing. The method which is here illustrated serves to lay stress upon the point, however, that the content should be of interest to the child, and of such a nature that he will write it as a whole. This, of course, is aside from the question of analysis which comes to the surface when definite form of drill is introduced. A further qualification which should be made is that the child is not well able at the outset to grasp a whole sentence. Practice may then be confined to individual words of a sentence for a time, after which very short sentences may gradually be introduced. If the content is chosen from the child's reading or from the other subjects, care should be taken at the beginning that the words are easy to write, that is, that they contain simple letters in easy combinations. The form in which this requirement is usually met consists in using only one-space letters for the early lessons and then gradually introducing the stem and loop letters and deferring the capitals until toward the end of the first year. This latter precaution is probably not wise since the capitals are necessary in writing sentences. If they are introduced somewhat gradually they will probably not involve special difficulty.

EDITORIAL NOTES

From July 6 to 12 the National Education Association will hold its annual meeting in the city of Chicago. For some years past the National Education Association has been the center of much discussion. The control of its offices has been more talked of than its educational activities. Indeed, those problems of school organization which have been in the hands of various committees have dropped entirely out of sight so far as the general reading public is concerned, and newspapers have been filled with accounts of partisan organizations and political strife. The educational public is worn out by this dispute about parties. The fact is that nobody cares very seriously about the control of an organization except in so far as that control or absence of control interferes with the educational functions of the National Association. There is a committee of the association on efficiency and economy of time. There is a committee on rural schools. There are other committees which mean more for the educational life of this country than the association, if the general organization is to be continually disrupted by political discussions. There are urgent problems of a professional character which the National Association ought to be taking up. For example, the whole matter of educational publication in this country needs to be discussed, and there ought to be developed at some center an educational journal which shall reach enough people to have a genuine influence in formulating the policy of the schools of the country. The appointments of teachers is at the present time dependent upon all sorts of chaotic influences. There never will be a teaching profession until some means are found of developing a professional spirit. The National Association used to promise by its organization and influence an improvement of the teaching profession, but there is at present little of this discussion heard at the annual meetings.

The National Education Association

Parties Should Be Eliminated

Everyone who is acquainted with the conditions under which the association came to the city of Chicago for its meeting this summer realizes that the association has reached a turning-point in its history. Either the organization is to suffer from the Chicago meeting a complete disruption and a neutralization of its influence, or it is to begin an entirely different type of existence. If either one of the so-called "parties" in the association dominates its councils at the coming meeting, there can be very little question that that party will be left to its own devices from this time on. It will be quite impossible for either of the extreme parties to gain control, and, at the same time, preserve the respect of the large body of neutral teachers who care nothing at all about the petty quarrels which have been persistently carried on during recent years. On both sides of this quarrel have been people who have contributed to American education, and who are respected within the spheres of their own activities. Why some one of them has not realized that leadership of American education is of more significance than leadership in a party is difficult for the lay member of the association to see. Is it not time for the lay members of the association, who have not been engaged in any of the disputes of the past years, to assert themselves, and see to it that the meeting is conducted as a professional organization ought to conduct itself? If the association could appoint three or four strong committees, if these committees could be set at work on some of the grave educational problems that confront us on every hand, the question of who are the officers at the summer meetings would sink into deepest insignificance.

Representative Bodies Should Govern

The only way in which an organization of the size of the National Education Association can do business is through some sort of representative body. The people who come together in a single auditorium at any time are not competent to represent the association as a whole. They should not presume to take action which is not sanctioned by a large representative group from all of the states. The organization of the association was designed with a view to securing for the major operations of the organization representative action.

This representative action ought to be respected. If the large body of members of the association make it known to their representatives that they will not tolerate any methods of organization within the society which do not recognize the justice of this contention, there is very little danger that anyone will be bold enough to try to gain control by methods other than those which can be recognized as truly representative.

These paragraphs are written in the optimistic hope that they represent the probable trend of opinion and action at the coming meeting. If the association could be brought to self-consciousness and if the approaching meeting could become the occasion for the expression of the sound views of the whole body of teachers in this country, the influence of the National Association would be very great. The influence of the Department of Superintendence is at the present time large in determining the educational activities throughout the country. That influence, augmented by the power of the general association, could improve professional conditions very rapidly. These much-to-be-desired results will not, however, be reached by a mere passive acquiescence on the part of the membership in political campaigning and the struggle for office and superficial control within the association.

Action Is Necessary to Secure the Hoped-for Results

CHARLES H. JUDD

BOOK REVIEWS

Psychology and Pedagogy of Writing. By Mary E. Thompson. Baltimore: Warwick & York, 1911. Pp. 128.

The aim of this book is to do for writing what Huey did for reading, that is, to make an analysis of the psychological processes which are involved in writing and to discuss critically the pedagogy of the subject in the light of this psychological analysis. The present effort, however, has not met with the success which attended the work of Huey. That this is true will appear from a survey of the book.

The book is divided in the main into three parts. The first includes an introduction and a brief description of the historical development of the alphabet; the second consists of a description of experiments which have relation to writing; and the third treats of the bearing of these experiments upon the teaching of writing. The description of the historical development of the alphabet, although much shorter than Huey's discussion of the same subject, occupies with the preface and introduction over one-fourth of the book. The subject is not very closely related to the development of writing in the child and the brevity of the discussion precludes a treatment which will have value in itself as compared with other treatments of the same subject.

This lack of relevancy appears also in the discussion of the experiments. This consists merely in a brief review of some of the investigations which have more or less bearing upon writing and in incidental remarks upon their application. The reviews themselves are not full nor clear. Some parts are even enigmatical—as for example the sentence which concludes the review of Meumann: "While increased speed causes fixed rhythmical pressure on parts of words and single letters, the child uses always a longer time [with increased speed?], and every stroke is made with approximately equal speed; absolute pressure therefore [?] is less important" (p. 79).

Some topics are given much less than their due space in this experimental section—the complexity of the writing movement for example is treated in two-thirds of a page—and many important investigations and discussions are not mentioned. Among the authors omitted are Abt, Awramoff, Binet and Courtier (except in the reference by McAllister), Diehl, Freeman, Gross, Goldscheider, Jack, Obici, Javal, M. K. Smith, and Starch.

The discussion of the pedagogy of writing consists of little more than a brief repetition of some of the experimental results mentioned in the preceding section, with a few practical applications. This discussion is not of a sort which will be of much value to the teacher. The rules laid down are sometimes vague and sometimes dogmatic and not organized so as to give any coherent view of teaching policy. The author even goes out of her way to assert that formal drill in spelling will not carry over to composition. Many quotations might be given to substantiate these criticisms but one or two will suffice. In discussing speed the author says: "Natural slant (elsewhere given as 80°) is the slope which allows the most rapid writing" (p. 100); but in discussing slant: "The greater the slant to the right the more rapid will be the writing" (p. 97). In another place the teacher is warned that "by having the child form one letter at a time the innervation of the mind is retarded" (p. 90); and is urged that the pupils be "trained toward a totality of will impulse" (p. 99). The writer is convinced that such ill-digested application of psychological experiments to pedagogy will retard rather than advance the cause of educational psychology not only in the eyes of practical educators but also in the eyes of scientific workers in this and other fields.

Frank N. Freeman

CURRENT EDUCATIONAL LITERATURE IN THE PERIODICALS[1]

IRENE WARREN
Librarian, School of Education, The University of Chicago

(An) agricultural kindergarten. Cur. Lit. 52:413–15. (Ap. '12.)

American School Hygiene Association. J. of Educa. (Bost.) 75:455–56. (25 Ap. '12.)

ANDREWS, BENJAMIN R. The school of arts of Columbia University. Sci. Am. 106:326–27. (13 Ap. '12.)

AYDELOTTE, FRANK. English as training in thought. Educa. R. 43:354–77. (Ap. '12.)

AYRES, LEONARD P. Measuring educational processes through educational results. School R. 20:300–9. (My. '12.)

BLISS, HENRY E. Departmental libraries in universities and colleges. Educa. R. 43:387–409. (Ap. '12.)

BOUGHTON, ALICE C. Administration of school luncheons. Psychol. Clinic 6:44–51. (Ap. '12.)

BRYANT, LOUISE STEVENS. The school feeding movement. Psychol. Clinic 6:29–43. (Ap. '12.)

(The) camp fire girls of America and their aims. R. of Rs. 45:577–81. (My. '12.)

(A) church play-garden. Lit. D. 44:887–88. (27 Ap. '12.)

COOKE, FLORA J. Colonel Francis W. Parker: an interpretation. El. School T. 12:397–420. (My. '12.)

For a university of religion. Lit. D. 44:939–940. (4 My. '12.)

FREEMAN, FRANK N. Current methods of teaching handwriting. El. School T. 12:427–36. (My. '12.)

FURST, CLYDE. Tests of college efficiency. School R. 20:320–34. (My. '12.)

GAY, EDWIN F. Tests of college efficiency. School R. 20:335–38. (My. '12.)

(The) geographical distribution of books. Outl. 101:14–15. (4 My. '12.)

GRADENWITZ, ALFRED. A school for colonial science. Sci. Am. Sup. 73:232–33. (13 Ap. '12.)

HENDERSON, WILSON H. Pre-vocational work a preventive of delinquency. The ounce of prevention. Voca. Educa. 1:332–43. (My. '12.)

[1] Abbreviations.—Cur. Lit., Current Literature; Educa. R., Educational Review; El. School T., Elementary School Teacher; English J., English Journal; J. of Educa. (Bost.), Journal of Education (Boston); J. of Educa. (Lond.), Journal of Education (London); J. of Educa. Psychol., Journal of Educational Psychology; Kind. R., Kindergarten Review; Lit. D., Literary Digest; Outl., Outlook; Pop. Sci. Mo., Popular Science Monthly; Psychol. Clinic, Psychological Clinic; R. of Rs., Review of Reviews; School R., School Review; School Sci. and Math., School Science and Mathematics; School W., School World; Sci. Am., Scientific American; Voca. Educa., Vocational Education.

HENIN, B. L. Jean Jacques Rousseau and physical education. Educa. 32:461–73. (Ap. '12.)

HENRY, NORMAN E. School libraries. Educa. 32:474–77. (Ap. '12.)

HILDRETH, HELEN R. Four months in a girls' trade school. Voca. Educa. 1:305–15. (My. '12.)

HINES, L. N. A study in retardation. J. of Educa. (Bost.) 75:460–61. (25 Ap. '12.)

HUDSON, J. H. A school camp in France. School W. 24:134–35. (Ap. '12.)

JACKSON, C. M. On the improvement of medical teaching. Science 35:566–71. (12 Ap. '12.)

JOHNSON, W. H. Reminiscences of a great educator. Dial 52:353–54. (1 My. '12.)

JONES, ERNEST. Psycho-analysis and education: the value of sublimating processes for education and re-education. J. of Educa. Psychol. 3:241–56. (My. '12.)

KETCHAM, JOHN L. What teachers can do to aid industrial education. Voca. Educa. 1:344–50. (My. '12.)

KEYSER, C. J. The humanization of the teaching of mathematics. Science 35:637–47. (26 Ap. '12.)

LEAVITT, FRANK M. Vocational education in the Boston public schools. Voca. Educa. 1:316–31. (My. '12.)

MCCRACKEN, ELIZABETH. American children. Outl. 100:925–35. (27 Ap. '12.)

MANNY, FRANK A. The arts in childhood. Kind. M. 22:579–84. (My. '12.)

Mathematicians growing modest. Lit. D. 44:931–32. (4 My. '12.)

MENZIES, ALAN W. C. General hygiene as a required college course. Science 35:609–12. (19 Ap. '12.)

MONROE, WALTER S. Colburn on the teaching of arithmetic. El. School T. 12:421–26. (My. '12.)

MONTESSORI, MARIA. Disciplining children. McClure 39:95–102. (My. '12.)

MOORE, CHARLES LEONARD. Do we know what we want in education? Dial 52:343–44. (1 My. '12.)

Moving pictures in the classroom. Lit. D. 44:683–84. (6 Ap. '12.)

Natural history in the Chicago schools. R. of Rs. 45:570. (My. '12.)

OLDS, GEORGE D. The opportunity of the teacher in the class room. School Sci. and Math. 12:355–64. (My. '12.)

OWEN, WILLIAM BISHOP. The opportunity of high-school English. English J. 1:193–202. (Ap. '12.)

PATTISON, MARY. Domestic engineering. Sci. Am. 106:330–31. (13 Ap. '12.)

PERRY, ARTHUR C., JR. Woman and "equal pay." Educa. R. 43:344–53. (Ap. '12.)

PHILLIPS, D. E. The child versus promotion machinery. Educa. R. 43:336–43. (Ap. '12.)

PHILLIPS, WILLIAM. Education in the new *Encyclopaedia Britannica*. J. of Educa. (Lond.) 44:281–82. (Ap. '12.)

Plans for teaching journalism. Lit. D. 44:884–85. (27 Ap. '12.)

READ, THOMAS T. University education in China. Pop. Sci. Mo. 80:441–48. (1 My. '12.)

RIORDON, RAYMOND. Interlaken, an outdoor school where boys through their own efforts learn how to think and how to work. Craftsman 22:177–86. (My. '12.)

RITCHIE, JOHN, JR. Shall my boy become an electrical engineer? Sci. Am. 106:408–9. (4 My. '12.)

ROSE, MARY SCHWARTZ. The training of the school dietitian. Psychol. Clinic 6:52–55. (Ap. '12.)

SARGENT, WALTER. Problems in the experimental pedagogy of drawing. J. of Educa. Psychol. 3:264–76. (My. '12.)

School and college. Dial 52:341–43. (1 My. '12.)

SMITH, P. A. Sex education in Japan. J. of Educa. Psychol. 3:257–63. (My. '12.)

SNEDDEN, David. The practical arts in liberal education. Educa. R. 43:378–86. (Ap. '12.)

———. Problems of health supervision in Massachusetts. J. of Educa. (Bost.) 75:458–60. (25 Ap. '12.)

SUTTON, W. S. On some current educational criticism. Educa. R. 43:325–35. (Ap. '12.)

TATE, W. K. Country schools for country children. World's Work 24:102–6. (My. '12.)

TAYLOR, CHARLES KEEN. Effects of coffee-drinking upon children. Psychol. Clinic 6:56–58. (Ap. '12.)

TERMAN, LEWIS M., AND CHILDS, H. G. A tentative revision and extension of the Binet-Simon measuring scale of intelligence. J. of Educa. Psychol. 3:277–89. (My. '12.)

THORNDIKE, EDWARD L. The measurement of educational products. School R. 20:289–99. (My. '12.)

TOMBO, RUDOLF, JR. Attendance at German universities. Science 35:648–49. (26 Ap. '12.)

Uncommon people and the common schools. Outl. 100:856–58. (20 Ap. '12.)

VOORHEES, O. P. A plea for a secretary of education. J. of Educa. (Bost.) 75:400–02. (11 Ap. '12.)

WEBSTER, F. M. The present educational system and the training of economic entomologists. Science 35:557–66. (12 Ap. '12.)

WILD, LAURA H. Training for social efficiency. Educa. 32:494–504. (Ap. '12.)

WINSHIP, A. E. Montessori methods. J. of Educa. (Bost.) 75:399–400. (11 Ap. '12.)

Fiftieth Annual Convention of the National Education Association

AT CHICAGO, JULY 6–12, 1912

PROGRAM OF GENERAL SESSIONS

All General Sessions will be held in the Auditorium Theater

MONDAY AFTERNOON, JULY 8, 2:30 O'CLOCK

Presiding—HARRY PRATT JUDSON, President of the University of Chicago, Chicago, Ill.

Invocation—THE VERY REVEREND WALTER T. SUMNER, Dean of the Episcopal Cathedral, Chicago, Ill.

Addresses of Welcome—FRANCIS G. BLAIR, State Superintendent of Public Instruction, Springfield, Ill.; HARRY A. WHEELER, President of the Chamber of Commerce of the United States of America, and former President of the Chicago Association of Commerce.

Introduction of CARROLL G. PEARSE, President of the National Education Association.

Response to Addresses of Welcome—THOMAS H. HARRIS, State Superintendent of Education, Baton Rouge, La.

President's Address—CARROLL G. PEARSE, Superintendent of Schools, Milwaukee, Wis.

The Half-Century Mark:

(*a*) **The Re-Birth of the Association in 1884**—THOMAS W. BICKNELL, Providence, R.I.

(*b*) **The Ideals of Half a Century**—(Speaker to be supplied)

(*c*) **The Monuments; the Achievements of Fifty Years**—JAMES M. GREENWOOD, Superintendent of Schools, Kansas City, Mo.

(*d*) **The Coming Half-Century**—ELLEN C. SABIN, President of Milwaukee-Downer College, Milwaukee, Wis.

TUESDAY FORENOON, JULY 9

Topic: The American High School.

1. **Its Relations to the Schools Below**—WALTER R. SIDERS, Superintendent of Schools, Pocatello, Idaho.

2. **Mortality in the Early Years: Some Administrative Remedies**—ADELAIDE STEELE BAYLOR, Assistant in the office of the State Superintendent of Public Instruction, Indianapolis, Ind.
3. **The Specialized or Vocational vs. the Composite High School**—ARTHUR D. CALL, Principal of Henry Barnard School, Hartford, Conn.
4. **Social Activities and Organization**—MILTON C. POTTER, Superintendent of Schools, District No. 1, Pueblo, Colo.
5. **What the Public May Expect in Dividends; Material, Civic, Social**—KATE UPSON CLARK, Brooklyn, N.Y.
6. **The Worship of "The Standards"**—WILLIAM HUGHES MEARNS, School of Pedagogy, Philadelphia, Pa.

TUESDAY EVENING, JULY 9

Topic: A National University.

1. **The National Association of State Universities and the National University**—EDMUND J. JAMES, President of University of Illinois, Champaign, Ill.
2. **A National University a National Asset; an Instrumentality for Advanced Research**—CHARLES R. VAN HISE, President of University of Wisconsin, Madison, Wis.
3. **A National University as Related to Democracy**—JAMES H. BAKER, President of University of Colorado, Boulder, Colo.
4. **Ways and Means; the Next Steps**—WILLIAM O. THOMPSON, President of University of Ohio, Columbus, Ohio.

WEDNESDAY EVENING, JULY 10

Topic: The Relation of the Public Schools to the Movement for Recreational, Social, and Civic Opportunity.

1. **The Schoolhouse as a Social and Civic Center**—FRANK P. WALSH, Kansas City, Mo.
2. **How a Community May Find Out and Plan for Its Recreational Needs**—ROWLAND HAYNES, Field Representative, Playground and Recreation Association of America, Minneapolis, Minn.
3. **The Relation of Schoolhouse Architecture to the Social Center Movement**—DWIGHT H. PERKINS, Chicago, Ill.
4. **The Public Library, the Public School, and the Social Center Movement**—ARTHUR E. BOSTWICK, Librarian, Public Library, St. Louis, Mo.

5. **The Organization and Administration of Recreation and Social Center Work**—ERICH C. STERN, Member of State Legislature, Milwaukee, Wis.
6. **The School as a Recreation Center**—JANE ADDAMS, Head Resident, Hull House, Chicago, Ill.
7. **The Social Center and the Rural Community**—HERBERT QUICK, Editor of *Farm and Fireside,* Springfield, Ohio.

THURSDAY EVENING, JULY 11

Topic: The Public Schools and the Public Health.

1. **The Duty of the State in the Medical Inspection of School; Results Which the Public May Rightfully Expect**—FLETCHER B. DRESSLAR, Specialist in School Hygiene, Bureau of Education, Washington, D.C.
2. **The Teaching of Hygiene in the Schools: Public, Personal**—DAVID STARR JORDAN, President of Leland Stanford Junior University, Stanford University, Cal.
3. **Sanitation in the Rural Community**—CHARLES E. NORTH, M.D., New York, N.Y.
4. **Medical Inspection and Medical Freedom**—CHARLES A. L. REED, M.D., Cincinnati, Ohio.
5. **Some Problems in Education, as Related to the Public Health**—HARVEY W. WILEY, Contributing Editor and Director of Bureau of Foods and Health, *Good Housekeeping Magazine,* Washington, D.C.

FRIDAY FORENOON, JULY 12

Topic: Rural Life Conditions and Rural Education.

1. **A Social and Educational Survey of the Rural Community**—WARREN H. WILSON, Director of Missions, New York, N.Y.
2. **What Is Being Done to Meet the Problem:**
   (*a*) **By the Schools of Guilford County, North Carolina**—T. R. FOUST, County Superintendent, Greensboro, N.C.
   (*b*) **By the State of Oregon**—L. R. ALDERMAN, State Superintendent of Public Instruction, Salem, Ore.
   (*c*) To be supplied.
   (*d*) **In North Dakota**—J. H. WORST, President State Agricultural College, Agricultural College, N.Dak.
3. **The School, the College, and the English Farmer**—E. J. RUSSELL, Director of Rothamsed Experimental Station, Harpenden, England.

4. **What the National Government Can Do**—PHILANDER P. CLAXTON, United States Commissioner of Education, Washington, D.C.

FRIDAY EVENING, JULY 12

1. **The Best Next Thing for the Teaching Profession**—ALBERT E. WINSHIP, Editor of *Journal of Education*, Boston, Mass.
2. **Peace and Arbitration**—BARONESS BERTHA VON SUTTNER, Vienna, Austria.
3. **The Camp-Fire Girls; the New Relation of Women to the World**—LUTHER HALSEY GULICK, Director of Department of Child Hygiene, Russell Sage Foundation, New York, N.Y.

NATIONAL COUNCIL OF EDUCATION

President

CHARLES H. KEYES, Executive Secretary, Committee on Safety of the City of New York, New York, N.Y.

Vice-President

WILLIAM M. DAVIDSON, Superintendent of Schools, Washington, D.C.

Secretary

ROBERT J. ALEY, President, University of Maine, Orono, Me.

Local Committee

WILLIAM B. OWEN, Principal of Chicago Normal School, Sixty-eighth Street and Stewart Avenue.

SATURDAY FORENOON, JULY 6, 9:30 O'CLOCK

President's Address—CHARLES H. KEYES, Executive Secretary, Committee on Safety of the City of New York, New York, N.Y.

Discussion.

Business Meeting.

SATURDAY AFTERNOON, JULY 6, 2:30 O'CLOCK

Final Report of the Committee on High-School Preparation of Students for Normal Schools.

Discussion.

SATURDAY EVENING, JULY 6, 8:00 O'CLOCK

Reports on Educational Progress of the Year: Five-minute Reports to be made from each of twelve states, upon the single item of greatest present educational importance in that state—(Speakers to be supplied).

Vol. XII JUNE, 1912 No. 10

The Elementary School Teacher

$1.50 a Year 20 Cents a Copy

THE UNIVERSITY OF CHICAGO PRESS
CHICAGO, ILLINOIS

AGENTS
THE CAMBRIDGE UNIVERSITY PRESS, LONDON AND EDINBURGH
TH. STAUFFER, LEIPZIG
THE MARUZEN-KABUSHIKI-KAISHA, TOKYO, OSAKA, KYOTO

The Elementary School Teacher

PUBLISHED MONTHLY EXCEPT IN JULY AND AUGUST

EDITED BY

THE FACULTY OF THE SCHOOL OF EDUCATION

WITH THE CO-OPERATION OF

THE FACULTY OF THE FRANCIS W. PARKER SCHOOL

Vol. XII   CONTENTS FOR JUNE, 1912   No. 10

The Elementary School Teacher is published monthly from September to June. ¶The subscription price is $1.50 per year; the price of single copies is 20 cents. ¶Postage is prepaid by the publishers on all orders from the United States, Mexico, Cuba, Porto Rico, Panama Canal Zone, Republic of Panama, Hawaiian Islands, Philippine Islands, Guam, Tutuila (Samoa), Shanghai. ¶Postage is charged extra as follows: For Canada, 30 cents on annual subscriptions (total $1.80), on single copies, 3 cents (total 23 cents); for all other countries in the Postal Union, 46 cents on annual subscriptions (total $1.96), on single copies, 6 cents (total 26 cents). ¶Remittances should be made payable to The University of Chicago Press, and should be in Chicago or New York exchange, postal or express money order. If local check is used, 10 cents must be added for collection.

The following agents have been appointed and are authorized to quote the prices indicated:

For the British Empire: The Cambridge University Press, Fetter Lane, London, E.C., England. Yearly subscriptions, including postage, 8*s.* each; single copies, including postage, 1*s.* each.

For the Continent of Europe: Th. Stauffer, Universitätsstrasse 26, Leipzig, Germany. Yearly subscriptions, including postage, M. 8.25 each; single copies, including postage, M. 1.10 each.

For Japan and Korea: The Maruzen-Kabushiki-Kaisha, 11 to 16 Nihonbashi Tori Sanchome, Tokyo, Japan. Yearly subscriptions, including postage, Yen 4.00 each; single copies, including postage, Yen 0.50 each.

Claims for missing numbers should be made within the month following the regular month of publication. The publishers expect to supply missing numbers free only when they have been lost in transit.

Business correspondence should be addressed to The University of Chicago Press, Chicago, Ill.

Communications for the editors should be addressed to them at The University of Chicago, Chicago, Ill.

Entered October 12, 1903, at the Post-office at Chicago, Ill., as second-class matter, under Act of Congress March 3, 1879

FINE INKS AND ADHESIVES
For those who KNOW

Higgins'

- Drawing Inks
- Eternal Writing Ink
- Engrossing Ink
- Taurine Mucilage
- Photo Mounter Paste
- Drawing Board Paste
- Liquid Paste
- Office Paste
- Vegetable Glue, Etc.

Are the Finest and Best Inks and Adhesives

Emancipate yourself from the use of corrosive and ill-smelling inks and adhesives and adopt the **Higgins Inks and Adhesives.** They will be a revelation to you, they are so sweet, clean, well put up, and withal so efficient.

At Dealers Generally.

CHAS. M. HIGGINS & CO., Mfrs.
Branches: Chicago, London
271 Ninth Street. Brooklyn, N. Y.
8

Breeze-Swept Long Island
"New York's Seacoast"

IT'S a real vacation place—with a shore line of over 400 miles on Ocean, Sound, and beautiful bays, and a delightful country inland for the carrying-out of every form of pastime sought by vacationist.

Trains leave the new Pennsylvania Station, in New York, for all Long Island Resorts, the same station in which Pennsylvania Railroad trains arrive from points south and west—a convenient transfer.

Send for our new book beautifully illustrated with the Island's beauty spots, and a tabulated list of hotels and boarding cottages, mailed on receipt of 10c. postage by the G.P.A., L.I.R.R., Room 341, Pennsylvania Station, New York.

6

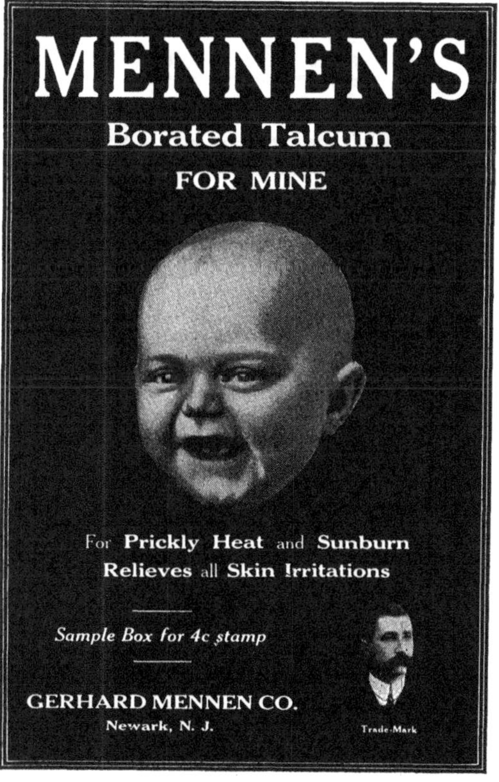

Intending purchasers of a *strictly first-class* Piano should not fail to examine the merits of

THE WORLD RENOWNED

SOHMER

It is the special favorite of the refined and cultured musical public on account of its unsurpassed tone-quality, unequaled durability, elegance of design and finish. Catalogue mailed on application.

THE SOHMER-CECILIAN INSIDE PLAYER SURPASSES ALL OTHERS
Favorable Terms to Responsible Parties

SOHMER & COMPANY
315 5th Ave., Cor. 32d St. NEW YORK

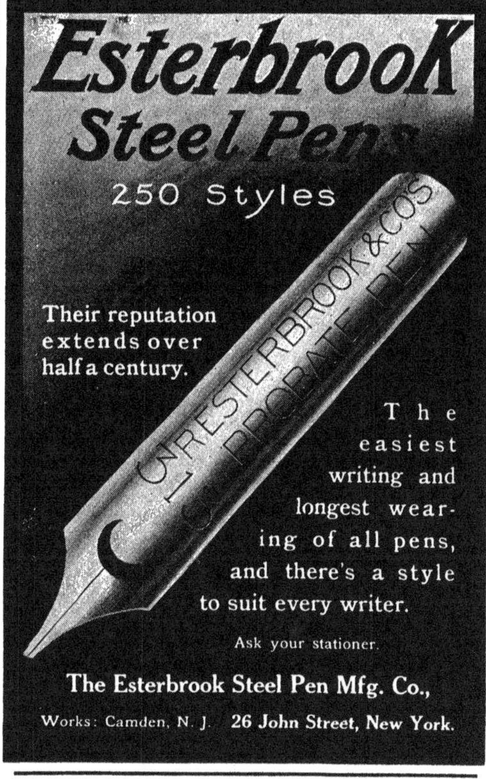

Esterbrook
Steel Pens
250 Styles
Their reputation extends over half a century.
The easiest writing and longest wearing of all pens, and there's a style to suit every writer.
Ask your stationer.
The Esterbrook Steel Pen Mfg. Co.,
Works: Camden, N. J. 26 John Street, New York.

The Chicago Association of Commerce

cordially invites

National Education Association

to hold their next convention

in the City of Chicago

A few concrete reasons for your consideration are outlined herei

Signed *George M. Spangl*

MANAGER BUREAU OF CONVEN

The above is a facsimile of the invitation accepted by the National Education Association to hold its summer m in Chicago, July 6–12 inclusive, and the "concrete reasons" on which such action was based are given

CHICAGO

CHICAGO IS CENTRALLY LOCATED

TWENTY-EIGHT GREAT TRUNK LINES CENTER HERE

CHICAGO CONVENTIONS ARE WELL ATTENDED

FIFTY-MILLION PEOPLE LIVE WITHIN A NIGHTS RIDE OF CHICAGO

CHICAGO HAS MAGNIFICENT HOTELS, THE BEST OF SERVICE, MODERATE

THREE HUNDRED CONVENTIONS MET IN CHICAGO LAST YEAR

CHICAGO IS ESPECIALLY ATTRACTIVE TO CONVENTION DELEGATES

THE HOSPITALITY OF CHICAGO IS EXTENDED TO YOU

JULY 6-12, 1912

BAKER'S
Breakfast Cocoa
Is of Unequaled Quality
For delicious natural flavor, delicate aroma, absolute purity and food value, the most important requisites of a good cocoa, it is the standard.
Trade-Mark On Every Package
53 Highest Awards in Europe and America
Registered U. S. Pat. Off.
WALTER BAKER & CO. LTD.
Dorchester, Mass.
Established 1780

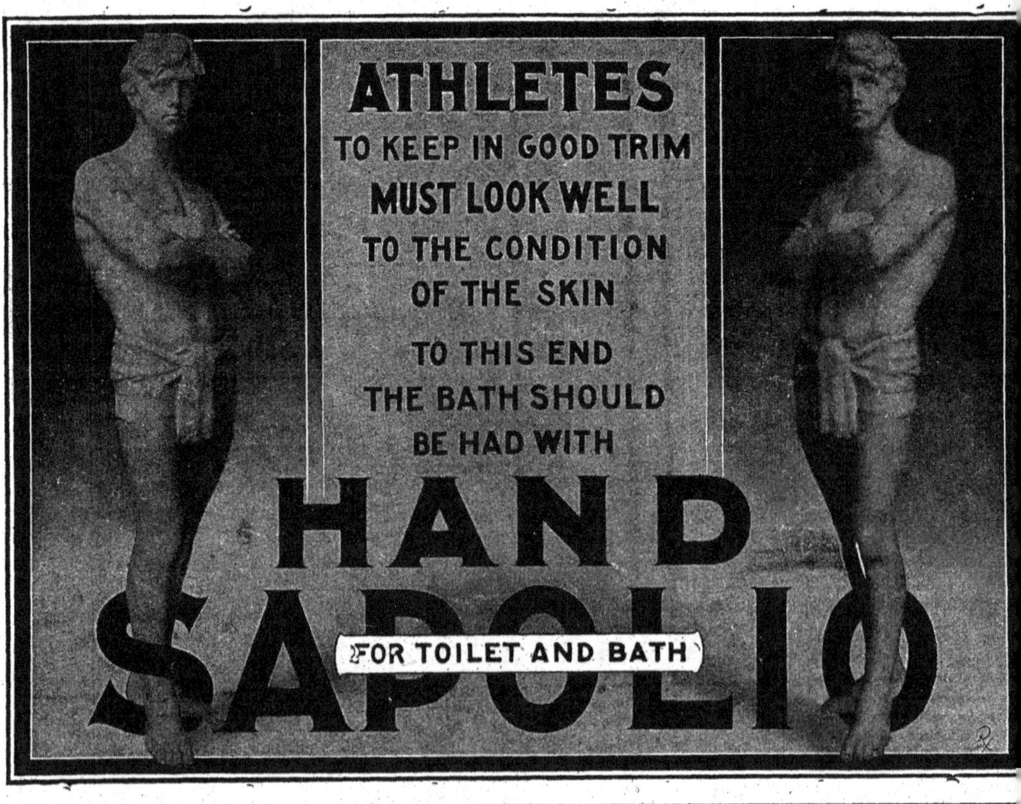

www.ingramcontent.com/pod-product-compliance
Lightning Source LLC
LaVergne TN
LVHW010524100826
845148LV00001B/81

* 9 7 8 1 4 2 5 5 7 3 6 9 0 *